BRAVE SOLDIERS,
PROUD REGIMENTS

Captain Jim DeCoste 2PPCLI epitomized the four virtues of a soldier: loyalty, integrity, truth and courage. He died on UN duty in Croatia in 1993.
Courtesy Katherine Taylor, Esprit de Corps.

BRAVE SOLDIERS,
PROUD REGIMENTS:
Canada's Military Heritage

by

ALLEN ANDREWS

foreword by

MAJOR-GENERAL
LEWIS MACKENZIE

RONSDALE PRESS

1997

BRAVE SOLDIERS, PROUD REGIMENTS
Copyright © 1997 Allen Andrews

RONSDALE PRESS
3350 West 21st Avenue
Vancouver, B.C., Canada
V6S 1G7

Set in New Baskerville, 11 pt on 14
Typesetting: Julie Cochrane
Printing: Hignell Printing, Winnipeg, Manitoba
Cover Design: Julie Cochrane
Maps: Courtesy of Pauline Veto

Permission to reproduce Charles Fraser Comfort's painting "Sergeant P. J. Ford" on the cover has been granted by the Canadian War Museum. (Catalogue Number 12282, Copyright Canadian War Museum; photography by William Kent)

Ronsdale Press wishes to thank the Canada Council for the Arts, the Department of Heritage, and the British Columbia Cultural Services Branch for their support of its publishing program.

CANADIAN CATALOGUING IN PUBLICATION DATA

Andrews, Allen.
    Brave soldiers, proud regiments

    Includes bibliographical references and index.
    ISBN 0-921870-50-7

    1. Canada — History, Military.   2. Battles — Canada.
3. Soldiers — Canada — History.   I. Title.
FC226.A52 1997   355'.00971   C97-910287-1
F1028.A52 1997

This book is dedicated to
the memory of

D. 82568 Pte. George Lowson
12 Platoon B Company,
1st Battalion Royal Highland Regiment of Canada

who died with his comrades on July 25, 1944
"the Black Watch way": facing the enemy

ACKNOWLEDGEMENTS

I wish to express my gratitude to a number of people who have assisted me with this book: especially Robert Shipley, who helped me select the biographies and histories which have been included, and Major-General (ret.) Lewis MacKenzie, who spent considerable time and effort ensuring that information in the chapter on himself as Chief of Staff of the United Nations Protection Force (UNPROFOR) in Yugoslavia and Commander, "Sector Sarajevo," was accurate. Additionally, I wish to thank Colonel Strome Galloway and Dr. R. H. Roy, Professor Emeritus of Military and Strategic Studies at the University of Victoria, for their expertise and kindness in reading and checking the manuscript. Nonetheless, I acknowledge full personal responsibility for any errors in fact or interpretation which this publication may contain.

Special thanks goes to my friend and colleague Pauline Veto, who researched and drew the maps which are included; likewise to my friend Lanny Miller, who shared in my excitement as this collection of essays developed, and quietly encouraged me to pursue my dream.

Charlie Chung, Mrs. Henry (Mamie) Fung, and Mrs. Faye Leung provided information and photos concerning the role of Canadian Chinese who served as special agents operating behind Japanese lines in South East Asia during World War II.

I also wish to express my appreciation to my wife Carol, who devoted her spare hours to helping make this a better book. I am deeply indebted to her for sound advice, penetrating insights, vigorous criticism, and her unflagging enthusiasm and emotional support during the considerable time I was engaged in this project.

CONTENTS

Private Michael James O'Rourke, VC; MM.
Ernest Fosbery — CWM Collection (Cat.No. 8163). Photography by William Kent.

FOREWORD

WE ARE A CURIOUS PEOPLE, we Canadians. Each year the United Nations determines the best of its 185 countries in which to live. For the last three years they have declared Canada to be number one and each time we have apologized! In 1996 when we took first place and Japan was declared number two, one Canadian wag exclaimed: "Japan has screwed us again — they took away our second 'place.'"

Why are we as a nation so reluctant to accept the praise of others based on our accomplishments? Is it our reflex reaction to living cheek by jowl with the world's great superpower where patriotism is a growth industry? Might it be the consequence of feeling just a bit guilty because of our good fortune compared to the rest of the world's population? I still believe that a nation's obligations abroad should be somewhat proportional to its blessings at home. That being said, Canada has a significant bill to pay and perhaps by playing down our domestic accomplishments we negate, at least in our own minds, some of our external responsibilities.

The same characteristic of misguided modesty applies to our military and our military history. Non-Canadians tell us, "You Canadians have the best soldiers in the world." We respond, "Oh *no*, you obviously haven't heard about Somalia!" The response is immediate, "Yes we have, there was a murder of a young Somali thief; it was terrible but you still have the best soldiers in the world!" Why can't we put our accomplishments in context; it seems everyone else can. I have my theory.

Before TV cameras ventured onto the battlefield, conflict, particularly between countries or groups of countries in support of great causes or against tyranny, was considered to be noble and glorious. Historians proffered their versions of events based on the records kept or verbally recalled by the participants. A number of the warts were removed in the interests of decency. Not so with TV coverage of conflict. It's in your face and spurs the electorate to action. We became embroiled in Sarajevo "thanks" to TV clips on the six o'clock news. I know that for a fact. Just think if someone could have smuggled a mini TV camera into Bergen Belsen at the beginning of the Holocaust and beamed pictures of the horror to a 24-hour worldwide news network. Would it have taken the Allies years to liberate the camps? I doubt it.

Canadians have discovered, a bit later than most, thanks to our geography, that war is a very nasty business and even "peacekeeping" can occasionally bring out the worst in human kind. We even perpetuate the myth that Canada is a non-military nation with little military history or tradition. What an appalling misrepresentation of the facts. This nation was born of conflict as recorded in the first chapter of Allen Andrews' *Brave Soldiers, Proud Regiments,* and throughout our history we have fought for great causes out of all proportion to our population. Canada's soldiers have excelled and this has made leading them both an honour and a pleasure.

And so, as we as a nation are praised by the international community, it's only appropriate that we take a pause from the current obsession with our warts and take pride in our military's significant contribution to our reputation as the world's most desirable country.

Surely it's O.K. to be proud of that!

MAJOR-GENERAL (RET.) LEWIS MACKENZIE

INTRODUCTION

CANADIANS FREQUENTLY THINK of themselves as "an unmilitary people," believing that our country was built by peaceful means rather than by war. While there is much truth in the image of the "peaceable kingdom," it omits important aspects of our history and distorts our present-day image of who we are. The country we know did not come into existence without a struggle, and it was from a military struggle, such as the early rivalry between French and English, or the armed resistance to American expansionist dreams. Indeed, it can be said that the American Revolution created not only one new country but two, for Canada developed in large part from the Loyalists' determination to resist American individualism. During the War of 1812, our early militia achieved great feats of prowess to protect the newly emerging Canada. Later, our countrymen performed truly exceptional service in both the Great War and Second World War, far exceeding what might have been expected from our population and resources. While wars exerted a major influence on the development of a distinct Canadian nation, and helped make us what we are today, the military heritage has operated when our ancestors have been at peace as well as when war threatened or occurred. Canadian society and the Canadian economy have been profoundly affected by military influences and institutions which we today often forget, or even deny.

The roots of Canada's military heritage really begin with our Native people. Recent research has enabled anthropologists to analyze in considerable detail the war organization and military techniques of aboriginals such as the Iroquois Confederacy. These tribes, occupying what is today called the St. Lawrence Valley, as well as the region to the south, organized themselves in a federation, or "Council of the Six Fires," both for political purposes and as a defence against their Huron rivals. On Canada's West Coast, too, the Haida, traditionally the most warlike of Pacific tribes, frequently raided and took slaves, in the process rowing their colourful dugout war canoes hundreds of miles. Prime place as warriors, though, must be accorded the tribes of the prairies, who developed possibly the most formidable and specialized military society of all. The functional rituals that these peoples created actually worked to minimize conflict between rival groups, and keep casualties, in numbers of wounded or dead, extremely low, especially when compared to modern warfare.

By the mid-18th century, the Blackfoot were acknowledged to be the most daring and accomplished horse raiders of the Western Plains. With banners streaming from his lance, ribbons and feathers bedecking the neck of his pinto pony, his eagle feather bonnet high and proud, a Blackfoot war chief at full gallop was a magnificent sight. Such warriors reminded the earliest Europeans of medieval knights of chivalry. No camp was safe from these and other horsemen, who like the Sioux, from whom they first acquired the horse, raided as far as today's south-western United States.

A distinctive feature of such plains Natives was their hierarchical military societies or orders. Members of military societies acted as camp police, regulating the behaviour of the people in hunting, war, and daily activities. Some tribes, the Blackfoot for example, possessed half a dozen such groups. Others, like the Assiniboine, had but a single warrior society. All, however, ranked

among the most warlike of prehistoric Canada's numerous aboriginal groups. For this reason, while natives further east were
forming alliances — the Hurons with the French, and the Iroquois
with the English — the plains tribes would be the last to abandon
their warrior tradition.

In the 16th and 17th centuries, the arrival of the French
added another layer of military prowess and institutions. The first
French settlers were not soldiers, and they had no wish to employ
the sword instead of the plough. Nor did they owe their seigneur
military service, as in France. Nonetheless, the early settlers would
develop their own highly effective military organizations. The continuing Iroquois menace, lack of adequate support from France,
and the tight hold the monarchy had on the colony, encouraged
the creation of both a militia force and later a force of colonial
regulars, the so-called *Troupes de la Marine*. Because of these military institutions, New France, which did not attract immigrants on
a large scale, was able to survive for more than a century. Indeed,
the French would expand until they encircled the more populous
English colonies to the south.

Other powerful military influences at work in New France expanded this heritage. In 1665, the Régiment de Carignan-Salières
arrived fresh from victory over the Turks at St. Gotthard in 1664.
Eventually numbering 1,200 soldiers once all companies of the
grey and chestnut clad troops had arrived, the regiment would
write a dramatic new chapter in the story of the colony, by attacking the threatening Iroquois, the allies of the English, in their
own villages, and effectively ending the threat they posed to settlers. When the Carignan-Salières were disbanded after their victory over the Iroquois, almost half of the regiment opted to stay in
Canada and thereby established the roots of a powerful military
tradition.

Military personages such as the colourful and fiery Louis
de Buade, Count Frontenac (1622–1698), added to New France's
growing military reputation. Renowned as the "Soldier-Gover-
nor," and for his daring excursions that threatened British America, he would be especially heralded for his triumphant defence

of Quebec against Colonial raiders in 1690 at the beginning of King William's War (1689–1697).

Any pantheon of French military heroes must also note the legendary achievements of the talented Pierre Le Moyne d'Iberville (1661–1706). Indeed, the "Paladin of New France," third son of Charles Le Moyne's numerous offspring, would enjoy a remarkable though controversial career. His conquests and colonizing activities ranged from Hudson Bay to the West Indies. He captured northerly Fort Nelson from the English, raided Schenectady, New York, and drove the New Englanders from Pemaquid, in today's Maine. But Iberville's most notable campaign would be the cruel, even bloody, attack by which he subdued Newfoundland during the winter of 1696–1697. His march across the Avalon Peninsula would prove an epic in its own stead. During the protracted winter's campaign, which shocks modern sensibilities despite its strategic brilliance, Iberville's force would destroy 36 settlements, including St. John's, and be primarily responsible for killing 200 persons. Additionally, the raiders took 300 captive and seized an immense amount of booty.

From the late 17th century onwards, the money that France poured into New France for its defence, for the support of troops, and the construction of fortifications far exceeded the revenues the colony earned from the fur trade. Also, it enriched the colony's contractors and sustained the economy until gold ceased to flow because the mother country had other priorities. As a major recipient of such largesse, Louisbourg symbolized France's grandiose imperial ambitions in the new world. Built in the early 18th century by French military engineers to safeguard the approach to the St. Lawrence, the imposing fortress situated on Cape Breton Island's eastern shore would be attacked and captured twice during its lifetime. First taken by Sir William Pepperell's New England militia in 1745, during the War of the Austrian Succession (1740–1748), it would be handed back to France at the conflict's conclusion. Soon it would be stronger than ever. Nonetheless, during the Seven Years' War (1756–1763), the great fortress, often called the "Dunkirk of the North," would fall a second time, on this occasion to a force led by James Wolfe, and commanded by his superiors Major-General Jeffrey Amherst and Admiral Charles Boscawen.

As W. J. Eccles has pointed out, in New France the ethos of a feudal nobility prevailed, despite its modification from the European model. Indeed, "the military virtues were extolled." Adding to the tradition, the officers of the regular regiments from France, who garrisoned the colony from 1755 to 1759, brought with them an aristocratic social attitude that reinforced an already well-established martial sense.

Personifying such military ardour was the oval-faced Commander, Louis-Joseph, Marquis de Montcalm (1712–1759). By the time he came to New France in 1756 the veteran campaigner had fought in a number of European wars and experienced many changes of fortune. His greatest victory, however, would occur in early July 1758 when he and the small force of regulars he commanded successfully repulsed a much larger British army led by General James Abercromby at Ticonderoga (or Carillon), in today's New York State. The General's sense of triumph was evident in the letter (with obvious exaggerations) he sent his wife soon after the battle: "Without Indians, almost without Canadians or colony troops — I had only four hundred — along with Lévis and Bourlemaque and the troops of the line, thirty-one hundred fighting men, I have beaten an army of twenty-five thousand." The General also wrote his friend Doreil: "The army, the too small army of the King has beaten the enemy. What a day for France! If I had two hundred Indians to send out at the head of a thousand picked men under the Chevalier de Lévis, not many would have escaped. Ah, my dear Doreil, what soldiers are ours! I never saw the like."

Montcalm's triumph would be short-lived. But even after Brigadier-General James Wolfe's victory at Quebec the following year, military considerations continued to shape New France. At the surrender in 1760, Brigadier-General James Murray announced that colonists enrolled in French units would be returned to France as regular soldiers. The French Canadians immediately laid down their arms in order to remain in their own country. Subsequently, the British military occupation forces employed the militia organization, headed by captains in each parish, to govern and administer the captured colony.

During the challenging decades before the American Revolution, two battalions of the 60th Royal Americans would be raised from *Canadien* volunteers, and placed under the command of a French Canadian. In addition, a dozen other young *Canadiens* from prominent families (Salaberry, Jachereau-Duchesnay, and Des Rivières) were given commissions in the British Army. In such manner, the British encouraged the continuation of New France's military institutions and spirit until the end of the American Revolution brought a complete demobilization in 1784. Later, when invasion came in 1812, and when Irish-American Fenians were a menace in the 1860s, French Canadians would be quick to take up arms to defend their homeland. And, although there has been a decline of military interest among the general body of Francophones, a number of families retain the military connection which their ancestors developed during the French Regime. Certainly the proud record of a famous French-speaking unit such as the Royal 22nd Regiment ("Van Doos") in the wars of the 20th century has deep historic origins.

British rule strengthened Canada's military roots in other ways as well. Although modern Canadians often choose to ignore the reality, the relocation of the American Loyalists, or those who elected to remain loyal to the British Crown, was essentially a military operation. In Upper Canada, especially, many of these so-called "displaced persons" or refugees were males who had been organized in provincial militia companies, and who had fled to the safety of Canada early on in the struggle in order to use it as a base from which to mount military operations against the American rebels. Following the war, many such provincial soldiers would help settle the new colony under the direction of Governor John Graves Simcoe, who earlier had led the Queen's Rangers fighting rebels in the war's southern theatre.

After the Revolution, the British also actively encouraged

loyal Indians, such as Joseph Brant and his Mohawk followers, to relocate to Canada. Traditionally, such Indian groups, or nations, have regarded their association with the British as a compact between sovereign powers, and have come to the assistance of the Crown to fight its enemies on many notable occasions since.

As a result of the groundwork laid by Simcoe, Sir Frederick Haldimand, the Governor-in-Chief of Canada (Quebec), and other administrators, our country would have a well-developed, British-style militia system almost from the beginning. In both Upper and Lower Canada, this militia organization would be strong enough to make a valuable contribution during the War of 1812, as it would later when the 1837 rebellions threatened the Canadas' civil administration.

In the 19th century, moreover, it was the British garrison that continued to provide Canada, as it had since Wolfe's victory, with its main military character and protection. As military historian Elinor Kyte Senior has written: "In the early nineteenth century Canada was an imperial frontier defended by a force roughly equal to the standing army of the United States." And, since we possessed a population smaller than our neighbour, Canadians were aware of the presence of such troops and the need for an imperial garrison. Far more important than the provincial militia and volunteers, regulars, stationed in garrison towns such as Halifax, Montreal, and Kingston, not only constituted our country's main line of defence against the growing power and population of the United States and the threat it posed, but also exerted their own distinctive influence on the colonies.

During the century or more from 1759 to Confederation in 1867, virtually all British units, save cavalry and Household Guards regiments, would be posted to Canada at one time or another. Indeed, it is calculated that Britain's garrisons on this continent constituted roughly a quarter of Britain's expenditure on overseas troops. One expert, C. F. Hamilton, has calculated that between 1841 and 1851 Great Britain "spent more in safeguarding the provinces [of Canada] than the [provincial] legislature did in administering it." Thus, in much the same manner as the earlier

French Regime, British authorities continued to ensure that military expenditures would account for the lion's share of government expenditure in Canada.

In addition to the obvious military and economic benefits it created, the omnipresent garrison influenced other aspects of Canada's society as well. During the early 1800s Canada's government was dominated by officers who had assisted the Duke of Wellington win the Battle of Waterloo in 1815: Sir Peregrine Maitland, who had stopped Napoleon's Imperial Guard; Sir John Colborne, commander of the famous 52nd Regiment; Sir James Kempt, whose brigades had withstood the great French assault, and other officers. In Nova Scotia, the custom prevailed of combining civil office with military command. Even when it became policy to appoint civilians to govern the Canadas, the tradition of a "court" social life, with military trappings, lingered. Most important, perhaps, was the "glamour and glitter of the garrison" — especially in its cultural and artistic impact.

The presence of British garrisons also helped foster English ways and ideas, and assist the process of resisting "Americanization" throughout Canada. Even after the "Recall of the Legions" in 1870, British artillery batteries and training units would continue to function in a number of locations throughout the Dominion. British garrisons continued for decades afterwards at Halifax and Victoria. British garrisons and settlements founded by ex-officers reinforced the innately conservative character established in Canadian society during the French regime and by the Loyalist settlement of Upper Canada. Indeed, the presence of the military strengthened ties with the mother country because the forces were not regarded as an enemy or occupying force.

By the mid-19th century, the presence and tutelage of British officers and British rule had created an environment that would nurture the ongoing development of Canada's own military forces. This was already noticeable in the great surge of enthusiasm for amateur soldiering which led to the establishment of dozens of new volunteer units during the 1850s and 1860s. As such, it provided the Dominion with an "outpost line" of patriots burning to resist any enemy of Britain.

In the decades to follow, given our deep military roots, Canadians were going to prove their claim of being "a military though not a warlike people."

Not surprisingly, given Canada's military background, Canada now provides its own troops on overseas service, and these troops relive some aspects of the experience of the British garrisons in Canada of over a century ago. So far has the ongoing story of our military heritage evolved.

Major-General James Wolfe, 1759.
Watercolour on paper by Brigadier-General the Hon. George Townshend.
(McCord Museum of Canadian History, Montreal)

1

MAJOR-GENERAL
JAMES WOLFE

The Most Perfect Shot Fired on a Battlefield

-

The Seven Years' War (1756–1763), the third great conflict fought between Britain and France and their allies in the 18th century, saw action take place in Europe, North America, India and elsewhere. In 1758, James Wolfe (1727–1759) accompanied Major-General Jeffrey Amherst to North America and participated in the successful assault against Louisbourg. Impressed, Wolfe's superior recommended that the young brigadier be selected to head the expedition against Quebec the following year. After a long and ineffective siege that lasted the better part of the summer, Wolfe chose the Anse au Foulon (Wolfe's Cove) as the best place to land his invasion force. On the morning of September 13, 1759, under the cover of darkness, his troops scaled the formidable cliffs. When Montcalm made the mistake of meeting him on the Plains of Abraham, immediately west of the town, Wolfe ordered his soldiers to hold fire until the enemy was within 40 paces. Then, on his command, the British redcoats defeated the onrushing French with what history has eulogized as "the most perfect shot fired on a battlefield." Like Montcalm, however, Wolfe was mortally wounded at his moment of victory, and would die shortly afterwards.

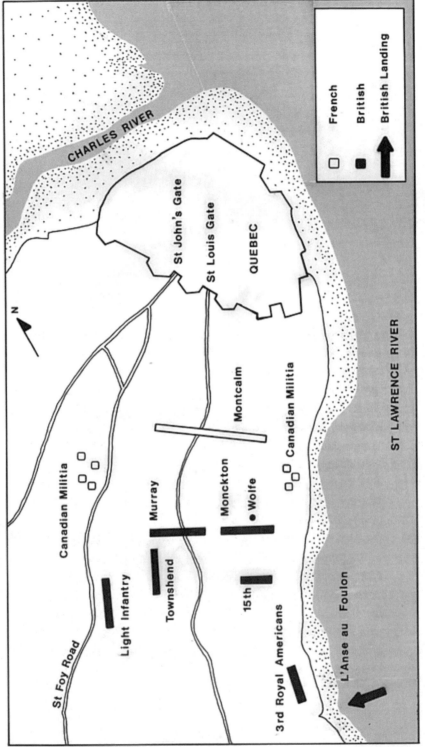

Battle of the Plains of Abraham, Sept. 13, 1759

A single light, hoisted to the topmost shrouds of *Sutherland*, lying off Cap Rouge, served as the signal for the transports to drop down and assemble between her and the St. Lawrence's south shore. Thirty minutes later, two lights from the flagship conveyed the signal to leave for the Foulon. The progress of the ship's boats, laden with armed men, was rapid. Soon the lead boats were bearing down on the sloop *Hunter*, anchored in midstream. Wolfe, who was in the lead boat, was alongside before its captain, expecting the French, could fire. Shortly afterwards, afloat on the river's darkened currents, the general would, according to account, utter his famous statement concerning Thomas Gray's *Elegy:* how he would "rather have written such a poem, than be the conqueror of Quebec." He repeated the phrase: "The paths of glory lead but to the grave"; and in his pocket were the lines transcribed from Alexander Pope's translation of Homer's *Iliad*, marked at a passage presaging death.

Soon the boats had crossed the mainstream, making now for the river's north shore. The huddled redcoats in the craft passed the first French post without alarm. At Point Sillery, however, a sentry's challenge rang out: *"Qui vive!"* Fortunately, Wolfe had placed Simon Fraser, a Highland captain who spoke excellent French, in the lead boat. After a series of challenges answered by acceptable responses, the sentry relapsed into a doubtful silence. And in the boats below, the redcoats breathed easily once again. The strong current bore the boats onwards. Exactly at seven minutes past four, Wolfe's own boat ground its keel on the eastern shore of the Anse au Foulon (later called Wolfe's Cove). As usual, the General was the first ashore, followed by Captain Delaune and his 24 men comprising the "Forlorn Hope," or storming party.

Certainly no one was less the typical soldier of popular imagination than James Wolfe. A six-footer with sloping shoulders, he had lanky limbs that conspired to make him seem even taller. Pale and fragile in appearance, he possessed carroty hair and bright blue eyes. As if in caricature, his forehead sloped back, his nose was long and slightly upturned, and he had inherited his mother's receding chin. Although he habitually held himself erect, his gait is recounted to have been awkward. Nonetheless, his mouth was firm, and his general expression most pleasant. As for his soldiers, they idolized him, and they also respected his drive and unflagging determination.

The serene heights above the Anse au Foulon were scarred by a great gully; but Wolfe had no intention of forcing this path, choked as it was with fallen branches. Instead, he quickly led the advance party to a projecting spur that he noted lay 150 yards farther east. "I don't think we can by any means get up here," he said, "but however we must use our best endeavour."

The path up the cliff face was steep, craggy, overgrown with clumps of cedar and spruce. It is evident from reports of the ascent, however, that it was not quite so bad as it appeared. Its difficulty lay in the conditions under which it had to be accomplished. Captain Delaune's force consisted of Highlanders from Fraser's and Montgomery's regiments. As the silent climbers proceeded, a soldier's boot would gain a tenuous foothold, only to be betrayed by a yielding shower of soft dirt and other obstacles. A pause would follow, and the Highlanders continued their ascent in relative silence.

Two hundred feet above, a Highlander, imitating Fraser, opened a parley in French. Before the startled sentry could respond, a strong party of Highlanders drove home with fixed bayonets.

To Wolfe, waiting below, the storming party's cheers denoted that the hoped-for surprise had been achieved. Now the redcoats crowded in the waiting boats were dispatched in immediate motion up a projecting spur leading to the top of the cliff, from whence Captain Vergor's post might be taken in flank and rear. Although suffering from tuberculosis, Wolfe somehow found the strength, among the files of Rangers, Highlanders, and Grenadiers, to drag himself up with the rest. By six o'clock Wolfe would have 4,800 men on the heights.

Meanwhile, transports, which had dropped down on the tide, began to disgorge troops packed aboard them, who were now being rowed ashore. Soon, these would be joined by 1,200 more redcoats, ferried across from the south shore, where they had awaited orders under Brigadiers Carleton and Burton. Under Moncton's direction, sweating soldiers would shortly commence to drag two field-pieces up the zig-zag two-foot-wide path. Once the debris the French had intentionally placed was cleared, the ascent was relatively easy for those who followed. In the grey dawn with its cool spray of rain, the long file of red-coated infantry moved quickly upwards, forming as ordered on the plateau above.

After reconnoitring, Wolfe chose for his battlefield the grounds between a low ridge, lying about a mile west of the town, and a second ridge, some 800 yards in front of its walls. It was named the Plains of Abraham, after Abraham Martin, a pilot who had once owned land there. Returning to his army assembled at the top of the Anse au Foulon, the General quickly marched the files of Highlanders and infantry by way of the Ste.-Foy road to the first ridge, abruptly wheeling their columns to form his line of battle. His extreme right, on the knoll, was held by the 35th; its duty would be to cover the flank of their own comrades. Next, thrown a little forward by the nature of the ground, were the three companies of Louisbourg Grenadiers. Then, in order, stood the 28th, the 43rd, the 47th, the Highlanders, the 58th and 15th. The latter, posted just south of the Ste.-Foy Road, secured the left flank. Behind them, Wolfe placed his Light Infantry, facing north towards the valley of the St. Charles in order to repel any attack from that quarter. His reserves consisted of the 2nd Royal Americans, just behind the 58th, and the 48th, across the road from Sillery. The 3rd Royal Americans guarded the vital path leading from the cove to the heights.

Despite the prevailing myth, it was not predominantly English soldiers who bested the French on the Plains of Abraham. Of the ten British regiments that took part in the Battle of Quebec, one was Scottish (Fraser's Highlanders, the largest and most formidable of Wolfe's regiments), one Irish (Otway's 35th Foot, nicknamed the Belfast Lilies), four American (the 60th Foot, or Royal American Regiment, consisting of two battalions; also the grenadier companies of Hopson's 49th Foot, Warburton's 45th Foot, as well as Lascelle's 47th Foot), and the remaining a polyglot of

Irish, English, Welsh, and Scottish (Bragg's 28th, Kennedy's 43rd, Amherst's 15th, and Anstruther's 58th). Additionally, Wolfe's small force was composed of 600 men of His Majesty's Independent Company of Rangers, raised in 1756, which had fought earlier at Louisbourg. There were also some 300 colonial pioneers, who arrived in July, to deal with the "paint and howl of the Indian menace." To his enduring credit, Wolfe would produce outstanding results from such a motley body of troops, but only after short, sharp training.

The firing line Wolfe presented to the French comprised 3,100 men. Over 1,000 of these, however, were chiefly placed or intended to protect his little army's flanks. The six battalions facing Quebec, destined to bear the shock of battle, were to cover a front half a mile wide with only 1,800 troops. Overextended as his troops were, Wolfe could not afford to deploy them three deep, a formation which in itself was thought exceptionally daring in its economy. Thus for the first time in a battle between the armies of two major powers, one side would fight with a line only two soldiers deep. As such, it was the authentic "thin red line," half a century before the formation would be officially authorized by the British army. Wolfe's force was in array by eight o'clock; he was ready to fight, though as of yet totally without the support of artillery, which was still being manhandled up the cliff.

As he checked the troops' deployment, Wolfe felt his ill and fevered mind leap back over his own short thirty-two years and events which, seemingly, had drawn him to this supreme test: how proud he had been at receiving his first commission at the age of fifteen; how as a nineteen-year-old captain he had campaigned against the Young Pretender in the '45; the subsequent lonely years spent in garrison duty in the cold and damp Highlands, during which he had mastered the basics of military command; and how as a junior officer during the ill-fated descent on Rochfort, on the French coast, he had learned how difficult it was to combine land and sea operations.

Undoubtedly, too, he recalled his second experience at combined operations, at Louisbourg in 1758 when, in his first outing as a brigadier, his brilliant improvisation had saved the day and brought about the surrender of the great French fortress on Cape Breton Island. As a result, William Pitt, the new prime minister, recognizing him to be a fellow neurotic, driven by the same mix of monomania, dejection and elation as himself, had placed him in command of this, his third combined endeavour.

Although he had criticized Amherst, his commander, for failing to capture Quebec following Louisbourg's fall, Wolfe himself had, to his chagrin, been badly stymied since landing at Quebec three months earlier. Frustrated by the fortress' natural defences, and by the formidable French lines stretching some eight miles east of the town, he was forced to alter his original plans. Throughout July he continued to change his strategy. Eventually he had attacked the Montmorency Heights, east of the town. But his grenadiers had been repulsed with heavy casualties. During the last days of August, Wolfe's health, never robust, had broken under the combined physical and mental strain. In the St. Lawrence's humid summer heat, he seemed to be withering away, consumed by indigestion, tuberculosis, and dysentery. As he fearfully confided to his surgeon: "I know perfectly well that you cannot cure my complaint, but patch me up so that I will be able to do my duty for the next few days and I shall be content."

Hastily convening a council of war, Wolfe had sought the advice of his brigadiers: Robert Moncton, of Acadia fame; James Murray, a brave, ambitious, envious officer; and the haughty yet talented George Townshend, the Duke of Newcastle's arrogant nephew. Rejecting their commander's proposals, they argued that Montcalm's communications must be cut, in order to force "the Old Fox" to come out and fight.

Shortly afterwards, Wolfe and Townshend had taken out a party of officers to reconnoitre the river. Surveying the commanding height of the plateau through a spyglass, Wolfe noted a long path that traversed the steep face of the precipice, and made his fateful decision to land his troops at its base.

Now, with the ascent behind him, Wolfe switched his mind back to the task immediately at hand. Always considerate of his men, he ordered the files of troops to lie down in the grass. As he awaited the enemy sortie, the General, accompanied by Townshend, attempted to gauge the build-up of Montcalm's forces. Aside from a little earlier sniping to their left, however, the redcoats suffered no annoyance from the enemy since they had captured the Samos battery, which had been firing on them. Clearly, the French continued to sleep, unaware of the British presence.

It would not be until after six o'clock that Montcalm, riding up from the Beauport lines to Governor Vaudreuil's headquarters near the St. Charles bridge, learned the full enormity of what had occurred. A sick officer, who had hastened from the General Hospital, informed him that the British had landed and were advancing along the Ste.-Foy road. Moments later, Montcalm himself spotted Wolfe's men on the horizon. Calling out all the troops that were nearby, he ordered the Guienne Regiment forward to reconnoitre. He also sent an officer to summon the French left wing from its position beyond Beauport. Vaudreuil, however, who commanded the troops that defended the river's shoreline below the town, ordered the forces to stay where they were. Only with difficulty did Montcalm succeed in getting the support of the Royal-Roussillon regiment, stationed in this sector. And when he asked the Sieur de Ramezay for 25 pieces of artillery to bolster the town's defences, the officer refused to send more than three, without the Governor's express orders.

Montcalm, alarmed by the confusion surrounding him on all sides, held an informal council of war. Should they attack immediately? Or would it be wiser to try to secure reinforcements of both men and guns? Should they await Captain Louis Bougainville and the force he commanded from upriver? With Wolfe only a mile distant, and brisk skirmishing commencing, Montcalm still remained ignorant of the enemy's strength and battle plan. While his troops assembled, the French Commander made a hasty reconnaissance. But having seen only the British left and centre — for the majority of Wolfe's troops were lying down — he decided that his opponent's force was quite small. They should be attacked before the British had the opportunity to strengthen their numbers. Also, if Montcalm did not act, he feared the British might seize the bridge across the St. Charles, effectively cutting the French forces in two. To the French Commander it appeared that whatever advantage might be gained by waiting would be more than counterbalanced by the increase in strength each hour's delay would provide the British.

Montcalm ordered forward an additional 1,500 skirmishers to assist the force comprised of *Canadiens* and Indians already engaging the enemy. Soon, firing on the British centre and right intensified. The British responded by sending forward sharpshooters of their own. This produced a lively exchange, in which the French and Indians appeared to hold the advantage.

Shortly after nine in the morning the British finally saw French regulars on the skyline in front of the town's fortifications. Riding at their head, Montcalm ordered his six battalions forward 100 paces before issuing orders to expand the advancing column into line to match the enemy's deployment. Unfortunately, it took more than half an hour to manoeuvre his men to his liking. Meanwhile, the densely packed French suffered heavy casualties from British skirmishers. Also, Captain York, commanding two 6-pound guns that had just reached the battlefield, began to direct a heavy fire against them.

The British line, two soldiers deep, stood motionless. When a redcoat was hit, a trooper advanced from behind to fill the gap. All the officers Wolfe had chosen were deployed for the struggle: Townshend commanded on the left flank; Murray was in control in the centre; Moncton commanded on the right; Guy Carleton was in charge of the Grenadiers.

Four years earlier, Wolfe had penned a prophetic letter to his mother, noting: "As I rise in rank . . . people will expect considerable performances, and I shall be induced . . . to be lavish of my life." Was he now deliberately exposing himself? Possibly he believed that he had but a short time to live or that a glorious death on the battlefield in the moment of victory was to be preferred to a lingering and painful death from illness. At any rate, the ungainly commander was actively in the forefront as the skirmishing proceeded. Elated that "Monsieur, le Marquis" had elected to engage his lobster-backs, he continued to stride resplendently up and down the lines, his lanky gait and tall figure rendering him terribly conspicuous. Attired in tricorne hat, embroidered waistcoat, scarlet frock coat, and gold-threaded sword belt, he moved quickly about, cane in hand, encouraging officers and men, checking their ranks, and cautioning the officers: "Under no circumstances are you to open fire until the order is given. Have your men hold fire until the enemy is within forty yards."

Wolfe also issued orders for soldiers to load their muskets with two balls, to increase the power of the volley at close range. Sore and harassed after weeks of skirmishing around their camps, and disgusted at the treatment of comrades who had fallen into enemy hands, the infantrymen were excited to be at last coming to combat with the enemy. In the centre, the Highlanders, in a riot of colour, pipes skirling, eagerly unsheathed lethal broadswords, anticipating hand-to-hand battle.

As Wolfe passed in front of the lines, a captain he knew was shot through the lungs by a sniper. Kneeling beside him, the General told him: "Do not despair. I shall see to it that you earn early promotion when you are recovered." Shortly after, Wolfe sent an aide-de-camp to General Moncton to inform him of the promise should he himself fall. Such gestures carried Wolfe's troops through every hazard of battle. They knew that any promise made by their Commander would be kept.

At about half-past nine, a sniper's bullet struck Wolfe's wrist, shattering it. He seemed scarcely to feel it, so delighted was he at bringing the enemy to battle. He calmly bound the wound up with a handkerchief an officer lent him. Then, walking across the line in his bright red coat, he gave his final instructions. Rumour has it that he was struck again, in the groin, in front of Bragg's regiment. Modern critics, however, discount this. Finally, for the coming battle, Wolfe took up his position on a small rise where he could enjoy a good view of the battlefield.

Riding back and forth in front of the French lines on his magnificent black charger, gleaming sword in hand, Montcalm rhetorically asked his men if they were tired. They answered their General, roaring they were eager to advance.

The great clock in Quebec's basilica marked five minutes past ten as the French prepared to advance. Montcalm gave the order to march, and the ensigns let the big silk banners fly under the sun, which had broken magnificently through the clouds. Drums rolled out the charge. Across the intervening space, British redcoats heard the troops' throaty cheer as they began to advance. The French regulars, in white uniforms and red waistcoats, came on rapidly (indeed, too rapidly). Roussillon, Languedoc, and La Sarre had blue facings; Guienne and Béarn, red. Captains and higher officers carried pikes; sergeants, halberds. Above each regiment floated its ensign consisting of a white cross quartered with a splash of colour, according to the unit. Quebec's grey-clad *Troupes de la Marine* advanced on the left, on the right came those of Montreal and Trois Rivières. The officers were mostly of good quality, as were the soldiers, though the colonial troops were somewhat lax in discipline. Infantry on both sides carried flintlock muskets armed with bayonets. Indeed, in equipment, there was little difference between the hosts.

In a single motion, the British line sprang to its feet, infantry moving forward about 50 paces to take their position. Overall, the numbers on both sides were about equal. But all of the French regulars were in the battle line which consequently outnumbered the British front, although being shorter.

Advancing with a shout, the French continued to come on at a double-quick pace. Captain York continued to work his guns until the last moment. One of these was handled with great daring by the officer himself, who ran it out along the Sillery road and opened on the French with grapeshot at a range of 300 yards. Such fire did much damage among the men of the Royal Roussillon and unsteadied the entire enemy line. The Captain continued to work his guns until the very last moment, before running the pieces back behind the British lines, which, after having risen, continued to stand motionless, with shouldered arms. At 300 yards, the French colonials on the flanks began firing without

Portrait of Louis-Joseph, Marquis de Montcalm.
19th century? Artist unknown. (NAC/C-027665)

orders. As was the custom, they threw themselves on the ground to reload. Some slunk off to join the skirmishers in the flanking woods. In the centre, worried French regulars, their ranks increasingly disarrayed, continued to advance. Their line was greatly overlapped by the British, and to protect their flanks Montcalm's troops moved increasingly outward from the centre.

Soon, the advancing lines of regulars began to lose their symmetry. Men stopped and fired without orders, paused to reload, and moved on a little way. Then the confused mass repeated its

ragged fusillade. In this manner, the five battalions of French regulars soon came within the 40 paces Wolfe had specified in front
of the British lines.

The General had placed himself in front of the gap separating
the Louisbourg Grenadiers and the 28th. As the enemy advanced,
he observed them "with a countenance radiant and joyful beyond
description." At Wolfe's orders, the redcoats stood as stone, muskets at the slope. Fortunately, they were spread so thin that casualties were relatively few. As the French continued their advance,
the British remained motionless. Suddenly, the infantry, in a single motion, unshouldered their Brown Besses, the Long Land
Pattern Musket, and the familiar loading orders were given:
"Handle cartridge, Prime, Load, Draw Ramrod, Return Ramrod,
Make Ready, Present."

On Wolfe's command, officers now issued the final order:
"Present — Fire!" Commencing on the right, from each of the six
battalions, a double-shotted volley crashed out. So perfect was the
redcoats' musketry that it seemed like six reports of a single
gigantic gun.

Nearly every man in the French front rank went down. As the
dense smoke cleared, the French tried to maintain some sense of
order. There was no respite. Having reloaded as ordered, the
British advanced 20 paces, and poured another series of volleys
into the now-retreating enemy, whose ranks were in disarray. Captain John Knox later reported that captured French officers
noted they had "never opposed such a shock." A distinguished
British military historian, Sir John Fortescue, would later write of
this action: "It was the most perfect shot fired on a battlefield."

Watching the French begin to waver, Wolfe shouted the order
to charge. But before he had proceeded ten paces, a ball struck
him in the chest. He asked two grenadiers to support him so that
the troops would not see him fall. With their assistance the
Commander walked 100 yards to the rear before sinking down.
Although he was painfully wounded, Wolfe refused a surgeon.
Minutes later, someone cried: "They run; see how they run!"
"Who run?" demanded the dying Commander, roused from slum-

ber. "The enemy, sir . . . they give way everywhere!" Wolfe now gave his final orders to cut off the fugitives: "Go . . . to Colonel Burton; tell him to march Webb's regiment down to Charles's River, to cut off the retreat from the bridge." Turning on his side, Wolfe reportedly said: "Now God, be praised, I die content." In the words of a 19th-century historian, "his gallant soul had fled."

A few minutes after the General's death, Montcalm, too, was mortally wounded. According to a French account, the commander was struck during the retreat, as he was swept away by his own men. But a British artillery officer would claim that he fell victim to grapeshot fired from one of the 6-pounders he commanded. It is quite possible that Montcalm, a prominent figure on the battlefield, was indeed sniped over open sights by British gunners. According to a French officer, the General was wounded in the lower part of his stomach and his thigh. Another officer saw him ride painfully back into the town on his great black steed, three soldiers holding him in the saddle. Although wounded beyond help, he would not die until the following morning.

Oblivious to Wolfe's plight, with a loud "hurrah" and a spine-chilling Gaelic war cry, redcoats and Highlanders broke into a run to pursue the retreating enemy. Some continued to fire, some relied on the bayonet, while Fraser's men wielded their dreaded broadswords. One witness who followed the Highlanders across the field later observed: "The bullet and the bayonet are decent deaths compared with the execution of the swords," and he noted further shocking details of the stomach-wrenching action, including heads that were neatly severed from bodies. Although rout had turned into slaughter, the Highlanders never caught up with the main body of enemy troops. Also, the British managed to capture only two French guns, and not a single standard.

On the northern flank, protected by a wooded area and the hill that slopes down to the St. Charles, the French made a final stand. As a result, they managed to check the British advance for some time. The Highlanders of the 78th, after pursuing their quarry to the town's walls, circled back through the woods to the battlefield. Soon they were engaged in a bloody fire-fight with a force of *Canadiens* on the edge of the Plains. A junior officer reported that the enemy "killed and wounded a great many of our men, and killed two officers, which obliged us to retire a little, and form again." Finally, assisted by the 58th and 2nd Royal Americans, British forces were able to drive the enemy down the hill and across the St. Charles. The tenacity of local militia, fighting from cover, made it possible for the beaten French regulars to escape across the bridges to the Beauport camp.

The battle resulted in heavy casualties for the small armies. Townshend recorded British losses as 659 all ranks, of whom 58 were killed. Among senior officers, Moncton, Carleton, and Isaac Barre were wounded; additionally, nine officers were killed. Fraser's Highlanders, which recorded 168 casualties, was the regiment that suffered most. On the French side, Vaudreuil reported the loss of some 600 men in addition to 44 officers. 350 were also made prisoner. Although it seems strange that the defeated side would have suffered casualties that were lighter than the victor's, quite possibly the Governor underestimated. In contrast, Townshend estimated French losses as high as 1,500 men.

The reason for the British triumph is not difficult to determine. A Scottish officer who was present would describe the clash as "the first regular engagement . . . ever fought in North America." It was Wolfe, however, who fully anticipated the nature of the battle. As records indicate, he had taken considerable care and trouble to prepare his troops and make them as perfect an instrument for war as time and circumstances permitted. Clearly, his was the better army.

Some critics also contend that superior armament in the form of the Brown Bess with its 46-inch, .75-calibre barrel, played an important part in the British victory. Certainly, it had some influence. Murray, for example, commented on the evident French fear of what they termed "the English musket" at Deschambault. Nonetheless, the effective firepower of a company depended more on massed rank firing and timing than it did on the accuracy of the individual soldier. Also, it should not be overlooked that the smoke created by the discharge of dozens of muskets, in an age before smokeless powder, would have effectively obscured the battlefield, rendering it difficult for a marksman to draw a bead on his target.

Impressive though it was, the British victory was anything but complete. As already mentioned, the greater part of the French forces managed to escape across the St. Charles, and would retreat to the west that evening. The loss of Wolfe was also a serious setback for the British. And, if our informant was accurate in describing the Brigadier's last moments, he possessed a critical appreciation of preventing the enemy's escape. It seems that neither Burton nor Townshend, however, ever heard their dying commander's final order.

In the present century, military historians have expended a great deal of effort assessing the professional competence of both Montcalm and Wolfe. Although Lévis, Montcalm's second-in-command, wryly remarked afterwards "a dead general is always wrong" (indeed, he might have added, a dead one is at a particular disadvantage), the reality remains that Montcalm did not need to attack at ten o'clock. Instead, he could have attacked at twelve or two. Although it would have given the British time to entrench as well as bring up additional forces, a delay would have enabled him to bring more artillery from inside the town onto the battlefield. Likely, it would also have given Colonel Antoine de Bougainville, Montcalm's subordinate, who commanded some of the best troops, the opportunity to join his chief in the Battle of the Plains.

Despite his bravery in and the successful outcome of the battle, Wolfe has had his critics. Colonel C. P. Stacey, a leading Canadian military historian, has criticized Wolfe's summer-long siege of Quebec: "As a strategist . . . Wolfe was painfully inadequate." But the same historian notes that he was "an uncommonly fine fighting officer, at his best under fire; and this accounts for his great reputation among junior ranks of his army, who knew nothing of his deficiencies as a planner." Stacey also observes that, once the army was ashore, "no mistakes were made. Wolfe was as decisive on the battlefield as he had been indecisive through the long weeks, when he was fumbling with his strategic problem." Such a judgement is likely as complete as any that it will ever be possible to arrive at concerning this controversial officer and his fabled role in the Battle of the Plains of Abraham.

For over two centuries, Wolfe has received far more adulation and attention than can possibly be justified. Why is this? Wolfe was especially fortunate in the construction of his image after his death, for he was immortalized by one of the age's most celebrated painters. Benjamin West's sprawling canvas *The Death of Wolfe,* done in London a decade and a continent removed from the action, set the stage for a heroic interpretation. Previously, West, a "history painter," had painted classical scenes from antiquity. This time, the painter's idea was that the people would appear in contemporary dress, not in the garb worn by the Ancients. Clothing apart, however, the painting contained virtually nothing in the way of historical fact, despite West's going to great trouble to paint the general as convincingly as he could. In the famous oil, Wolfe lies swooning in the arms of three officers in the centre of a crowded scene. Clustered figures include (somewhat incongruously) a kneeling, meditative and noble-appearing Indian and a colonial frontiersman. Despite its inaccuracies, West's evocative creation forms a projection of far-reaching and epic conquest. As such, it captured the imagination of Britain's upper classes. So apparently real was the painter's depiction that, when future generations of both British and Canadian schoolchildren grew up drilled in the "truths" of imperial history, it was West's heroic scene that they and their teachers envisioned, more than any more literal rendering.

A century later, another heroic version of Wolfe and Montcalm would be added to the record. It was provided by New England historian Francis Parkman and his well-known book *Montcalm and Wolfe,* a magnificent study. Indeed, Parkman's brilliant portrait, in which he tried to imbue his story with the life and spirit of the time, events, and people described, derives much of its heroic character from his account of Wolfe's determination to complete a gigantic mission despite the appalling state of his physical health. Not least, Parkman, who himself was going blind, injected into the work his own intense identification with the General and his struggle to overcome his handicap.

Even today, Wolfe's intense and fevered personality continues to perplex and challenge us. One thing is certain, though: his victory ensured the triumph of British arms. Five days after Wolfe's death, the Chevalier de Ramezay yielded the ruined fortress of Quebec. The next day, Brigadier-General James Murray led the main body of British troops into the battered city. Murray, although only the junior brigadier, would of necessity assume the military governorship of the captured fortress. The next spring, he would almost lose it once again to a besieging French army commanded by General Lévis. Five months later, fortune would be dramatically reversed. Now, there would take place the final act in the drama of the "fading of the Lilies." Three British armies, commanded by Murray, William Haviland, and Amherst, totalling 16,000 troops, converged on Montreal, the headquarters of French resistance, in a vast and perfectly-coordinated pincer movement.

On September 8, 1760, close to a full year after Wolfe's initial success, General Amherst, the commander-in-chief, took the final surrender of the colony of Quebec from Vaudreuil. Lévis, however, furious at the British commander's refusal to accord the French honours of surrender because of atrocities committed by their Indian allies, ordered his troops to burn their colours. The following day, a detachment of the British army under Colonel Frederick Haldimand entered Montreal and took formal possession of the town. In accordance with the surrender's terms, French regulars and officials were repatriated to France. Several years later, the capitulation would be officially confirmed by the Treaty of Paris, agreed to by both Britain and France in 1763. Henceforward, it would be British soldiers and British guns that would defend the St. Lawrence Valley, and protect both Canada and the French from invasion.

SELECTED READINGS

Bishop, Arthur. *Canada's Glory: Battles that Forged a Nation.* Toronto: McGraw-Hill Ryerson, 1996.

Keegan, John. *Warpaths: Travels of a Military Historian in North America.* Toronto: Key Porter, 1995.

Liddell Hart, Sir Basil Henry. *Great Captains Unveiled.* New introduction by Max Hastings. London: Greenhill Books; Novato, Ca., U.S.A.: Presidio Press, 1990.

McCulloch, Ian. "With Wolfe at Quebec: Who Fought on the Plains of Abraham?" *The Beaver* 72:2 (April–May 1992): 19–25.

Schama, Simon. *Dead Certainties (Unwarranted Speculations).* New York: Knopf, 1991.

Stacey, C.P. *Quebec 1759: The Siege and the Battle.* London: Pan Books, 1973.

Butler's Rangers, British Provincial Army, ca 1777.
By Charles Lefferts. (The New-York Historical Society Neg. No. 16618A)

2

ONTARIO'S LOYALIST
SOLDIER-FOUNDERS

A Mark of Honour

*Mythology concerning the 40,000 United Empire Loyalists
who emigrated to British North America during and after
the American Revolution (1776–1783), and who established the colonies of Upper Canada and New Brunswick,
tends to be ingrained. Instead of images of the dogged, sometimes even ferocious, fighting and the frontiersmen whom
necessity forced to become soldiers, we usually picture loyal
civilians marching out of the victorious United States at the
end of the conflict to settle in what would in time become
Canada. But this stereotype causes us to overlook the fascinating story of one group of Loyalists: the soldier-settlers who
founded Upper Canada, today's Ontario. By the time the
treaty of separation was signed in 1783, four full-strength
regiments were serving in the Provincial Corps of the British
Army. Also, a fifth corps contained three complete companies.
At the American Revolution's conclusion, all of these units
would contribute personnel who would help establish the
new jurisdiction, or colony, of Upper Canada.*

Only in the last decade or two have historians constructed detailed accounts of just who the Loyalist Provincials were and what they achieved. The fact is, however, that the clash in which British redcoats and colonial minutemen exchanged shots at Lexington and Concord, on Boston's outskirts, in April 1775, initiated not only a rebellion in North America, but also a cruel and bitter civil war. From the very beginning, colonial Americans would fight one another in an internecine rivalry destined to become increasingly savage and bloody. Loyal Americans — men and women who supported the royal cause — made such a decision for a number of reasons. Many genuinely believed in the superiority of British political institutions and the benefits of preserving the unity of the Empire. Some were motivated by social considerations of preserving their privileged position. Others would be persuaded to follow prominent, influential, even charismatic Loyalist leaders. All, however, were to either a greater or lesser degree moved by the simple credo they had been taught in childhood: to "Fear God and Honour the King."

In the northern theatre, some of the largest and most active units during the course of the struggle would be regiments such as the Royal Highland Emigrants, the King's Royal Regiment of New York, Butler's Rangers, rangers of the Northern Indian Department, as well as several smaller corps. All operated from bases situated either in British North America, north of the St. Lawrence and lakes, or else close to today's Canadian-U.S. border. And, contrary to prevailing stereotype, the typical Loyalist who took service in such "provincial" units was a recently arrived, illiterate subsistence farmer of either German or Scots background, dwelling in one of New York's frontier colonies. Following the war, substantial numbers of such soldiers from Loyalist corps would become the founding fathers of present-day Ontario.

From the very beginning of the troubles — with the British garrison in Boston besieged by 20,000 angry American farmers, even before the colonies declared independence — British authorities began to look to loyal supporters to assist the Crown. Strange as it may seem, because of his background, one of the first men that the commander-in-chief General Thomas Gage turned to was an open-faced fifty-year-old officer, Lieutenant-Colonel Allan Maclean. Possibly because he was an avowed Jacobite, or supporter of the Stuart cause, his name has been allowed almost to disappear from our history. Still, this officer's life remains one out of which a novel might well be crafted. As a young man of twenty, Maclean had been "out with Prince Charlie" at the Battle of Culloden. Following the romantic and bitter defeat of the Stuart cause, he had taken service with Holland's Scots Brigade. Afterwards, when King George III extended an amnesty to Jacobite officers, he had served in America. During the Seven Years' War, he was wounded twice, at Ticonderoga and Niagara. He also served with Wolfe's force besieging Quebec.

Maclean was entrusted with raising a regiment to help quell the growing unrest in the colonies. Having "taken the King's shilling, and eaten his bread," the near-legendary officer was not the kind of man who would betray his royal employer. Gage's "beating order" authorized Maclean to raise a regiment among "our subjects who have, at different times, emigrated from the North West parts of Great Britain and have transported themselves to New York." Eventually, the regiment would consist of two battalions of ten companies each, recruited from Scottish settlers in a number of the provinces of North America, including Quebec and Nova Scotia. Appropriately, its name would be the "Royal Highland Emigrants."

Recruits had still to receive their much-coveted Highland uniforms when they and personnel from the British Indian Department (the forerunner of the present Department of Indian and Northern Affairs Canada) were thrown into a desperate attempt to block the advance of American Richard Montgomery and his rebel army northwards up the Lake Champlain-Richelieu River route in the autumn of 1775. Two hundred and fifty provincial Highlanders, who were at Montreal, would fall back to Quebec following Montgomery's capture of the former town. Here, the intrepid Allan Maclean would play a major role. Not only did he steel the resolve of Governor Sir Guy Carleton's deputy to resist the rebels' demands in the Governor's absence, but once Carleton himself managed to return to the besieged city, Maclean continued to encourage the inhabitants to resist. The siege finally ended on New Year's Eve, when Montgomery's and fellow rebel Benedict Arnold's combined forces assaulted the walled city in a two-pronged attack, both parts of which defenders successfully beat back in the Lower Town. The botched effort cost Montgomery his life and Arnold was wounded.

After a British fleet relieved Quebec in the spring, Maclean's Emigrants took part in mopping-up operations. Following this, a detachment of Maclean's regiment would not only serve in Quebec but would assist in defending the Great Lakes' frontier. Later, a second battalion would be employed in the Atlantic region.

The growing crisis in the colonies soon promoted the formation of a second, more prominent, Loyalist regiment. The powerful and charismatic Johnson family of New York gathered its supporters — the closest thing North America possessed to a feudal force — in the Mohawk Valley. In June, Guy Johnson, superintendent of the Northern Affairs Indian Department, which was closely tied to the British Army, moved his operations base north to Montreal. Meanwhile, his cousin, Sir John Johnson, remained behind in order to raise a battalion to assist the King's cause.

In early 1776, Sir John, too, at last escaped to Canada, accompanied by a large number of fellow Tories, a few Mohawks, and scouts. Following an arduous, hunger-plagued journey through the Adirondack Mountains of New York, during which members subsisted on wild onion roots and the leaves of beech trees, the party of 170 arrived safely at Montreal.

The thirty-four-year-old Johnson was a relative stranger at this time, even to many who would later serve under his command. As the son of the famous, even formidable Sir William Johnson, he had been sent as a young man on a prolonged tour of England. Later, he had returned to North America, served in the Seven Years' War, and married an heiress and lady of fashion. By the time he arrived in Canada, the Mohawk Valley baronet, who had been awarded a title while abroad in the Mother Country, had emerged as a "confident, aspiring, enterprising man," determined to restore the fortunes of his family and army of retainers, or followers.

Upon arriving in Canada, Johnson received a warrant from governor Guy Carleton authorizing him to raise a regiment. The King's Royal Regiment of New York was the second regiment raised in the Northern Department. Eventually, it would number 1,290 men, making it the largest Loyalist provincial corps.

The green-clad "Royal Yorkers" 1st Battalion was pressed into action almost immediately, assisting Carleton who was attempting to expel the rebels from Canada and push down Lake Champlain. In August, 1777, Johnson's provincials and other Loyalists would play an important role in the bloody battle of Oriskany Creek, in New York, which both sides claimed as a victory. Governor Frederick Haldimand, Carleton's successor, remained cautious, however, concerning the suitability of such provincial units for major campaigning. Thus the regiment would be employed in only three other important expeditions directed against the Mohawk Valley.

It was Butler's Rangers, though, rather than Maclean's Highland Emigrants or Johnson's regiment, that ultimately would prove to be the indisputably most successful and feared provincial regiment. John Butler, the son of an Irish officer, had seen extensive service as a youth during the Seven Years' War. By the time of the American Revolution, although growing corpulent, he still remained active in the field. Courageous, ambitious, and driving, Butler had, by 1777, turned his considerable energies to encouraging the Iroquois, who had put off taking sides, to resist the Americans. Most importantly, he convinced 300 Seneca warriors to participate in the escalating struggle. This finally broke the neutrality that had prevailed on the part of the Indians.

As the third corps of provincials raised to operate from Canada, Butler's Rangers would ultimately comprise eight companies, two of which were composed of frontiersmen familiar with Indian customs and languages. During the half dozen years following the Rangers' commissioning, Butler himself, appointed a lieutenant-colonel, served as the tireless leader of the corps. As already mentioned, despite being middle-aged, he frequently served in the field, personally leading raiding parties. Otherwise, he organized strategy for the Indian Department's Headquarters, situated at Niagara. Additionally, Walter Butler would serve as his father's captain from the autumn of 1779 until his untimely death in October 1781, during one of the last raids made in the war.

Following British General "Gentleman Johnny" Burgoyne's disastrous march south, at the head of a British army, and his humiliating surrender at Saratoga, in upcountry New York, in 1777, the Mother Country would mount no more major offensives. From this point onwards, the entire nature of the conflict along the Great Lakes frontier was drastically altered. Posts such as Montreal, Oswegatchie (Ogdensburg), Carleton Island (where Lake Ontario enters the St. Lawrence), Oswego, Niagara, Detroit, and Michilimackinac, situated in the far west at the juncture of the Great Lakes, would serve as bases for mounting raids southward into New York and Pennsylvania, as well as westward into Illinois and Ohio. For the next five years, Tory raiders, including an increasing number of frontiersmen and loyal Indians, would sweep down from Canada in a punishing war directed against poorly defended American frontier settlements.

Both existing Loyalist corps as well as Butler's new Rangers, organized to serve alongside Indians, would be used in such delaying or punishing actions. The tactics Butler employed had earlier been used with devastating success by the famous ranger hero Robert Rogers during the Seven Years' War. Also, in the Revolutionary War's southern theatre of operations, Major John Graves Simcoe's Queen's Rangers were on active service. But the task of Butler's men was markedly different from that of the troops led by the future first lieutenant-governor and founding father of Upper Canada. Ranging far and wide in scouting operations remote from civilization, enduring hardships for long periods of time, Butler's raiders harassed the enemy, destroyed his crops, and obliged Commander General George Washington to transfer troops from the seaboard to defend the frontier. Other objectives of Butler's Rangers included assisting persecuted Loyalists to escape, and driving cattle and horses to Niagara.

Surprise was the Rangers' hallmark. Penetrating at will, small companies bypasssed garrisoned forts in order to direct crippling blows against isolated settlements deep within enemy territory. Before the American militia could respond, they would be gone. The Ranger byword was "hit and run," "strike and escape," especially if a situation began to deteriorate. Rogers' methods, and Butler's modifications of them, bear an uncanny resemblance to modern commando tactics. Indeed, they established the basic pattern employed by their modern counterparts when operating in dense forest or jungle and sparsely settled regions.

Butler's men, in contrast to regulars and other provincials, operated year round. In summer they marched or travelled in bateaux and canoes, braving the pests and diseases encountered in the swamps and bogs of uncleared country. For food they subsisted on Indian corn, crushed between two stones and boiled, seasoned on occasion with meat or fish, if they were lucky enough to obtain such. In winter Rangers employed sleighs, skates, or snowshoes. At nightfall they would scrape the ground bare with their snowshoes, and bank the snow to protect themselves against the wind. Small branches of spruce, fir, and hemlock served both as bedding and to cover the shelter they constructed under the lee of a bank of snow. Since the beds and slanting roof retained the fire's heat, a single blanket was all that was required for comfort.

A Ranger travelled with a minimum of equipment to impede him, and his uniform consisted of whatever was comfortable and practical. For weaponry, a Ranger was usually armed with a smoothbore musket that fired buckshot or bullets. Commonly, he wore a short, dark green jacket, carried a tomahawk, powder horn, and scalping knife. A leather bag or bags filled with shot dangled from his belt. Some Rangers had a small compass fastened to the bottom of their powder horn. Although Ranger uniforms included parade dress, Rangers usually substituted long hunting shirts, leather leggings or overalls, and moccasins when operating in the woods. For headgear, Butler's men wore low flat caps bearing plates monogrammed "G. R." (George Rex: George III) encircled by "Butler's Rangers." When possible, Butler encouraged his men to carry rifles, either their own or drawn from government stores, for they were a superior and far more accurate weapon than the smoothbore. Quite often, to boost firepower and to provide themselves with a weapon capable of breaching fortifications and heavy doors, a company of Rangers going into battle would tow a three-pound cannon, called a grasshopper, behind them on a tump line, or rope, to provide leverage and make it easier to drag through the bush.

Moving through wooded country, Rangers followed rules laid down by Robert Rogers, already mentioned above, the Massachusetts-born originator of guerilla warfare who earlier fought alongside the British during the 1740s' War of the Austrian succession, and in the later Seven Years' War. Scouting, Rangers would proceed in a single file, leaving a space between each man, so that only one of them could be targeted by an enemy marksman. When crossing swampy ground, they usually moved abreast, in order to confuse trackers. Rangers were trained to make camp when darkness had fallen, never before, and to situate it where sentries would have a clear view. When a force consisting of several hundred was out, Rangers usually split into three columns, each marching in single file, with outer columns at least 20 yards distance from the inner. Scouts, deployed forward, to the rear, and along flanks, watched for indications of an ambush. Spread out in such a manner, Butler's men were extremely difficult to surround. In a firefight, Rangers employed other unconventional tactics. If encircled, a company formed a square and held out until darkness afforded them an opportunity to steal away. Whenever the enemy pursued them night or day, Rangers commonly turned and circled back in the hope of catching their attackers in an ambush. Sentries were generally deployed in groups of six, a couple on duty at a time, while the others slept. Such a practice avoided the sending out of fresh sentries, which often tended to inform spies that a camp was nearby.

In addition to hunger, fatigue and sudden changes in weather, the Rangers were commonly beset by the pests and diseases that prevailed in the swamps and bogs of uncleared country. "Muscetoes" of incredible size and voracity were a constant problem. Malaria, called swamp fever, or ague was endemic. Colonel Butler related how an officer "was so ill with Ague that he was under the necessity of having himself tied to his horse." When ill, Indians would make rattlesnake soup "which operated as a cure to attack the ague." Such venomous snakes, commonly used for food by the natives, infested the country in great numbers. Taking a leaf from their Indian allies, Rangers killed them with a sharp stick, which they ran through the head. Wild Solomon's seal as well as broad leaf plantain were employed as effective antidotes should a Ranger be bitten.

Unlike officers of the Rangers, who kept formal journals of their expeditions, Indian leaders and aboriginals, because of their lack of facility in writing English, reported only the results of their expeditions. Except when rebel informers or prisoners identified acquaintances following a raid, the exploits of Indian raiding parties remain unrecorded. As a result, the activities of Scots such as Daniel Rose, Archibald Thomson, James Park, and John Chisholm, whose names appear briefly in surviving records, along with hundreds of other such whites who fought alongside loyal Indians have mainly passed into oblivion. We know, however, from their own statements that all four "volunteered the most dangerous Enterprises," and were "almost unremittingly on actual Service" throughout the war.

Rangers were usually alert and armed by dawn, the choice time for Indians to attack. When travelling, they avoided forts. They also kept a safe distance between themselves and streams or rivers, so attackers could not pin them against the water. When Rangers travelled by water in summer months, they usually rested during daylight hours and moved by night.

Because of Butler's tactics, rebels watched at home or took turns standing sentinel when labouring in the fields. The Americans would be continually harried by conflicting rumours. Often the first intimation that Butler's raiders or Indians were in their midst was the glare of a neighbouring farmhouse bursting into flames. Although their opponents' fears proved an asset to the Rangers, they also inspired many tales of ferocity and atrocity. Most contain little truth. The rebels' bitterest complaint, that white men disguised themselves as Indians, certainly was not new. Both sides had employed such tactics throughout the earlier French wars.

Butler tested his new corps and methods when the first phase of his operations commenced in June 1778. At the head of 200 Provincials and 300 Indians, he swept down the Susquehanna River bound for Pennsylvania's Wyoming Valley. The area was a hotbed of rebel resistance, having been settled in the main by Connecticut Yankees. Butler quickly forced several smaller forts in the Wyoming Valley, Wintermute's and Jenkins', to surrender. When the defenders of nearby Forty Fort refused to yield, Rangers lured them out and ambushed them. The cost was 300 American lives. In total, Butler's raiders destroyed all eight forts in the region, and gutted 1,000 farms. Despite the fact civilians were left in peace, so long as they were disarmed, both the New York and Pennsylvania frontiers were in panic. Indeed, rebel leaders feared the entire region would soon be deserted.

That autumn, Butler and Joseph Brant (whose exploits will be examined in the next chapter) continued the pressure with pinprick raids. The Americans responded by raiding the upper Susquehanna, burning the village of Oquaga, and ravaging the wife of an Oneida chief. Butler's arrogant son Walter now moved on Cherry Valley in New York, a major supply depot, with 200 Rangers, a detachment of the 8th Regiment, as well as 400 enraged Senecas. Until Cherry Valley, the Indian-Tory raids had been fairly humane by the standards of guerilla warfare. But during the attack, the younger Butler's first independent command, the Indians killed 32 men, women, and children. Although Brant tried to halt the killing, and Butler himself actually rescued some survivors, the damage had been done. Henceforth, "Cherry Valley" became a byword for Loyalist butchery. Rebels as well as opponents of the war in Britain itself used the incident to full advantage. Also, generations of American historians would attribute the bloody act to Butler himself. In fact, however, he had remained with the main body of the force engaged in besieging the fort, and had no role in the attack on the civilians.

The following year, 1779, Loyalist forces repeated their successes in a series of similar raids. In response, Major-General John Sullivan would lead an American army of over 5,000 through Iroquois territory in a "scorched earth" campaign. Since Butler's force of Indians and Rangers was helpless to stop them, the Continentals destroyed more than 40 Indian villages and 160,000 bushels of corn. Subsequently, more than 5,000 Iroquois fled northwards from their territories to the protection of Fort Niagara, where the Indian Department fed and clothed them.

Responding to Sullivan's blow, Butler's Rangers now began the second stage of their operations, a period of rigorous retaliation destined to last until the final British surrender at Yorktown, Virginia, in the autumn of 1781. Because the Loyalists who had earlier supplied Rangers with food had by this time either fled or been imprisoned, small bands of Rangers were now obliged to be self-sufficient. Usually, the raiders were mounted. This gave them the option of subsisting on horse-flesh as necessity demanded. Also, they sometimes drove cattle along with them. When accompanied by Indians, Rangers usually attacked rebels who remained in fortified dwellings or villages. On such forays they also sought intelligence.

In the spring of 1780, raiders struck even more forcibly along the northern frontier than they had earlier. Accompanied by 200 Indians, Johnson's Royal Yorkers, relatively inactive since the early stages of the war, unleashed their fury on their leader's old neighbourhood of Johnstown, utterly destroying a 13-mile strip on the north shore of the Mohawk River. Following this, they hit Little Falls. So devastating was the damage that the Iroquois who had sided with the rebels began increasingly to waver. As well, many Onondagas and Tuscaroras now openly declared for the British. That summer, Brant's forces burned the remaining Oneida and

Tuscarora villages, forcing a number of Indians to seek the refuge offered by Fort Niagara. Indian support for the rebel cause virtually ceased at this point. The bloody and desperate frontier war continued, unabated. Later the same year Loyalist forces destroyed more than 1,000 homes, 100 barns, and 60,000 bushels of grain. Except for a few scattered settlements, the once-flourishing Mohawk Valley had been reduced to a string of smouldering ruins.

After Cornwallis's surrender at Yorktown, the third stage of Butler's Rangers operations began. To offset the advantage the rebels had gained in the conventional war, as well as to exploit the superiority the Loyalists enjoyed in frontier fighting, Butler's and the other groups of Rangers pressed the battle home. In 1781 no fewer than 64 Ranger war parties were out attacking likely targets on the frontiers of New York and Pennsylvania, in addition to the Ohio region. Along with destroying settlements the rebels had rebuilt, raiders hit new targets as well. Loyalist parties were able to penetrate almost to Albany and Schenectady in New York, and even into New Jersey. The Americans were also forced to abandon Fort Stanwix and the main post at Cherry Valley. In October, while Barry St. Leger led a diversionary attack down Lake Champlain, Major John Ross, an officer of the regular army, directed a mixed force of Loyalists — including Butler's Rangers as well as British and German regulars from Oswego — against the Mohawk Valley. After burning Warrensborough on the river's south side, the Tories fought their way back through Whig militia and Continentals at West Canada Creek and ultimately escaped to Fort Carleton.

During the last four years of the struggle, a more far-ranging and discontinuous, yet equally savage war raged farther west, in the Ohio and Illinois Country. Although Indian warriors played a more prominent role here, the most notable white Loyalists would be Matthew Elliott, the legendary Samuel Girty, and Alexander McKee. All were former Indian traders in the region who had joined the Indian Department. Fifty Butler's Rangers moved into the region as well in 1779. The next year a further company of Rangers would be sent to serve as scouts.

In the northern states, British arms had triumphed, thanks to the efforts of Butler's Rangers, Johnson's Royal Yorkers, and the regulars who supported them, such as Allan Maclean's Royal Highland Emigrants. Indians and Indian Department officers had played a major role as well. In 1782 Butler's Rangers would be mainly involved in operations in the Ohio Country. Andrew Brant's raid on Wheeling, West Virginia, would be Butler's Rangers' last action during the Revolution — indeed, probably the last involving provincials in the drawn-out struggle. In May, Guy Carleton arrived at New York as commander-in-chief, with instructions to bring the conflict to an end. Soon he began withdrawing all units from the coastline to New York. He also ordered Frederick Haldimand in Canada to permit only defensive operations.

In addition to the three major provincial units whose roles have been detailed, two other provincial units also assisted in defending Canada. In November 1781 the Loyal Rangers, or Jessup's Rangers, became a regiment. Edward Jessup, its new commander, along with his brother Joseph, had served earlier in its predecessor unit, the King's Loyal Americans. During this early period the force had been commanded by their older brother Ebenezer. By the end of 1782, the newly constituted corps attained its full battalion strength of ten companies, thus becoming the fourth provincial unit officially on the books of the British Army's Northern Department.

Several years earlier, in 1779, an effort had been made to organize another unit, the King's Rangers, commanded by the fabled hero of the Seven Years' War himself, Robert Rogers. By this time, however, Rogers was addicted to alcohol, and possibly senile. Thus, little came of the effort, and during the corps' four-year existence it was not really considered an official part of the Northern Department. Nonetheless, it is appropriate that Rogers' name not be forgotten or omitted from the seldom-told and little-appreciated story of the activities of the King's Men. As mentioned before, he was the very best of the Rangers who had been active during the Seven Years' War. Not least, he formulated the techniques employed so successfully by Loyalist raiders during the revolutionary struggle we have been narrating.

Today, the bright chapter the King's Men wrote during the epic struggle continues to speak for itself. During nine years of fighting to defend their homeland and Canada, they provided unwavering service, and achieved an almost unbroken string of victories. At war's end, they actually controlled the northern frontier regions. It was sacrifices like theirs that Carleton had in mind when he later recorded that it was his wish "to put a mark of honour upon the families who had adhered to the unity of Empire, and joined the Royal Standard in America before the Treaty of Separation in the Year 1783."

Fortunately, Frederick Haldimand, the tough-minded but sensitive soldier-administrator of Upper Canada, afterwards realized the importance of settling European Loyalists in their military units. Essentially, he believed that the hard-won "mutual loyalties of comrades in war," as he put it, were far too valuable "to throw away in the days of peace."

Since the Loyalists could not be settled in existing seigneuries, Haldimand decided to purchase land from the Indians, and, as was the custom in his native Switzerland, determined that divisions or "cantons" should be established on neat ethnic and religious lines. The Governor's ambitious plans called for 13 townships to be laid out, and surveyed. Eight of these were located along the St. Lawrence's upper region, five on Lake Ontario's Bay of Quinte.

In order to economize on transportation expenses, provincial troops near the inland forts were settled close to bases where they had served. Butler's Rangers remained at Niagara, the 2nd battalion of the King's Royal Regiment of New York, at Cataraqui, today's Kingston. Beyond the vacant buffer zone that separated the westernmost French seigneury and the easternmost Loyalist township, the 1st battalion of the King's Royal Regiment of New York was moved to the initial five, or as they would shortly be deemed, "Royal Townships," named after members of King George III's numerous family (Charlotteburgh, Cornwall, Osnabruck, Williamsburgh, and Matilda). Most of the Loyal Rangers were settled in townships further west (Edwardsburgh, Augusta, and Elizabethtown).

In the Bay of Quinte region, the first township (Kingston) was allocated to Michael Grass's party; the second (Ernestown) to the Loyal Rangers; the third (Fredericksburgh) to the 2nd battalion of the King's Royal Regiment of New York and the King's Rangers; the fourth (Adolphustown), a peninsula a mere quarter the size of other townships, was assigned to Peter van Alstyne's group; and the fifth (Marysburgh) was assigned to German regulars who wished to stay in Canada and some Royal Highland Emigrants.

Later, two additional townships (Niagara and Stamford) were surveyed for Butler's Rangers. At Detroit, in the far west, no townships were laid out, since the number of settlers was small, consisting mainly of Indian Department personnel, Royal Highland Emigrants, and William Caldwell's company of men from Butler's Rangers. Later, when a problem arose over ownership, Caldwell's men would be relocated to the north shore of Lake Erie (Colchester Township).

In the decades to follow, such soldier-founders of the province of Ontario would fight, and indeed win, perhaps their hardest battle: the struggle against the Canadian wilderness, which in the end produced a vital new society. Today, no stauncher an expression of this spirit to endure exists than in Ontario's proud and sonorous Latin motto: *Ut Incepit Fidelis Sic Permanet:* "Loyal she began, loyal she remains."

SELECTED READINGS

Allen, Robert S., ed. *The Loyal Americans: The Military Role of the Loyalist Provincial Corps and Their Settlement in British North America, 1775–1784*. Ottawa: National Museums of Canada, 1983.

Fryer, Mary Beacock. *Allan Maclean, Jacobite General: The Life of an Eighteenth Century Career Soldier.* Toronto: Dundurn, 1987.

————. *King's Men: the Soldier Founders of Ontario.* Toronto: Dundurn, 1980.

Moore, Christopher. *The Loyalists: Revolution, Exile, Settlement.* rev. ed. Toronto: McClelland and Stewart, 1994.

Thomas, Earle. *Sir John Johnson: Loyalist Baronet.* Toronto: Dundurn, 1986.

Thayendanegea, Joseph Brant, the Mohawk chief.
By George Romney. (NAC/C-011092)

3

CAPTAIN JOSEPH BRANT (THAYENDANEGEA)

The King's Loyal Indians

Legend contains no more remarkable a story than that of Mohawk chief and ally of George III, Captain Joseph Brant (c. 1742/43–1807), also known by his Indian name, Thayendanegea. No other Native leader approached the task of leading his people to resist the white man's encroachments in so focussed a manner. Conversant in Latin and Greek, a devout Anglican, he was used to associating with the powerful and presented himself with all the dignity benefiting a head of state. But there was also the "warrior" side to this steely, dedicated leader who spoke at least three, possibly as many as six, Native tongues. During the American Revolution, Brant's Indian raiders swept down on the American frontier, establishing a fearful record of vengeance and destruction. Afterwards, Brant showed his flexibility and statesmanship by leading his dispossessed people northward into Upper Canada. Here, they became settled and loyal allies of the British King. Brant, however, would ultimately fail in his dream to establish an independent Indian state, situated between the Ohio River and the Great Lakes, that would serve as a buffer between Canada and the United States, and preserve the status of the natives as a distinct and sovereign nation, or group of nations.

Aside from the many striking portraits of Joseph Brant painted by
a bevy of famous 18th-century artists, the best present picture we
have of the mature Mohawk leader is the description recorded by
a Continental officer from the Mohawk Valley who met him while
in the guard house at Niagara:

> He was . . . of fierce aspect — tall and rather spare — well spoken,
> and apparently about thirty years of age. [Brant was thirty-
> eight.] He wore moccasins, elegantly trimmed with beads — leg-
> gings and breech-clout of superfine blue — short green coat,
> with two silver epaulets — and a small, laced, round hat. By his
> side hung an elegant silver-mounted cutlass, and his blanket of
> blue cloth, purposely dropped in the chair on which he sat to
> display his epaulets, was gorgeously decorated with a border of
> red.

Indeed, the last sentence tends to confirm the report that Brant
was even prouder of his rank in the British Army than the honours conferred upon him by his own people.

Brant's origin and pedigree remain a tantalizing mystery.
According to his own account, he was "descended from Wyandot
prisoners adopted by the Mohawks on both the father and
mother's side." However, it was commonly (if erroneously) assumed on both sides of the border that his father was the legendary Sir William Johnson, head of the British Indian Affairs
Department, who is reported to have fathered over 100 Native offspring.

The known circumstances of Brant's birth do little to clear the
fog. He was born in 1742, or thereabouts, in the forest country of
the Upper Ohio. The next dozen or so years of his life he spent
totally immersed in the Native lifestyle: fishing, hunting, swimming, camping, trapping, canoeing and playing Indian games,
which strengthened his fine physique. When Molly, his spirited
sixteen-year-old half sister, caught Johnson's fancy, and went to
live with him at Fort Johnson, located in New York's Mohawk Valley, young Joseph's world changed overnight. Accepted as a member of Sir William's intimate family, the bright youngster quickly

adapted to the new and imposing lifestyle. Like some European feudal baron, the Mohawk magnate held court in a fortified house secured by armed Highlanders, was courted by swarms of delegates from various Indian tribes, and visited by a continual procession of powerful guests.

During the ensuing Seven Years' War, Joseph would accompany Sir William on a number of hinterland campaigns. At the war's conclusion, the prospects for Brant appeared so bright that Johnson packed off the youth, now nineteen, along with his own acknowledged natural son, to the Indian school run by the celebrated Ebenezer Wheelock at Lebanon, Connecticut.

As he had earlier, Brant experienced little difficulty in again changing his lifestyle, this time from the martial din of camp and field to the classroom and Christian chapel. Associates would be markedly impressed by the eager, gentle scholar's nature. As portraits of this period indicate, the young man's softly rounded face is suggestive more of a philosopher's nature than his future calling of a warrior. A sudden roll of thunder in the West, however, soon disrupted such ambitions and scholarly concerns. The Indian leader Pontiac, chief of the Ottawa nation, had revolted and the Western Indians of the Ohio Valley and upper Great Lakes flocked to join him. He led them in a series of successful attacks on eight British outposts in 1763. Pontiac's conspiracy, as it was called, soon ended, but young Joseph, who had opposed the revolt, would not return to his studies. In the years that followed, he settled at Canajoharie, married twice, and was twice widowed.

By the mid-1770s, Brant was becoming increasingly aware of the threat white settlers posed to aboriginals dwelling beyond the frontier of white settlement. When his mentor Sir William died suddenly in 1774, the event magnified Joseph's importance rather than reduced it. Soon, the shots fired at Lexington and Concord would thrust enormous new responsibilities on the handsome Native's broad young shoulders. Upon his decisions would soon rest the fate of his people, along with the lives and fortunes of every settler dwelling in the vicinity of the New York-Pennsylvania border.

When American armies invaded Canada, Brant and Indian Supervisor Guy Johnson (Sir William's nephew) argued that the assistance and services of the Indians should be employed immediately. But both William Butler, chief translator of the Indian Affairs Department, and Governor Guy Carleton opposed employing the Indians in the growing hostilities. Because of their reluctance, Brant, Johnson, and their associate Daniel Claus journeyed to England in late 1775 to carry their plan directly to the cabinet.

In London, Brant was hailed by press, public, and society at large as "King of the Indians." In the capital, the visitors cut an exotic, fascinating figure. One day Brant would appear dressed as an English gentleman; the next, in the colourful regalia of the Mohawk chief that he was. Doors, both official and unofficial, opened. Everywhere he was greeted with enthusiasm, even applause.

After meeting with Lord George Germain, the new secretary of state for the colonies, and explaining Iroquois land grievances and expectations of military assistance, Brant was assured of "every Support England could Render Them," following the suppression of the rebellious American colonists. This promise apparently satisfied the Mohawk leader. Indeed, he became convinced that the Indian people, in order to ensure their future protection and survival, needed to conclude a military alliance with the British against the American colonies. On returning to North America, Brant also decided the time had come for him to assume his appropriate place at the head of the Iroquois' war effort. A problem, however, existed. A war chief achieved his rank only by acclamation, and, since some factions opposed him, he could not muster such support. At length this Gordian knot was severed. On this occasion, the sacred council fire of the Iroquois nation, which had burned for centuries, was ordered formally extinguished to deal with the crisis. With the ancient confederacy's traditions suspended, Brant could become his people's temporary leader. Equally important, he was assured that many hundreds of Iroquois, if not all the aboriginals, would follow him against the

Americans the following spring.

After Burgoyne's disaster (detailed in the preceding chapter), the British would not repeat the obvious mistake of attempting such great formal invasions. Instead, a bloody frontier struggle now commenced. Indians, intent on avenging their losses, would play a vital role in it, assisted, as we have seen, by John Butler's Rangers and Sir John Johnson's "Greens," or the King's Royal Regiment of New York.

Until early 1778 no New York settler had died defending his homestead. Now this prolonged immunity was about to end. Indeed, the first Indian onslaught would strike with a vigour that had not been experienced to date. On May 30, Brant emerged from the shadows of the wilderness on the crest of the ridge above Schoharie. From this commanding vantage point, he and his followers could enjoy the superb prospect of ancestral Mohawk homelands stretching to the east, as well as imposing views to-

Lieutenant-General John Burgoyne Addressing the Indian Allies, Summer 1777.
Drawn by H. Warren, engraved by J.C. Armytage. (NAC/C-017514)

wards Johnson Hall to the northeast, and his own home, Cana-joharie, to the north. With Brant were some 300 Indians and a number of Tory partisans.

Brant's first strike was against the hamlet of Cobleskill. Following such a thrust, an Indian raiding force normally retreated rapidly back into the wilderness, but Brant now withdrew his followers only a few miles, while he selected his next target. During the next two months, he continued to march and counter-march among the wooded hills that separate the intricately intertwined watersheds of the Mohawk, the Susquehanna and the Delaware. Every district of New York's frontier dreaded that it might be the next to suffer, and defenders were forced to remain deployed among the garrisons of the district's numerous forts and stockades. Sometimes Brant detached small parties to raid exposed farms and communities. On other occasions, he boldly struck at towns employing his full strength. His objectives were simple and direct. He sought to maximize the spread of terror in order to confuse attempts to organize a defence. Other goals included seizing cattle and grain to stock both his and Butler's commissaries, destroying food and property that could not be carried off by the enemy, gathering in Tory recruits, rescuing Tory families, and singling out for punishment rebels who were notorious for persecuting Tory neighbours.

The Indian leader's next major stroke was at Springfield on July 18. Here he torched houses and barns, even wagons, ploughs and haystacks. His raiders also drove more than 200 head of cattle and horses down the Susquehanna to Butler's forces. Following Springfield, Brant wasted the settlements around Otsego Lake. Even memories of earlier days he had happily spent here before the war did not deter his hand. Indeed, his devastations were as thorough as elsewhere.

This done, Brant now turned most of his force over to Butler for the campaign in Pennsylvania, already described in the previous chapter. Still, it did not end his own raiding. With a few selected followers he continued his own highly effective covering and flanking operation. In early July he confiscated cattle and grain far down the Delaware. Such raiding took him within 35 miles of the headquarters General George Washington had established on the Passaic following the Battle of Monmouth. Two weeks later, on July 18, the far-ranging Brant burst from the forest 150 miles north, to burn Andrustown. This time, a hastily assembled detachment of local militia pursed his relatively small force, but in the end it failed to catch him.

Brant's success in maintaining a raiding force in continuous contact with the frontier for so long a period was unprecedented. For two months he succeeded in keeping 150 miles of American border territory in turmoil, its inhabitants in flight, and its defenders confused and distracted. In his summary he reported his force had killed or taken prisoner 249 enemy. All of those who had been killed were armed men encountered in action. Most prisoners he had released after lecturing them on the evil of rebelling against their king. Notably, there are no contemporary American complaints accusing Brant or his Indian followers of the indiscriminate murder of women or children, or other noncombatants, during the campaign.

Strategically, Brant's raiding produced brilliant results. It materially reduced an important supply source, for Washington's army depended on both beef and wheat from the Mohawk Valley. Brant's destruction of stores and interruption of seasonal harvesting seriously dislocated enemy operations.

Overall, the rigour of the Indian leader's devastations can be accounted for by the delight his aboriginal followers derived from such a warlike challenge as well as by Brant's own strong emotional conviction that he was striving to recover the homes of both his people and his Tory companions in arms. Such confidence in the righteousness of the King's cause was fortified by the intensity of his loyalist beliefs. A good insight into the inner workings of his mind is provided by a letter he wrote that spring. In it, Brant observes: "I mean now to fight the cruel rebels as well as I can."

In early 1779, Brant, who fought as a war chief, and his Mohawks repeated their earlier successes in similar raids, striking from Vermont in the east to Ohio in the far west. Vivid stories of his reputed ferocity made him a legend in the minds of terrified rebels along the northwest frontier. Other war chiefs, too, such as Blue Jacket of the Shawnee, Little Turtle of the Miamis, and the Cherokee's Dragging Canoe, inspired by his example, likewise employed British arms to harry and raid rebel forces and encroaching settlers.

In late 1779, Major-General Sullivan, heading an army of more than 5,000 Americans, swept through the Iroquois territory, subjecting natives to fire and sword. As has already been mentioned, Butler's small forces of Indians and Rangers could offer little effective resistance to the punitive foray. Eventually the Colonials burned over 40 Indian towns and some 160,000 bushels of corn. As a result, more than 5,000 Iroquois sought refuge at Fort Niagara.

But far from crushing the Six Nations, Sullivan's actions only increased their determination for revenge. Numerous native raiding parties struck far and wide, spreading terror through American frontier settlements during 1780. In July of the same year, on the recommendation of Guy Johnson, Governor Frederick Haldimand made Brant, who hitherto had not held an official commission, "captain of the Northern Confederate Indians." In August 1781, in the Ohio Country, Brant, with 100 whites and Indians, would utterly defeat an equal number of men under Indian fighter George Clark, killing or capturing all of them. Brant's final service would come in 1782, when he and his warriors assisted Major John Ross's men to repair Fort Oswego. Later, in July, he set out with a large party of Indians and a company of light infantry to harry American settlements, but he would be summoned back after the announcement of peace negotiations.

When the peace treaty of 1783 ceded the Indians' traditional territory south of the Great Lakes to the newly independent United States without consulting the Native Americans, their plight suddenly became acute. The Iroquois, who considered themselves "a free people subject to no power upon Earth," were shocked to learn of the British government's arbitrary decision, which effectively rendered them a stateless people. Indeed, aboriginal leaders have continued to the present day to regard themselves as a distinct nation, or group of nations, despite the mind set of many Canadians, who would deny them such status.

Fortunately, Haldimand, dealing with problems on the spot, was sensitive to the problems of the Mohawks and other Iroquois. Aware that they had contributed more to the war effort on a per capita basis than any other group, he ordered land to be set aside for the Natives north of Lake Ontario. Initially, Brant favoured settling both his own family as well as his people on the Bay of Quinte. But by the spring of 1784 his vision had shifted westward to the region of the Grand River Valley. His new preference was based on a larger hope, although it was destined to fail. This was that the location, in the southeast Niagara Peninsula, would enable him to maintain close communications with the western Indians in the Great Lakes region, who continued to look to the Iroquois for guidance.

But not all Iroquois shared Brant's vision. In Quebec, a band of Mohawks led by John Deseronto, who had encamped at Lachine, chose to go to the Bay of Quinte on Lake Ontario's north shore. The remainder of the Mohawks, under Brant, would be somewhat slower in taking up their rich new grant, consisting of 570,000 acres. Still, by 1784–85 the general shape of the new Grand River settlement had come into being. In the main, the various tribes settled in groups. The Mohawks took up land in the vicinity of Brant's Ford (a crossing in the river). The other groups were strung out along the course of the river: the Onondagas and Senecas on its west bank, the Tuscaroras and Oneidas on its east, and the Cayugas at its mouth where it flows into Lake Erie. Also, small numbers of the Iroquois' Indian allies, as well as Loyalist whites who had fought alongside them during the struggle, were invited to settle at Grand River.

To commemorate their triumphs and tribulations, and to celebrate their Christian faith, the Mohawks constructed St. Paul's, the first Protestant church to be built in what would become Ontario, in 1785. They also agreed to share the silver communion service Queen Anne had originally presented to their chiefs, prior to her death in 1713. Four of the valuable pieces went to the Grand River settlement, the other three to Tyendinga, part of the township Haldimand had assigned Deseronto and his followers on the Bay of Quinte. Also, Brant himself, who read the Classics and wrote poetry, would translate the Gospel of St. Mark, as well as both the psalm book and liturgy of the Anglican church, into the Mohawk language in his later years.

Ever the statesman, the Mohawk chief made a second trip to England in the mid-1780s, seeking additional compensation for his people. Although he refused to kiss the King's hand, arguing that he was "a king in his own country," he obtained the pension as well as £15,000 Sterling he had requested. Some time later, Brant visited George Washington, the American President, who received him as a visiting head of state.

By the late 1780s and early 1790s, however, it was evident that the Indian confederacy Brant had envisioned was not functioning as he had planned. The Americans had ignored it, and insisted on making treaties with smaller groups of Indians. The whites' continuing extortion of huge land grants encouraged growing resentment and division among the Indians, and eroded the unity Brant sought to establish. After the failure of negotiations between the Indians and the Americans on how to divide the Ohio and Great Lakes country, war was inevitable. In 1794 the Western Indians would be resoundingly defeated at Fallen Timbers, in today's Indiana, by Major-General Anthony Wayne's army. The Treaty of Grenville, conducted by Wayne in 1795, effectively wrote an end to the grand plan for Indian unity.

Brant, who had given unstintingly both of his time and energy, now realized that he had failed completely in his dream to make his people a strong, independent native race with its own territory. Ironically, the principles that had successfully governed the actions of the Six Nations Confederacy had not been effective in the larger union. In consequence, the Indians' future, as well as that of various other tribes, would be seriously imperilled during the decades that followed. One must ask, however, whether the idea of a separate Indian state, situated between the Ohio

River and the Great Lakes, designed to act as a buffer between Canada and the United States, was ever really a feasible concept. Indeed, as one modern expert, Robert S. Allen, reminds us, the Algonkian tribes and Six Nations Iroquois had a long and rancorous history of mutual distrust and conflict. Even the common threat to their survival was going to prove insufficient to preserve the confederacy and prevent the advance of the American frontier westward.

Until Brant's death in 1807, such concerns were foremost in his mind. So, too, was the question of the future of his Mohawk and Iroquois followers. Suspecting what was likely to happen to them, his last recorded words would be: "Have pity on the poor Indians." Such a statement takes on added force, given the epic struggles and sacrifices Brant and his followers made, both during and after the Revolution, when they served as loyal and unfailing allies of King George III and his white Loyalist supporters. Indeed, without Brant the Americans might have successfully overrun the colonies to the north. Had this been the case, the country we know today as Canada would never have come into existence.

SELECTED READINGS

Allen, Robert S. *His Majesty's Indian Allies: British Indian Policy in The Defence of Canada, 1774–1815.* Toronto: Dundurn, 1992.

Fryer, Mary Beacock. *King's Men: the Soldier Founders of Ontario.* Toronto: Dundurn, 1980.

Kelsay, Isobel Thompson. *Joseph Brant, 1743–1807: Man of Two Worlds.* Syracuse, N.Y.: Syracuse Univ., 1984.

Van Every, Dale. *A Company of Heroes: The American Frontier 1775–1783.* Toronto: Mentor, 1962.

Sir Isaac Brock, 1904.
By Alfred Sandham. (NAC/C-114549)

4

MAJOR-GENERAL
SIR ISAAC BROCK

Saviour of Upper Canada

Isaac Brock (1769–1812) was born in Guernsey, in the Channel Islands, and first came to North America in 1802. In 1811, he was promoted major-general and made provisional administrator of Upper Canada. As such, he was officially in charge of the colony on the eve of the War of 1812. Ironically, just before hostilities broke out, Brock, who wished to join the Duke of Wellington in Spain, had obtained leave to depart Canada. Instead, the young officer chose to stay. Within a short period, he and his forces, numbering at best a few thousands, would earn a fame of their own, swooping on Michilimakinac and capturing Detroit. Such decisive actions thwarted President James Madison, who had declared war on the British Empire, hoping to seize Canada without firing a shot. Tragically, Brock would die a hero's death at Queenston Heights on October 13, when he was shot by a sniper while repulsing American invaders. Today, an impressive monument dominates the battlefield, and reminds us how close we came to losing our country. It was not the first instance, nor the last, that the British Army would assist us in preserving our territory and help establish the framework for Canada as we know it today.

A Proclamation

Inhabitants of Canada! . . . The army under my command has invaded your country . . . . To the peaceable, unoffending inhabitants, it brings neither danger nor difficulty . . . . I come to protect, not to injure you . . . . In the name of my country, and by the authority of my government, I promise protection for your persons, property and rights. Remain in your homes . . . raise not your hands against your brethren . . . . No white man found fighting by the Side of an Indian will be taken prisoner — instant destruction will be his lot . . . . The United States offers you peace, liberty, and security. Your choice lies between these and or, slavery and destruction.

So read the bombastic proclamation the American general, William Hull, issued on July 12, 1812, when his army crossed from Detroit and invaded Sandwich, Upper Canada (today's Windsor). Earlier, President James Madison, believing that concentration upon real or imagined failings of the British or some other foreign power could be relied upon to gain badly needed votes, had officially declared war on the British Empire and its North American possessions. The majority of Americans believed that Canadians, many of whom were recent emigrants from the Republic, would welcome invaders with open arms, and that victory would be "a mere matter of marching." Also, at the beginning of the conflict, Canada's defenders were shockingly outnumbered and ill-prepared to fight a major struggle. As events would shortly demonstrate, however, her populace started with some distinct assets: discipline, purpose, training, and not least, a leader.

Major-General Isaac Brock, a forty-three-year-old career officer, possessed all the essentials of greatness. Destined to symbolize in the eyes of 19th-century Canadians the very ideal of a hero and personification of duty, he towered an impressive six-feet-two-inches and was well proportioned. In his own estimation, he was "hard as nails," though possibly beginning to suffer a bit of middle-age stoutness. Earlier, as a young officer, he had established a reputation for horsemanship, athletic ability and strength, as well as for his legendary feats of endurance. Strikingly handsome in appearance, Brock possessed fair, curly hair and a narrow face. Blue eyes were set off by a long distinctive, knife-blade of a nose. Indeed, there was a certain magnetism about him that today would be described as charisma. Outwardly pleasant and self-assured, at ease with both himself and others, he was also capable of extreme inward self-control: able to keep his own counsel when events dictated that he do so. The General enjoyed a great popularity in Upper Canada. His superiors both liked and respected him. Most telling, the adulation of his troops stopped just short of worship, and the Commander returned their love in full measure.

A decade earlier, Brock had first sailed up the St. Lawrence with his regiment as a young colonel, following a stormy ocean voyage, and had marvelled at the rocky heights of Quebec. Crowned with its imposing fortress, it doubtlessly reminded him of the stirring events that had taken place there just four decades earlier. Still, the young officer could have had no premonition that, like General James Wolfe, he himself would find fame and death on another height in this majestic new land. Fresh from fighting the French in Europe, Brock had already commenced making a name for himself, transforming his regiment, the 49th "Green Tigers," from the worst to one of the best in the British army. After serving aboard ship as part of the marine force that accompanied Britain's idol Nelson at the Battle of Copenhagen, young Brock had been posted to the Caribbean.

Brock's next stationing — in Canada — was supposed to be merely a routine tour of duty. But it was evident that work needed to be done, and as a devout pupil from the school of General Sir Ralph Abercromby and Admiral Horatio Nelson, he set about doing it in the best possible manner. During the ensuing decade, Brock would make his impression on both Canada's military and administrative life, serving both at Quebec and Montreal, prior to accepting his posting to the wilderness of Upper Canada. He had laboured mightily to strengthen Canada's fortifications, improve the forces' commissary and correct glaring problems in army finances. With characteristic enthusiasm, as well as his fluent command of French learned in his native Guernsey, Brock came in time to possess a detailed knowledge of the raw young country. He also came to love it.

Brock, however, was becoming restless. As he privately remarked to his brother in 1811: "You who have passed all your days in the bustle of London, can scarcely conceive the uninteresting and insipid life I am doomed to live in this retirement." He longed to be with his idol the Duke of Wellington in Spain, where officers his age were winning promotion and establishing reputations. Instead, stuck in the backwater of Upper Canada, he lacked the basic amenities he had enjoyed earlier at Quebec and Montreal. They included good food and drink, a moderately sophisticated society, and books. Brock, who was reasonably well connected, had continued communicating with friends and fellow officers in the hope of arranging a transfer to Europe. As fate would have it, he obtained leave to depart Upper Canada just as war seemed imminent. Now, whether from ambition or a sense of duty, he decided he could not abandon the responsibilities of command.

Brock's superior General Sir George Prevost, Governor General and Commander-in-Chief for the Canadas, had been able to do little to prepare the colony for war during his brief tenure. Problems remained at the most basic level. Most important, there was no coin to pay the troops. Thus, Prevost had to persuade the legislature to issue paper currency. Nor was the Commander-in-Chief able to supply the growing numbers of militia with needed rifles, let alone other equipment. A ship sent from Bermuda to Halifax carrying 6,000 stand of arms foundered in a storm. Given the prevailing global crisis, the mother country's first priority was to supply Wellington's army. Also, Canada remained short of experienced officers. There were only two generals in Lower Canada, Prevost himself and Baron Francis de Rottenburg. In the Upper Province there were but two more, Brock and Roger Sheaffe.

The opposing strength of the United States' regular army

amounted to about 13,000, although on paper its numbers exceeded 33,000. Additionally, in the event of war, the Republic, with its superior population, could call into service some 450,000 militia. Opposing such, the two Canadas were defended by a force comprising a mere 7,000 regulars. Of these, five battalions of the line were deployed in the Lower Province to protect the colonies' lifeline, the St. Lawrence. But since the majority of American soldiers were recent recruits, the Americans' total force was not superior to the British regulars in Canada.

The crisis point was Upper Canada, as Brock was aware. If Major-General Henry Dearborn could solve his supply problem and concentrate his forces, the invaders possessed the capability to strike simultaneously at three fortified points: Detroit, the Niagara frontier and Kingston. To deal with this worst case scenario, Brock commanded but a single British line regiment, the 41st (now the Royal Welch Regiment). The only other regulars in the province consisted of a substantial detachment of the 10th Royal Veteran Battalion, another of the Royal Newfoundland Fencibles (chiefly employed as marines on the Lakes), and a single company of artillery. In addition, there was the provincial militia, consisting of all men of military age — organized on paper at least — in battalions. Even on the eve of war, however, such units remained almost totally untrained.

For his part, Prevost presented a marked contrast to Brock, who wore the "two hats" of military and civil administrator in Upper Canada with some difficulty. More diplomat than soldier, Sir George had worked his own type of miracle in Lower Canada. He had conciliated the French Canadians following his predecessor Sir James Craig's "Reign of Terror." He had regained their loyalty, and even managed to arm and encourage them to resist the growing threat from the U.S. But, as Brock realized, Prevost had no real stomach for a struggle with the Americans.

Portraits of the two Generals reveal much concerning their personalities. Despite his attractive appearance, the forty-four-year-old Sir George, with his oval face, high forehead, and dark sideburns, appears introspective and cautious. Furrows creasing his brow tend to reinforce the impression of uncertainty. There is a certain casual quality, unsuited to a military officer. Certainly there is none of the knife-edge sharpness and sense of command that characterizes the few surviving portraits of his subordinate Brock, who appears so confident and resolute in temperament.

Stories concerning Brock's notorious determination and audacity only fuelled Prevost's concern. One recounted how, when the 49th was stationed in Barbados, an officer, who was a confirmed braggart and skilled duellist, habitually insulted his fellows and fought them at a dozen paces' distance. According to accounts, Brock intentionally provoked him, accepting the resultant challenge. But instead of proceeding to fire at the standard distance, the brave Guernseyman produced a handkerchief. He demanded that they both grasp a corner and fire at point-blank range. The bully panicked and refused to fire. Shamed, he soon left the regiment. This had been Brock's intention all the while. There were other tales as well: how Brock had challenged his own equestrian skills by riding to the very summit of Mount Hillaby, 1,200 feet above the Caribbean, and how in 1803 he had personally pursued three deserters across Lake Ontario in an open rowboat in a storm.

On his part, Prevost liked and admired Brock. Still, he worried about how to keep his enthusiasms in check. British strategy did not envision the seizure of American territory. More importantly, Prevost wished to avoid provoking the enemy. To contain Brock, he had consciously decided to keep the regular force in the upper country to a minimum. Upper Canada would be sent 500 reinforcements, no more. And as Sir George cautioned, Brock must promise that these numbers would not be employed in offensive operations, "unless . . . solely calculated to strengthen a defensive attitude."

President James Madison did not officially declare war until June 18, 1812. Thus, even as he opened a special session of the province's legislature in early August at York, its capital, Brock did not know whether the Declaration of War had been passed by Congress. Resplendent in his dress uniform of crimson and gold, the General managed only by a supreme act of self-control to mask the frustration, despair, even contempt, boiling within his breast. However, to encourage his audience, he spoke in encouragingly bland and generalized terms. He especially stressed the need for loyalty and support on the part of the citizenry.

Brock's apprehensions were reflected in a communication he had sent earlier to the Adjutant General at Headquarters in Lower Canada:

> My situation is most critical, not from anything the enemy can do, but from the disposition of the people — The population, believe me, is essentially bad — A full belief possesses them all that this province must inevitably succumb — This prepossession is fatal to every exertion — Legislators, Magistrates, Militia, Officers, all have imbibed the idea, and are so sluggish and indifferent in all their respective offices.

> What a change an additional regiment would make in this part of the Province! Most of the people have lost all confidence — I however speak loud and look big.

As the General realized, sheer numbers seemed to dictate that Upper Canada would be incapable of resisting any American show of force. The British population of the Canadas numbered a mere half million. Additionally, many of Upper Canada's inhabitants were recently arrived American immigrants. In contrast, America's population was between six and eight million. Brock calculated that his best weapon to counter the disparity lay in surprise. If he could move before the enemy was ready, he might indeed be able to deal the enemy a blow for which he was not prepared. Success would solidify support within the Indian population and ensure that the Natives joined the British side. This might convince the faltering settlers that they could resist the enemy and even repulse the invaders.

As Brock realized, though, Prevost had no real stomach for a struggle with the Americans. Five days prior to Hull's invasion of Canada, Prevost still believed the U.S. was too divided to pose a

real danger. Even three weeks after war's outbreak, he was ordering his subordinate not to attack. Specifically, he forbade Brock
from "committing any act which may even by construction tend to
unite the Eastern and Southern states" into an effective force. A
less able commander would likely have adopted a passive and
defensive attitude. Brock's greatness lay in the fact that he refused
to let circumstances discourage him. Instead, he realized the best
hope of carrying out his strategy lay in assuming a vigorous local
initiative. But before he could launch a series of bold offensive
strokes with limited objectives, he had to know where the main
threat to Canada lay.

When he first learned that General Hull had crossed from
Detroit on July 12, and invaded nearby Sandwich, in the Lake Erie
region, Brock moved instead to the Niagara frontier. His motive
was to repulse a possible second enemy foray. Since there appeared to be no immediate threat in this sector, however, the
General returned to York in late July. Here he summoned the legislature to deal with the emergency. By the time the short session
was prorogued, the military picture had defined itself. The main
threat to Upper Canada lay indeed on the Detroit frontier. Thus,
Brock revived the plan he had conceived six months previously.
His target would be not only Detroit, but also the American-con-
trolled fur post of Michilimackinac, located to the northwest, at
the top of Lake Huron. Unless both strong places were in British
hands, he would have little hope of successfully defending the 800
miles of frontier for which he was responsible, with the mere
1,200 troops he commanded.

On July 28, Brock informed Prevost that he was sending a
force to relieve Amherstburg. The little British fort, situated just
down the river from Sandwich, remained in British hands. The
following day, Brock received news from Quebec, informing him
that war had been officially declared by President Madison on
June 18. Now, he at least knew the game he was playing. From the
far west there also came galvanizing news. Captain Charles Roberts, stationed at St. Joseph's Island, commanding a hastily assembled force of 180 voyageurs, his own small garrison of 45 regulars,

and some 400 Indians, had swept down and captured Fort Mackinac. Its American defenders had been so surprised that they had offered no resistance whatsoever!

Brock now called for volunteers to accompany him to Amherstburg. As he recorded, more than 500 rushed to apply, "principally the sons of Veterans, whom His Majesty's munificence settled in this country." Brock could take only half this number, however, due to a shortage of transport. Nonetheless, the York Volunteers, a regiment that included among its officers the sons of such famous Upper Canada families as Rideout, Jarvis, and Robinson, would soon become the Commander's favourite military unit.

Earlier, Brock had seen to it that an effective system of convoy had been established on the inland waterways. This ensured that additional regiments and material could be brought upriver from Quebec and Montreal. During the spring, recruitment efforts had also produced an entirely new provincial corps. As such, the Glengarry Light Infantry was already 400 strong. Between that district and Kingston the General had ordered every man capable of shouldering a musket to hold himself in readiness. And, at both York and Niagara, he had called out flank companies of militia, which he ordered to train like regulars so they could be used in heavy fighting. In a crisis, these 800 untested, poorly equipped soldiers, many lacking even boots, would have the crucial task of defending the Niagara River line. This would enable British regulars to be moved up from Quebec and Kingston. That is, assuming such regiments could be spared from the colossal struggle Britain was engaged in against Napoleon.

Prior to hostilities, Brock had also taken steps to purchase 2,000 bushels of Indian corn from the American side of the border. In this way, diminishing stock on the Canadian side could be avoided. The General had also encouraged Upper Canada's farmers to sow more grain than they ever had before. Additionally, he had modified military duty, so as to minimize demands made on farmers. Measures had also been taken to encourage women to assist with field labour.

On August 6, Brock left York with the York Volunteers. Arriving at Burlington Bay, the force travelled overland to Long Point on Lake Erie. Here it was joined by the Norfolk Militia, under George Ryerson. Embarking 260 militia and 40 soldiers of the 41st Regiment in a collection of leaky boats, Brock then proceeded to Port Talbot, where the force was augmented by Peter Talbot and his riflemen.

As the flotilla moved silently through the dark Lake Erie night, its Commander carefully studied papers found aboard *Cayahoga,* an enemy ship recently captured by the British. Containing Hull's correspondence to the Secretary of War, they had been swiftly forwarded to Brock at Fort George. As he read the letters, Brock took confidence from Hull's apparent despondency and lack of initiative. Also, when he arrived at Amherstburg just before midnight on August 13, Brock would find other cheering news waiting. Tecumseh, the Shawnee chief, with 25 warriors, had ambushed a party of 200 Americans sent out from Detroit to escort supplies. Not only had the Indians captured precious provisions bound for the fort, but they had also seized a second batch of the hapless General's correspondence. These documents, too, confirmed the enemy commander's growing doubts and fears.

A week earlier, Hull had learned of the dramatic news of Mackinac's surrender. He was shaken, for he realized that the northern bastion securing the American frontier no longer existed. Fearing "the northern hive of Indians" was about to come "swarming down in every direction," the aging Commander, who lacked Brock's gambler instinct, decided to retreat. He commenced his pull-back to Detroit on August 7. Four days later he had completed the operation. It was but a bare month since he had first set foot on Canadian soil.

The British Commander now met with his Indian counterpart, Tecumseh. If accounts are accurate, the fabled midnight encounter, conveyed to posterity by a variety of pens and paintbrushes, forms one of the most dramatic moments in our nation's history. An unidentified writer's account which has survived captures the colour of the scene:

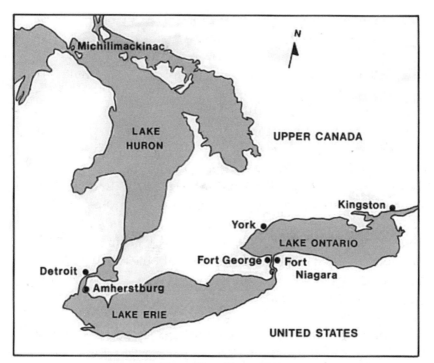

Upper Canada, ca. 1812

Rising, he extended his hand to his ally. The British general towered over the lithe figure of the Shawnee. Impeccable in his
scarlet jacket, blue and white riding trousers, and Hessian boots,
Brock was large-limbed, blue-eyed, and fair of complexion.
Tecumseh, a tense, sinewy five-foot-nine, was smaller, but sup-
ple, and perfectly built. He was dressed in a plain suit of tanned
deerskin, fringed at the edges, and wore leather moccasins,
heavily ornamented with porcupine quills. In his nose were
three silver ornaments in the shape of coronets, and around his
neck, hung on a string of coloured wampum, he wore a large silver medallion of George III.

Born within a year of each other, yet with backgrounds a world
apart, both were joined with a common purpose. Ironically, each
was destined to die within the year. From the moment of this first
meeting, however, a unique rapport united the two. Each took the

other's measure and was impressed. Brock later wrote Lord Liverpool: "A more sagacious and gallant warrior does not I believe exist." Tecumseh's judgement, delivered to his followers, was even more pointed: "This," he said, "is a man!" Later, he would again express his admiration for Brock in equally concise language: "Other chiefs say, 'Go' — General Brock says, 'Come'."

Tecumseh urged that Detroit be attacked immediately. Tracing the lines with the point of his knife on a birchbark roll, he drew the river, the hills, the clearings, the muskeg and the forest, as well as a network of trails that would serve Brock's forces. But at the private counsel of war Brock afterwards convened with his officers, the General was unable, despite his arguments, to convince them to attack. Suddenly he ceased talking and simply announced: "I have decided on crossing, and now gentlemen, instead of further advice, I entreat of you to give me your cordial and hearty support." Next morning when Brock informed the Indians of his decision, it caused Tecumseh to remark approvingly that their great father George III had "awakened out of a long sleep." The Indian leader's hatred of the Americans knew no bounds. Members of the 4th U.S. Regiment, who garrisoned Detroit, were his especial foes. Less than a year earlier, under General William Harrison, they had slaughtered half-armed men and women of his tribe while he and his warriors were absent.

Upon occupying Sandwich, Brock dispatched two aides-de-camp across the river with a dispatch addressed to Hull. It demanded his immediate surrender. Brock wrote: "It is far from my intention to join in a war of extermination, but you must be aware that the numerous body of Indians who have attached themselves to my troops will be beyond control the minute the contest commences." The wording was intentional, meant to panic Hull. Earlier, however, Brock had obtained Tecumseh's promise that he and his followers would not resort to scalping the enemy. Neither was it Tecumseh's practice to employ torture, making him a rare exception among North American Indians.

While awaiting Hull's answer, Brock ordered a heavy battery constructed opposite Detroit. It consisted of a single long 18-

Tecumseh, the Great War Leader of the Shawnee. (NAC/C-007042)

pounder gun, two long 24-pounders, and a couple of mortars. They were conveniently hidden behind a building and some oak trees. When the aides returned, bearing Hull's response that he would not surrender, the screening trees were chopped down. The brisk cannonade, the first shots fired in the war, continued well after dark. Both sides hurled hundreds of pounds of cast iron across the river. Despite this, little damage was inflicted on either force.

Next morning, August 16, dawned a calm and beautiful Sunday. Arranging his little force composed of 220 regulars and

400 militia, the General prepared for the difficult river crossing. Luckily, Major Thomas Evans had devised a crafty ploy. It involved clothing the militia in 300 cast-off uniforms of the 41st Regiment. As a result, the anxious Hull was deceived into believing that Brock's small number of regulars was double their actual strength. Five pieces of artillery supported the army during its crossing. Also, to spread the risk of its suffering disabling casualties, Brock divided his force into three miniature brigades. Two consisted of militia stiffened with regular detachments, while the main body of the 41st Regiment formed the third. Having already crossed, the Indians lurked in the forest, threatening to attack Hull's flank and rear should he attempt to impede the passage of the regulars and scarlet-clad militia.

Covered by artillery fire from several British ships as well as the Sandwich battery, Brock's passage proceeded in routine manner. Shielded by Indians skirmishing in the woods to his left, Brock mustered his men. Forming up, the column moved forward in sections. Since the General had doubled the space between them, it made the diminutive force he commanded appear larger. Light artillery, consisting of three 6-, and two 3-pounders, moved forward immediately behind the advance guard. At its head the procession was preceded by fluttering standards and rolling drums.

Brock's plan was to outwait Hull, draw him out of the strongly built fort, and do battle in the open. Here his regulars could devastate the American militia. No sooner had Brock's force landed on the enemy shore, however, than a scout rode in. He bore the unwelcome news that 300 enemy horsemen had been spotted three miles to the rear. Since he risked being caught between a strong fortification and an advancing column, Brock, without hesitation, changed his plans. He decided to attack immediately.

Drawn up more than 1,500 strong in line on an overlooking rise, the enemy watched the British march. Additionally, the Americans had placed two 24-pounders loaded with grapeshot in the roadway commanding the approach to the town.

At the head of the march rode Brock himself on his grey

charger. His brilliant uniform flashing in the morning sun presented a shining mark. The rat-a-tat-tat of kettle drums, the clear-cut whistle of fifes, resonant roll of big drums, and the steady tramp of armed men orchestrated the British advance.

Fort Detroit's guns and Hull's field-pieces continued to point their threatening black muzzles at the British column. Unperturbed, Brock rode up and down in front of his men, encouraging them with a command here, a kindly rebuke there, a word of cheer for all ranks.

Suddenly, one of the officers, acting Quartermaster General Nichol, rode forward. "General," he said, "forgive me, but I cannot forebear entreating you not to expose yourself. If we lose you, we lose all. I pray you, allow the troops to advance, led by their own officers." Turning to return the gallant officer's salute, Brock replied: "Master Nichol, I fully appreciate your kindly advice, but I feel that, in addition to their sense of loyalty and duty, there are many here following me from a feeling of personal regard, and I will never ask them to go where I do not lead."

Still, the fort's guns had not fired. The steady, onward tramp, tramp of crimson lines, raw recruit and grizzled veteran, struck fear into Hull as he watched. Although his defenders outnumbered the besiegers three to one, Brock's intention was all too apparent. The American General could gain no comfort from the scarlet wall, solid and bristling with steel, advancing in battle array, with even, ominous tread.

Hull occupied an exceedingly strong position. Consisting of 300 houses, the town was enclosed on three sides by a stockade of 14-foot pickets. Three massive gates restricted entrance. The fort itself, situated to the northeast on high ground, covered three acres. A double palisade, a 26-foot rampart with four bastions and a glacis protected it. A ditch, six feet deep and twelve feet wide, surrounded the entire fort. In total, Hull had in excess of 40 cannon, including three 10-inch howitzers, and an immense supply of ammunition. Although a 400-man detachment commanded by Colonels McArthur and Cass had not returned, he still commanded 1,700 troops. Indeed, Hull should have realized that, excellent as Indians were as fighters in their native forests, they were seldom effective in attacking fortifications. Detroit was a formidable objective. In the Peninsula, British, French, and Spanish garrisons had successfully defended weaker positions for weeks.

Suddenly Brock ordered his troops to wheel to the left. Quickly, he marched them into an orchard and ravine that screened the attacking force from the enemy guns. Although the American position appeared impregnable, the General planned to employ a secret weapon — psychology. Having already deceived Hull concerning the number of regulars he led, he now employed a second stratagem. He ordered Tecumseh and his followers to march in single file across a gap in the woods, out of range of the garrison. After sprinting across the meadow in full view, the natives circled back and repeated the operation three times. Hull's alarmed officers, incapable of distinguishing one Indian from another, continued their count. To their growing alarm, they reckoned that 1,500 "painted savages" were indeed present.

Hull was close to collapse. Since, as mentioned, several officers had not returned, and others were indisposed, he had no battalion commanders to assist him. Already the commander of the Michigan Militia, Elijah Brush, had stated that his men would flee rather than fight. As well, the fort was jammed with civilians as well as soldiers and cattle. All sought refuge from the British bombardment, which now commenced in earnest.

Inside the palisade, Hull, who had seen blood spent during the Revolution, became quickly unnerved by the cannonade. A 16-pound cannonball, bouncing over the fort's parapet, skipping across an open space, cut an officer (appropriately named Blood) in two. Continuing on, it sliced both legs off a nearby surgeon's mate, before mangling a second man. Another cannonball dispatched two more soldiers, splattering blood and brains over walls as well as the gowns of some women seeking refuge nearby. One collapsed, others began to scream.

Fearing for his daughter Betsy and her child, who had sought refuge in the fort, Hull panicked. He found his brain, confronted with the heat of battle, overloaded with information. Half-seated, half-crouched, the battle-shocked Commander chewed on his tobacco furiously. Absent-minded, he added quid after quid, until brown juice dribbled down his beard and clothing. His imagination conjured up any number of ghastly outcomes: troops deserting to the enemy, women and children starving in a protracted siege, cannon fire dismembering soldiers and civilians alike. Most chilling of all was the prospect of Tecumseh's warriors ravaging, burning, and killing all within the fortress.

At ten o'clock, with shells continuing to scream overhead, Hull ordered his son to run up a white flag. He wished to arrange a parley. However, as Captain Hull was about to haul down the Stars and Stripes and hoist a white towel in its place, a senior officer intervened. The towel was too dirty. Also, to replace the American ensign would mean the complete surrender of the fort. Better to find a bed-sheet and drape it over the southwestern bastion.

Crossing the Detroit River under a flag of truce, the younger Hull carried a message to Brock: "I propose a cessation of hostilities for one hour to open negotiations for the surrender of Detroit — W. M. Hull, B. Gen." But the Brigadier had little concept of his opponent. Accompanied by an escort, Brock was well in advance of his army, within a few hundred yards of the fortress, surveying its ramparts. When Hull's message finally reached him in the field, General Brock sent his aides Lieutenant-Colonel John Macdonnell and Captain James Glegg into Fort Detroit to arrange its surrender. But it would be on his terms. His orders were that the fort be surrendered within three hours. Otherwise he would commence the assault.

Hull accepted all of Brock's demands. Although Brock was glad to achieve a bloodless victory, his professionalism was so outraged by such a shameful surrender that he refused the enemy commander the customary honours of war. At noon, the Americans stacked their weapons and filed sullenly from the fort. Some smashed their rifles, rather than surrender them intact. And, when Colonel Cass returned to find the fort had surrendered, he broke his sword across his knee and cried.

Fife and drums playing "The British Grenadiers," the victors marched in. The American flag was run down, and the Union Jack raised in its place. Then a small military band struck up "God Save the King." Such ceremonies finished, Indians poured through the town. As promised, Tecumseh honoured his pledge to keep his followers disciplined. As they rode through the fort, Brock and the Indian leader presented a memorable picture. The giant General, in his black cocked hat, crimson uniform, and gilt epaulettes, contrasted strongly with the simplicity of his Shawnee ally. A legend would soon spring up claiming that an elated Brock tore off his military sash, and presented it, along with two pistols, to Tecumseh. But there is no evidence to corroborate such an anecdote.

Terms of capitulation, as agreed to, included the surrender of a general officer and 2,500 men of all ranks (nearly 600 of them regulars), until recently, the would-be conquerors of Canada. Captured material consisted of 2,500 muskets, 500 rifles, 33 artillery pieces, the brig of war *Adams,* as well as immense quantities of stores and munitions, amounting to the princely sum of £40,000 Sterling. Fort Shelby was surrendered, along with the town of Detroit, and 69,000 square miles of U.S. territory. To the wild joy of Tecumseh's warriors, the fort's standard, the colours of the hated 4th Regiment, also changed hands. Today, the captured flag, once the possession of the self-styled "heroes" of the Indian massacre at Tippecanoe, is proudly displayed in the Welch Regiment Museum, Cardiff, Wales.

Canada was saved! As Brock wrote Prevost: "When I detail my good fortune your Excellency will be astonished." But more than luck had ensured the campaign's success. Brock's energy and boldness had proven decisive. Brock also wrote his family in Britain, telling them he hoped to be able to contribute more to their physical comfort from his share of the prize money. Earlier, he had signed over his regimental pay to help support the family, following the collapse of a London bank in which his brother William had been a partner.

Overnight the strategic situation reversed itself. The Americans had lost their western forts, a major army and any hope of winning the Indians to their cause. In Canada, morale soared. The population took heart. Officials no longer had to tolerate pro-American attitudes. Authorities could insist that everyone perform militia duty. Not least, the Six Nations Indians, who had played a minor role, would drop their neutrality and support the British cause.

Instead of accompanying the long train of captured American soldiers, weapons and supplies in its triumphant progress to Montreal, Brock hurried east. Arriving at Fort George a scant eight days following Detroit's surrender, he found hostilities temporarily suspended. To his chagrin, Prevost had negotiated an armistice. Meanwhile the Americans hastily reinforced their posts. By the time the cease-fire ended, the enemy had amassed 6,800 troops to Brock's 1,700 along the 33-mile Niagara front, extending between Lakes Erie and Ontario.

Early on the morning of October 13, Brock would spring from his bed, awakened by distant gunfire. Crouched low over his charger Alfred's neck, he galloped down the road to Queenston, seven miles distant. Bursting into the village in dawn's half-light, he rallied a handful of troops to resist the enemy, who were beginning to swarm ashore. Then, galloping up the nearby Heights, which dominate the Niagara River, he would come upon the single British cannon that was stubbornly peppering the enemy below, who managed to make the easy 200-yard crossing. Suddenly there were shouts from the rear. Three hundred Yankees had discovered an obscure path up the Heights, circled behind and were charging. "Spike the gun!" Brock cried. This done, leading his horse, he ran downhill with the gunners.

Gathering 100 men in the bright morning sunshine, Brock led them to the bottom of the hill. He said: "Take your breath, boys, you'll need it." Then, abandoning Alfred, he led a sword and bayonet charge to recapture the towering heights. He caught a bullet in the wrist, but ignored it. An American sniper, stepping from the nearby bush, took deliberate aim and shot him in the chest. He died almost instantly. Ironically, he would never know that his capture of Detroit would win him a knighthood.

The Battle of Queenston Heights, October 13, 1812.
By John David Kelly. (NAC/C-000273)

The war would last two and a half more years, and involve repeated American attacks in the vicinity of Lake Erie, on the Niagara frontier, along the vital St. Lawrence River route between Kingston and Cornwall, and south of Montreal. Upper Canada's capital, York, would be attacked, and Niagara would be torched, as would St. David's and Port Dover. In retaliation, the American capital, Washington itself, would be burned by the British, and there would be counter-thrusts, raids, and reprisals on neighbouring American territory. Additionally, there would be crucial naval conflicts on the Great Lakes. But the worst danger to Upper Canada had ceased by the end of 1812. Thanks to Brock's strategy, the colony had been preserved, as well as all the lands to the West, including their Indian population. In the final judgement, the Americans would lose the war due to their own unpreparedness, but also due in large measure to Brock's early initiative.

Carefully studied, the Detroit campaign demonstrates a number of lessons that form the essence of military science. Especially "Maintenance of Morale, the Dividends of Offensive Action and Firepower, Concentration of Force and Economy of Effort, as well as the Principle of Flexibility." To these must be added "Effective Intelligence, the Employment of Deception," and the benefits to be derived from "Psychological Warfare."

Not least, Brock, whom Canadians have honoured by adopting as a native son and one of our country's few genuine heroes, was a great leader and brilliant officer. His favourite motto, often repeated to young soldiers he led, such as James FitzGibbon, stated: "Nothing should be impossible to a soldier; the word impossible should not be found in a soldier's dictionary." He lived and died by that credo. Today, when Canada faces so many impossibilities, we forget it at our peril.

SELECTED READINGS

Berton, Pierre. *The Invasion of Canada 1812–1813*. Toronto: McClelland & Stewart, 1980.

"Sir Isaac Brock." In Canadian Historic Sites: Occasional Papers in Archaeology and History, No. 11. Ottawa: Indian and Northern Affairs, 1974.

Turner, Wesley. *The War of 1812: The War that Both Sides Won*. Toronto: Dundurn, 1990.

Zaslow, Morris, ed. *The Defended Border: Upper Canada and the War of 1812*. Toronto: Macmillan of Canada, 1964.

Lieutenant-Colonel Charles de Salaberry, ca. 1818–1836.
By Anson Dickinson. (NAC/C-009226)

5

LIEUTENANT-COLONEL CHARLES DE SALABERRY

Hero of Châteauguay

Lieutenant-Colonel Charles-Michel de Salaberry (1778–1829) was a French Canadian aristocrat, whose grandfather fought against General James Wolfe. His father Louis was severely wounded fighting against American invaders in 1775. Aided by their patron the influential Duke of Kent, Salaberry and his brothers became officers in the British Army. After serving in the West Indies and fighting Napoleon, Charles returned to Canada in 1810 as General Baron Francis de Rottenburg's aide, and raised a corps of light infantry, the Canadian Voltigeurs, at Quebec. On October 26, 1813, leading a force of regulars and other units, he repulsed a superior American force at Châteauguay in the Eastern Townships. Some experts regard the encounter as more important than either General Brock's and General Sheaffe's repulse of the Americans at Queenston Heights in 1812, or the hard fought battle of Lundy's Lane in the Niagara Peninsula in 1814. Throughout our history, French Canadians have played an important role in the protection of Canada. The story of the "hero of Châteauguay" is but one example of soldiers who have served their country bravely.

In the autumn of 1813 American Major-General Wade Hampton and 4,000 American regulars moved threateningly down the Châteauguay River, situated in today's Eastern Townships, towards Montreal, which they intended to capture. Opposing them, Lieutenant-Colonel Charles de Salaberry, a French Canadian professional who had served with the British Army in many parts of the world, was busy constructing entrenchments along several streams that ran into that waterway, one behind another. Despite claims that most were civilians, recent research has shown that the majority of troops manning the position were either French Canadian regulars or near regulars.

Salaberry himself, thirty-four years of age, was a unique product of Quebec. Although an aristocrat, he was no ballroom fop. His commander, Major-General Baron Francis de Rottenburg, liked to call him "my dear Marquis of cannon power." Short in stature, barrel-chested, and muscular, he was notorious for meting out strict, sometimes brutally harsh discipline. Salaberry was a proud man, to whom "honour" meant everything. His temperament could never allow him to forget how General Sir James Craig, the previous British governor, had quarrelled with his father and sought to destroy the rights of French Canadians. Also, his brow bore a scar incurred when he had dispatched the German duellist who had killed his best friend.

Due to the influence and patronage of the Duke of Kent, father of the future Queen Victoria, Salaberry received his first commission at fourteen. Later, he campaigned in the West Indies and fought against Napoleon in Europe. Three of his brothers had died abroad, fighting the British King's wars. When Charles himself was a young headstrong officer, the Duke had personally intervened to prevent him from marrying foolishly. Later, he chose a seigneur's daughter.

The site Salaberry had chosen to defend, employing his beloved grey-clad Voltigeurs and units of the Select Militia, was the best possible one. It was situated on the Châteauguay's north shore, about 35 miles southwest of Montreal, where the road squeezed between dense woods and the river. Half a dozen gullies crossed the area, cutting their way through sandy soil at right angles to the river.

Salaberry deployed his Voltigeurs, composed of sturdy young French *Canadiens* who were used to fighting bare-footed, in the front defensive ranks. By mid-day on October 22, axemen had constructed breastworks of felled trees and tangled branches on the forward tip of each of the gullies running into the Château-guay. Also, he had ordered his axemen to destroy all bridges that might assist the enemy's advance. Additionally, woods on the right flank of Salaberry's lines provided cover for a handful of Indians and buglers.

Despite such precautions and good intelligence, Salaberry was surprised when Major-General Hampton launched a flanking attack on the morning of October 25. Clearly he had not expected the American assault so soon. Nonetheless, upon hearing the roar of gunfire around 10 a.m., the Canadian Commander moved up quickly to reinforce axemen strengthening the two forward abatis, consisting of cut-down sharpened trees, that he had

Battle of Châteauguay, 1813. By Henri Julien. (NAC/C-003297)

ordered placed a mile or so in advance of the front line. They
extended in an arc from the river's mouth on the left to a swamp
in the forest on their right and were intended not only to slow
down the American advance, but also warn Salaberry's main force
of an attack. Cheering lustily, the Americans pushed forward.
However, they were halted by the Voltigeurs' steady musket fire.

After several hours' pause, Hampton ordered the attack to
resume. Behind their breastworks, the Canadians watched a tall
American officer ride forward. He cried: "Brave Canadians, surrender yourselves; we wish you no harm!" Salaberry himself fired.
The officer fell from his horse, and battle was joined.

To get a better view of the battlefield and command his men,
the French Canadian Commander mounted a huge tree stump.
Later, tongue-in-cheek, he would write his father: "I have won a
victory mounted on a wooden horse" (indeed, contemporary pictures depict him standing on a log, waving his sword, and gestur-
ing in grand style in the enemy's direction). Certainly he had chosen his ground well. Although American attackers outnumbered
his troops in the firing line four to one, it was evident it would
take a very determined force to drive them from their position.
Fortunately, the attackers did not possess such mettle.

As was his style, Salaberry kept his eye on everything. Seeing a
soldier raise his musket, the Colonel stood behind him to check
his marksmanship. The Voltigeur fired, but the man he had
aimed at remained stubbornly standing.

"Is that what you came here for, Jerome?" demanded the
Colonel, gruffly.

Demanding he might be. But the commander knew his men's
names by heart, and knew how to get the best out of them. As
Brigadier-General George Izard advanced along the road in an
attempt to turn the Canadian flank, Salaberry moved behind one
of his companies. Chiding and encouraging them simultaneously,
as was his manner, the Colonel shouted: "Show them what you're
made of, my old rascals. If you can't face them down, you're not
men at all."

Confused by the cries of a small band of Caughnawaga (Kahnawake) Indians hidden in the woods on the Canadian right, the enemy concluded the main force to be concentrated there. Discharging their weapons in platoons, as if on parade, the Americans poured volley after crashing volley into the bush. Most of the lead balls, however, whistled harmlessly through the treetops.

Suddenly, Lieutenant-Colonel "Red" George Macdonnell, leading the Select Embodied Militia reinforcements he had brought from Kingston, sounded his bugles. It signalled Salaberry that he was advancing. Responding, the colonel ordered other buglers, situated in the nearby woods, to trumpet in all directions. This caused the Americans to conclude that they were heavily outnumbered.

Two other tricks reinforced Izard's misconceptions concerning the Canadians' numbers. A group of Macdonnell's men, clad in red coats, disappeared into the woods. Shortly they reappeared, having reversed their jackets, and now clad in white flannel. In addition, Salaberry, conscious of the ploy General Isaac Brock had used the year previous against Hull, sent 20 Indians to dash through the forest, tomahawks in hand. The fearful Americans believed hundreds of natives, decked out in war-paint, were lurking in the woods, waiting for an opportunity to attack.

While Izard's force busied itself for an hour or more in ineffectual sniping, another skirmish was developing on the other, or south, side of the river. Here, the evening previous, Hampton had ordered Colonel Robert Purdy's force to attempt to flank Salaberry's defence lines from the south by way of a ford.

Two Canadian companies, having driven off Purdy's forward skirmishers and advanced towards his position, were now commencing to tangle with the main force. Hurrying to the river bank, Salaberry shouted orders in French to Captain Charles Daly of the Embodied Militia. Meanwhile, he quickly deployed his own force, consisting of Voltigeurs, Indians, and Beauharnois militia, along his side of the river. Their orders were to fire on Purdy's troops should they emerge from the woods.

Sensing themselves threatened by Daly's little force in the swampy forest, Purdy's overwhelming body of crack soldiers responded with a shattering volley. Fortunately, Daly had ordered his men to kneel before firing. The order saved their lives. Most of the blast passed over their heads.

After stopping to reload, Purdy's American force employed the momentary pause to sweep forward on the Canadians' river flank. Their intention was to storm the defenders' position from the rear. The *Canadien* militia, however, suddenly burst out of the woods onto the river bank. At this, Salaberry, watching through his glass, issued the order to fire. The brush on the river's north side erupted into a sheet of flame. The invaders, exhausted after fourteen hours of struggling through heavy bush and swamp in addition to fighting, could struggle no more.

Hampton believed that no less than 5,000 to 6,000 men opposed his advance. Rather than incur the heavy casualties required to storm their positions, he opted to withdraw. Ironically, the defenders comprised only a small fraction of that number. Salaberry had perhaps 300 Voltigeurs in his position, Macdonnell about 200 more Embodied Militia in reserve. The remainder, numbering no more than 600 additional troops, were several miles back at Lafourche. For reasons either planned or unplanned (it is not certain), they had not been committed to battle.

As Salaberry commented in a letter sent to his father, the battle was "a most extraordinary affair." Four hundred troops had forced the retirement of 4,000 well-trained infantry. A handful of Voltigeurs, and English and French Canadian Embodied Militia, assisted by civilians and Indians, had turned back the greatest invasion of the war, at almost no cost. Indeed, Canadian casualties numbered a mere 5 killed, 16 wounded, 4 missing; American losses, about 50. Most important, the Canadian defenders had thwarted Hampton's plan to reach the St. Lawrence and join with Major-General James Wilkinson's advancing army to capture Montreal. Had they succeeded in doing so, Upper Canada, deprived of both its communications and supply line with Great Britain, would have been seriously threatened, despite victories won there.

Salaberry, awarded a gold medal as well as the Order of the

Bath for his victory, later served in Lower Canada's Legislative Assembly. He died at his seigneury at Chambly at the age of forty-nine. Although regarded as an epic figure in Lower Canada, he has never received the national recognition due him as our first Canadian-born war hero. Today, most general histories in English continue to ignore the brave officer who saved Canada on the wooded banks of the Châteauguay.

SELECTED READINGS

Berton, Pierre. *Flames Across the Border 1813–1814*. Toronto: McClelland & Stewart, 1981.

Bishop, Arthur. *Canada's Glory: Battles that Forged a Nation*. Toronto: McGraw-Hill Ryerson, 1996.

Turner, Wesley. *The War of 1812: The War that Both Sides Won*. Toronto: Dundurn, 1990.

Wohler, Patrick. *Charles de Salaberry: Soldier of the Empire, Defender of Quebec*. Toronto: Dundurn, 1984.

Sir John Colborne, Field Marshal Lord Seaton.
Painted by G. W. Fisher, engraved by James Scott. (NAC/C-010889)

6

MAJOR-GENERAL SIR JOHN COLBORNE

The Road to St. Eustache

Major-General Sir John Colborne (1778–1863), a deeply religious officer, was a hero of the Peninsular Wars against Napoleon as well as Waterloo. Following a term as Governor General of Guernsey, he became Lieutenant-Governor of Upper Canada, where he actively promoted public works and immigration. About to return to England, Sir John was suddenly appointed commander of British forces in the Canadas, in response to growing unrest in both colonies. An officer known for his self-discipline, high intelligence, and focussed energy, he personally led the military response that suppressed the 1837 Rebellion in Lower Canada. Although the response appears harsh by modern standards, we should not ignore the reality that at the time a vigilant administration mistook Patriote leader Louis-Joseph Papineau's sudden flight from Montreal as a sortie into the countryside to rouse armed support. In the end, the rebellion, ineffectually planned and almost accidentally begun, was quickly snuffed out as a result of effective military assistance to the civil power. When a second rising broke out, Sir John promptly crushed it as well. In 1839, Colborne returned to England, and in recognition of his services to Canada was elevated to the House of Lords, becoming First Baron Seaton.

On the sunny, yet freezing morning of December 13, 1837, curious Montrealers gathered to watch a rare spectacle, even for that sizable town. A military parade consisting of more than 2,000 British regulars and militia was about to set off from the city's Quebec Gate Barracks bound on a half-day march that would take them to the village of St. Eustache, which had become a centre of insurgency. Riding easily at the column's head, Major-General Sir John Colborne, the fifty-eight-year-old Commander-in-Chief, who insisted on leading the strike force in person, created a minor sensation. Nonetheless, his presence did not surprise those who were aware of his outstanding military record, especially his service in the Peninsular War. The small army Coiborne commanded consisted of two brigades of marching, great-coated infantry, including elements of the Royals, 32nd, 83rd, as well as two militia units, the Royal Montreal Rifles and Globensky's Volunteers. In addition, the force included the Montreal Volunteer Cavalry, as well as half a dozen field guns and their ammunition wagons. In marked contrast to the bumbling British commanders during the American revolution, Sir John, short on regulars, had decided early on to make full use of available militia.

The unrest that had been growing in the colony, which suddenly exploded into a state of apparent insurrection, had been developing for some time. Since 1835, it was clear that in Upper Canada the fiery Scot William Lyon Mackenzie and his followers were moving towards revolt. Unable to influence the Legislature's executive, unheeded by the Colonial Office, the editor of the *Colonial Advocate* was increasingly extolling the virtues of the American system of government. Meanwhile, in Lower Canada, Louis-Joseph Papineau, the Speaker of the Assembly and the principal advocate of reform, was leading a similar movement. Although a seigneur, he spoke for the farmers and small business and professional people of his province and race. An extensive reader, Papineau was an outspoken admirer of British institutions, but he was also acquainted with the French Revolution's idealism, as well as the workings of American democracy. Increasingly, the French Canadian leader was convinced that democracy was needed in Lower Canada's government. Also, many of his followers, fearing the domination of the Château Clique, or British-dominated establishment, wished to defend the old laws, the old institutions — especially the French language, as well as the seigneurial land holding system. The growing unrest, however, was fuelled most strongly by the savage economic depression that had struck both Canadas during the summer of 1837. At this stage, revolutionary talk was bound to spark action, and indeed it had. By late November and early December 1837, a series of bitter clashes between self-styled *Patriotes* and British detachments sent to the chief centres of rural unrest, as well as Papineau's and his followers' flight, had produced the perception on the part of the British authorities that revolt was on the verge of breaking out everywhere in Lower Canada.

As excited onlookers watched the tramping columns march out of the city, Colborne and staff officers riding alongside, many sensed that what they were witnessing was, indeed, living history. Certainly, it was likely the last campaign of one of the finest officers who had ridden with Sir Arthur Wellesley, the famous Duke of Wellington, the British commander who had broken the pride of Napoleon and his Eagles two and a half decades earlier. Colborne's almost uncanny resemblance to the famous Duke only added to the atmosphere. Although much larger than Wellesley, his former chief, Sir John conveyed the same natural reserve, tempered with a quick will-to-action, as well as a sense of natural command. He also carried himself with the same military bearing, and had the same noble stature as did his mentor. In marked contrast to Wellington's aquiline features, though, Colborne's firm face was moulded on predominantly straight lines. His massive forehead, through his long nose, linear mouth, and imposing square jaw-line conveyed an extremely stern demeanour. Watchers also noted, with approval, that riding with the Commander-in-Chief, as aides-de-camp, were his two sons. James, the elder, was a twenty-two-year-old lieutenant in the 24th, and Francis, the younger, a twenty-year-old lieutenant in the 15th. From this first exposure to battle, both would follow in their famous father's footsteps, rising to the rank of generals in the British Army in decades to come.

The road Sir John was taking to St. Eustache had, in a sense, begun four decades earlier. In the last decade of the 18th century, Colborne, as a youth, was a carefree, six-foot, fair-haired young giant. He also possessed the qualifications that would speed his promotion in the military, whether he realized it or not. Initially, he received his first commission, as ensign in the 20th Foot, through the influence of his stepfather's patron, the Duke of Warwick. Following this initial step, Colborne would win subsequent advancements through the rank of field-marshal, without resorting to purchase. At this period, this was an almost unheard-of achievement. Although he was not the type to promote himself unduly, the young officer did not lack confidence or determination. On more than one occasion, he had drawn the attention of his superiors to an advancement he felt he had truly earned.

The onset of the Napoleonic wars only hastened the talented young officer's advancement. Promoted captain-lieutenant in 1799, Colborne saw active service in the Netherlands, and also served in Egypt, Malta, and Sicily. As military secretary, first to General Fox and later the legendary Sir John Moore, he mastered half a dozen languages, including Swedish. Colborne was at Moore's side during the Spanish campaign, including the epic British retreat to Corunna on the coast. One of the mortally wounded General's final requests was that Colborne, who had served him so faithfully, be promoted. As a result, he would be gazetted lieutenant-colonel.

Later, Colborne returned to Spain with Moore's famous successor, Sir Arthur Wellesley, mentioned earlier. The young officer commanded the 52nd Oxfordshire Light Infantry in a number of famous actions. He also won a reputation for possessing "a singular talent for war," in the words of Sir John Napier, historian of the Peninsular War. Seriously wounded in the siege of Cuidad Rodrigo, one of the two gateways that blocked the advance into Spain, Colborne was permanently disabled in his left arm. Upon returning to active service, he headed a brigade during the forcing of the Pyrenees and the advance into southern France. At Waterloo, the 52nd would be part of General Sir Frederick Adams' Light Brigade, charged with protecting the British right from being bent by Napoleon's famed Imperial Guard. When the

Guard moved menacingly forward, Colborne suddenly advanced his battalion downhill, simultaneously swinging it in a dramatic charge that swept the elite French troops back in confusion. Witnessing the rout, the rest of the French army soon collapsed. Although Colborne's feat remained unacknowledged by Wellington, himself hotly engaged in the "fog of battle," the "colonel of the 52nd" would be widely acclaimed, and subsequently decorated by England, Austria and Portugal.

Had the conflict continued, opinion was that Sir John himself would likely have succeeded his master Wellington as Commander-in-Chief of the British forces. Instead, he gained valuable experience as Guernsey's governor, before Wellington's recommendation dispatched him to Canada, where many of the Duke's protégés served in the decades following 1815. Here, he quickly established a sterling reputation as Upper Canada's ablest administrator. His major accomplishments included encouraging immigration and public works, founding Upper Canada College, an elite boy's preparatory school that continues to this day, and endowing the province with 40 new Anglican parishes.

In the spring of 1836, an unexpected dispatch from Lord Glenelg, the Colonial Secretary, altered Colborne's plans to return home. It appointed him Commander-in-Chief in the Canadas. Journeying dutifully back to Montreal, Sir John, as was his style, put public service before personal desire. Against the background of rapidly escalating civil unrest in Lower Canada, Colborne's presence made itself immediately felt. In the estimate of one contemporary, the Waterloo hero "was equal to 10,000 disciplined troops." Another would describe him in almost Arthurian terms — as an officer *sans peur* and *sans reproche*. Overstatements such might be, however the General's steadying presence did much to counterbalance the weak and vacillating actions of Lord Gosford, the colony's over-conciliatory civil-administrator.

As noted, Colborne possessed a personality not unlike Wellington's. He was an officer of upright character, high principles, and great energy. Like all the Duke's conservative-minded officers, however, he bore a reluctant suspicion of innovations in government. A strong member of the Church of England, he naturally sympathized with the concept of a class-ordered society. Overall, the Commander-in-Chief's abrupt nature, coupled with his formidable military bearing, a natural reserve and a "quick and imperious manner," made him a formidable personage to deal with. Fortunately, this cold and distant image was balanced to a degree by Lady Colborne's natural charm and graciousness. Most important, the Colborne household was famous for its warmth, simplicity and generosity.

French Canadian radicals, however, continued to under-rate the General and the authority he so evidently represented. Some *Patriotes* openly mocked Sir John for his strict beliefs, also his "constant praying and psalm-singing." To their peril, they overlooked the Cromwellian inner-resolve of the man. Although Colborne has left precious few records of his inner thoughts, existing evidence suggests that his dutiful and controlled nature was shaped by a combination of influences. Among such were several personal bereavements, his own vigorous military training, and, above all else, a deeply held religious faith. Three of the General's close family — his stepfather, father-in-law, and brother-in-law — were clergy. Colborne's own beliefs were simple and straightforward, typified by advice he gave to his son James: "Attend to the study of Christ and yourself, which is the wisest preparation for all that may happen to us." As Rebellion historian Elinor Kyte Senior notes: "There was something almost Puritan in the severe self-discipline, a discipline that brought him out of bed at four in the morning to study foreign languages." Clearly, a man of such Cromwellian resolve would not brook insurrection lightly.

From his first arrival in Montreal, Colborne tolerated no interference with the military prerogative. Sir John and Lord Gosford, the governor, would personally clash over a number of points. Colborne always won, however. After the rebellion was crushed, Gosford complained that he was often "left to learn from common rumours the movements contemplated among the forces . . . or . . . [was] allowed to remain in ignorance until they had been wholly or partially executed." Lieutenant-Colonel Charles Grey, son of the famous British prime minister, would note of his superior officer: "Though a most excellent man . . .

[he] is somewhat sulky." Luckily, Colborne would find a like-minded soul in the colony's equally demanding and effective attorney-general, John Ogden. The two trusted one another implicitly, and this was to be an important bonus during the coming troubles.

As already mentioned, in politics Colborne subscribed to the same credo as Wellington: that to grant the colonies local government would be incompatible with British interests and sovereignty. Still, he refused, at least initially, to take alarm over Louis-Joseph Papineau's increasingly heated speeches demanding self-government for French Canadians. Although Sir John thought the radical spokesman's utterances to be "of a very seditious character," he remained convinced that they would "produce little effect here." Soon, however, Colborne came to view growing *Patriote* agitation with concern. Especially when agitators, copying the American model, refused to purchase British products, clothed themselves in *pure laine,* the traditional habitant's undyed woolen homespun, in the Assembly, and escalated their protest further by boycotting British courts.

To the alarm of many persons of British origin, the *Patriotes* soon had their own flag as well. The new red, green and white *tricolore* evoked memories of the French revolution and Napoleon in Colborne and other officers' breasts. Agitators also began singing their own songs, and increasingly looked to the classically educated Papineau as both their hero and leader. To add further alarm, in the minds of British officers at least, radical *Patriotes* began raising so-called liberty poles topped with the red Phrygian cap of revolution in front of homes. The escalating disorder in the colony glaringly contradicted the atmosphere the fresh and serious-minded new monarch Victoria, who had just ascended the throne in 1837, wished to encourage. In August, the reform-dominated Assembly brought things to a head by refusing to vote supplies (a budget). In response, Gosford dissolved it. It would not be convened again prior to the rebellion's outbreak.

Meanwhile, Colborne resurrected the town's police force, which earlier had disintegrated due to lack of funding. The Commander-in-Chief strengthened Montreal's garrison to 1,000 troops. Additionally, he ordered Quebec City's forces raised to 1,700 officers and men. But as Sir John and the *Patriote* leaders knew, the total number of regulars in the colony constituted an exceedingly small force to police a sprawling province like Quebec, with a population of 650,000 — especially considering the fact authorities feared the entire populace might soon attempt to overthrow the colony's legitimate government.

Sir John continued to strengthen his command during the autumn of 1837. In Upper Canada, Sir Francis Bond Head, the governor, agreed to send him the last remaining regiment of regular troops to assist in maintaining order in the Lower Province. Colborne also prepared for the possibility he might have to wage a winter campaign. He stockpiled 100 sleighs, ensured runners were available to be fitted to artillery wagons, and saw to it that soldiers were equipped with snowshoes and moccasins. For safety, he ordered Quebec's long-neglected gates shut. Canadian veterans of Colborne's old regiment, the famed 52nd, turned out to drill enthusiastically. Regular officers reconnoitred the roads leading to the Eastern Townships. Also, the secret service was expanded, and many local contacts were cultivated in the colony's bilingual society. However, when Colborne attempted to suppress Montreal's vitriolic *Patriote* newspapers *Vindicator* and *La Minerve,* which continued to inflame revolutionary sentiment, he failed.

As unrest continued, the General observed: "The game which Mr. Papineau is playing cannot be mistaken and we must be prepared to expect that if four or five hundred persons be allowed to parade the streets of Montreal at night singing revolutionary songs, the excited parties will come to collision." Not long afterwards, as predicted, the first stage of the revolution began with a riot, when youthful members of the Sons of Liberty, Papineau's supporters, collided with young men of the rival Doric Club, or British faction. Almost immediately, military pickets took up posts throughout the town, and the Montreal Royal Artillery patrolled the streets. Six days later, in the face of continuing agitation, Colborne issued a proclamation forbidding unsanctioned gatherings. Authority was also given to raise volunteer bodies of riflemen, artillery and cavalry to support the authorities. By November 9, Sir John had established his headquarters in Montreal, and consolidated all aspects of the colony's government under his control. Additionally, he now took the major step of issuing warrants to arrest *Patriote* leaders for treason. Such decisive actions, supported by Gosford, came none too soon, for the situation appeared to be rapidly worsening. Indeed, Lady Colborne observed in a private communication: "The whole country has . . . apparently changed its nature in the short span of the last fortnight and become interested in revolution."

The apprehension of two proscribed rebels, Dr. Davignon and Pierre-Paul Desmaray, in the village of St. Jean d'Iberville in the Eastern Townships, only added to the perceived alarm. Members of the Montreal Volunteer Cavalry, a French Canadian unit equipped only with sidearms, were sent to protect the arresting magistrates and escort the prisoners back to town. The troops were attacked, however, and overwhelmed by rebel sympathizers who released the duo. The outrage was the first act of open defiance. The rebels' shots fired on the occasion signalled the beginning of armed revolt. And, like the skirmish at Lexington and Concord in 1775, news of the attackers' success spread rapidly through nearby parishes. Not least, it greatly encouraged hundreds of rebels assembling in the villages of St. Denis and St. Charles in the Richelieu region, south of the St. Lawrence.

Colborne's response was to order a strong body of regulars to return to the spot where the troopers had been attacked. The General's unequivocal order to them read: "Should they resist the civil power or fire on the troops, you will fire on the rebels, also destroy any house from which they might fire." In issuing such a directive, the Commander-in-Chief was adhering to standard British practice of the period. This sanctioned the seizure of assets and papers of rebel leaders, and also specified the burning of homes and other quarters from which rebels either operated or fired shots at forces of the Crown. Sir John's senior officers were well acquainted with such procedures, for many of them had employed such measures to suppress rioting in other parts of the Empire, especially Ireland and Jamaica.

Soon, intelligence reports confirmed that rebel forces were, indeed, concentrating in the Richelieu Valley, south of Montreal. Others were hidden in the Two Mountains Region northwest of the town. As a veteran officer, Colborne realized that, given the relatively small force at his command, overall success would depend on striking at the rebel leaders before they could augment their numbers.

On November 22, Colborne ordered his quartermaster, Sir Charles Gore, to take a force of 250 regulars, plus militia, down river to Sorel, on the St. Lawrence's south shore. His orders called for him to ascend the Richelieu to St. Denis, where a local rebel leader, Dr. Wolfred Nelson, was hiding. Sir John also ordered Colonel George Wetherall, with 350 men, to Chambly, on the river's south shore directly south of Montreal. His orders called for him to proceed to St. Charles, some eight miles south of St. Denis, to arrest another ringleader, Thomas Brown. On paper, at least, the plan appeared simple enough. Gore would ascend the Richelieu River and drive the rebels from St. Denis. Wetherall would descend it and dislodge the rebels around St. Charles. As the two converging columns closed, any rebels who managed to escape would be swept into a swiftly closing pocket. Still, the operation suffered from serious shortcomings. Troop movements had to be made in darkness over roads deep in mud; as well, both forces lacked adequate guides. Major Augustus Gugy, accompanying Wetherall's column, recorded that only a single man spoke French. Nor did either force possess wagons to enable it to transport supplies or wounded. As Gugy complained, troops advanced "without a dollar, without a loaf of bread, and without a spare cartridge."

Greeting Gore's advance, *tricolores* and eagles painted on tavern doors graphically reminded the Commander and other veterans of the Napoleonic wars. As the night-time march proceeded, horses drawing the column's two field guns sank shin-deep in mud, and cold rain changed to wet, chilling snow as morning beckoned. Even more dispiriting, as weary troops slogged forward, church bells warned the insurgents of Gore's advance. Their chimes also summoned armed bands of *habitants* from the surrounding countryside. Finally, however, after the British strike force had engaged the rebels, who were protected in a strongly fortified stockade, for five hours, Gore decided to retreat. British casualties were 24 wounded or killed. Incredibly, Dr. Wolfred Nelson's *habitants,* assisted by a handful of veterans of the Voltigeurs of 1812, had stood their ground, repulsing red-coated veterans led by officers who had served under Wellington himself. Early next morning, Papineau, the rebel leader, who had been present but had taken no part in the combat, accompanied by fellow rebel Edmund O'Callaghan, escaped across the nearby American border.

Although it was larger and better led, Wetherall's force achieved little more, at least initially. When it was seven miles short of St. Charles, its Commander received word of Gore's repulse. In response, Wetherall returned to Chambly. Two days later, on the night of November 24/25, he again moved on St. Charles, this time with a reinforced column. As at St. Denis, local rebels had erected a loopholed barricade and posted marksmen in a nearby house. The sight of British regulars, however, caused rebel leaders to flee. Once Wetherall's artillery drove their followers from the stockade, his 400 bayonet-equipped troops encountered little difficulty in storming the barricade. Goaded into a frenzy by defenders' fire, which had been directed at them from houses and barns during their advance, regulars and volunteers destroyed the enemy camp. Although the manor house the rebels had employed as headquarters was spared, 20 other buildings were torched.

Upon being informed of Wetherall's success, Colborne now ordered a reinforced Gore to mount a second strike against St. Denis. But Nelson, Brown and other principals sought by the Crown had fled. In response, troops destroyed Nelson's fortified house, as well as a nearby brewery owned by the rebel Commander. But when redcoats discovered the body of Lieutenant George Weir, a dispatch rider who had gone missing the week previous, their anger could not be contained. Weir, taken prisoner by the rebels, had jumped, while still tied, from a wagon and been dragged on his knees. Startled by Weir's sudden attempt to escape, rebels wounded him fatally with blows from their swords, before a leader dispatched the British officer with a *coup de grâce* from his pistol. Afterwards, to keep Weir's horribly mutilated corpse from being discovered, the rebels had weighted his body with rocks and sunk it beneath the nearby river's waters. Because of this grim discovery, British regulars would adopt the shouted slogan: "Remember George Weir." Many subsequent atrocities would trace their roots to the unfortunate incident. Despite such reprisals, however, reports filed by regular officers make absolutely no reference to a state of indiscipline prevailing among troops. Only a single British soldier, convicted of deliberately firing on individuals along the line of march, was ordered sentenced to 200 lashes and dismissed without pay or pension.

The nearby Two Mountains region, situated northwest of Montreal, had long been excited by Papineau's justifiable, though fiery rhetoric, as well as the reformers' numerous demands as detailed in the *Patriote* press. Upon learning of Gore's defeat at St. Denis, the region exploded in open revolt. Fortunately, government spies had already warned Sir John that sizable rebel forces were concentrated here. Their leader was Amury Girod, a Swiss, who had earlier served as a cavalry officer in turbulent Mexico. Bearing a commission that Papineau had personally signed, he had made St. Eustache his headquarters. After quarrelling with moderate leaders, he had chosen a young idealist, Dr. Olivier Chénier, fired with the dream to fight and die for liberty, as his lieutenant. As in the Richelieu valley, gangs of *Patriotes* roamed from village to village. Their main activities consisted of forcing local officials to destroy their commissions, terrorizing citizens who did not support the rebel cause or who wished to remain neutral (the *chouayens*), as well as scouring the countryside for weapons and food. A number had already looted the nearby Indian village at Oka of a substantial stockpile of weapons.

Before dealing a blow against the Two Mountains insurgents, Colborne needed to ensure no new outbreaks were likely to flare up elsewhere. By early December, some 3,000 volunteers were under arms in Montreal and nearby communities. The excitement led John Durnford of the Ordnance Department to comment: "All the young folks are military mad. Uniforms and side arms in all directions." Near the Vermont frontier, the Missisquoi Volunteers, 250-strong, were patrolling to prevent hostile excursions into Canada. Also, in the eastern portion of Upper Canada, all the English-speaking militia corps had volunteered their services. Such included the Glengarry Highlanders, the Grenville Militia, the Leeds Regiment, as well as Perth's Volunteer Artillery.

Earlier, Colborne had implemented full martial law in Montreal and vicinity. He had also requested fellow Peninsular veteran General Sir John Harvey, commander at Fredericton, to send the 35th Regiment "without possible delay" to follow the 43rd, dispatched earlier, to reinforce Quebec's garrison. Including militia, as well as friendly Mohawk Indians, Colborne could count on a combined strength of over 8,000 troops. In early December, the last requirement of the Commander-in-Chief's carefully planned strategy was finally in place. Freezing temperatures now solidified waterways in and around the island city, simplifying the logistics of moving men and supplies across various surrounding river obstacles.

Having, as mentioned, served with Sir John Moore, the officer who pioneered British light infantry tactics, as well as having gained valuable experience commanding a battalion in General Adam's Light Brigade, Colborne was no stranger to the art of rapid manoeuvre. He was more than confident that the rebels, despite their growing numbers, could be dealt a quick blow by effectively handled infantry. The operation against St. Eustache would be undertaken by two brigades. The first, composed of the 32nd and 83rd Regiments augmented by the Montreal Volunteer Cavalry, was under the command of Lieutenant-Colonel Sir John Maitland. The second, commanded by Lieutenant-Colonel George Wetherall, the conqueror of St. Charles, consisted of the Royals, the Montreal Rifles, as well as St. Eustache Loyal Volunteers. In addition, the strike force was stiffened by 78 members of the Royal Artillery, manning half a dozen cannon, commanded by Major Jackson. In total, the Crown force consisted of an impressive 1,280 regulars and 220 volunteers.

As its brigades marched out from the Quebec Street Barracks, the beaten path leading northwards was only wide enough to allow two great-coat clad soldiers to march abreast. Thus, the brigades would take different routes for the first dozen or so miles of the march, to St. Martin on Isle Jésus. Troopers of the Royal Montreal Cavalry provided escort for Colborne and his headquarters staff, including his two sons. The unusual route towards St. Eustache had been mapped out by the Superior of the Sulpicians, a religious order. After crossing the river on the ice and following its north shore, the force would be able to move against St. Eustache without difficulty by avoiding the ordinary road the insurgents expected an attacking force to take. Some of the bridges had been damaged by local rebel leader Dr. Jean-Olivier Chénier's men. But Colborne's troops managed to repair such breaks sufficiently to march over them. Near St. Rose, however, the crossing of the ice was so hazardous artillery horses had to be detached from their traces. Gun carriages and ammunition wagons were dragged forward by hand. A tumbril and several horses broke through the ice, but they were recovered by the marchers.

Approaching St. Eustache, Globensky's detachment was spotted by Amury Girod's sentries. In response, Girod ordered Chénier and 500 rebels to cross the ice and intercept them. But Colborne's main force, approaching from the northeast, sighted the insurgents on the ice. To deal with them, he ordered artillery to sweep the rebel force with grape. Thrown into confusion by the brisk cannonade, Chénier's men, exposed on the broken ice, now clearly saw the size of the force moving against them. Commanded by Sir John himself, riding at its head, it sprawled fully two miles along the shore, composed as it was of infantry, cavalry, gun carriages, ammunition tumbrils, and supply wagons.

When 500 of their followers began to retreat, many of them fleeing with their arms, Girod and Chénier, drawing their swords, forced a number to assume defensive positions in the village's substantial stone church. Eventually 200 to 250 rebels garrisoned the town's convent, presbytery, church, and manor house. As well, small skirmishing squads were situated in nearby homes. After rallying fleeing rebels at the back of the village, Amury Girod lost his courage in the face of the imminent military threat posed by Colborne's force, mounted his own horse and fled. Later, in Montreal, the brains behind the rising would place a pistol to his head and take his own life.

Sir John's investing army now commenced a slow, circling movement. Its objective was to surround the village, denying the rebels any further opportunity to retreat. Once the village was encircled, the General sent cavalry forward to parley with Chénier and his hard core of determined followers. The rebels answered by opening a heavy fire. Responding, Sir John ordered his artillery, including Peninsular-vintage Congreve rockets, to bombard St. Eustache's centre. But the hour-long shelling produced little appreciable effect. At last, one of the aged Congreve missiles exploded. Its body broke off, and its whistling head narrowly missed Colborne and his staff. The Commander now ordered the softening-up process suspended. When it resumed, bombardiers employed less spectacular but far more effective cannon shot.

For a fleeting moment, the near-fatal accident caused Sir John to remember a similar near-miss at Waterloo. A cannonball, passing exactly over the head of a whole column of his old brigade, the 52nd, caused the soldiers to bob their heads. To hearten them and divert their thoughts away from the peril of the moment, he had called out: "For shame! for shame!" In an instant every man's torso went straight as an arrow.

Despite the pounding, St. Eustache remained uncannily silent as dusk fell on this late December afternoon. Maitland, employing his spyglass, confirmed that the formidable stone church was still occupied by a sizable force. Drawing on his experience in Spain, Colborne ordered the Royal Artillery to move one of their heavy howitzers up the village's main street to attempt to smash in the building's main doors. Such had been standard practice in the Peninsula when the enemy had barricaded himself behind heavy fortifications or walls.

Two companies of Royals rushed forward, providing cover for the gun crew. Riflemen soon cleared William Scott's and other fortified houses along the main street. They also kept sharpshooters barricaded in the church from firing. Colborne now ordered a second battery to commence firing from a position 280 yards north of the church. But the hour's cannonade that ensued again accomplished little. Meanwhile, encircling infantry, shivering and impatient, remained out of the rebels' range on St. Eustache's outskirts.

At last, a small detachment of Royals, commanded by Lieutenant Ned Wetherall, the surgeon son of the brigade's leader, managed to burst into the presbytery and set it afire. Under cover of the flames and smoke, the Royals' Grenadier Company carried at bayonet point the manor house that faced the presbytery. Covered by their fire, Wetherall's troops stormed the church's sacristy from the presbytery. Chénier's rebels, who had destroyed the stairs inside the church, continued firing from the gallery where they had taken refuge in desperation. In response, Wetherall's men, chopping pieces of wood from the altar, hastily built a fire to drive the insurgents out.

As flames spread rapidly through the structure, trapped and desperate rebels jumped from the windows. Many were severely wounded. In despair, Chénier rallied four remaining defenders in a heroic attempt to continue resisting. Outside, British regulars, shouting "Remember Jock [George] Weir," the name of their

Front view of the Church of St. Eustache occupied by the insurgents.
By Charles Beauclerk. (NAC/C-000392)

slain colleague, continued to pour a murderous musket fire into the building's casements. The muscular Chénier, struck in the chest by a musket ball, would shortly die of the wound.

This fiery final assault on the musket- and artillery-pocked church ended the four-hour standoff. Rebel casualties numbered 70 dead, 15 wounded. Additionally, 115 were captured. Nearly all of the 50 insurgents still occupying the church lay dead. In contrast, Crown casualties were remarkably light for a storming force. Only one British soldier was killed during the siege. Two of eight wounded died soon afterward, however.

The inferno illuminating St. Eustache as the December dusk fell gave the village the eerie aspect and feel of a hot summer's day. Only two rebel houses, belonging to Scott and Chénier, were officially ordered burnt. Following standard practice that prevailed when insurgents had invited bloody assault by refusing to surrender, Colborne now ordered his forces to "Free Quarters." This allowed troops to requisition whatever billets and provisions they could. Maddened by the ferocity of the struggle, the length of the siege, as well as the intense cold they had endured since morning, the fatigued soldiers now gave full vent to their rage and disgust. Hungry regulars seized a sizable quantity of beef that rebels had requisitioned and salted down. Soon, the search for other provisions turned to outright looting. In the excitement, rioters stripped the bodies of dead *Patriotes* and even stole pieces of the church's belfry clock. Strangely, though, when the priest's strongbox was found next day, it still contained £250 Sterling. Such random insanity moved a Peninsular veteran present to record that the devastation "equalled if not surpassed the sack of Badajos." Over 60 homes and barns, Loyalist as well as *Patriote,* were torched. By the time morning dawned, St. Eustache, ranked behind only Quebec and Montreal as a social and cultural centre, had been reduced to little more than a pile of smoking ashes.

Rumours concerning the postmortem that military surgeons had conducted on Chénier's body only added to the sense of outrage. Unrepentant *Patriotes* spread the false account that authorities had ripped out the rebel leader's heart, quartered it, and placed the grisly remains on display in a nearby tavern. Repeated in both contemporary accounts as well as histories of the rebellion, the lurid tale would continue to cause great bitterness not only among the disaffected, but also among French Canadians in general.

It must be stressed that much of the savage arson and looting that was St. Eustache's lot was probably due to the actions of volunteers and civilians, rather than British regulars. During the month of occupation leading up to the village's liberation, the local population had suffered extensively at the hands of Girod and his followers. Now, they had taken retribution. In balance, though, Colborne and his officers do not appear to have taken any special precautions to prevent the rigorous punishment that such irregulars now exacted. Likely, the commander wished to remind the French Canadian population that rebels who took up arms against established authority could expect little mercy from authorities.

Next day, at nearby St. Benoit, Colborne's troopers lined up suspects, threatening them, with a brace of cannon placed in the doorway, to reveal where leaders were hiding. Colborne himself warned local rebels "if one shot is fired by any insurgent, the village will be put to the sword." After the regulars had moved on, a loyalist force meted out its own harsh vengeance. Eighty-nine buildings, including the priest's house, were torched. Drunken volunteers, parading in the priest's vestments, smashed religious statues, forced open the tabernacle, ground the sacred host under heel, and desecrated altar vessels. Lady Colborne would later write (perhaps somewhat simplistically) of these horrendous acts, especially the torching of the village: "Happily as everyone thinks, for Sir John would not order, partly by accident, and partly by the indignation of the volunteers, the whole was in blaze so rapidly, the wind being so high, that they had some difficulty in escaping . . . the smoke so thick and fires bursting out on every side, they were afraid they should not get their horses and they could not go back." Evidence suggests the Commander himself only learned of the fiery reprisals and other incidents after they had taken place. The outcome was that guilty parties were never identified or punished. Doubtlessly, however, Colborne, with his strong religious sensibilities, must have been as revolted as others were by the drunken savagery vented on St. Benoit's church and altar plate.

So ended the first stage of the "Rebellions in the Canadas." In Upper Canada, the crisis had peaked a week previous, when Colonel FitzGibbon, Allan MacNab, and Governor Head himself, along with 600 militia, drove William Lyon Mackenzie's ragtag army back, and burned Montgomery's Tavern, the rebel head-quarters north of Toronto. In the Lower Province, too, the series of pitched battles detailed here effectively ended the major threat to the colony's legitimate authority.

A number of factors had both hampered and inflamed the operation. They included the *Patriotes'* guerilla tactics, the grue-some though unplanned murder of George Weir while he was attempting to escape his captors, as well as the frustration and fatigue of soldiers campaigning in the Richelieu area without proper transport and commissary. Even army veterans were un-used to fighting in bitter weather such as had prevailed. Colborne faced additional problems due to the disruption of commun-ications between headquarters and Gore and Wetherall, his field commanders. As a result, he had left great discretion to them. In the final balance, though, it was the rebels' resorting to strongly constructed stone buildings and houses as positions of defence in all three instances in the Lower Canada fighting that had obliged investing forces to resort to both artillery and hazardous frontal assaults, including bayonet charges.

Afterwards, French Canadians christened Colborne "le Vieux Brûlot," literally, "Old Firebrand." Generations of historians, none however a military specialist, would condemn him for his fanati-cism, brutality, and anti-Catholicism in suppressing the Lower Canada rebellion. Ironically, the judgement overlooks the Com-mander's personal qualities, outstanding military service, and many contributions to Canada. Not least, Colborne's operation, undertaken in extraordinary conditions, in difficult weather, and with relatively small forces, offers a classic study in effective "mili-tary assistance to the civil power."

The home government, alarmed, now rushed elite Grenadier

and Coldstream Guards, as well as cavalry units, to bolster Canada's garrison. As a result, when a second rebellion broke out in Lower Canada in 1838, Sir John crushed it within a week. As previously, he relied upon loyal Glengarry Scots as well as Caughnawaga (Kahnawake) Mohawks to bolster his regulars and strike terror into the hearts of the insurgents. The new round of risings resulted in a full-blown program of dragooning in the region south of the St. Lawrence. Previously, Colborne's leniency had resulted in no executions and the freeing of all but eight prisoners. Now, however, 111 prisoners were brought before military courts, a dozen ultimately going to the gallows. In one noteworthy instance, a member of the General's staff was embarrassed to find his superior on his knees praying for the condemned. But Charles Grey, another of Colborne's staff, thought he was much too lenient with many involved in the risings.

Despite the extremely conservative beliefs of Colborne and other Peninsular veterans who served under him, such as Sir James Macdonnell, Sir Charles Gore, John Clitherow, and Sir Randolph Routh, the cost of the two rebellions was mercifully low. Casualties numbered only 325 dead, 27 of these soldiers of the Crown, the remainder rebels who had resisted authorities. Also, there were 13 executions, one of them (as we have noted) being George Weir's, carried out by the rebels. Colborne's prompt action — one might better describe it as military professionalism and thoroughness — had effectively brought an end to the rebellion. In restoring domestic peace, he also indirectly laid the groundwork for responsible government, which would be granted the French Canadians, as it was the English in Upper Canada, in 1848–49. Most importantly, his actions ensured that grievances in the province would not become a festering wound for decades to come, such as was the case in Ireland.

On October 23, 1839, Sir John took his final leave of Canada, riding down to the ship awaiting him at Montreal through cheering throngs of well-wishers. Shortly afterwards, elevated to the peerage as Baron Seaton, he chose as supporters to his personal arms the image of a soldier of his old regiment as well as that of a Canadian settler with an axe. This coat of arms would serve him well during two more decades of public service, culminating in his appointment as Commander-in-Chief of the garrison in Ireland between 1855 and 1860. Although it appears very few French Canadians realized it, they possessed a loyal friend in the tall, austere officer who had suppressed the risings with such firmness. Shortly after he had assumed his seat in the House of Lords, Seaton eloquently, though unsuccessfully, opposed the measure Parliament passed in 1840–41, uniting English and French Canada. In his scholarly and cosmopolitan mind, he realized the French Canadians in British North America regarded themselves as a distinct and unique race. As a result, they would never accept the ill-conceived measure, stemming from Lord John ("Radical Jack") Durham's report, drafted in response to the rebellions, that recommended they be assimilated as soon as possible into the faster-growing, more "progressive" population of Upper Canada. Tory in mind-set and military officer though he might be, Seaton was also a man of conscience. Thus, he realized a quarter century prior to Confederation that further unrest could be forestalled best by allowing the French Canadians their own distinct identity within a form of government that would safeguard and protect it. Such rare, even insightful, clarity of vision entitles Sir John to a better place in our nation's history than he has hitherto enjoyed.

SELECTED READINGS

Schull, Joseph. *Rebellion: Rising in French Canada 1837.* Toronto: Macmillan of Canada, 1971.

Senior, Elinor Kyte. "Suppressing Rebellion in Lower Canada: British Military Policy and Practice, 1837–38." *Canadian Defence Quarterly* 17:4 (Spring 1988): 50–55.

——— . *Redcoats and Patriotes: The Rebellions in Lower Canada 1837–38.* Canadian War Museum Historical Publication, No. 20. Stittsville, ON: Canada's Wings Inc. in collaboration with the Canadian War Museum, National Museum of Man, National Museums of Canada, 1985.

Wade, Mason. *The French Canadians 1760–1967.* 2 vols. Rev. ed. Toronto: Macmillan of Canada, 1975–1976.

Colonel Alexander Dunn, VC.
Half-tone by W. Goode. (NAC/C-005081)

7

CORONET (SECOND-LIEUTENANT) ALEXANDER DUNN

Light Brigade Hero:
Canada's First Victoria Cross

The Victoria Cross, the British Empire and Commonwealth's highest award for military valour, has been awarded to only 1,348 individuals. Coming as they do from a wide variety of backgrounds, both rich and poor alike, recipients possess a single characteristic in common: "conspicuous bravery in the face of danger." Alexander Dunn (1833–1868), the younger son of an influential Toronto family, the first of a select company of ninety-three countrymen, set the example for future generations. As a second-lieutenant in the elite and aristocratic 11th (Prince Albert's Own) Regiment of Hussars, he won the coveted new award for the great gallantry he demonstrated in the famed and courageously foolish Charge of the Light Brigade on October 25, 1854, at Balaclava, in Russia's Crimean Peninsula. Later, during the Indian Mutiny, Dunn used his fame to help raise the 100th (Prince of Wales' Royal Canadian) Regiment in Canada. After commanding the unit in Gibraltar, he would die under mysterious circumstances in a hunting mishap in Abyssinia.

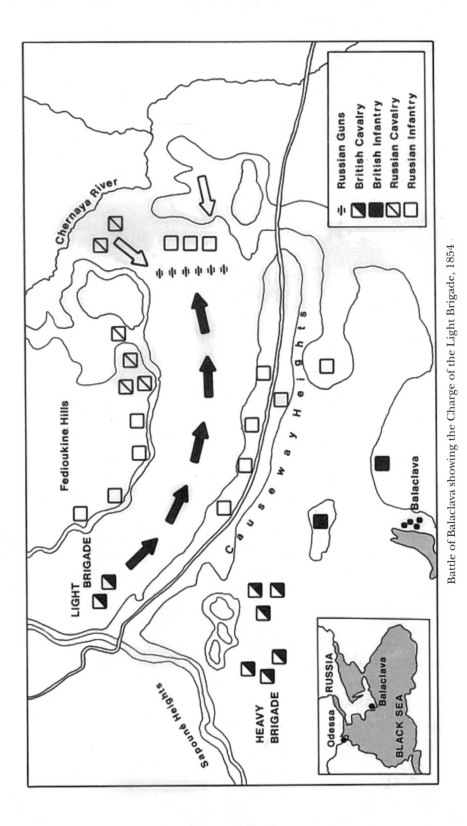

Battle of Balaclava showing the Charge of the Light Brigade, 1854

Educated at Upper Canada College and Harrow, Alexander Dunn had been granted an opportunity available to few youths born in colonial Canada. The second son of a wealthy and powerful family, he joined the British Army at the age of nineteen. Through the influence of his father, Henry Dunn, Upper Canada's Receiver General, he was gazetted coronet (second lieutenant) in the crack 11th Hussars (Prince Albert's Own). More informally, the regiment was dubbed the "Cherubims," or "Cherry Bums," because of the tight, cherry-coloured riding breeches for which it was famous. Commanded by the Earl of Cardigan, it was one of Britain's most exclusive units, and Dunn was determined to live up to its illustrious history. Although only average in the classroom, he had matured into an impressive-looking man, endowed with tremendous strength, standing six-feet-three-inches tall. Headstrong but courageous, the blonde young officer with drooping moustache showed every indication of becoming a splendid trooper. Shortly after his appointment, the regiment moved to Ireland, where it remained until the outbreak of war against Russia in the Crimea. Following his unit's arrival in the Crimea, Dunn participated in the battles of the Alma and Inkerman, and also witnessed the siege of Sebastopol. Although he had come under minor fire, he had experienced little real action. This only fuelled his impatience and desire for battle.

His opportunity would come at Balaclava, a small village situated just outside Sebastopol, the site of the main British camp. About a mile above the settlement, the main road opened into a wide space, known as the plain of Balaclava. Some two miles by three miles, the location forms a natural amphitheatre, enclosed on all sides by hills. Mounds and hillocks form a ridge, or hog's back, running from west to east, which the British called the Causeway Heights. Two valleys on either side of the feature were termed the South Valley and the North Valley. It was the latter that would be the scene of the famous charge of the Light Brigade, in which Dunn would shortly ride.

For centuries, the concept of military glory had seized men's imaginations and set their blood afire. But such dreams of trumpets, plumes, chargers, battle's excitement, and the exhalation of victory was not a dream for the common man. Essentially, war was an aristocratic trade or occupation, and its glory was reserved for aristocrats and rich men's sons. Courage was esteemed to be an essential military requisite and held to be a virtue exclusive to society's leaders. Indeed, the class was educated to courage, trained as no common man was by years of practice in dangerous sports. The Victorians praised the concept, and even worshipped it; believing that battles were won by valour, they saw war as the supreme adventure. It was a dream destined to die hard. The incompetence of the Light Brigade's leader Lord Cardigan, however, would greatly hasten the growing disenchantment with military glory.

Popular and bursting with energy, Dunn personified the cult of "muscular Christianity" and the worship of heroic valour that was so characteristic of Victorian society. In particular, he excelled at athletics, especially swordsmanship, riding and marksmanship, all requisite skills for an officer. His youthful sense of adventure and sheer bravado also ensured that he did not back away from challenges. One story recounted how, during his school days, he placed a small cap on the head of a favourite servant. Then, firing at the target from a distance of 16 yards, he hit it 36 out of 40 times. The other four shots narrowly missed the hat. Although the story seems foolish to us today, only testifying to the youth's impulsive nature which at times verged on foolhardiness, it also illustrates how Dunn possessed the rare ability to inspire confidence in those close to him. This would be true both then and later.

On the day Dunn would become a hero at Balaclava, a gray haze obscured the normally azure skies that usually gave the Crimea a theatre-like setting. But the clouds had little effect on the tall, handsome young Canadian. He sat happily astride his glistening mount, surveying the lines of British cavalry, arranging themselves in ordered ranks at the entrance to a long valley. Like the young Lieutenant, his fellow troopers were eager for action. Red and blue uniforms created a defiant splash of colour against the dark background. Troopers' faces were full of anticipation. Certainly no one foresaw that they would shortly hack their way across one of military history's bloodiest, silliest, and most heroic pages.

Waterloo excepted, the Charge of the Light Brigade was destined to be the most famous event of British military history during the 19th century. As a battle, it was hardly more than a moment. *The Times's* correspondent, William Howard Russell, recorded that the brigade formed up for the charge at precisely 10 minutes past 11. At 35 minutes past 11, hundreds of dead and dying British cavalrymen, also their mounts, would crowd the bloody ground in front of the Muscovite guns.

Why had such a tragedy occurred? A century after the Charge of the Light Brigade, Cecil Woodham-Smith would provide an answer and detail the disaster in her much-celebrated book *The Reason Why.* Due to an ambiguous and misunderstood order, Lord Cardigan, its commander, led his brigade in a heroic and incompetent attack which even the better-equipped and mounted Heavy Cavalry would not have attempted: in short, he and his troopers charged head-on, in their mistaken ignorance, against the Russian artillery and cavalry mustering at the end of Balaclava's North Valley.

Coronet Dunn had waited all his young life for an opportunity to savour combat's excitement as now seemed momentarily developing. Since his boyhood in Toronto he had always wanted to be a soldier. Now, he would get his chance. This would be his first time in action against the Russian enemy. And, mixed with his obvious anticipation was a twinge of anxiety. For only 2,000 yards ahead, a 12-gun Russian battery was drawn up hub to hub, gun carriages blocking the narrow gap at the valley's end.

In addition to the enemy battery, Dunn could see a huge concentration of Russian cavalry waiting down the valley. Also, extending for more than a mile on either side, the valley's flanking slopes bristled with more Russian troops and artillery. Between the surrounding heights, the valley appeared to be a partially hidden death trap of varying width, closing in on the battery that blocked its end. Still, Dunn had no idea that during the next 15 minutes he would establish himself as a military hero. Nor could he have possibly guessed that he would become Canada's first winner of a new award Queen Victoria would establish for valour, the coveted Victoria Cross.

Lord Cardigan, Dunn's commanding officer, also surveyed the valley. He had misgivings concerning the somewhat confusing order he had just received to attack any enemy within his command's reach — which appeared to be the Russians at the end of the valley. Because of his concerns, he now narrowed the front line of the cavalry, drawing the Light Brigade's troopers up in two lines: the first consisted of the 13th Hussars, the 11th Hussars, and the 17th Lancers; the second, the 4th Light Dragoons and the main body of the 8th Hussars.

At the last moment, however, Lord Lucan, the field commander and Cardigan's superior, in his usual fussy and interfering manner, decided to narrow the brigade's front yet again. Without consulting Cardigan, he moved the 11th Hussars from the front line back to reinforce the second. In doing so, he placed Dunn, along with some of the more reliable troopers, on the left flank to protect and cover the advance. Quickly surveying the deployment, Dunn noted the Light Brigade's new formation. Instead of its earlier two lines, the newly deepened Brigade now comprised three distinct parts. The first line consisted of the 17th Lancers on the left and the 13th Hussars on the right. Dunn's own regiment, the 11th Hussars, formed the second line. Directly behind the Lancers, the third line consisted of the 4th Light Dragoon Guards on the left and the 8th Hussars on its right. Each regiment was drawn up in two ranks. Overall, the interval separating the lines was 400 yards. On this momentous morning, the Brigade's effective strength was down from the original 1,250 to a mere 670, so severe had been the effects of cholera and dysentery.

Now, while Dunn and others watched, Major-General the Earl of Cardigan, the Light Cavalry Brigade's Commander, rode forward and took his position ten yards in front. Splendid in appearance, he sat in what cavalrymen termed the long style, yet nonetheless tall and upright in the saddle astride Ronald, his charger. Behind Cardigan rode a group of staff officers, followed by the Brigade's front line.

Sabre drawn, Cardigan sat quietly, looking straight ahead, as final adjustments were made in the ranks behind him. Exactly at ten minutes past eleven o'clock, the Commander turned and faced his men. Simultaneously, he issued the final order in his habitually strong, hoarse voice: "The Brigade will advance. Right squadron of the 17th Lancers will direct!" Then, turning to the trumpeter of the 17th Lancers, Cardigan commanded, "Sound the advance!"

Automatically, Trumpeter Britten sounded the "walk-march." Later, Dunn would remember feeling his own heart pounding and how the hair on the back of his neck stood erect as he eased his charger forward.

At Cardigan's nod, the trumpeter sounded "trot" and the pace quickened. "The 600," later memorialized in Alfred Lord Tennyson's famous poem, were now heading straight down the valley. The moving mass of men and horses seemed a single, living thing with a soul of its own. Sensing himself part of it, Dunn grasped the hilt of his sword, spurred his horse forward, and rode resolutely into the coming havoc.

An eerie stillness descended on the battlefield as the Light Brigade commenced its charge. Artillery fire momentarily ceased. Only the faint jingle of curb chains and bits could be heard as the trotting horsemen advanced in perfect formation. The sun pierced the mists of early morning, enabling watchers on the heights to identify individuals in the ranks below. Veterans of famous British battles such as the Sikh Wars and even far-off Waterloo, looked on silently, hearts beating with emotion, as they witnessed the Light Brigade's troopers, armed with little more than the traditional weapons of chivalry, lances and swords, commence their perilous ride. Seemingly, it would take them right into the muzzles of General Liprandi's waiting army. Silence continued for 100 or so yards. Even the Russians could scarcely credit their eyes as the squadrons advanced, as if on parade.

According to standard formula, light infantry, when defending itself from cavalry, had to begin firing at 600 to 800 yards. By the time advancing horsemen had reached 710 yards, each artillery piece should have fired seven spherical case shots (hollow iron spheres containing a number of bullets, as well as charge and fuse). These would be fused to burst several yards above ground. When the riders were at 380 yards, and commencing their final charge, two round shots had to be got off, also two more case shots in the time that remained. The entire bombardment had to be compressed into six minutes, the approximate duration of a cavalry charge. Procedure called for cavalry to cover the initial 780 yards at a trot, the middle 430 yards at a gallop, and the final 430 yards at full charge.

Almost hesitatingly at first, the Russian artillery opened fire. However, it soon commenced to respond more rapidly and with increasing accuracy once gunners and artillerymen found their range. Suddenly, an artillery shell exploded to Cardigan's right, just in front of the 17th Lancers. Dunn now saw a horse, its rider apparently pierced through the heart by a piece of shell fragment, wheel to the right. The mount continued to gallop back through the ranks of the 13th Hussars, body upright in the saddle, sword arm raised. When the dead trooper's corpse finally fell, someone said it was Captain Lewis Nolan, the aide who had carried forward Lord Raglan's original command to advance. Later, Dunn realized the irony: the officer who delivered the devastating and disastrous order was the first to die. (Many, however, believed that the officer, having realized the error of the message, had heroically ridden across the front of the advancing brigade so as to direct Cardigan and his troopers to the real target, the Causeway Heights, to their right, in order to support the Heavy Brigade in its pursuit of retreating Russian cavalry.)

The Brigade, with Dunn and other troopers of the 11th Hussars in its middle, continued to ride forward at a trot. But now the horsemen found themselves exposed to the withering fire from Russian riflemen on the Fedoukine Hills on the left, as well as those deployed on the Causeway Heights. Round shot swept through the ranks, shells burst overhead, as well as among the squadrons, wreaking havoc on riders and horses. Onlookers on the heights had expected the Brigade to swing right and charge the Causeway Slope. However, it became obvious that by some colossal blunder they were continuing right down the valley.

Spectators were horrified. Hardened soldiers held their breath in anticipation as they helplessly watched the spectacle. A French officer on the heights is purported to have exclaimed: *"C'est magnifique, mais ce n'est pas la guerre"* ("Magnificent, but it isn't war.") Meanwhile, Cardigan, angered, could think of little, aside from Nolan's apparent insolence in attempting to ride across his front. Was he trying to assume command of the Brigade? It did not cross the Commander's mind that the officer might have been desperately attempting to prevent a disaster.

Momentarily disengaging his fury, Cardigan nodded to Trumpeter Britten to sound the "gallop." Before he could do so, the trumpeter fell from the saddle, fatally wounded. Now, in addition to the storm of enemy bullets and artillery fire, Dunn and his comrades felt enemy artillery on either side open up on the squadrons of British horse.

Sensing they faced oblivion, the riders instinctively quickened their pace. In their race with death, Dunn and the others rode straight for the guns at the valley's end. Dead and wounded men and horses began to litter the valley's floor, forcing second and third lines either to leap over the carnage, or swing round the fallen, as they rushed past.

In front, Cardigan, obeying orders, checked his men from going too fast. They seemed almost to be on parade. A Russian battery opened fire on the British horse. Tongues of flame and smoke spurted from the ranked guns followed by the menacing hiss of shells slicing towards their targets. Additionally, musket fire on the flanks brought down individual troopers with a thundering crash, littering the plain with dead and dying. The very air seemed to hiss with bullets. In front where he now rode, Dunn could see the cannons blowing great gaps in the advance lines of cavalry. Whole sections fell, leaving gaping openings in the ranks.

Cardigan continued to work desperately to keep the 17th Lancers in orderly lines and from surging ahead in disordered groupings. Behind the Light Brigade's leader, ragged lines of the various regiments began cheering wildly as they closed towards the Russian battery. As men and horses were struck, Dunn and other officers, as well as NCOs, cried: "Close in! Close in!" to fill the gaps, and to maintain some semblance of order. Finding himself surrounded by wounded and riderless horses that at one point threatened to take him down, young Dunn had to employ the flat of his sabre to drive them off.

A quarter of a mile from the guns, the 17th's lancers, whose trumpeter had been a casualty, lowered their sharp-tipped weapons in anticipation. However, Cardigan, admonishing the Captain who had given the order, continued to call for the troopers to close "stirrup to stirrup."

Soon after, and two miles distant on the Chersonese Plain, *The Times's* correspondent saw a flashing halo of steel. Cardigan had issued his final order to charge and the troopers of the Light Brigade had drawn their sabres or lowered their lances. Suddenly, however, the cavalry seemed to disappear in a haze of smoke and blinding flashes as Russian gunners fired a point-blank salvo into the remains of the cavalry's front line. But the survivors of the 13th and 17th had reached the Russian battery. All was pandemonium. Cardigan, at one point almost cut down by the blast several yards in front of the guns, was the first rider in and through the battery. Then, as the second line of the 11th on the extreme left outflanked the Russians, the third, led by the 4th Light Dragoons and finally the 8th Hussars, crashed over the Russian guns. Fierce hand-to-hand fighting ensued. Despite Russian attempts to remove the guns, they would soon be over-run.

On the Brigade's left, Dunn and his troopers rode right through the gun position. In the process they sabred down enemy gunners who had survived the depleted first line's crashing assault. Lieutenant-Colonel John Douglas, the 11th's Commanding Officer, Dunn and two other officers swiftly led the regiment, now reduced to a mere 80, to a position behind and clear of the cannon. All was now swirling confusion. No orders had been given for action behind the enemy lines. Lord Cardigan, who had already ridden back, was nowhere to be found. Spotting a huge mass of enemy cavalry and artillery at the base of the Fedoukine Hills, Douglas formed his troops in a line. "Give them another charge, men. Hurrah!" he shouted. Lord George Paget, the brigade's second-in-command, recorded: "The Cherubims advanced

'Flash'd all their sabres bare, flash'd all at once in air."

There is little doubt that, on the memorable October 25, 1854, Lord Raglan intended the light cavalry to charge the Russians on the Causeway Heights, from which he believed they meant to remove our guns that they had captured that morning. Lord Lucan (who could not see the heights from his position) mistook the meaning of the order and charged the guns at the east end of the valley. Captain Nolan, who carried the order, was the first to be killed. For over a mile and a half the cavalry rode beneath a murderous fire from the Russian army in position

THE CHARGE OF THE LIGHT BRIGADE, BALACLAVA

The Charge of the Light Brigade, Balaclava. "Flash'd all their sabres bare, flash'd all at once in air." Half-tone by George Thomas. (NAC/C-026012)

against the entire force of the enemy cavalry! Indeed, the Russian army!"

The Russians held, momentarily. Then they turned and broke, riding back towards the Tchernaya River. Here they re-formed in a ravine. The 11th pursued them. By this time, though, their horses were so tired that to attack was impossible without additional support. Casting about desperately, Douglas spotted lancers to the rear. He was elated. Troopers heard the Commander's cry rise above the noise of battle. "Hurrah, it's the 17th Lancers!" For an instant the brave remnant thought it was saved.

The men of the 11th, however, quickly realized from the green and white pennants on their lances that the six squadrons of approaching cavalry were Russian, not British! Even worse, they were drawing up to cut off any possible chance of retreat!

Douglas shouted: "Every man for himself now." The 11th's remnants, with a few officers and men from other units, responded instinctively. Forming a rough semicircle, they faced the enemy lancers. With the best chargers to the front and centre, the troopers made a last desperate charge. Riding stirrup to stirrup, heads close to their horses' necks, sabres at the guard position, the cavalry charged straight for the enemy. When the lead riders reached the Russians, enemy lancers allowed them to pass through their ranks. But as the weaker horses came abreast, the enemy closed in, attacking from both sides. Desperately, the tiring British attempted to fight their way out of the trap. Some fell, but others succeeded, fighting ferociously, to break through the ranks of encircling Russians.

Dunn and other officers brought up the rear. The powerful young Canadian, having emptied his revolver at the Russians, now defiantly flung it at them and resorted to his sabre. He was a formidable adversary, with his strapping physique and his powerful horse. In addition, he wielded a specially made sword that exceeded regulation length by many inches. His heroic conduct inspired all around him with courage.

Voices shouted: "Sergeant Bentley's cut off!" Without hesitating, Dunn turned, spurring his charger back towards the beleaguered sergeant, who was attempting to parry the blows of a trio of Russian dragoons. Dunn knew the risk he faced. Aside from dead and dying, they were the last of the brigade left on enemy ground. But seeing Bentley standing alone facing fearful odds, the young Canadian now chose to hazard all in a desperate attempt to save him.

Clenching his teeth, Dunn spurred straight for the first dragoon, sabring him out of the saddle. The action allowed Bentley to recover his legs, while Dunn turned his attention to the two other Russians. The sunshine breaking through the clouds illuminated the three mounted figures as they closed, hacked, and circled round and round. Now and then, Dunn's gigantic and nervous charger lashed out, almost unseating his rider. Blood and foam mingled, flecking rider and steed.

In only a minute or two Dunn dispatched both adversaries. Seconds later, he saw an enemy swordsman overcoming Trooper Levett, also of the 11th. Again, Dunn charged and saved a second life. Tragically, Levett's rescue was short-lived. He would be killed just minutes later.

Having lost his giant mount, shot out from under him shortly after rescuing Levett, Dunn mounted a horse belonging to the 13th. This second mount was also shot, obliging the Canadian to escape on foot. Now the long trek through the desolated valley began. Injured and wounded dragged themselves across the ground over which they had proudly advanced but 20 minutes earlier. Paget, one of the 11th's few surviving officers, graphically described the retreat: "What a scene of havoc was the last mile, strewn with the dead and dying and all friends." Survivors saw their old comrades, "some running, some limping, some crawling." They also witnessed horses from their regiment "in every position of agony, struggling to get up, then floundering back again on their mutilated riders."

673 horsemen rode in the charge, hurling themselves against some 25,000 Russian troops powerfully defended with artillery. But only 198 returned for roll call. Dunn's regiment, which had paraded that morning with 110 all ranks, at sunset could muster a scant 25, including Dunn himself. Out of the 673 horses that had ridden in the charge, close to 500 had either been killed or else had to be destroyed. Because of such horrendous losses, the Light Cavalry Brigade ceased to exist as an operational unit in the Crimea.

Despite his heroism, the ensuing months would bring their problems for Dunn as well. Following the slaughter at Balaclava, two replacement troops were sent to augment the 11th Hussars. One was given to the regiment's first lieutenant. But Dunn, who expected that he would be given the second, was passed over due to a liaison he was openly having with Lieutenant-Colonel Douglas' wife Rosa Maria. Instead, its command was given to a staff officer who lacked battlefield experience. Dunn protested, but was told he was too young for such a responsibility. Anger at the oversight spread amongst the regiment. When the story leaked out, the British press took up the cause. It claimed a regimental favourite had been given precedence over a hero who had proven himself at Balaclava. Dunn requested permission to resign his commission. Although this initial request was refused, early in 1855 permission was granted. Now free, Dunn and Rosa Maria Douglas eloped from the Crimea. In order to escape publicity, the couple chose to cross the Atlantic and take up residence in Toronto.

For two years following, Dunn and his love lived a quiet existence in Canada. As a hero, he was much sought after by the public, hostesses, and family friends. Usually, though, he turned aside questions about his experiences in the Crimea with a modest: "It was nothing, really. I did no more than my duty."

The summer following Balaclava, Dunn had participated in the first great Victoria Cross parade and investiture ceremony, in Hyde Park, London. On the historic occasion, 62 officers and men, Dunn included, stood shoulder to shoulder, irrespective of rank. As the huge and distinguished audience cheered, the diminutive Queen Victoria, brushing away tears of emotion, stooped from the saddle of her charger and pinned the coveted new decoration on the breast of each recipient. Although only a little Maltese cross of bronze, cast from enemy cannon taken at Sebastopol, the award possessed a significance far beyond its modest material value. The citation that accompanied the Canadian's decoration read:

> (Lieutenant Dunn) for having in the Light Cavalry charge of the 24th October, 1854, saved the life of Sergeant Bentley, 11th Hussars, by cutting down two of three Russian lancers who were attacking him from the rear, and afterwards cutting down a Russian Hussar, who was attacking Private Levett, 11th Hussars.

Befitting the occasion, the cavalry was commanded by the indomitable Lord Cardigan. He led the final march-past at a thundering full gallop. The spectacle delighted the madly cheering crowd, who took it as a fitting salute to the heroism of the charge of the Light Brigade. For a moment, recriminations and denials about the wording of the order he had received, and who had blundered, were willingly forgotten.

The great parade with its heroes would soon serve an added purpose. In 1857, the Horse Guards or British military office found itself hard-pressed to fill the increased manpower requirements the Indian Mutiny was creating throughout the Empire. In response, it approved the re-establishment of the old 100th as an Imperial regiment to be raised in Canada. Dunn was placed in charge of the ambitious project. The title of the unique regiment was designated "The Prince of Wales' Royal Canadian Regiment." Its predecessor, the 100th Regiment of foot (the Prince Regent's County of Dublin Regiment), had sailed for service in Canada in 1805 during the Napoleonic Wars. Following service in both Quebec and Ontario, the unit had fought in the War of 1812 in the Niagara campaign, earning distinction, but suffering heavy casualties. Once the Napoleonic wars ceased, many of its officers and men, following a tradition earlier established by both the famous Carignan-Salières and James Wolfe's veterans, settled in Canada, taking up land grants in the Ottawa Valley.

After he had arrived home with his Victoria Cross, Dunn received a hero's welcome. It was expected this would greatly assist recruiting. But the challenge he faced was formidable. Labour was scarce, wages high. Nor were Canadians, despite the collective thrill citizens experienced at Colonel John Inglis' heroic defence of Lucknow's Residency (detailed in the following chapter), especially threatened, emotionally or economically, by the potential loss of India.

Although rich, socially prominent and now a famous soldier, Dunn had to muster all his charm and persuasion to assist recruiting. He spent his personal fortune on equipment and travel, and he employed his magnetic personality to attract recruits. Eventually, his countrymen flocked to serve under such an officer. As his reward, Dunn, who had never held the rank of captain, was gazetted major.

Many of the 400 men who composed Dunn's quota were

either sons or grandsons of veterans of the original 100th. Among them was the son of its old commanding officer. Thus the regiment was, indeed, a reincarnation of the famous regiment, whose battle honour "Niagara" it would later be authorized to bear on its new colours.

Ultimately 1,200-strong, the regiment would consist of picked men, averaging five feet eleven inches in height. This was certainly noteworthy by the standards of the time. Indeed, the formidable physiques of both officers and men helped offset the reality that the unit's original clothing consisted of old coatee, or coat-like uniforms, which had been in storage for decades.

Once regimental training was underway, Dunn and a companion officer escaped from the social protocol of Toronto, setting off on a hunting trip that took them into the wilds of the Rocky Mountains. For several leisurely months, the duo gave themselves over to adventure, shooting bear and moose as well as buffalo, living among trappers and Indians, camping on the Alberta plains or beside fragrant alpine streams. As such, quite likely they were among the first of many gentlemen and officers who would discover and revel in the excitement mid-19th century Western Canada had to offer.

Meanwhile, Dunn's love affair seems to have run its course. The only mention concerning his personal life appears in the history of the 33rd Regiment. It merely alludes to the fact that he had "other adventures" during this period. The close cloak of Victorian respectability had been cast over his "indiscretion."

Under its first commanding officer, the formidable Baron de Rottenburg, the Royal Canadians soon departed Quebec City en route to England. By this time, mopping-up operations were underway in India. Thus the unit would not be needed on a war front. Dunn and his companions were posted first to Shorncliffe, later Aldershot. Here, at the Empire's premier war camp, Dunn received a unique honour. He was presented with the sword of the illustrious General James Wolfe, recently uncovered on the Plains of Abraham, which had earlier been displayed in the Great Exposition's Canadian section. Almost immediately, the distinction was followed by another. Baron de Rottenburg, a veteran of the War of 1812, retired, and Dunn, promoted lieutenant-colonel, succeeded him. The Canadian officer had achieved a truly rare distinction. He had attained command of an infantry regiment at the tender age of twenty-seven. Despite earlier transgressions, it seemed his military career was back on track.

When the Prince of Wales' Regiment was transferred to Malta in 1864, Dunn became full colonel. He was now the youngest colonel in the British Army. While in Malta, Dunn's elder and only brother John, a subaltern in the regiment, died of fever. This left Dunn heir to the family estate. But his despondency over the loss of his brother, coupled with the inactivity of the "cribbed and confined" garrison life on the island led him to seek action. He transferred to the 33rd Regiment (the Duke of Wellington's Own), stationed in the hill country at Poona, in India. He was made second lieutenant-colonel, with his superior being promoted to brigadier-general. Thus Dunn soon found himself acting colonel of the unit.

But even India, with its hunting, polo, and other inducements, could not fulfil Dunn's desire for excitement. He had high expectations when the regiment, placed on active service, was chosen to form part of General Charles Napier's Expeditionary Force to Abyssinia, in East Africa. But his anticipation was darkened by a sense of despondency.

Was he continuing to wonder why he had survived the Charge, when so many others had not? Did he just feel his luck had run out? Or was he suffering from guilt and possibly drinking heavily? Unfortunately, the answer will never be known. It remains buried with him in the desert. Despite his emotional depression, Dunn was too much an officer and gentleman to hide himself away in secret. On the morning of January 25, 1868, apparently in good spirits, he set out with the regiment's medical officer and two native bearers on a hunting expedition. Members of the party became separated when Dunn followed some elusive deer. Tired, he sat on a rock and asked his servant for a brandy flask. Exactly what ensued remains at best a tantalizing mystery.

Was it an accident or did Dunn shoot himself? As commonly, even conveniently, reported afterwards, the stopper was stuck. When Dunn struggled to open the bottle, his gun slipped, discharging both barrels. The shot tore through his upper right chest. An hour later, when the panicked servant returned with the doctor, he was dead.

Two days later Dunn would be buried at Senafe with full military honours. The entire camp attended his funeral. Following Victorian practice, fellow officers cut locks from his hair as mementoes, and kissed his cold face. Afterwards, a comrade wrote a letter to Dunn's sister in England: "In no regiment was ever a commanding officer so missed as the one we have unhappily lost — so perfect a soldier, so fine a gentleman, so confidence-inspiring a leader. He was a friend and felt to be such by every man in the regiment. The regiment will never again have so universally esteemed a commander."

Dunn's remains were buried in a small cemetery at Senafe, among the rugged hills of Abyssinia (now Ethiopia). A special correspondent of *The Times* recorded:

> I found Senafe on my arrival yesterday full of a terrible tragedy which cast a gloom over all the camp. One of the most popular and promising officers attached to the Abyssinian force, Colonel Dunn, V.C. of the 33rd Regiment had two days before shot himself — the whole army has sustained a heavy loss in the death of Colonel Dunn. He was the youngest colonel in it and his career had already given sufficient promise of distinction to justify the belief that the highest military appointments were within his reach. In the ever memorable Charge of the Light Brigade, he won the Victoria Cross, conferred upon him by the unanimous vote of his comrades. Though a strict disciplinarian, he was greatly beloved by his soldiers and all under him.

Dunn's kit was auctioned the day following his burial. Every item in it was purchased by comrades at prices described as "utterly fantastic." Decades afterwards, his Victoria Cross, medals, and portrait, painted by Desanges, were sold at auction in London. A century after his death, however, General Wolfe's sword still remained a cherished heirloom of his sister's family in England.

Today, this brave Canadian officer's remains continue to rest under a rough rock in Senafe, far from England and Canada, the countries he loved. The site is neat and tidy. The headstone plain, but quite legible. The simple inscription reads: "In memory of A. R. Dunn, V.C., Colonel 33rd Regiment, who died at Senafe on the 25th day of January, 1868, age 34 years and seven months."

Several years prior to Dunn's tragic death, the regiment he helped raise, the 100th, Prince of Wales' Royal Canadian Regiment, returned to Canada for two years' service. Its purpose in being sent to Canada was to protect the colony, threatened by the Fenian raids which had commenced in 1866. The return to its homeland, however, coincided with the expiration of the terms of service of its "originals." Henceforward, as the Leincester Regiment (Royal Canadians), it would it would revert to being a truly British unit. Nonetheless, officers and men would continue for decades to honour its Canadian traditions. Dominion Day especially was marked by the decoration of its Colours. On this special holiday, all ranks also wore maple leaves obtained from Canada. Certainly, Dunn would have approved of this symbolism, which continued to link the regiment he helped raise to its Canadian roots.

SELECTED READINGS

Bishop, Arthur. *Our Bravest and Our Best: The Stories of Canada's Victoria Cross Winners.* Toronto: McGraw-Hill Ryerson, 1995.

Earl, Marjorie. "Canada's Light Brigade Hero." *Weekend Magazine* 4:43 (1954): 11–19.

Thomas, Donald. *Cardigan: The Hero of Balaclava.* London: Routledge & Kegan Paul, 1987.

Wheedle, H. M. "Canada's Forgotten Hero." *The Beaver* 71:2 (April–May 1991): 6–15.

Woodham-Smith, Cecil. *The Reason Why.* New York: Dutton, 1960.

Sir John Inglis.
Public Archives of Nova Scotia. (ACC. NO. 9075)

8

LIEUTENANT-COLONEL
SIR JOHN INGLIS

A Bishop's Son Defends Lucknow's Residency

Today, most Canadians have forgotten their heroes. But in the mid-19th century, soldiers who earned their honours on far-distant battlefields and in sieges in which British armies participated were household names. In addition to Toronto's Alexander Dunn, who, in the Charge of the Light Brigade, won Canada's first Victoria Cross, British North America's most honoured sons were two Nova Scotians. General Sir William Fenwick Williams' defence of Kars in northeast Turkey in 1854 held up the advance of a Russian army that might have overwhelmed that country during the Crimean War. Even more famous, however, was Sir John Inglis (1814–1862), whose defence of the Residency at Lucknow in 1857, during the Indian Mutiny, saved the lives of numerous civilians, including women and children. Because of his action, Inglis attained the status of a Victorian hero; the defence also came to be mythologized in the eyes of 19th-century British and other imperially-minded Empire citizens, as the "Epic of the Race." In 1858, as a result of the Mutiny, the East India Company would be abolished, and the British government would assume administration of India. Not until Independence in 1947, however, would India's people gain the right to govern themselves.

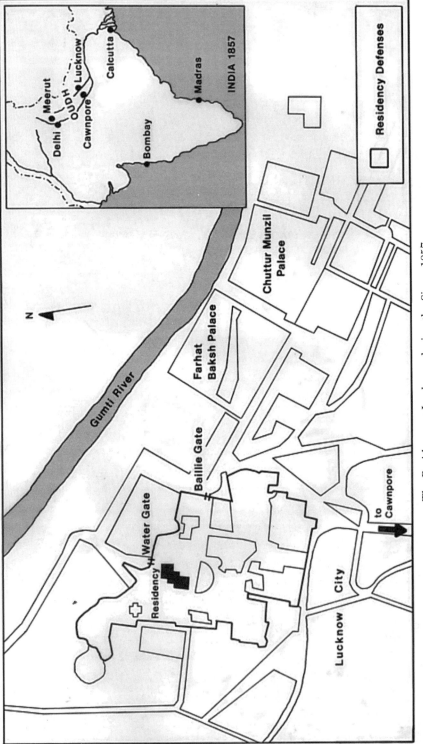

The Residency at Lucknow during the Siege, 1857

Although the siege of Lucknow was not, as was claimed at the time, the greatest siege in history, it was one of the most curious and fascinating. After news arrived of the initial mutiny at Meerut, some 60 miles north of Delhi, Indians and British continued to live, side by side, in increasingly uneasy proximity, for a period of 15 days. Both groups knew they could soon be at one another's throats. During this eerie prelude, the Europeans who were about to be besieged laboured feverishly, assisted by Indian troops and servants, to prepare the Residency to resist an attack. When it actually came, the defence would be conducted in the main by Lieutenant-Colonel John Inglis, the son of the third Bishop of Nova Scotia, grandson of the first. Following an epic stand-off of 87 days, a British army would arrive to rescue the defenders. After fighting its way through the enemy, however, it would be unable to extricate itself. Finally, while both public and empire waited in breathless anticipation, Sir Colin Campbell, the Commander-in-Chief himself, would arrive with a second army and finally relieve Lucknow.

In 1857 news that cartridges for the new Enfield rifle were lubricated with tallow which could contain fat from pigs and cows stirred up unrest in the Bengal Army, which had been in a state of dissatisfaction for some time. During the months of February, March, and April, the rumour spread and grew among sepoy, or Indian, troops: the British, it was alleged, had coated the cartridges with animal fat to undermine the religions of both Muslims and Hindus and thus convert them to Christians. Cartridges were normally torn open with the teeth, before loading them with their powder charge into a musket's barrel. For a Hindu to eat the fat of a sacred cow or for a Muslim to consume pig fat was a crime too horrible to contemplate. And there was truth to the rumour. Not through malice or design, but from sheer ignorance, someone in London had authorized cartridges covered with animal grease to be sent to India.

Officers in the Indian Army responded quickly by withdrawing the offending cartridges. And, in order to placate sepoys' fears, the Governor General issued a proclamation denying any attempt by the British to destroy the caste system or offend religious beliefs. Orders were also issued for a new loading drill that would allow troops to tear open cartridges with their fingers instead of teeth. The damage had been done, however.

Fanning British fears, even paranoia, was the overwhelming numerical disadvantage they faced. Of the British army's 151,000 men, only 23,000 were European troops. Thirteen thousand of these were in the Punjab, and not immediately available to fight the mutineers. The majority of the remainder were concentrated in Calcutta, Meerut, and Delhi, and a handful were scattered throughout hill stations in northern India. Thus, in the 900 miles between Meerut and Calcutta — an enormous distance when covered by bullock cart — there were fewer than 5,000 European troops to face close to 55,000 sepoys.

Sir Henry Lawrence, a brilliant administrator who had made his reputation in the Punjab, before being posted to Oudh, of which Lucknow was the capital, was one of the few senior officers in northern India aware of the discontent among the sepoys. Disturbed by it, he attempted to monitor the course of the approaching storm by opening mail, employing spies, and questioning loyal Indian officers. On May 3, 1857, exactly one week before the outbreak at Meerut, which marked the Great Mutiny's commencement, it almost began at Lucknow.

Lieutenant-Colonel John Inglis, forty-three, accompanied by his twenty-three-year-old wife Julia, was driving to church at about five o'clock in the afternoon, when an aide rode up in a state of great excitement. The aide told Colonel Inglis that he and his regiment were required at nearby Moosa Bagh. Inglis immediately turned his horses about and raced back, calling to men he encountered in the streets to return to barracks. Inside an hour, he had assembled the regiment, and, leaving a guard for women and children, he marched to Moosa Bagh, where Sir Henry had proof that the 7th Oudh regiment was planning to mutiny.

During the dramatic evening, all the European troops, including artillery, would be sent to Moosa Bagh, to back up Inglis' force. The native infantry would be sent as well, on the theory that it was safer to have them with the British soldiers than back in defenceless Lucknow. Taken by surprise by Inglis and the others, the 7th grudgingly formed ranks, throwing down their weapons as ordered. Indeed, the disarming parade might have passed routinely, save for the fact someone (certainly not Lawrence or Inglis) had given the order for the gunners to light their fire ports, or matches, employed to light muzzle-loading cannon. Seeing this, the irregulars, fearing they were about to be blasted by the artillery, ran for their lives. All in all, it was very indecorous. Nonetheless, the offending regiment had been disarmed.

Not until May 15 did the British at Lucknow learn that mutiny had broken out at Meerut, some 280 miles northwest, and as mentioned just north of Delhi, five days earlier. On May 19 a rumour spread that the 71st Native Infantry planned to mutiny at two o'clock, but nothing happened. On the evening of May 21 a fire broke out in the artillery lines, but sepoys helped extinguish it. Four days later, on Lawrence's orders, all the women and children, numbering about 500, were sent to the Residency, a large stone building situated in Lucknow's heart, on the southern bank of the Gumti River. Also, cartloads of grain, ammunition and other supplies were brought in. Preparations were now commenced to withstand a possible siege.

Even after he had learned about the mutiny at Meerut, however, Lawrence did not attempt to disarm any of his native regiments at Lucknow, for he feared it would only precipitate further problems. For the next 15 days a strained spirit of co-existence prevailed in the city.

Under Lawrence's and the engineers' direction, a roughly diamond-shaped enclosure about 37 acres in extent was rapidly constructed around the Residency and its dependencies. Where possible, existing walls were employed, so that all the buildings, including several smaller ones, were soon linked together by earthworks, trenches and palisades. The defenders also placed elaborate obstacles outside the ramparts. Since the defensive perimeter measured about 2,000 yards, over a mile in length, the makeshift fortifications were too long to be properly manned by the available troops, which numbered only about 1,700. On the other hand, the area the defences enclosed was too small to contain easily both the troops and the large number of noncombatants. The British had abandoned some of the lower ground, leading Julia Inglis to record in her diary that it "all seemed very crowded and uncomfortable." Unfortunately, from a defensive standpoint, several tall mosques and temples continued to overlook the area. From a strictly military point of view, they should have been demolished, but Lawrence and Colonel Inglis feared that to take such a step would only confirm the sepoys' suspicions that the British intended to destroy the Indians' religion.

In the second week of May the rising at Meerut was followed by Indian troops' seizure of Delhi itself. When the mutineers restored the Mogul Dynasty, the British authorities at Calcutta finally awoke from their lethargy to find their existence in the subcontinent under serious attack. At last, at the end of May, the rebellion arrived at Lucknow itself. As expected, the bulk of four native regiments mutinied. But the rebellious troops were successfully driven off by Lawrence. A week later, at nearby Cawnpore, 50 miles to the southwest, the sepoys rose, occupying General Wheeler's ill-prepared position. Henceforward, one by one, the British would lose control of the outlying portions of Oudh, leaving Lawrence and his force effectively cut off in Lucknow.

The British, with Lieutenant-Colonel Inglis second in command, were forced to seek shelter in the Residency. Lawrence's force consisted of women and children, a single weak battalion of European infantry (the 32nd), and a handful of odds and ends, as well as civilian volunteers.

Every dark face was now suspect. Most Indian troops were disarmed and sent to their homes. Only some 700 were allowed to remain, including some Sikhs, a number of servants, and approximately 180 old Indian army pensioners, who had journeyed from their villages to assist their old masters.

On June 29, the British, led by Inglis, sallied out to attack the rebel forces rumoured to be near Lucknow. They found them, but in the ensuing battle the British were routed. Although Julia Inglis was in bed with smallpox, when a wounded officer came in with the alarming news, she dragged herself from her bed and stood by a window to view the defeated troops' return. "The greatest excitement and consternation prevailed," she recorded. "They were straggling in by twos and threes, some riding, some on guns, some supported by comrades. All seemed thoroughly exhausted. I could see the flashes of muskets, and on the opposite side of the river could distinguish large bodies of the enemy through the trees." The waiting and apprehensive women and children soon learned news, good or bad, of their husbands' and fathers' respective fates. Rarely in war would soldiers' families be so close to the battle. But at Lucknow the battle would soon come to them with shells bursting inside the Residency. The anticipated siege had commenced.

Just two days later, a howitzer shell, crashing into the Residency, seriously wounded Sir Henry Lawrence in the thigh. Since the wound was so high, it was not possible to amputate his leg. After two days of intense suffering, he died. On the evening of his death, there was a noisy thunderstorm and rain. Above the thunder, shouting and screaming could be heard in the city outside the Residency. It was the sepoys plundering the town. "It was fearful to think how near the wretches were to us," Julia Inglis recorded.

Colonel Inglis, whom Lawrence would specifically charge with the defence of the Residency prior to his dying, had spent his entire military career, since he was commissioned at the age of nineteen at Quebec, attached to the 32nd Foot, which he now commanded. He had served with his regiment during the Canadian Rebellion of 1837. In India, he had seen considerable action during the Second Sikh War. He was known throughout Northwest India as both a keen and capable regimental officer, a crack shot, and ardent sportsman. A half dozen years before the mutiny, he had married Julia Thesiger, whose famous soldier-father would become the First Lord Chelmsford. She and their three children would be with Inglis at Lucknow. Although Inglis was not particularly noted for his originality, neither was he foolish. He was an unassuming officer, friendly, kind, and, not least, brave. Indeed, the very model of a Victorian regimental officer.

Fortunately, Inglis would be assisted in the Residency's defence by Major Anderson, an exceedingly capable engineer, although he would die later during the siege. Also, Inglis' subordinates would serve him well. Most importantly, he could take advice. As one chronicler has observed, Inglis was "a delightful man to have in command, pleasant-tempered, agreeably mannered, attending to everything asked, giving if possible, saying at once why it could not be given if he thought it undesirable."

Inglis' standing orders, issued to his men, were as follows: keep under cover, always be on the alert, and never fire unless you can see your man. At the siege's beginning, full rations were issued. These consisted of a pound of meat and a pound of flour per soldier per day. No vegetables were available. The allowance was soon reduced to twelve ounces, then six, and, before the long siege was finished, four. There was no chivalrous nonsense concerning food. The men who were fighting came first. Women were assigned three-quarter rations, and children, half.

Julia Inglis' description of embattled civilians' hardships may at first raise a smile today: "Our ladies were many of them put to sore straits as the siege continued; they had no servants, and had to cook their own food and wash their own clothes." Still, the hardships were real enough. And rise to the situation the ladies did. They tended the wounded, they kept reports on rations, and they noted the casualties. They even loaded muskets for the men on the firing line, while they themselves were exposed to almost constant bombardment. Not least, they witnessed their men and children die, either of wounds, or from the ravages of cholera, scurvy, smallpox and dysentery, which shortly broke out.

Enemy shells accounted for almost daily losses. Ironically, among the wounded was Dr. Brydon, the sole European to survive the famous march from Kabul that had occurred 15 years previously. Some persons became despondent, and there were several suicides. Morale in general remained high, however, and an air of good humour prevailed among the besieged. To the garrison's amusement, one of the refugee officers, who earlier had lost his clothes escaping through the jungle, cheerily cut and sewed himself a suit of Lincoln green, made from the cloth of the Residency's deserted billiard table.

The mutineers' numbers varied between eight and fifty thousand. From the start, the Residency and its surrounding strongholds came under intense bombardment. Enemy artillery fired from well-dug-in emplacements, at virtual point-blank range. Although lacking round-shot, the mutineers soon substituted all manner of missiles, including bits of iron, pieces of telegraph wire, also huge blocks of wood. Seeing some of the latter coming, the defenders would humorously shout: "Here comes a barrel of beer at last!" Throughout the siege, both Residency and surrounding buildings would be subject to bombardment and close sniping, especially on its eastern and southern perimeters, due to the proximity of surrounding buildings the mutineers had occupied.

Within the defensive lines, individual posts were manned by 14 independent units. Not only did each of these separate garrisons have to repel enemy attacks, personnel also had to improve their own defences, as well as make local sorties as might be required. In addition, soldiers had to serve on general fatigue duties.

The defenders' fatalities numbered ten or so per day. Lieutenant-Colonel Inglis, his staff officers, as well as engineering officers, were more exposed to the enemy's fire than others. The brave commander made his rounds once a day as well as once a night, accompanied by whichever officers he might require.

Doubtlessly, Inglis's stubborn defence was spurred by the fact his young wife was among the brave women who were refugees within the Residency. Having just recovered from smallpox herself, the Colonel's wife had her work cut out for her: ministering to the couple's two small boys, as well as the baby, in addition to helping the other women with their duties. When the Lucknow garrison learned that Nana Sahib, one of the rebel commanders, had butchered all of the women and children at nearby Cawnpore, and ordered their body parts thrown down a well, many of the women feared that "a most horrible death" awaited them, too. Some even planned to take their own lives, employing laudanum or prussic acid. Since she was the wife of the senior officer, Mrs. Inglis refused to endorse such desperate measures, arguing that, in such an eventuality, "God . . . would put it into [their hearts] how to act." As she recorded in the very detailed diary she kept of the siege, her husband talked in private of blowing them all up should it be necessary to save them from dishonour or a worse death. "It was strange how calmly we talked of these subjects."

As early as the first week of July, cholera appeared. Both it and smallpox, as well as other illnesses, would claim victims regularly. Due to the lack of a balanced diet, as well as the prevailing monsoon conditions, the garrison suffered a wide range of health problems: painful boils, gastritis, skin rashes, persistent colds, as well as symptoms of scurvy. A woman observer noted that Colonel Inglis, who had not slept with his clothes off for more than three months, looked "as though he would not be able to stand the wear and tear much longer"; indeed, his hair had "turned quite grey."

Even during the initial, damp days of the siege, before the tribulations of the broiling summer's heat commenced, some defenders easily surrendered themselves to a "sullen, obstinate, silent despair." Seeing others die, they, too, hoped they might shortly meet their deaths. Inglis "found it impossible to make these men careful." Seeming "quite reckless," they "walked slowly and quite upright past gaps that were constantly watched by enemy snipers." There was also the opposite problem: some of the more obstinate, and racially conscious Englishmen simply could not motivate themselves to run for cover when fired upon by native marksmen.

By now the heat was ferocious, the bombardment unremitting, and one could scarce move a foot in the open without becoming the target of a sniper from over the walls. One by one, buildings tumbled until the entire compound was a wreck. Rations were running short. The air stank with carrion and excrement. Many of the women had taken refuge in cellars, where they were plagued by mice and rats and often fell into gloomy fits of foreboding.

On July 20, Inglis and his men successfully repulsed the enemy's first general assault thrown against their positions. This attack was announced by the sepoys' detonating their first mines, which had been tunnelled under the garrison's defences. Henceforth, much of the siege would consist of an elaborate campaign of mine and countermine. Fortunately, the 32nd was a Cornish regiment (indeed, it would later be renamed the Cornwall Light Infantry), and many ex-miners were in its ranks. The Sikhs, too, would prove themselves able tunnellers.

This first assault cost the enemy many hundreds of lives. Among the defenders, four Europeans were killed and twelve wounded. Additionally, a dozen or so casualties were recorded among the Residency's Indian troops. Following the fighting, Inglis commended the force "on the determined manner in which the attack made on the position was repulsed. . . . It is invidious to draw comparisons; but the manner in which the garrison outposts drove back the enemy is worthy of the highest commendation."

Two days later, Inglis himself led a daring sortie to determine whether the enemy was constructing additional mines from outside a portion of the defences. No trace of mining activity was found. At Inglis's direction, however, the retreating raiding party set the roofs of nearby buildings afire before withdrawing within their own lines.

On August 10, enemy forces mounted a second assault on Lucknow's defences. This time the defenders' casualties were even lighter than on the occasion of the first attack, since they had mastered the art of defence. But the enemy's casualties were more severe than they had been on July 20. Indeed, from this time onwards the defenders whom Inglis commanded would feel that, despite the mutineers' overwhelming numbers and ample material, they lacked the ability to carry Lucknow's insubstantial and crumbling defences. Nevertheless, the battering the Residency's top floor endured, as well as the constant damage to its portico and surrounding buildings, spawned an ever-present anxiety concerning just how long the defenders would be able to hold out.

By mid-August Inglis and the garrison expected to be relieved by the force commanded by Sir Henry Havelock, a dogmatic tee-totalling Christian commander. On August 16, Inglis sent a detailed communication through the lines describing his position. As he reported, the garrison's strength consisted of 350 able-bodied European men and 300 loyal sepoys. In addition he had 120 sick and wounded, 220 women and 250 children. He also informed Sir Henry that the garrison's rations were running out, and that the enemy's mining and artillery were severely reducing both the defences and the number of defenders. On August 28 Inglis received a message from Havelock who said that he was waiting for reinforcements, and that he expected to reach Lucknow in 20 to 25 days. To Inglis and the people in the Residency, this seemed like a long time to wait.

The longer the siege lasted the greater the anxiety in Inglis' and other officers' minds concerning the loyalty of the sepoys. Despite, even because of, the appalling prospects they faced, the English knew that they must find the fortitude to continue to resist. But they were not so sure that their Indian comrades regarded the threat to their own lives as equally serious. Indeed, there were some desertions. On the evening of August 30, a party of 16, that included the King of Oudh's former musicians as well as some servants, went over to the enemy. In explanation they left the message "Because we had not opium" scribbled on walls in several places. Their needs, however, were dramatically ended when the rebels executed them.

On September 16, Inglis sent Havelock a second desperate letter, describing the firing, both day and night, to which the garrison was exposed. He also referred to the explosion of two large mines. A notable passage stated: "My weekly losses continue very heavy both in officers and men. I shall be quite out of rum for the men in eight days, but we have long been on reduced rations, and I hope to be able to get on pretty well till about the 1st proximo. If you have not relieved us by this time, we shall have no meat left." Inglis continued: "my men [cannot] perform the heavy work without animal food." And he noted, "I am most anxious to hear of your advance to enable me to reassure our native soldiers."

At long last the relief, or at least assistance, arrived. On September 24 the besieged garrison could hear the sound of distant guns. That evening, Julia Inglis "could not sleep for excitement and anxiety." By this time the Residency was a shambles. Its walls had been knocked down, roofs were wrecked, and the incessant bombardment had collapsed some buildings. Also, there were many weaknesses in the under-manned defences. Inglis and others feared that the rebels might make a last, violent attempt before the rescuers could arrive.

The following day, September 25, would be an intense and exciting one for Inglis' small force. Inside the Residency, civilians and troops could now hear the crisp crackle of musket and rifle fire as Henry Havelock's relief force fought its way through the city to the Residency's Baillie Gate. Soon, the defenders saw through the musket and cannon smoke two kilted Highlanders fighting their way towards them, and above the battle din they heard bagpipes skirling. Inglis' orderly rushed into his master's quarters to fetch the sword his master had not worn since the defeat at Chinhat. At six o'clock in the evening, Julia Inglis, who was with other women attending to the dying child of a friend, heard loud cheers. Shortly afterwards, she saw her husband walking towards her, accompanied by a "short, quiet-looking, gray-haired man, who I knew at once was General Havelock." At last, the Colonel, his family, and persons within the garrison could breathe easier. Mrs. Inglis was moved to record in her diary: "Yes, we are safe, and my darling husband spared to me."

Havelock's reinforcements came none too soon. At the beginning of the siege, the garrison's total strength had been 1,720; by September 25 it had been reduced to 979. Of these, 537 were Europeans, 402 Indians. Of 240 women who had begun the ordeal, five had been killed, and 11 had died; of the 270 children, 54 were dead. Abroad, news of the defence had inspired British and Europeans, as well as both Americans and Canadians as an example of European fortitude in the face of appalling conditions and overwhelming odds. Although the British changed their tactics after 1857, memory of the epic resistance would continue to divide British and Indians for a century to come.

The defenders of the Residency thought that salvation had arrived and that they would be brought out. But this was not to be. It was soon obvious that Havelock's and General Outram's force was not strong enough to drive the mutineers from the city. Also, there was not enough transport to move the sick, the wounded, and the women and children. Although the relieving force had brought additional men, guns, and ammunition to defend the Residency, it possessed very little food. The old defenders were already on short rations. Ironically, it seemed that the arrival of the relief force now meant that they would be starved out all the sooner. No novelist writing such a tale would have dared to provide the solution that now actually occurred. As a result of errors on the part of the commissariat, the defenders discovered that there was, in fact, far more grain than had been calculated. Incredible as it may seem, no officer had actually examined the stores until this juncture. When Colonel Robert Napier (later Lord Napier of Magdala) did so, he located a great pit of grain that Lawrence had prudently ordered hidden away, the existence of which had been unknown.

Major-General Sir James Outram, "The Bayard of India," who had temporarily placed himself under Havelock's orders, so that Havelock could have the honour and glory of relieving Lucknow, now took command, although wounded. He paid a handsome compliment to Inglis and his defenders of the Residency who had held out for 87 days. The General told them that "the annals of warfare contain no brighter page than that which will record the bravery, fortitude, vigilance, and patient endurance of hardships, privations and fatigue displayed by the garrison of Lucknow."

For another 53 days after the arrival of Havelock and Outram the siege would go on. By now conditions were desperate. Although, fortunately, more grain had been located, people were reduced to eating sparrows, also smoking dried tea or straw. Surgeons, who had run out of chloroform, were reduced to performing operations in common sleeping quarters. Disease was rife, so were lice. Many of the defenders had shaved their heads, but this only heightened the sense of horror. By this time, most structures were mere shells. Everything was riddled with balls like smallpox, as the garrison chaplain noted. Into the ruins now poured the torrential rains of the monsoon, moisture dripping into every shelter and clouding everything in a damp haze.

Meanwhile, rebel sappers continued to mine everything beneath the compound. The besieged could often hear the clink of pickaxes below their feet. The enemy drove 20 mines under the compound. In turn, the British responded by driving 21 counter-mines. Additionally, sappers on both sides often fought macabre hand-to-hand battles deep in the clammy depths.

During the three months of his defiant stand, Colonel Inglis had kept the Union Jack flying from the top of the Residency. There, it had been the favourite target of marksmen. Bullets rid-dled the bunting, cut its halyards, splintered the staff. But after dark the flag was always patched and refitted. Each morning, onlookers took strength from seeing it flying. Outram, too, would continue the practice of his predecessor. Through the long autumn weeks, the Union Jack would continue to fly from the Residency tower, defiant among the ruins.

At the end of October, word arrived that a second relieving force, under General Colin Campbell, was approaching from the north. At last, on November 18, Sir Colin, the Commander-in-Chief, arrived, at the head of a combined force of five to six thou-sand men of all arms. This time, the relieving force, as arranged, did not attempt to fight its way in to join the garrison within the compound, but merely kept Lucknow quiet, so that the survivors could be safely withdrawn. First came women and children, mov-ing through the lines of the riverside palaces to the British lines. Some were in wagons, some in litters, some walked. The survivors moved under constant fire, assisted and jollied along by the sailors of Campbell's naval brigade. Sometimes they were ushered into trenches; sometimes they passed through camouflage con-sisting of canvas screens. With them came the crown jewels of the Kings of Oudh, and some £250,000 Sterling worth of treasure from the British Residency.

Finally, at midnight on November 22, Inglis' old garrison

marched out, carefully breaking step so as to avoid rousing the rebels' suspicions. At last, the rearguard, consisting of a few hundred gunners and Highlanders crept past the Baillie Gate to join the army outside the city. As a distraction, they had left their camp fires burning in the Residency's deserted ruins. The long siege of Lucknow was over. By dawn next day, a six-mile-long procession consisting of soldiers, bullock carts, litters, elephants, horsemen, sepoys and camp followers was crossing the silent plain towards Cawnpore.

At the end of the Residency's evacuation, a moment had occurred when Outram and Inglis jockeyed for the honour of being able to say: "I was the last man to leave the Residency!" Although Outram was the senior, and might have claimed the privilege, Inglis modestly requested: "You will allow me, sir, to have the honour of closing my own door."

Smiling, the urbane Sir James purportedly shrugged, then, holding out his hand, said, "Let us go out together." After shaking hands, the Commanders walked side by side down the slope that led away from the battered Baillie Gate. At last the long ordeal was over.

For his central role in the siege, Lieutenant-Colonel Inglis was made a major-general and Knight Commander of the Bath (KCB). The citation honouring him read: "For his enduring fortitude and persevering gallantry in the defence of the residency at Lucknow for 87 days against overwhelming forces of the enemy."

Julia Inglis survived Lucknow, came under fire again at Cawnpore, and finally reached Calcutta safely. From there she took ship for England. Although she was shipwrecked off the coast of Ceylon, she would survive that experience as well, and live on until 1904.

Half a world away, the Nova Scotia legislature would present its second native son to command a heroic siege, within the span of only a few years, with a sword of honour, its blade appropriately forged from the finest Nova Scotia steel. Since there was already an Inglis Street in Halifax, Lucknow street was named in his honour. Although Inglis shortly returned to command, he was not destined to live long. A scant few years afterwards, in 1862, he died of fever at Hamburg, in Germany, while travelling. He was only forty-seven.

A second Nova Scotian, William Hall, a descendant of black slaves from the Chesapeake, also demonstrated his own brand of heroism during the Mutiny. A member of HMS *Shannon's* Marine artillery company, which had accompanied Sir Colin's force on its desperate overland march to relieve Lucknow, he continued, even after coming under heavy fire from the mutineers, to command the single remaining howitzer that eventually blew a hole in the Residency's wall. This enabled the Highlanders to advance through the breech and eventually relieve the garrison. For his bravery, Hall would be awarded the Victoria Cross. The much-esteemed medal would be Nova Scotia's first, and, following Dunn, the second VC won by a Canadian.

For nearly a century following Lucknow's siege, the ruined Residency, where Inglis' small garrison, with its women and children, resisted an overwhelming force of mutinous sepoys, would serve as the supreme sanctuary of Britain's imperialism. The siege's story and the fabled relief was familiar to every Victorian student, as immortalized in Tennyson's stirring ballad "The Defence of Lucknow":

> Banner of England, not for a season, O banner of Britain,
>   hast thou
> Floated in conquering battle or flapt to the battle-cry!
> Never with mightier glory than when we had rear'd thee
>   on high
> Flying at the top of the roofs in the ghastly siege of Lucknow —
> Shot thro' the staff or the halyard, but ever we raised thee anew,
> And ever upon the topmost roof our banner of England flew.

Schoolchildren in Canada and the rest of the Empire memorized these stirring lines. And the scene of the great siege itself soon became the site of a pilgrimage. From Hill's Imperial Hotel, the Civil and Military Hotel, the Royal or the Prince of Wales', visitors from London, Toronto, and Halifax would proceed to the old

William Hall, a Canadian Black who won the VC. (NL/C-018743)

Residency compound. Here, the battlefield was preserved in the very same condition it had been when Havelock's Highlanders fought their way in finally to relieve Inglis' desperate garrison:

> Saved by the valour of Havelock, saved by the blessing
>   of Heaven!
> "Hold it for fifteen days!" We have held it for eighty-seven!

On the compound's highest point, stood the Residency. Half destroyed, it was still imposing, with the remains of its tower. An air of proud authority lingered, emphasized by rubble lying all around. Standing proud sentinel, a few artillery pieces gleamed under the sun. And, night and day down through the years, as it had through the long siege itself, the Union Jack continued to fly from the broken battlements. Only on August 15, 1947 would it cease to fly, bringing an end to two centuries of British imperialism.

Modern historians see the siege differently. Some view it as the first blow for independence, although this is probably incorrect. Most recognize it as a turning point in Britain's governance of India and the other colonies. Thereafter, the British realized that they would have to send more officers of Inglis' calibre and begin to train a civil service staffed by Indians. These moves would allow Britain to govern successfully in India until the Independence movement. One final lesson seems clear: not only is history a moving and inspiring account of an event, it is also a matter of perception.

SELECTED READINGS

Edwardes, Michael. *A Season in Hell.* London: Hamilton, 1973.

Farwell, Byron. *Queen Victoria's Little Wars.* New York: Norton, 1972.

Hibbert, Christopher. *The Great Mutiny: India, 1857.* New York: Viking, 1978.

Inglis, Lady. *The Siege of Lucknow, a Diary.* London: Osgood, 1893.

Morris, James. *Heaven's Command: An Imperial Progress.* Harmondsworth, Middlesex, England: Penguin, 1984.

Battle of Ridgeway, Canada West. Desperate charge of the Fenians under Colonel O'Neill near Ridgeway Station, June 2, 1866. Litho. by the Sage, Sons & Co. (NAC/C-018737)

9

PRIVATE FRED MCCALLUM

The Queen's Own Marches
Against Fenian Invaders

On June 2, 1866, Lieutenant-Colonel Alfred Booker led 900 Canadian militia, including young Fred McCallum, into battle against 800 Fenians at Ridgeway, in the Niagara Peninsula. Most of Colonel John O'Neil's Fenians were Irish veterans of the U.S. Civil War, whose goal was to assist their fellow Irishmen's fight for independence by striking at Great Britain. In marked contrast, the majority of Canadian militia were university students, like Fred, who typified the earnest but largely unprepared part-time soldier of the pre-Confederation period. Although the Canadians fared well at first and were even on the verge of victory, a sudden change of fortune cost them the battle. Their inexperience would also result in 10 dead and 38 wounded. Ridgeway, however, was a watershed in Canadian military preparedness. After the near-disaster, Colonel Garnet Wolseley and Captain William Otter, of the Queen's Own, commenced a program that within a few years produced major improvements in the battle-readiness of Canada's rapidly growing number of citizen volunteer militia battalions. In 1870, when Fenians struck across Quebec's border on two occasions, the invaders were easily repulsed.

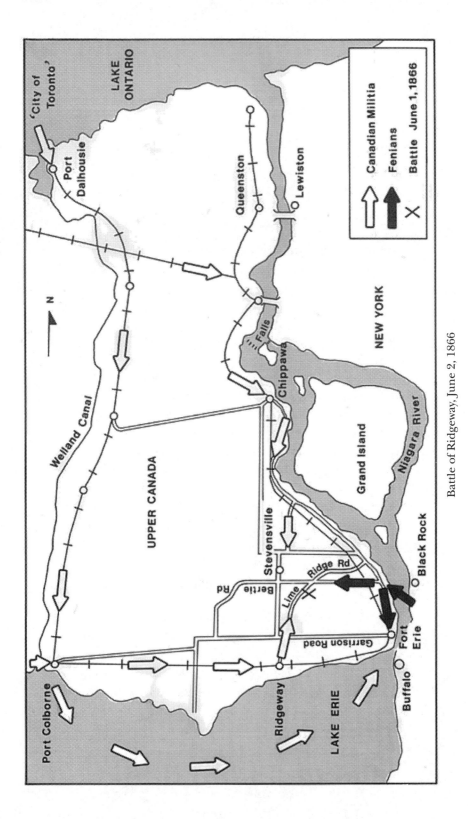

Battle of Ridgeway, June 2, 1866

Saturday, June 2, 1866: 6 a.m. Already the morning is warm. Soon it will be hot. There is a cloudless sky, no wind. Up towards Lime Ridge, the loudest sound is from the bees and other insects already buzzing above the bright carpet of spring wild flowers.

No sounds come at all from the few prosperous-looking farmhouses spread along the dusty road that runs down the slope to Ridgeway. At the station, however, near bedlam prevails. Tired, stiff, unshaven militia are rapidly disgorging from boxcars. The soldiers, some in red tunics, others such as Fred McCallum in dark rifle green, grab personal equipment from piles of muskets, greatcoats, and assorted bundles, then hurry across the road hastily to form in line. Already, they are beginning to sweat under their thick woollen uniforms. A trio of thirsty soldiers break ranks, scooping up muddy ditch-water with caps and bare hands. A few minutes later, shouting officers cajole and pester them back into line. Soon, the dark uniforms of Toronto's Queen's Own Rifles and the red coats of Hamilton's 13th Battalion are sorted out and formed into ranks — ready to march.

In 1865, when the Fenian Brotherhood, Irish Civil War veterans, threatened Canada with invasion from the United States, militia soldiering became a serious matter. Several provincial battalions composed of drafts from various militia units, including the 2nd Battalion of the Queen's Own, were placed on full-time patrol on the frontier. In March, there was a general stand-to of all militia. Once the invasion threat appeared to subside, though, the provisional battalions were released from duty. Then suddenly, in the early morning hours of May 31, a force of Fenians crossed the border near Fort Erie, at the Niagara's south end.

The first alarm that "General" John O'Neil's Fenians had descended on Port Colborne, on the Lake-Erie side of the Niagara Peninsula, was given by a few men who were out night-fishing. Sensibly, five elderly British veterans, the only British troops on the spot, made themselves scarce. Next morning, at Toronto, Captain Durie, deputy Adjutant General, instead of trying to create a new composite unit, simply ordered out the Queen's Own Rifles, his old corps. The unit would shortly be joined by a number of other militia battalions, which were again mobilized to deal with the emergency.

Fortunately, Major Charles Gillmor and Captain William Otter, the adjutant, found many of the men at a banquet. Fred McCallum, a tall, lanky seventeen-year-old private in No. 5 Company was one of a handful of youths who found themselves presented with a list of names and orders to have their fellow militia on parade by 4 a.m. the following morning. McCallum managed to hunt down 28 of 30 names on his list. The battalion mustered 356 officers and other ranks. Thanks to Otter's efficiency, by 7:30 a.m. they were aboard the steamer *City of Toronto,* heading across Lake Ontario to Port Dalhousie, on Lake Ontario's southwest shore.

The haste with which the Queen's Own had been mobilized hid a number of weaknesses. First, no arrangements had been made to provide the volunteers with food. Nor did Fred and most of his companions even possess haversacks to carry rations. Fortunately, he had a water bottle, but most of the militia lacked even this essential item. In addition to the lack of cooking equipment, there were no tents or blankets. Nor were there stretchers, or men designated to carry them. Most of the troops, McCallum included, had brought their own military greatcoats. But lacking means to strap such to their backs, they either wore them, as he did, or carried them over their arms. This task alone proved hard work on a scorching, hot day. The regiment's officers shared some of the blame. Otter and others should have insisted that boys like McCallum take time for a decent breakfast. They should have realized that it would probably be the last meal the excited youngsters would have the opportunity to eat during the next several days.

By 10:30 on June 1 the Queen's Own had disembarked in Port Dalhousie. Here, they boarded trains to take them to nearby Port Colborne, southern terminus of the Welland Canal. Suddenly, however, there was a change of command. Major Gillmor was replaced as the unit's commander by Lieutenant-Colonel J. Stough-

ton Dennis, a militia brigade major from Toronto. Even neo-
phytes such as McCallum had heard stories about this infamous
officer, who was known as a "red tape courtier." While Dennis
waited for orders, McCallum and other personnel were distributed throughout the town in uncomfortable billets. Available
food was soon gone. Indeed, Fred and others in his company were
obliged to go to bed without a single bite. Still, some resourceful
officers managed to find a good supply of liquor from some secret
source.

Fortunately, more militia units were arriving in the Niagara
Peninsula. Most, however, were sent to reinforce Lieutenant-
Colonel George Peacocke's force of regulars, who were marching
steadily south. By evening, Peacocke's exhausted regulars and
militia managed to make camp at Chippewa, a village near the
Niagara's mid-point. Other units, including the York and Cale-
donia Rifles, as well as the 13th Battalion, which arrived at 11 p.m.
from Hamilton, travelled to Port Colborne. To the troops' amusement, it was now Dennis' turn to be chagrined. For the 13th's
commander, Lieutenant-Colonel Alfred Booker, was one of the
most senior officers in Upper Canada's militia, and, as such, easily
out-ranked the rank-conscious Dennis.

Colonel Peacocke had issued orders for the militia assembling
at Port Colborne to rendezvous with his own regulars at Stevens-
ville, mid-way between them. But after learning from a railway
crew that the Fenians had deserted Fort Erie, Dennis quickly
developed his own plan. Local militia would be loaded on a steam
tug and sent around to the village, thereby cutting off the
Fenians' escape route. In Dennis' mind, the drunken, demoralized Fenians would be hopelessly trapped. But all this had been
done without Peacocke's approval.

Having loaded his men, including McCallum and No. 5 Company, into boxcars at 1 a.m. as part of Dennis' plan, the new commander, Alfred Booker, simply left them there. In addition to
their hunger, Fred and his fellows spent a miserable night. It was
hot, the cars, which evidently had been employed to carry cattle,
were crowded and foul. Although they were exhausted from the

day's gruelling march, McCallum and the others were kept awake by the loud singing of the unruly minority who had uncovered the local liquor supply. Despite this, they were heartened by the arrival, around 4 a.m., of 135 fellow soldiers of the Queen's Own. Prodded by Captain Charles Akers, R. E., Peacocke's intelligence officer, Booker, edgy with excitement and lack of sleep, was as impatient to move as his cooped-up charges. Shortly after 5 a.m., on his orders, the long train began to move.

Meanwhile, O'Neil, the Fenian leader, finally learned of the forces moving against him. At 3 a.m. he ordered his column to resume its march, this time towards Ridgeway, a village situated a few miles west of Fort Erie, where he planned to strike against the weaker of the two columns converging on him. But the Fenians, too, were experiencing their own problems. By morning's light, of 800 followers, who had started out the previous evening from Fort Erie, only 500 remained. Suddenly, the sound of a steam whistle, bugles, as well as men shouting, clearly audible from over the hill at Ridgeway, brought the Fenians to an alarmed halt.

At Ridgeway's little station, confusion reigned. Although ammunition had been brought from Port Colborne, there was no way to transport it. For a fleeting moment, the idea went through McCallum's mind that he and other volunteers should seize a few carts from one of the prosperous-looking barns in the area. However, he knew that the officer in charge of the operation, a respectable Hamilton businessman, would never consider such a heresy. Instead, this officer ordered a few rounds handed to young privates such as McCallum, who had enough room in their pockets to carry the extra cartridges. Then, he ordered the remaining ammunition returned to Port Colborne, to ensure its safety.

A pair of locals galloped up to report that the Fenians were close at hand. But the florid-faced Booker, who had borrowed a horse from Major James Skinner of the 13th, simply pronounced the information as "unreliable." At 6:30 a.m. the march resumed, with the Queen's Own in the lead, although its officers had left their horses behind, fearing that they might prove a nuisance when the unit was moving through bush.

The day previous, June 1, a few cases of Spencer repeating rifles had been discovered aboard *City of Toronto*. Major Gillmor now ordered them to be distributed to McCallum and his companions in No. 5 Company, to replace their heavy muzzle-loading Enfields. With the efficient new weapons, but possessing only a few packs of ammunition each, McCallum and the others were posted as an advance guard, 1,000 yards in front. Behind them, the dark green-and-red-coated main column tramped along. Already, a few youngsters felt faint and dizzy, both from the morning's heat, already substantial, as well as from lack of food and sleep. At Ridgeway, a kind villager, noting their exhaustion, offered the tired men biscuits and herring, to be shared round. But lacking any means of alleviating their thirst, most refused.

The road along which McCallum, the advance guard, and the others marched sloped upward until it met the Garrison Road, leading off to Fort Erie on the right. At the crossroads was a dingy tavern, the Smuggler's Hope. A half-mile further along, near a prosperous brick farmhouse, another road merged at right angles to the militia's route of march. On either side of this road, trees, as well as orchards and clumps of forest interspersed with fields, limited visibility. Thus, the waiting Fenians could hear the advance of McCallum and the other Canadians long before they could see them. Even though most of O'Neil's force were veterans who had seen action in the Civil War, morale was plummeting. On the other hand, the 800 heavily laden sweating Upper Canadian volunteers, McCallum among them, who were now marching into their sights, were raw militia who had never experienced a shot fired in anger.

Suddenly, two mounted men spurred towards McCallum and the advance guard. They told Captain Edwards that they were Canadian government detectives, and that behind them were 800 Fenians. McCallum and his fellow skirmishers continued to advance. Meanwhile, the riders galloped on to warn Colonel Booker. But this was hardly necessary. As McCallum and the others passed the Smuggler's Hope, the Fenians opened fire. McCallum and the others spread out, and, rushing forward, took cover behind a convenient fence. During the next several minutes, both sides engaged in a furious, largely unaimed fire-fight. On the Canadian side, Ensign Malcolm MacEachren, struck by a bullet that passed through his stomach, crumpled to the ground. A few men half-lifted, half-carried him to the rear, where he died 20 minutes after.

Major Gillmor rattled off orders as fast as Otter could scribble them into his field book. Nos. 1 and 2 Companies would move forward, and join up with No. 5 Company, where McCallum and others were already under heavy fire. Nos. 3 and 4 would move up and assume a supporting role. No. 6 Company would move out, and attempt to flank the enemy on the right. No. 7, supported by No. 9, would do the same on the left flank. Nos. 9 and 10 were to remain in reserve.

As the various companies deployed, however, Colonel Booker received disconcerting news. Peacocke would be delayed. The scheduled rendezvous would be postponed for an hour. Although one of the government detectives now offered to ride across country to summon assistance, Booker suddenly realized that the morning's battle would be his alone. The regulars would not be arriving.

Still, it appeared that they might not be required after all. As McCallum and the advance company spread across the field, and others moved up, the fusillade intensified. But save for the unfortunate MacEachren, almost no one was hit. McCallum and the others began to advance. Half-an-hour of cautious movement brought them to the Fenian advance line, running along the Bertie Road. By then most of the riflemen of the Queen's Own were out of ammunition. Also, Gillmor's reserve had been employed to clear some patches of woodland on the far right. Clearly, it was time for 13th Battalion to play a part. Three of its leading companies now raced forward to replace Nos. 1, 2, and 5 in the front line. While McCallum and others fell back to catch their breath and hopefully replenish their ammunition, the advance continued.

To the Fenians' alarm the Canadian militiamen had not taken to their heels. They came on at a determined pace. Soon, McCallum and others rejoined the main body of the advance. All at once, it occurred to the Fenians that the soldiers they were viewing pushing through the woods and orchards were not militia at all, but seasoned British regulars. The Fenians began to flee, drifting back in ones and twos. Panic in the front ranks soon became general. With the contagion threatening to spread to the Irishmen's main body, a furious O'Neil and other mounted officers galloped forward to rally the men. If they failed, the battle would be over in a few minutes.

Only a quarter of a mile away, Colonel Booker dismounted from his uncomfortable perch. Now, as he stood flanked by Gillmor and Otter, the militia commander was about to be shocked indeed. All at once, on the road ahead, came shouts of "Cavalry! Look out for the Cavalry!" At the cry, a few men of the 13th came running helter-skelter down the road, their growing fear driven by a glimpse of horses in the bush ahead. "Cavalry," shouted the red-faced Booker, "Prepare for Cavalry!"

Only a week previously, the Queen's Own had practised the single response to such an order. Gillmor snapped out orders, bugles blared, and the five companies of riflemen, including that of McCallum's in the centre, doubled forward to form a square. In less than two minutes, as rehearsed, they had transformed themselves into a defensive clump of close-packed troops, half standing and kneeling, the sun glistening off fixed bayonets. A few redcoats from the 13th mingled in the green-clad mass. Astonished, the Fenians could scarcely believe their fortune. McCallum and his fellows now presented their first real target of the entire morning. Quickly abandoning any thought of retreat, the Irish veterans commenced to pump bullet after bullet into the dense cluster of militiamen.

Booker immediately recognized the error of his order. "Extend," the Colonel shouted, "Reform column." Two companies, Nos. 1 and 2, managed to do so. But the other three, including McCallum and the rest of No. 5, continued to stand where they were. Realizing that they must be moved back out of the line of fire, Gillmor barked out orders to the bugler. "Sound the retreat," he cried. The notes blared forth, repeated by other buglers in earshot. But the order continued to be ignored by McCallum's company as well as the others which continued to maintain their formation. Booker ordered the call repeated.

A shiver of apprehension spread through McCallum and the other young militiamen. Why retreat? For most of the troops within sound of the bugles, the battle appeared to be going perfectly. Still the order was all too clear. The three companies forming the square's centre now turned about. Their backs bravely to the Fenians, McCallum and the rest began to march. As they moved back, they could see scarlet tunics through the woods to the rear. "Reinforcements!" a militiaman beside McCallum shouted. The cry was taken up along the line as the young militiamen's excitement instantly overcame their parched throats.

Unfortunately, the soldiers they spotted were not reinforcements. They were the three companies of the 13th, which so far had seen little of the battle. They had glimpsed the square composed of McCallum and his fellows forming through the smoke that hung over the windless battlefield. Now, without explanation, it was disintegrating. McCallum and other Queen's Own militiamen were marching back directly at them, shouting. All at once, the battle appeared lost! The frantic bugle calls proved it. For the raw youngsters of the 13th looking on, such was evidence enough. Their ranks collapsed, they ran for their lives.

Witnessing the spectacle, McCallum and others in the retreating companies of the Queen's Own felt a sudden parallel sense of fear rise in their own chests and throats. Behind them, almost invisible in the trees and smoke, they could hear the gasping, pounding feet of running, panicked men. It was the 13th's forward companies, racing back to rejoin the main body. But for Fred McCallum and the Queen's Own, it meant something else. Instantly, McCallum and his fellow soldiers, too, broke ranks and sprinted down the hill towards Ridgeway's comparative sanctuary.

A few seconds of inexperience and miscalculation had transformed the battle. For senior officers such as Gillmor, Otter, as well as Booker, it was bewildering. Utterly dismayed, they, too, turned and followed McCallum and the rest of the terrified throng down the hill.

Some officers attempted to rally the fleeing men. A few companies and squads held for scant minutes and then disintegrated. Ensign William Fahey, sheathing his useless sword, grabbed a discarded rifle. Before he could fire it, a bullet struck him in the knee. Captain James Broustead of No. 3 Company was trampled by panic-stricken soldiers as he struggled to mount a rail fence. At the foot of the hill, Lieutenant Arthurs, seizing Booker's horse from its groom, mounted it and drew his pistol, threatening the scared volunteers. A few hundred paused and attempted to form a firing line. But the effort quickly collapsed when a sweating Gillmor arrived and ordered the retreat to continue. As McCallum and his friends looked on, an angry Arthurs climbed down from his horse, and gave it back to Booker. Then the trio of young militia officers and others continued their hurried flight.

A few hundred yards further on, it was all over. McCallum and

Presentation of a sword to volunteer officer, Lieutenant P.G. Routh, Fenian raid hero, at Hamilton, Canada West. (NAC/C-021302)

dozens of his comrades suddenly felt the mad panic end. Their lungs on the point of bursting, hearts pounding, they stopped running. But nothing — threats, promises, or insults — could convince them to remain on the spot where they stood. Just ten minutes previously, terror had overpowered them. Now, as an overwhelming sense of shame worked through their minds, they continued walking. To McCallum, it seemed they were seeking to escape humiliation alone.

Fortunately, the Fenians' pursuit was half-hearted at best. That evening, an improvised train brought most of the militia back to Ridgeway. McCallum and his two companions, hungry, thirsty, and totally exhausted, all exhilaration of battle drained from their fatigued and bruised bodies, threw themselves down to sleep. Next day, they were elated to learn that Captain Akers had assumed command of the militia, after Booker had been located in a state of near-collapse. At Port Colborne, McCallum and the other survivors of Ridgeway were soon reinforced by two more battalions of militia. After a false alarm at 1 a.m. on June 3, Captain Akers roused the Queen's Own at dawn. Loading them once more on trains, he set off for Fort Erie at 6 a.m. After disembarking at Sherkston, McCallum and his fellows would march the rest of the way to Fort Erie. One of the fresh battalions took the lead, and the Queen's Own brought up the rear. Disgraced as they felt, McCallum and his comrades could at least take encouragement from the fact that 13th Battalion, in even deeper disgrace, had been left behind in Port Colborne.

With the sudden departure of the Fenians and their unexpected arrest by U.S. authorities as they attempted to return across the border, the excitement was quickly over. After spending a day and a half camped at Fort Erie, McCallum and the rest of the Queen's Own found themselves loaded aboard a train and sent chugging and huffing off to form a slightly mysterious "camp of observation" the authorities had established at Stratford.

The camp would be commanded by Colonel Garnet Wolseley, the brightest and best British officer in Canada. The demanding schedule of military exercises the dapper officer would put the

Queen's Own and other demoralized militia regiments through during the next few weeks would not only serve to restore confidence, but also establish a new standard of what might be expected of properly prepared volunteer units.

In addition, the hot morning's near-disaster convinced Captain Otter, the adjutant of the Queen's Own, that every measure should be taken to ensure that young volunteers like McCallum and his comrades, who had fled white-faced down the road from Lime Ridge, would never again be led into battle like innocent sheep. In a country where peacetime soldiering and discipline remained suspect, Otter had already glimpsed the future. In the decades to come, as we shall see, he would not rest until he had made the Queen's Own, composed of youngsters such as McCallum, the very best regiment the Dominion had to offer, indeed, the model for Canada's rapidly expanding numbers of volunteer militia battalions.

SELECTED READINGS

Chambers, Ernest J. *The Queen's Own Rifles of Canada: a History of a Splendid Regiment's Origin, Development and Services, Including a Story of Patriotic Duties Well Performed in Three Campaigns.* Toronto: E. L. Ruddy, 1901.

Morton, Desmond. *The Canadian General: Sir William Otter.* Ottawa: Canadian War Museum, Historical Publication No. 9. Toronto: Hakkert, 1974.

Packard, Major L. H. "The IRA: North American Version." *Esprit de Corps: Canadian Military Then and Now* 5:12 (July 1997): 10–11.

Senior, Hereward. *The Last Invasion of Canada.* Toronto, 1991.

Lieutenant-Colonel Garnet Wolseley, First Viscount Wolseley.
Photograph: R. Notman. (NAC/C-020658)

10

LIEUTENANT-COLONEL GARNET WOLSELEY

The Apprenticeship of a British Officer

Lieutenant-Colonel Garnet Wolseley (1833–1913), a talented and ambitious Anglo-Irish officer, served with the British Army in India, the Crimea and China before being posted to Canada in 1861. Wolseley thoroughly enjoyed the posting, using his leisure time to read widely and formulate ideas that shaped his later career. In 1870, the young officer gained distinction by leading the Red River Expedition, sent to defeat Louis Riel. The remarkable campaign, a classic imperialist military operation of the period between the U.S. Civil War and the Great War, was the longest amphibious expedition a British force ever made, carrying all of its arms, rations and other supplies without naval support. Although Wolseley and the bulk of British regulars were withdrawn from Canada permanently a few years after Confederation, he left his mark of professionalism on the Dominion's militia, which would profoundly influence the development of our country's evolving military forces.

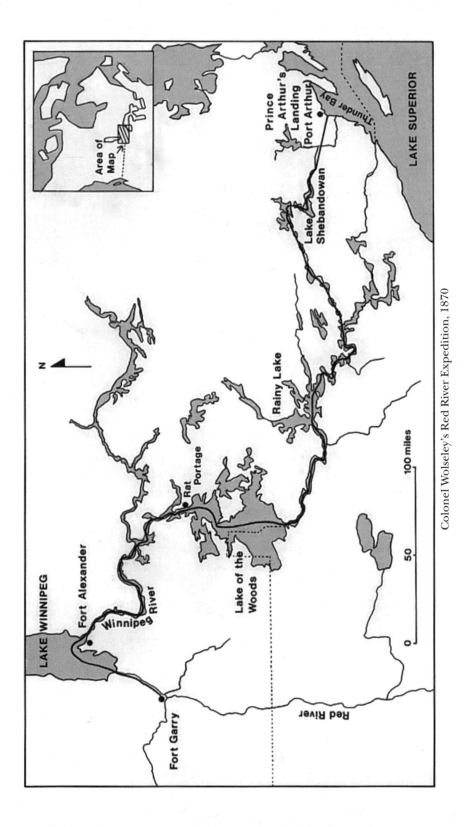

Colonel Wolseley's Red River Expedition, 1870

When Garnet Wolseley in 1857 became one of the first officers to reach the beleaguered defenders of Lucknow's Residency, commanded by Halifax-born Colonel John Inglis, none could have foreseen the role he would play in Canada's history. Although not yet evident, great things lay ahead for the young lieutenant. Not least, during nine short years in this country, he would transform the Dominion's moribund military establishment into the beginnings of a modern defence force. In the process, Wolseley would streamline procedures, improve training, and inject new ideas at every level. Also, he would help guard against Fenian depredations in Ontario. Most important, he would lead the bloodless suppression of the Red River Rebellion, with its nation-threatening potential, in distant Manitoba. Decades later, as Commander-in-Chief of the British Army, Wolseley was destined to revolutionize the Empire's military practices. In addition, his soldierly image would provide the model for comic operetta-writers Gilbert and Sullivan's "very perfect Major-General."

Garnet Wolseley was born near Dublin on June 4, 1833. He was one of seven children in a straight-laced Anglo-Irish military family, whose history was amply sprinkled with soldiers. Tragically, his father died when Garnet was only seven. Although he was an excellent student, determined on a military career from the start, the future field marshal, now penniless, found himself hard-pressed to obtain a commission. He was only fourteen when he applied for a commission without purchase, as the "son of one who gave great service to the nation." But he would not receive his colours, prophetically from Wellington himself, until four years later.

Although he stood only five-foot-seven, Wolseley was clean-cut and athletic — a resolute soldier who believed that all British gentlemen, not least himself, possessed the qualities to lead men into battle. Since he lacked the necessary funds to purchase advancement, he determined to succeed by seeking constant combat, by daring, as well as by constant study of his profession. In addition to hard work and luck, his rapid advance would be assisted by a number of assets. These included considerable strength of character, his uncanny ability to cultivate and judge men, and, later in life, unabashed social climbing. Not least, Wolseley, a fervent Anglo-Irish Protestant, considered himself "God's soldier always." He approached the innumerable battles of his imperial career with a courage that was formidably buttressed by piety.

Wolseley's courage and presence of mind won him recognition. In Burma, his initial proving ground, he was struck in the thigh by a ball as big as a plover's egg. He continued, however, to conduct the attack. In the battle of the Redan in the Crimea, a shell drove a large stone through his jaw, laid open his face and permanently blinded him in one eye. It wounded him in the leg and wrist as well. He was promoted captain after less than three years service. This was a rare, not to say spectacular, rise for a young man without either wealth or connections.

Hard on the heels of the Mutiny, the dashing young lieutenant-colonel, chest ablaze with medals, was off to China. Here he took part in the storming of the Taku Forts. He was also present at the looting of the Summer Palace, though his share was nominal.

The lesson Wolseley learned from these campaigns, both as a regimental officer and on the staff, was simple but important. There were glaring shortcomings in the organization and operation of the British Army in the field. Most notably, the ignorance and lack of military professionalism and training among the bulk of officers he encountered appalled him.

In 1861 Parliament dispatched 8,000 troops to Canada in response to the *Trent* incident, when a U.S. warship had removed two Confederate agents from a British steamer, and war seemed likely with the Union. Wolseley, who accompanied the reinforcements, was appointed Assistant Quartermaster General of the Canadian garrison, but by the time he reached Halifax the affair had been resolved.

Posted to Montreal, Wolseley chafed in the garrison, wanting to be in the forefront of battle, as was his custom. Meanwhile, the largest war ever fought on the continent raged to the south. Nonetheless, the nine years the young Assistant Quartermaster General spent in Canada were a happy time. It was also a crucially formative period in his own development as the Empire's foremost advocate of modern military thought and practice. In perspective, the quiet, reflective interlude spent in relative exile allowed the brilliant, though sometimes snobbish officer the opportunity to digest his practical war experiences of the 1850s. He would also assimilate and formulate the principles of modern army organization and practice that he would later implement both at home and abroad.

Despite his restless and impatient nature, Wolseley described Canada as a "soldier's paradise," with its hunting, fishing, tobogganing, ice-skating and amateur theatricals. Other officers quickly fell in love with the Dominion's fresh-faced young women, but the prudent and socially conscious Wolseley formed no serious liaisons.

For Wolseley, the U.S. Civil War was the real attraction. Most European observers thought it offered little in the way of tactical

Reinforcements for Canada: the Guards crossing Westminister Bridge on their way to the South-Western Railway Station. The Illustrated London News. (NL/C-006503)

lessons, although it would ultimately cost North and South a total of 623,000 lives. Nonetheless, the visionary and imaginative Wolseley was fascinated by all he saw and heard concerning the conflict. Later, Wolseley noted that the two soldiers he "prized above all the world" were Generals Robert E. Lee and Stonewall Jackson. He visited the Confederate forces in person and was highly impressed by the southern farm boys who formed the bulk of Lee's army. Back in Montreal, Wolseley recorded his impressions in an article he wrote for *Blackwood's Magazine* over the signature "An English Officer." Already, a year earlier, he had commenced his prolific literary career by publishing *The Narrative of the War in China in 1860.*

Wolseley also read diligently and regularly, entering in his diary a list of books that impressed him. Nor did he limit his reading to military treatises alone. A passage he recorded in 1866 remains just as valid today (perhaps even more so) as it was for the age in which it was written: "A man who aspires to command men must know all about men and their ways, if he means to lead them, and not about soldiers and their ways only, for he will have plenty to do with men who are not soldiers."

Since the *Trent* affair in 1861, mentioned earlier, both Canada and Britain had taken a quickened interest in the continent's defence concerns. At the Governor General's urging, the government now set to work to reorganize the colonial militia forces, expanded a decade earlier to meet the Crimean War crisis and the Indian Mutiny. Under the direction of Colonel Patrick McDougall, Wolseley (who had been breveted colonel in 1865) accepted command of the first Canadian officer training camp, at LaPrairie, in today's Quebec. This new responsibility made him feel useful again. As he later affirmed: "It was at the LaPrairie Camp that nearly all the best Militia officers of that generation were drilled and given some practical knowledge of military duties."

The demanding young officer not only instructed his colonial charges, he also learned from them. Proud of his students, Wolseley observed: "They were thinking and practical men, without any of the pedantry which too often clings to the young officers of all

Regular Armies." And, with his peculiar gift of clear-eyed pro-
phecy, Wolseley would later note, "My own experience of Canada,
and of its fine loyal, manly people, has taught me that England
can always depend upon the Canadian Militia to supply her with a
first-rate division, under Canadian officers, who are not to be surpassed in military characteristics of a high order by any other
troops."

Wolseley's practical talents would soon be required to deal
with a real military contingency. Following the debacle involving
the Queen's Own Rifles at Ridgeway (treated in the previous chapter), he would be designated, as we have seen, to "advise" General
John Napier, the British Commander in Canada West, on how to
deal with the Fenian threat. Employing his diplomatic but effective manner, Wolseley persuaded Napier to take such actions that
the invasion threat was soon decisively ended.

His next task was commanding an encampment on the Welland Canal, conveniently sited to counter any Fenian thrust from
across the border. Simultaneously, he both evaluated and improved the effectiveness and training of most of Canada West's
militia regiments. When the Fenian threat subsided, he returned
to England, intent on resuming his long-postponed courtship of
Louisa Erskine.

Not long afterwards, he was summoned back to the new confederation called the Dominion of Canada, and promoted to succeed Colonel Daniel Lysons as deputy Quartermaster General. At
thirty-four, Wolseley was the youngest officer ever to receive so
high a staff position. Still, he managed to snatch two months' leave
to return home and marry Miss Erskine. A clever and beautiful
woman, well-educated and fluent in French, she would prove
exceptionally helpful to his career. Not only would she assist her
husband socially, but on a more practical level, she would also polish his spelling and grammar. Theirs was a marriage of confidence
and devotion, destined to last the remainder of their lives.

Meanwhile Wolseley continued his active career. Soon, the
ambitious colonel would establish himself at the forefront of military reform by publishing *The Soldier's Pocket Book for Field Service*

(1869). Additionally, he busied himself with other writing, military cartography and further upgrading the Canadian militia. Its new-found effectiveness would be demonstrated when units beat back a second Fenian threat in 1870.

Still, it remained a dull period for British officers everywhere in the Empire's globe-encircling pink-coloured map expanses. So slow were things, a humorously inclined officer was moved to write: "There was not a shadow of war in the North, the South, the East or the West. There was not even a Bahote in South Africa, a Beloochie in Schinde, a Bhootea, a Burmese, or any other of the many 'eeses' or 'eas' forming the great colonial empire of Britain which seemed capable of kicking up the semblance of a row."

Things were about to change, however, for in 1870 a storm was gathering in Western Canada. And it would sweep in with the speed and force of a summer thunderstorm. The year previous, Ottawa had taken over large sections of the prairie, including Manitoba's Red River region, from the Hudson's Bay Company.

The Métis inhabitants, who objected to this, chose Louis Riel to be their leader. Riel's response was to establish the Republic of the Northwest with its headquarters at Fort Garry (today's Winnipeg). He also ordered his forces to execute a minor Canadian official, Thomas Scott. Additionally, the rebel leader's followers prevented the area's newly appointed lieutenant-governor from entering Riel's territory.

Although the Métis leader was backed up by fewer than 1,000 armed supporters, the newly formed Dominion government took his actions seriously. In its estimate, the rebellion was dangerous. Riel's secretary was a Fenian, and it was suspected that the U.S. might use the uprising as an opportunity to annex the western plains. Clearly, something had to be done quickly and decisively. Wolseley was named to lead a 1,200-man-strong military expedition against Fort Garry. Its object was "to restore Her Majesty's sovereign authority." His first independent command, it was also destined to be the last British military operation undertaken in North America. Thereafter, the young Dominion would have to rely on its own forces.

The thirty-seven-year-old Wolseley, avid imperialist that he was, reduced the issue to its simplest black and white terms. In his judgement, the Métis were attempting to block the westward march of empire by imposing a French-speaking Catholic province of their own. The Commander's blunt judgement of Riel was that he was no more than a "noisy idler," a dupe of the "clever, cunning, unscrupulous" Catholic bishop at Red River. Also, the entire affair appeared to be a conspiracy between French clerics in the field and French Canadian plotters in Ottawa. As such, the rising must be extinguished by force, and its leader must be humiliated, if possible.

No evidence exists that Wolseley's small force of 1,200 men was specifically recruited to punish Catholics and French-speaking inhabitants of the Red River. Still, its composition certainly suggests that such a motive was not far from Ottawa's military minds. As his intelligence officer, Wolseley chose the mercurial Lieutenant William Butler, a fellow Anglo-Irish Protestant. The green-clad King's Royal Rifle Corps, or 60th Rifles, provided a third of the strike force. A light infantry unit, its predecessor unit had first been raised in North America during the Seven Years' War. Most pointedly, it had earned its battle honours participating against the French and their Indian allies at Fort Duquesne, Louisbourg, Quebec, Montreal, as well as Bushy Run. The Dominion forces, forming the remaining two-thirds, included a battalion of Ontario militia whose personnel were avid Canadian expansionists and rabid Orangemen. Nearly all were anti-French and pro-Empire. Wolseley himself summed up the expedition's attitude when he wrote: "Most of us felt we had to settle accounts quickly with Riel who had murdered the Englishman, Mr. Scott."

As in future campaigns, Wolseley's guiding hand was evident in the officers he chose to assist him. The "Wolseley Ring," the group of highly intelligent and daring officers the Commander would later select to accompany him on his wars throughout the Empire, began in Canada. In addition to Butler, who would establish a reputation as one of the most literate soldiers in the Victorian army, Wolseley's assistants for the expedition included

Lieutenant Redvers Buller of the 60th Rifles and Lieutenant Hugh McCalmont, on leave from the 9th Lancers. Of Buller, who would later command in South Africa, Wolseley was to note, "He was the only man with us of any rank who could carry a 100 pound barrel of pork over a portage on his back." Although not destined to become an inner member of "the Ring," Lieutenant-Colonel Louis-Adolphe Casault, a talented Canadian veteran of both France's Foreign Legion and the British Army, commanded the Quebec Regiment, which composed part of the strike force's militia.

Logistically, the Red River expedition posed problems that amounted to a "veritable nightmare," as a modern military commentator describes the situation. Nonetheless, the jaunty Wolseley carefully planned every single detail of the entire operation. In this, he was assisted by General James Lindsay, General Officer Commanding Her Majesty's Forces in the Dominion, specially rushed across the Atlantic.

Even though he was accustomed to travelling light, Wolseley did not neglect to bring along his own personal portable library. In addition to *The Soldier's Pocket-Book,* it consisted of The Bible, Shakespeare, *The Imitation of Christ, the Book of Common Prayer,* as well as Marcus Aurelius' *Meditations,* a favourite of the new imperialists. The essential collection would be a constant travelling companion of its owner on subsequent campaigns.

Wolseley's single-minded drive to prove his theories of command correct in the field would be greatly assisted by the fact that planning proceeded relatively free of interference by the War Office. In this regard, both geography and lack of effective communication proved a boon. Still, the expedition's organizer did not underestimate the formidable problems the campaign posed. As he wrote many years afterwards, "I doubt whether any British force ever began so serious an undertaking under blacker prophesies of impending disaster, which in some instances seemed meant as threats."

Even today, from a military perspective, given the fact that no railway existed linking east to west, the expedition seems truly formidable because of its geographical scope and daring. The final stage of the 1,200-mile journey from the Lakehead to Red River was longer than Napoleon's celebrated march from the Niemen River to Moscow. The problems Wolseley encountered and the experience he gained would be employed by the Commander in successful campaigns he later conducted in West Africa and Egypt, campaigns that would lead to his being appointed Commander-in-Chief of the British Army between 1895 and 1900.

But the Red River Expedition's most singular feature was that it was first and foremost an amphibious operation. Of major importance as well was the time factor. It detailed that troops traverse the great distance separating Toronto and Fort Garry, then return to their starting point, between spring break-up and the first autumn freeze of water routes. Along the way, as will be seen, a multitude of geographical and physical obstacles posed a serious problem to easy navigation.

Every single item of arms, ammunition, rations, equipment, as well as general supplies would have to be carried on the backs of officers and men, or dragged by their own as well as the boatmen's combined efforts. As contrasted with British military expeditions in India or Africa, there would be a complete absence of native bearers, animal transport or civilian labour.

Most notably, the Royal Navy and Royal Marines were absent from the campaign. In this instance the British Army was literally going to have to paddle its own boat. The disposition of sick and wounded would be an added problem, for the terrain through which the force was destined to move was utterly bereft of settlements.

As the expedition unfolded, a unique aspect would be its total absence of disciplinary problems. It was also remarkable, given the incessant rainfall and hordes of flies and mosquitoes that caused the troops annoyance. In fact, there would be no cases of malingering or discontent. Of their conduct Wolseley would state, "No men on service have ever been better behaved or more cheerful under trials arising from exposure to inclement weather and excessive fatigue." The bottom line, however, was that the

Commander, then as later, respected his troops, seeing them as far more than mere automatons in uniform. He recognized their capabilities, realizing they would perform best if well treated and properly motivated. Strict disciplinarian though he was, Wolseley never forgot that "without common soldiers, there are no armies."

In addition to short rations, troops had to undergo two added privations almost unheard of in the military service. No provision was made for either tobacco or rum ration. Despite the rain, fire remained a constant threat in the wilderness. Thus the men were allowed to smoke only the little tobacco they carried in their personal packs, at day's end, about camp. The expedition's teetotal nature was a deliberate experiment suggested to Wolseley by Butler. Not only did it conserve space and weight, it copied a practice common to Canadian woodsmen. Generally they drank hot tea, rather than alcohol, when isolated and engaged in arduous labour in the bush.

Once underway, the force travelled the 94 miles separating Toronto and Collingwood, on Georgian Bay, by railway. Then its members travelled across Lake Huron and through St. Mary Locks to Thunder Bay, at the head of Lake Superior, a distance of some 535 miles. Here, the real journey began. A rough road had to be hacked out of the bush to carry the troops over the 48-mile, 849-foot-elevation, stretch of watershed that separated Lake Superior from Lake Shebandowan. Following this, the route was by boat for 310 miles. Seventeen portages, some a mile or more, linked Rainy River to Lake of the Woods, and ran north across Lake of the Woods to Rat Portage. Then the journey continued, down the beautiful, dangerous and difficult Winnipeg River, terminating at Fort Alexander on Lake Winnipeg. The final stage consisted of the short ascent of the Red River, arriving at Fort Garry itself. In total, the force would traverse approximately 650 miles from Prince Arthur's Landing, on Thunder Bay, through land hitherto known only to Indians and Hudson's Bay Company employees.

On May 26, Colonel Wolseley landed in a small clearing the Canadian Public Works Department had made on the shore of

Portaging, August 26, 1870. The Canadian Illustrated News. (NL/C-056441)

Thunder Bay. West of the Lakehead, especially, the Expedition had to transport all the supplies it required. Here, it was impossible to obtain provisions along the way. Each boat was carefully packed. In addition to two or three Indians or Canadian voyageurs, it carried eight or nine soldiers, as well as supplies, ammunition, and 60 days' provisions. These consisted of salt pork, beans, preserved potatoes, flour, biscuit, salt, tea, and sugar. Each boat also carried entrenching tools, cooking pots, blankets, tin plates, boat builders' tools, white lead to patch holes in the hull, and double-bitted American-style axes that the commander had ordered substituted for the standard single-edged British army axe.

In total, the western odyssey from the Lakehead to Red River would take 96 days. As alluded to above, a good deal of it would be in torrential rain, most of it troubled by blackflies and mosquitoes. As he would later do during the Ashanti Campaign in West Africa, the innovative Wolseley provided special hot weather supplies. "Mosquito oil" and "veils" protected personnel from blackflies, mosquitoes and sand flies they would encounter in the Shield. It seems, however, that soldiers seldom employed either for the purpose intended. Instead, they used the veils to strain scum from the lake water they drank, and burned the mosquito oil in lamps.

Decades later, the Commander would always remember the campaign's special strangeness and romance. Soldiers shouted "For Fort Garry!" as they pushed off from the shores of Lake Shebandowan. Then they paddled onwards across the still blue water, boat after boat, each crammed to its gunwales, oars dipping, the big sails bravely spread, rifles stacked in the stern, and the colourful voyageurs crouching forward. As Wolseley would nostalgically record: "It brought to my mind the stories read in boyhood of how wild bands of fierce Norse freebooters set out for some secluded bay in quest of plunder or adventure."

Men grew fitter, more skilful and happier as the weeks passed. They would rise at dawn and travel until dusk. By the end of the epic journey, the clumsiest English rifleman, as well as the flabbiest militia member, was routinely mending his boat, catching and cooking fish over a campfire and ranging the forest. Uniforms were in tatters, faces and arms burned black by the sun. But not a single man fell sick — an unbelievable record for a late-19th-century military expedition.

Wolseley himself, in a light birchbark canoe crewed by sinewy Iroquois, was always in the lead. Later, Butler would record the following memorable picture of his Commander:

[Wolseley was] . . . somewhat under middle height, of a well-knit, well-proportioned figure, handsome, clean-cut features, a broad and lofty forehead over which brown chestnut hair closely curled; exceedingly sharp, penetrating blue eyes . . . the best and most brilliant brain I ever met in the army. He was possessed of a courage equal to his brain power. . . . I never knew him tired, no matter what might be the fatigue he underwent. I never knew his eye deceived, no matter how short might be the look he gave a man or plan.

Of his Chief's command style, Butler presciently observed that "he never knew of a man upon whom command sat more lightly than it did Wolseley . . . one would no more think of questioning an order he gave than why the birds of the air sang or fish in the stream swam." These would be perhaps the most descriptive words ever spoken by anyone concerning the great commander.

Upon arriving in mid-August at Fort Alexander, situated on the east shore of Lake Winnipeg, Wolseley was more than ever persuaded that the expedition's mission was, in fact, war. Riel, he learned, had assembled some 600 fighting men at the fort. As the Commander recorded, this was news which "cheered our men's hearts," for it suggested that the rebels were, indeed, prepared to fight.

Now Wolseley pushed on at top speed with only the regular troops, whom he ordered embarked in 50 boats. The advance force sailed and rowed along the shores of Lake Winnipeg, reaching the mouth of the Red River on August 20, and ascending it as far as Stone Fort, some 20 miles downstream from Fort Garry. Landing before noon, the Commander unloaded the better part of his supplies, distributed arms and ammunition, and detailed B Company of the Royal Rifles to serve as a mounted infantry flank guard.

Mounted on wiry horses they had commandeered in the vicinity, riflemen and detachments rode forward. Their task was to scout both banks of the Red River, as well as to cover the main party's water-borne advance, scheduled for the following morning, August 23. The use of riflemen as mounted infantry was a practice that had not hitherto been employed by the British Army with great success. But Wolseley had seen the technique used by both Union and Confederate forces during the 1860s Civil War. Later, the U.S. Army would employ it in Indian campaigns on the frontier.

In the early morning hours of August 24, troops landed a short distance from Fort Garry. It was Wolseley's intention to approach the fort from the west, surround it, and catch Riel and his band in the right angle formed by the Red's and Assiniboine's junction. But the expected climax was pathetic. As dawn broke, the sky was grey, the ground deep in mud. It was pelting rain. Wet through, soldiers laboured up the soggy bank, dragging their little brass cannon behind the commandeered and creaking Red River carts. Everything appeared run-down and deserted. At the fort in front of them, there appeared to be no sign of life. It was all too apparent that the rebel leader had not waited to be encircled. Two mounted troopers galloped through the fort's open south gate. No one opposed them, and the fort was quickly occupied.

Wolseley's force now completed the formal takeover of Fort Garry. The Union Jack was hoisted, and a Royal Salute fired from the guns, in lieu of more exciting fusillades. As Wolseley observed: "Personally I was glad that Riel had not come out and surrendered, as he at one time said he would, for I could not then have hanged him as I might have had I taken him prisoner while in arms against his sovereign." Lacking both hindsight and historical perspective, the Commander never really grasped the true implication to the country of the Red River rising. In fact, it was a last, desperate attempt by Canada's Métis and Indians to preserve their traditional style of life, which was under assault by the forces of white civilization. As one modern historian, James Morris, notes: "To such an Imperial soldier it was rebellion pure and simple."

Lieutenant Butler recorded that, personally, he was "disgusted at having come so far to hear the band play 'God Save the Queen.'" But as Wolseley had told the men before they left Toronto: "Our mission is one of peace, and the sole object of the expedition is to secure Her Majesty's sovereign authority."

In such dispirited fashion, Wolseley's little force effectively put an end to the threat posed by the Métis rising. By August 28 the last Canadian Militia units arrived at Fort Garry. Immediately, they assumed the duty of providing a permanent garrison. (In fact, both the Ontario and Quebec battalions were to remain in the west during the winter of 1870–71.)

Regulars had it better. After quite literally drinking the settlement dry following their months in the bush, they departed for Thunder Bay on August 29. Their schedule demanded that they reach Eastern Canada before the early snows, for even a quarter of an inch of ice on the river-ways would have seriously damaged their boats. By October 15 the 1st Battalion of the King's Royal Rifles was safely back at Toronto's barracks.

Once Adams Archibald, the new Lieutenant-Governor, was installed at Red River on September 2, Colonel Wolseley's mission was complete. He turned official command over to Colonel Jervis of the Ontario Rifles, and commenced his return to Eastern Canada.

From Toronto, the 1st Battalion of the King's Royal Rifle Corps immediately proceeded to Quebec. Here, in late autumn, 1871, the unit embarked for Halifax aboard HMS *Orontes*. It was strangely fitting that the regiment, which had been with Wolfe at the surrender of Quebec in 1759, and which had seen the Union Jack first hoisted on the flagstaff, would be the last British unit to be garrisoned in Canada. At the unit's departure, it witnessed the replacement of the Imperial ensign by the new Red Ensign with Canadian badge of the Dominion.

Wolseley credited the expedition's success against incredible odds to the fact, already mentioned, that it had been planned and organized far from War Office influence and meddling. But thoroughness and luck doubtlessly played a part as well. The effort cost the modest sum of £100,000 Sterling, quite likely making it the cheapest military campaign Britain mounted in the late 19th century. The effort had been extremely arduous, as well. Nonetheless, the War Office would not issue a campaign medal until thirty-nine years afterwards.

Although Garnet Wolseley was a hero in Canada, in Britain scarcely a newspaper alluded to his epic march, for the Franco-Prussian war monopolized attention. Awarded a knighthood,

Wolseley was left to languish on half-pay for some time. Characteristically, however, he employed the interlude to write on military subjects, furthering his reputation as both a thinker and reformer.

Edward Cardwell, Prime Minister Gladstone's war minister, would soon bring Sir Garnet Wolseley into the War Office as an assistant Adjutant General. In this capacity he played a major role in reforming the British Army during the early 1870s. The entire military system was remodelled from top to bottom. Most notably, the purchase system, whereby ranks had been bought, was abolished. Also, regular and reserve forces were welded into a homogeneous army of "linked" battalions for both overseas and home service.

When he was promoted general, Wolseley's Canadian experience prepared him to fight in turn both Ashantis and Zulus, and to organize in 1884–85 the Egyptian Campaign. Unfortunately, troops arrived too late to rescue General Gordon (the "Christian General"), surrounded at Khartoum on the Upper Nile by the Mahdi's Dervish followers. Still, the specially recruited Canadian boatmen, upon whom Wolseley relied to transport the relief force up the great river's perilous cataracts, performed admirably.

At the end of a lifetime of distinguished service, Wolseley had not forgotten the little campaign of 1870. Nor the men he had personally led through the Dominion's wilderness to Fort Garry. In the relatively little time he could spare from the Empire and its troubles as Commander-in-Chief of the British Army, he liked to drift down the Thames in a canoe. On such occasions, he would reminisce about his carefree time in the Canadian bush. In his *Story of a Soldier's Life,* published some four decades after the Red River expedition, he would sum up the apprenticeship which had so effectively shaped his thought and military philosophy:

> I can draw no distinction between the relative merits of the military value of the regular soldier and the Canadian militiaman who went with me to Red River; each had arrived at Prince Arthur's landing with special attributes peculiarly their own, but

by the time Fort Garry had been occupied each had acquired the military virtues of the other. What it is that a large army of such men under some great leader could achieve, I for one, know not.

Wolseley's vision concerning the potential of the Dominion's citizen-soldiers would prove prophetically accurate. Little more than a decade after the field-marshal penned the above assessment, tens of thousands of our country's young men demonstrated they deserved to rank among the best soldiers in the world, under the inspired leadership of Lieutenant-General Sir Julian Byng, a British professional, and Lieutenant-General Sir Arthur Currie, a former militia officer from Victoria. In addition to his great contributions to the British Army, Wolseley's example and his reorganization of Canada's militia had laid the essential groundwork for Canada's efforts in World War I.

Today Wolseley's memory is enshrined in Canada in the name Wolseley Barracks, at London, Ontario, the home of the Royal Canadian Regiment since 1883. Fittingly, Wolseley himself was appointed Honourary Colonel of the RCR from 1899 until he died in 1913.

SELECTED READINGS

Bumsted, J. M. *The Red River Rebellion.* Winnipeg: Watson & Dwyer, 1996.

Farwell, Byron. *Eminent Victorian Soldiers: Seekers of Glory.* New York: Norton, 1985.

Morris, James. *Heaven's Command: An Imperial Progress.* Harmondsworth: Penguin, 1984.

Willock, Roger. "Green Jackets on the Red River." *Canadian Army Journal* 13:1 (January 1959): 31–53.

Wolseley, Viscount. *The Story of a Soldier's Life.* 2 vols. London: Constable, 1903.

Major-General Frederick D. Middleton (1825–1898) in 1884.
Photograph: William James Topley. (NAC/PA-025531)

11

MAJOR-GENERAL
SIR FREDERICK MIDDLETON

The Dominion's Militia
Prove Themselves on Saskatchewan's Plains

In 1885, the Northwest Rebellion's outbreak greatly tested the leadership abilities of General Frederick Middleton (1825–1898), who had recently succeeded as General Officer Commanding Canadian Militia. Competent but old and portly, the commander led his troops in a deliberately cautious manner against the outnumbered Métis and Indians. The General's organization was excellent, but he did not possess the imagination and tactical skills to confront the prairie marksmen and Native warriors. Following an indecisive action at Fish Creek, the militia themselves brought an end to the rebellion by breaking ranks and rushing the enemy at Batoche. Although Middleton was successful, at least in the eyes of Easterners, and was rewarded, it was the ordinary Canadian militia who emerged as the emergency's real champions. Having proven themselves, our countrymen would be henceforth confident in their ability to provide for the Dominion's home defence.

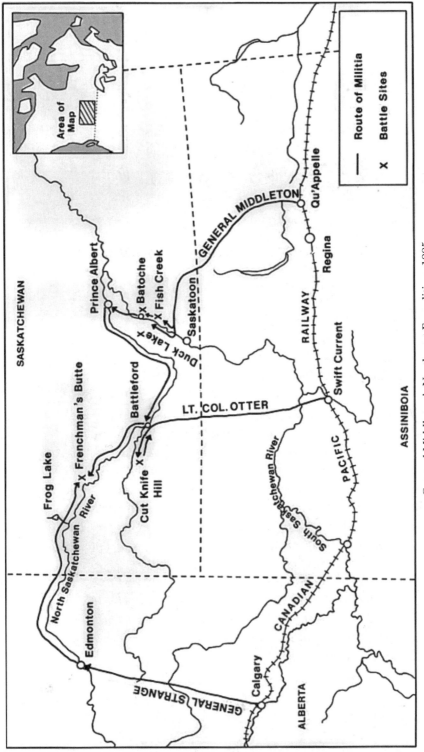

General Middleton's Northwest Expedition, 1885

In 1884, when Frederick Middleton became head of Canada's militia, he was delighted to be appointed to the post. In the middle-aged officer's mind, he would enjoy the local rank of Major-General and its accompanying status in a colonial society that worshipped all things British. Not least, he judged the appointment would not be especially challenging, for, although no stranger to physical courage, he had reached the point in life when set routine offered more attraction than a life of adventure.

Born to an Anglo-Irish military family (as were so many soldiers profiled in this collection), Middleton was educated at the Royal Military College, Sandhurst. Following his training, he joined the British Army in 1884. But promotion was excruciatingly slow in the mid-19th century, an age of unchallenged British superiority. Despite obvious skills and outstanding bravery, young Frederick found himself on half-pay from time to time. Like Garnet Wolseley, he had distinguished himself during the Indian Mutiny, had been mentioned in dispatches four times, and recommended twice for the Victoria Cross. After serving in both New Zealand and Burma, however, he found himself threatened with early retirement. Thankfully, service in Canada had saved him from this fate. Posted to Montreal, he had wed Eugenie Marie Doucet, daughter of a French Canadian lawyer, in 1868. Six years later, he returned to England. Here, he became Sandhurst's Commandant. He remained in the comfortable appointment for a decade. However, it, too, came to an end, leaving Middleton in an awkward predicament. As a sixty-year-old colonel, he could look forward to retirement only on half-pay.

Thus Middleton arrived back in Canada on July 13, 1884. Interested Canadians soon learned that the new General was exceedingly short, quite corpulent and very red-faced. Outwardly, it seemed he was quite friendly. Middleton, too, was delighted by his favourable reception by the Dominion's society, although he confessed to the Duke of Cambridge, the British Army's Commander-in-Chief, that he did not know how long the mutual enchantment might last. As he reported, "I cannot help thinking that your Royal Highness has read these people a lesson, by employing General Luard [his predecessor] and not listening to the barking and yelping at him and that to a certain extent I shall benefit from it."

Meanwhile, though, the General wished to please. To Militia Minister Adolphe Caron he appeared both obliging and constructive. Following a series of quick visits to Eastern Canada's military establishments, the General compiled the most flattering annual report on the Department since Colonel Patrick Robertson Ross' reports of the early 1870s. In Middleton's opinion the new militia and artillery schools had "performed wonders." The new military college at Kingston he especially praised: "There are very few institutions of a similar character equal to it in Europe and none is better," he reported. Clearly, he was setting out on the right foot to woo his new employers.

While his first year in his new post was relatively quiet, Middleton's slumber would be rudely interrupted in March 1885. Startling news arrived that serious trouble had broken out in the Northwest. Following the uprising of 1869–70, a Canadian garrison had remained in the Red River until 1877, when it was finally disbanded. The Manitoba Force, as it was called, was a lonely and forgotten detachment — in some sense the Canadian counterpart of scattered American army garrisons sprinkled throughout the west, south of the border, following the Civil War. When the newly established North West Mounted Police (NWMP) dispersed across the Northwest Territories, commencing in 1874, the troops at Red River, with little to do, soon found themselves redundant.

But in 1884, the torpor enveloping the "Great Lone Land," as William Butler had earlier termed it, changed virtually overnight. Convinced he was on a divine mission, Louis Riel, estranged leader of the short-lived Métis government that had established itself at Fort Garry in 1870, returned to his people at their new settlement of Batoche, on the North Saskatchewan. He had been invited back by the military leader Gabriel Dumont and two other Métis, who summoned him from his quiet existence as a teacher in nearby Montana. Soon rumours and reports of a new Métis rising, this one dimensionally more serious since it was supported by Indians, were pouring into Ottawa. The bad news could not have come at a worse time for Sir John A. Macdonald's Conservative government. The Canadian Pacific Railway was virtually bankrupt, and the Dominion's credit, tied to the CPR, was likewise in trouble. Desperate, the cabinet hoped the new wave of aboriginal unrest would blow itself out. Conservative newspapers tried to assist, pronouncing reports of rebellion "a monstrous exaggeration." Or, as Montreal's *Gazette* termed it, little more than "a petty riot."

A much larger story lay behind the growing unrest. The Métis, who 15 years earlier had abandoned their traditional lands in the Red River and moved to Saskatchewan to escape a wave of white settlers, wanted the boundaries of their new farms respected by Ottawa. In addition, the Indians whose land the government had sold, and who had been starved as the government broke its promises, were growing desperate, especially as the buffalo disappeared from the Plains.

On March 26, a small North West Mounted Police detachment, stiffened with volunteers, clashed with a Métis party near Duck Lake, north of Batoche. When the government force at last managed to escape, it left behind ten wounded, victims of Métis marksmen. As news of the so-called "massacre" spread, the Mounted Police abandoned Fort Carleton. Hundreds of white settlers now took refuge in Prince Albert. On April 2, a band of braves, purportedly led by Chief Big Bear, a Cree leader, murdered nine persons, including two priests and the local Indian Agent, at Frog Lake, further west. Indeed, one of the rebellion's tragedies would be that whites overestimated Big Bear's hostility towards settlers. The Indians also took other whites, including three women, prisoner. Afterwards, Indians surrounded the police post at Fort Pitt, obliging the garrison to flee to Battleford. Here, more police and 500 scared settlers had crowded into the little stockade. Like a rampaging prairie fire suddenly gone out of control, terror now spread rapidly across the Canadian prairies, as Indians pillaged Hudson's Bay Company stores and seized cattle and horses. Inflamed by rumours of the massacres (which were heightened by recent memories of Indian wars of extermination on the American plains), whites from Winnipeg to the Rockies reacted in panic.

In Ottawa, after studiously ignoring growing danger signals for months, Macdonald's government now moved decisively. After Duck Lake's disaster, Edgar Dewdney, the Northwest's lieutenant-governor, formally requested that a "military man" be appointed to deal with the burgeoning emergency. The Prime Minister, aware of hard-working Lieutenant-Colonel Charles Houghton's shortcomings (he was a habitual drinker with little judgement), decided that cabinet would have to rely upon his superior Middleton's planning alone.

The stout Middleton was now suddenly rooted out of his comfortable existence in Ottawa with orders to start immediately for the West. Although he was a competent military commander, he was not especially happy about the prospect of having to direct an army composed entirely of untrained amateur militia against so elusive a force as the Métis plainsmen under their wily military leader Gabriel Dumont.

The mobilization plan the General adopted was both simple and direct. Troops were to be moved from the east to western Ontario by rail. The gaps that existed in the track between Red Rock, on Lake Superior, and Winnipeg would be covered either by marching or by sleigh, as conditions permitted. The force would include both batteries of regular artillery from Quebec City and Kingston, as well as regulars of C Company, Infantry School Corps, later the nucleus of the Royal Canadian Regiment, senior infantry unit of the Canadian permanent force. For the first time in the country's history, however, the bulk of infantry and cavalry would consist of militia regiments. These varied widely in both efficiency and equipment. Two Toronto battalions, the Queen's Own and the 10th Royals, were the first to be cabled. They were wealthy enough to purchase the weaponry and accoutrements a niggardly government had denied them. For political reasons, it was also important to include French Canadian units. Thus, the next to be called were two French-speaking city battalions commanded by Conservative MPs, the 9th Voltigeurs from Quebec, and the 65th Caribiniers from Montreal. Secretly, though, the government possessed grave doubts concerning how such troops might fight against French-speaking rebels. To satisfy rural

Ontario, two composite battalions were organized as well. Additionally, the 7th Fusiliers from London, Ontario, the Montreal Garrison Artillery, Colonel George Taylor Dennison's Governor General's Bodyguard from Toronto, and a composite battalion from Halifax were sent to the Northwest.

Before he headed west, Middleton took the trouble to have his official photograph taken. The uniform he posed in, preserved for posterity, was one he had personally devised for the arduous campaign. As historian James B. Lamb observes: "It consisted of a simple tunic, breeches, a forage cap, setting off his walrus moustache and comfortable paunch, for he was striving to play down the tendency of militia officers to overdress in 'too much fur and feathers.'"

Hurrying west, Middleton reached Winnipeg on March 27. The city was convulsed with rumours and alarms. Finding that Houghton had already departed for the territories along with a company of the 90th Rifles, the General soon followed. Accompanied by the remainder of the battalion, he made camp at Qu'Appelle, the nearest point on the CPR to Batoche.

The problem of transporting an expedition from the East had been simplified by the CPR's construction. Still, while conditions were very different from what Colonel Wolseley had faced in 1870, they were by no means free of hardship. The railway was completed between Toronto and Qu'Appelle with the exception of three main gaps — one of 42 miles and two of 15 each — and several minor ones along Lake Superior's north shore. Men, supplies, horses and guns would have to be moved over such gaps, a difficult task in the late March conditions and deep snow that prevailed in the region. On William Van Horne's orders, the Hudson's Bay Company would aid the transfer between railheads by providing both hot food and warming fires, as well as the teams and sleds required to move troops and supplies. Nonetheless, Lieutenant-Colonel Montizambert, who commanded the artillery, later noted the extreme difficulties involved in embarking and disembarking guns and stores from flat cars to country team sleighs, and vice versa. Indeed, there would be 16 operations of this nature, in cold weather, with the thermometer dipping to -50°F (-45.5°C).

At Qu'Appelle, while awaiting the arrival of eastern troops, General Middleton saw to the organization of the expedition's transport, commissariat and medical services, and arranged his plan of campaign. The latter was no light task. Between Winnipeg and Alberta were a number of widely scattered settlements which needed to be protected. Also, the enemy's strength was practically unknown. Riel was doing his best to arouse the Indians, and if he succeeded the difficulties of the campaign would be increased immeasurably. Most importantly, Middleton had to distribute his forces to meet virtually all emergencies that might develop in an immense field of operations.

As a result, he decided to divide his men into three columns. The principal column, which he would command himself, would march on Batoche, the rebel capital. The second, under Lieutenant-Colonel William Otter, whose Queen's Own Rifles was one of the Dominion's most effective militia units, would proceed by rail to Swift Current, about 150 miles west of Qu'Appelle, where it would ultimately form a junction with the main column. The third, under Major-General Thomas B. Strange, would establish a base at Calgary and then move north to relieve the panic that had broken out at Edmonton. After the first and second columns had attacked Riel at Batoche, they were then to proceed separately to Prince Albert and Battleford. Once they had cleared the enemy out of this part of the country, they would march west, form a junction with the third column, and dispose of the Indian threat. Alarming reports from Battleford, however, would necessitate a change in the program. As a result, Colonel Otter would consequently be dispatched to march directly to Battleford from Swift Current.

Certainly Captain Bedson had organized an efficient transport service. Lord Melgund, the expedition's chief of staff, in the account he later wrote of the expedition, noted that "towards the end of the campaign we had in General Middleton's line of communications 745 teams, working in perfect order, in connection with a system of depots." Overall, the transport service, which had sprung into being virtually overnight, would employ 1,771 men and over 4,000 animals, and contribute greatly to the ultimate success of Middleton's field operations.

Middleton's plan and strategy were excellent. His tactics, however, proved another matter. On April 12, Lieutenant-Colonel Otter, accompanied by 500 men, left Swift Current bound for Battleford. It would take him five days to move his troops and their long wagon train across the South Saskatchewan. But by April 24, Otter's column had relieved Battleford, after marching on average 30 miles a day.

The General's main column, which departed Fort Qu'Appelle on April 6, would not make nearly such good progress. Despite the excellence and efficiency of the transport system, weather and conditions for marching were atrocious, at least at first. Soaked by rain and sleet, the men travelled only 12 miles the first day. That night, the temperature plummeted. By morning, the mercury stood at -23°F (-30°C). But perverse as conditions were, this was only the prelude. The march would lead militiamen through blizzards and force them to wade through sloughs up to their waists. Finally, on April 17 the General's struggling column reached Clark's Crossing, situated on the South Saskatchewan. Its slow progress enabled several contingents from eastern Canada to catch up with the force commander. At first, Middleton regretted the absence of the men accompanying Otter. But now he felt sufficiently strong to split his force, deploying half of it to move along each side of the river. Such a deployment was an essential part of his strategy to trap Riel at Batoche. Unfortunately, the steamer that Middleton counted on to maintain communications between the two wings as they advanced did not arrive. The *Northcote*, laden with reinforcements, supplies, even a field hospital and Gatling gun, left Swift Current only on April 22. By this time, the spring run-off had already crested and moved down the river. Its level, shallow at best, was falling. The Captain calculated that it would take him a mere four days to reach the force's Commander. In reality, it would take him fourteen.

On April 22, Middleton's force, now divided by the river, departed Clark's Crossing for Batoche. Two days later, at Fish Creek, the commander's wing encountered the first Métis resistance. Here, he would be fought to a standstill by a small force led by Gabriel Dumont, and ultimately forced to withdraw with a loss of 8 dead, and 49 wounded, 4 of whom died afterward. The Métis' casualties would be a mere 4 dead and 1 wounded. They would, however, lose 55 horses, their most significant casualty. Middleton's untrained militia had managed to hold their ground. Still, the overall loss of 57 was heavy for a force numbering a mere 350.

The real cost of the skirmish was that it severely eroded the General's previously high degree of confidence. Their two wings re-combined, the troops camped on the battlefield. While he waited for the steamer to arrive with reinforcements and medical assistance for the wounded, the chastened Middleton scribbled off a note of explanation to Caron. In it, he attempted to justify his action, as well as to argue that without his presence the battle would have ended in disaster:

> You probably have heard that I exposed myself needlessly. This is not the case. I was perfectly aware that it would have been dangerous not only to my troops but also to the N.W. territory if I was knocked over and I can assure you that I did not want to be knocked out, but I saw that one of two things had to be done: either I must retire the men which would have ended in a rout, or I must do my duty to the Government and run certain risks. I did so and I am glad to say was successful, ably and energetically aided by my 2 aides who deserve well of Canada.

Nonetheless, the Governor General, who received reports directly from the dashing Lord Melgund (later Lord Minto) accompanying the expedition, was well aware how close to disaster Fish Creek had been. Personally, he remained convinced that the aged Middleton should have been kept in Ottawa. Also, that Melgund himself, a younger, more imaginative officer, should have been given command in the Northwest.

While Middleton's men waited impatiently at Fish Creek, the

Northwest Field Force's two other columns were busy. Without informing his chief, Colonel Otter decided to attack the nearby Cree camp at Cut Knife Hill. In his opinion, such an action would have the benefit of discouraging the Indians from continuing their attacks on property around Battleford and also dissuade them from joining Riel. Setting out from Battleford, Otter and a large detachment reached the Indian encampment on May 2. But surprise had been lost, and Otter's men failed to press home their attack. This enabled Chief Poundmaker's Crees to recover sufficiently to infiltrate Otter's ranks. Worse still, the Natives surrounded the hill itself. In the end, good fortune intervened to save the little force. Its Gatling gun, which continued to spew a rain of bullets, enabled Otter to retire his men. Additionally, the restraining hand of Poundmaker himself ultimately saved the retreating militia from further casualties. Still, the cost of the foray was high: 8 soldiers killed, and 14 wounded. When Middleton learned of the setback, he was understandably displeased.

At Calgary, the "Buckskin Brigadier," General Strange, cobbled together his own field force — although only with considerable difficulty. Contrary to Wild West legend, the local cowboys owned few weapons suitable for serious battle. Only after his force was reinforced by militia battalions from Winnipeg and Montreal, was Strange ready to depart Calgary, on April 20. Ten days later, he reached Edmonton. Meanwhile, his men had dragged their wagon train across swollen rivers, as well as through swamps and prairie gumbo. Strange would spend the next two weeks fortifying the town and constructing makeshift barges to convey the force down the North Saskatchewan. These tasks done, Strange's Alberta Field Force commenced the pursuit of Big Bear in earnest on May 14.

By May 7, Middleton, appropriately reinforced, felt at last able to resume his advance. But the General seemed unsure of himself. His movement towards Batoche proceeded at little more than a crawl, so fearful was he of having the raw militia he led caught and attacked in the open. Ironically, though, the Métis were going to surprise the whites with their defensive capabilities.

Most importantly, the slowness of the General's advance gave them ample time to fortify their little capital and construct skilfully sited rifle pits. Upon arriving at Batoche on May 9, the Commander appeared completely stymied by the rebels. Despite his impressive force, consisting of 850 men, 170 wagon loads of supplies, as well as supporting artillery, steamers, and a military staff, he seemed to lack a plan to deal with the defenders. However, modern readers should not overlook the fact that Middleton's only-too-obvious caution and indecision stemmed from his awareness that he was leading an army composed mainly of militia who possessed little or no experience in fighting aboriginals in their own environment.

After hesitating, Middleton decided on a plan of attack which he attempted on May 13. It was to draw the enemy from the strong position they occupied, employing a feint from the plain north of the village. All of the mounted men, with one of the guns and the Gátling, would be engaged in this diversionary flank movement which the General himself would command. Lieutenant-Colonel Bowen van Staubenzie, meanwhile, would remain in command of the infantry. As soon as he heard firing from the north, this officer would engage the enemy with all his troops. Although Middleton's flank attack was executed as planned, through some misunderstanding, van Staubenzie failed to order the general advance.

Furious, Middleton marched his men back to camp. But early in the afternoon, in circumstances that have never been totally explained, the troops in the battalions guarding the front began to advance. As militia swept forward, others in the camp rushed to reinforce them. And, in their gun pits dug into the reverse slope, the Métis, out of ammunition and unprepared to resist the assault, now fled. Scattered resistance would continue in Batoche itself, but it was evident that the Métis rebellion had collapsed.

The performance of the river force conspired to add a farcical dimension to the display. After beginning its attack an hour late, the steamer *Northcote* struck a wire that the Métis had stretched across the river. As masts, funnel, and wheelhouse sheared off, it careened helplessly downstream.

Lieutenant Arthur Howard behind a Gatling Gun used during the 1885 Riel Rebellion. Photographer unknown. (NAC/C-001882)

Still, the overall attack quickly overwhelmed the enemy defences, and Batoche was captured. When, two days later, Riel gave himself up, it was clear that Métis forces had surrendered. Still, the quelling of the Métis rising had not lacked its surprises. At Duck Lake, Cut Knife Hill, Fish Creek, as well as Batoche, Native forces had caught white troops in the open, surprising them. In fact, all the commanders involved — Superintendent Crozier of the North West Mounted Police, Otter, and Middleton himself on two occasions — had been caught at a serious disadvantage by Natives firing from cover.

After Batoche, however, all was anti-climactic. At Frenchman's Bluff, Middleton lost a golden opportunity when he refused to order additional cavalry forward to support Mounted Police Inspector Sam Steele's scouts, "the best light cavalry in the world," in their pursuit of Big Bear and his main body of Crees. Militia soon became frustrated with blundering through the north Saskatchewan bush, pursuing Indians, or guarding mounds of hay, or cannon or beef along the CPR's right-of-way. An editorial in an eastern newspaper correctly caught the mood when it charged: "It would be an outrage for men to be detailed from their professional or other profitable business avocations for a longer period than the exigencies of public service demand." The government, too, was anxious to end the expensive operation. On June 22, after the last white prisoner had been freed, elements of the Field Force proceeded to return home. Middleton, hoping to burnish his image, planned to conclude the campaign with a triumphant review in Winnipeg. But his hopes were drowned under a torrent of rain. In compensation, the mayor allowed the town's taverns to remain open all night. Thus the troops, like those in Garnet Wolseley's earlier expedition of 1870 who had been denied liquor throughout the campaign, enjoyed a more congenial celebration. By July 20, the last militia units had entrained and were on their way home. This left only permanent troops as well as some local militia to ensure that the dying embers of revolt would not burst into flame again.

General Middleton emerged as a hero, if not in the eyes of most of those who served with him, at least in the estimate of the general public. The government, too, had good cause to appreciate his overall conduct of the campaign. Certainly, the collapse of Métis resistance was a tremendous accomplishment. The entire expedition had been a remarkable feat of improvisation for the young Dominion. An army had been organized, and more than half of them brought from eastern Canada over the uncompleted CPR. This in bitter cold and winter conditions. Altogether some 5,885 men, of whom 5,330 were militia and 555 Mounted Police, had seen military service in one capacity or another. More importantly, the entire operation had occupied just three months. The costs were real enough for a country the size of Canada: 26 men killed and over 100 wounded. The bill for the military side of the operation amounted to a not-inconsequential $3,000,000. Still, until Batoche fell, Ottawa anticipated a far worse ending. In thanks, a grateful Parliament voted Middleton $20,000. Also, the British government made both Caron and his General Knight Commanders of the Most Distinguished Order of St. Michael and St. George (KCMGs). Not least, a thankful War Office confirmed Sir Frederick in his British rank of major general.

After much lobbying, a medal for the suppression of the Northwest Rebellion was authorized. A suitable design was chosen, and a medal struck in Britain, to be bestowed by the Queen's proxy. The Canadian government was expected to assume the cost, a trifling £1,500. This, however, it declined to do. Thus, the British government picked up the cost of this award for both troops and civilians who had participated.

The real though relatively unsung champions of the Northwest Field Force were, of course, the ordinary militia. They had endured cold and hunger, performed impressive feats of marching, and quickly developed both the discipline and endurance to overcome their lack of training and equipment. Eventually a clasp bearing the single word "Saskatchewan" was authorized and issued to 2,250 soldiers who participated in the actual fighting. Once again, the trifling cost was borne by British taxpayers. Pensions for disabled soldiers were meagre. So, too, was the $80 cash or grant of bald prairie that active service veterans received.

Lieutenant-Colonel Otter returned to the obscurity of the Canadian militia staff where he remained until the outbreak of the Boer War in South Africa in 1899. As detailed in the chapter that follows, he would establish his reputation leading the first contingent to go overseas: the 2nd (Special Service) Battalion, Royal Canadian Regiment.

The most important question concerning who ordered the final charge that subdued Batoche remains unanswered. But many of those present continued to insist that it was due to

Canadian initiative — especially that of Colonel Arthur Williams, a Conservative MP, whose men were among the first to attack. Unfortunately, Williams died shortly before the campaign's conclusion, but this only encouraged militia officers to claim him as a martyr. After awarding both Caron and Middleton knighthoods, British authorities, judging the campaign by the standards of "Victoria's little wars," authorized only three additional, minor decorations. As a result, the dissatisfaction of officers remained.

Riel was denied the show trial he envisioned, where he could advertise his people's plight to the world. Instead, six months after the rebellion's end, he found himself on trial for his life in Regina's grubby little courtroom. Stubbornly, he denied the obvious plea of insanity, urged by his lawyers, which the government now offered. Inevitably, he was found guilty of high treason. In the end, he died on the gallows in Regina's courtyard, along with half a dozen members of Big Bear's band.

Meanwhile, Charles Bremner, a mixed-blood fur trader arrested at Battleford, had complained about Middleton. When he was released, the trader found his furs impounded. The trail led directly to Middleton and his officers. In 1887, Middleton answered the charge of theft with a flat denial. But by 1890 further evidence had accumulated. Middleton responded to such charges in his typically bluff manner. As he told a select committee of the Commons: "I thought I was the ruling power up there" . . . [and] "that I could do pretty much as I liked as long as it was within reason." The committee's judgement, however, was that the confiscations were "unwarrantable and illegal."

Growing criticism would ultimately oblige the Conservative government to sacrifice Middleton on the altar of political expediency. After being forced to resign in humiliation, he bundled his family and himself back to England in a huff. In 1896, however, the "failed general" would be rewarded when he was appointed Keeper of the Crown Jewels in London's Tower. It was the Crown's rebuke for those who had harried him from the Dominion like a common thief.

One final irony remained. In contrast to his predecessor

Major-General Sir Richard Luard, who ultimately ran into problems by having too high a profile, Middleton, a "competent placeman," as Desmond Morton describes him, came to grief as well. Despite markedly different styles of command, both officers failed in the end to win the trust of subordinates or the protection of superiors. The lesson was obvious. Given the Canadians' proven record and growing confidence in their own ability to provide for their country's defence, a Canadian was required for the office.

SELECTED READINGS

Beal, Bob and Rod Macleod. *Prairie Fire: The 1885 North-West Rebellion.* Toronto: McClelland & Stewart, 1994.

Flanagan, Thomas. *Riel and the Rebellion: 1885 Reconsidered.* Saskatoon: Western Producer Prairie Books, 1983.

Lamb, James B. *Jingo: The Buckskin Brigadier Who Opened Up the Canadian West.* Toronto: Macmillan Canada, 1992.

Morton, Desmond. *The Last War Drum: The North West Campaign of 1885.* Toronto: Hakkert, in cooperation with the Canadian War Museum, 1972.

——— . *Ministers and Generals: Politics and the Canadian Militia.* Toronto: University of Toronto Press, 1970.

Stanley, George F. G. *The Birth of Western Canada: a history of the Riel Rebellions.* Toronto: Univ. of Toronto Press, 1992.

Lieutenant-Colonel William D. Otter. Canadiana Military Events Album.
(NAC/C-005366)

12

BRIGADIER-GENERAL SIR WILLIAM OTTER

Canada's First True Professional

Sir William Otter (1843–1929) is often described as Canada's first professional officer. Indeed, his biography reads like a Victorian "official life." From humble birth in the Huron Tract and a minor clerkship, he rose by his own efforts to become a member of the Order of the Bath and the Dominion's first general. Enlisting in the Queen's Own Rifles in 1861, Otter would follow a career path that parallelled the development of the Dominion's Army during the late 19th and early 20th centuries. The Battle of Ridgeway taught young Will the need for discipline and professionalism, a lesson that would be reinforced by the close call his column experienced at the hands of the Cree Chief Poundmaker at Cut Knife Hill in the 1885 Northwest Rebellion. During the South African War, Otter commanded the Dominion's first overseas contingent and participated in the Battle of Paardeberg. Afterwards he served as the first Canadian Chief of General Staff from 1908–10. During the Great War he came out of retirement and directed Internment Operations. Following a record 59 years' service, Otter at last retired in 1920.

The Plains of Abraham: Friday, July 24, 1908. The Dominion's tercentenary celebrations, commemorating the 300th anniversary of Champlain's founding of Quebec and the 200th anniversary of the death of Bishop Laval. Across from the reviewing stand there spreads an enormous checkerboard of uniforms, arranged in brilliant colour, interspersed with the gleam of polished brass and steel. To the left, cavalry have just returned to their place in line, leaving behind a thin cloud of dust hanging in the noon's heat. Already, guns and ammunition limbers are commencing to assemble in the space beside them. Beyond the troops, visible only to those occupying the highest seats, the dark shapes of cruisers are evident in the St. Lawrence.

Massive, heavy-shouldered, erect, General William Otter, Canada's Chief of General Staff (CGS), relaxes astride his big broadbeamed bay charger as he chats with the distinguished guest of honour, the Prince of Wales. As he proudly surveys the smartly marching ranks of his old regiment, the Queen's Own Rifles, the General wonders if people notice his flush of pride. The crowd bursts into appreciation as the long procession of sailors, marines, gunners, cavalry and infantry proceeds. A special hand of applause goes to their favourites, the cadets from Royal Military College and Lord Strathcona's Horse, the Permanent Force's newest unit.

Twice, "Bobs" (General Lord Roberts), the Empire's pre-eminent soldier, trots out to lead troops past the Prince of Wales and the reviewing stand, ablaze in gold-braid dress uniforms, summer dresses and a sea of huge flowered hats. At the very end of the parade, on Otter's explicit order, the Royal Canadian Regiment brings up the tail. Its position, marching at the parade's end, puzzles the Prince. However, Otter explains: "I wanted the tail to equal the head." Finally, at the very last, two batteries of Permanent Force artillery race across the field, bringing the great review, pregnant with symbolism, to an impressive ending. As Otter rides out to meet the huge mass of Imperial scarlet, rifle green and navy blue uniforms, he cannot help feeling satisfied.

Excelling in the hard, physical sports of rowing and lacrosse, young Will Otter was the very model of mid-Victorian Canada's "cult of manliness." He also possessed a sense of solid integrity that would give his career a "kind of moral straightness" in an age when militia politics was subject to corrupting influences. Yet as a result of his family's financial problems, there was also a dark side to Otter's personality. He demanded much of both himself and others. His goal, largely fulfilled, was to re-establish himself and his family name, to eradicate the haunting memory of his father's career failures. He was a hard taskmaster, uncritical of authority. Admirers called him a great disciplinarian. Others condemned him as a martinet. Men who served under him in South Africa called him "Black Bill," indicating that he was not entirely beloved. And he believed that a hard-won bonus of his life was the opportunity to associate with persons whom we today would describe as "rich and famous."

Otter enlisted in Toronto's Queen's Own Rifles in 1861, when the *Trent* affair threatened imminent war between Great Britain and a warlike American Union. The youth's membership in the militia soon came to represent much more than a mere opportunity to show off his uniform and good looks, or to associate on terms of equal footing with the city's best society. Otter later recorded: "On the first day of my enlistment in the corps I became imbued with an ardent desire and love for order, system, and discipline pertaining to and necessary in a military organization, and as I advanced in experience, rank and service the advantage of such grew with me." In fact, Otter's advance was remarkable. In 1863, after attending a school run by the British garrison, he qualified as a sergeant. Following further training he was gazetted a lieutenant in 1866. Soon, he was an adjutant, responsible for training officers, as well as supervising every detail of the prestigious battalion's operations.

Otter's conception of military preparedness would, however, be severely challenged by the Fenian rout of the Queen's Own at Ridgeway in early June 1866, described in a previous chapter. Henceforth, he was determined that Canadian soldiers would never again be sent into battle like innocent sheep.

In 1869, when the crucial decision was made to withdraw British troops from Canada, Otter was promoted to major. The very same year the militia revenged the humiliation of Ridgeway by repulsing renewed Fenian threats on Quebec's border. The following year, when Canada's militia played a major role in crushing the Red River Rebellion, Otter and Colonel Gillmor, his colleague, journeyed to the head of Lake Superior to observe Wolseley's expedition.

Over the next decade, the Queen's Own, commanded by Otter as lieutenant-colonel, established a reputation as the best volunteer unit the Dominion possessed. With his broad chest, curly brown hair and moustache, and immaculately tailored green uniform, the unit's commander cut an impressively handsome figure. But his growing reputation was not based on his looks alone. His 15 years' military experience was evident in the crack regiment's day-to-day operation. His practical style was also reflected in *The Guide,* a useful handbook he prepared. It contained detailed information on every aspect of military life, from how to conduct divine service to how to measure an officer for uniforms.

Otter's philosophy differed markedly from that of most Canadian military experts of the age. While others preached that their countrymen were imbued with a natural talent for war, Otter saw things differently. If anything, he argued, the colonial Canadians tended to be mesmerized by the British Army. They copied, however, only its superficial characteristics: "Its uniforms, its ceremonial drill, its regimental etiquette and internal snobberies." But, he concluded: "Soldiering is not easy or even glamorous; it [is] a matter of routine, discipline, and even subordination."

During the 1885 Northwest Rebellion, Otter would experience near catastrophe again when his little column overran Poundmaker's camp at Cut Knife Hill. Thanks to discipline, though, some impressive leadership on the part of individual officers, and the Commander's own attention to Ridgeway's teachings, the small force was saved. To the end of his life, however, the chastened officer would keep a portrait of Poundmaker on his study wall as a graphic reminder of the well-deserved lesson the wily old Cree chief had taught him.

Over the following decade and a half, Otter commanded the

Dominion's most populous and prestigious military district: Toronto, the Peninsula and the counties of central Ontario. He was one of the first Permanent Force officers to implement a serious and practical program of training to prepare the militia's elite for future eventualities. Under his direction, Toronto especially would emerge as a bustling centre of military activity and efficiency. In addition to a hectic annual schedule of camps, church parades, field days, tournaments, and lectures, Otter established the Canadian Military Institute in the city in 1892.

To his chagrin, Otter was passed over when Colonel Walker Powell, senior Canadian-born officer in the force, retired. Nonetheless, his fortunes were about to change dramatically. In 1899 the South African War broke out, triggered by Boer President Paul Kruger's high-handed treatment of "outlanders" (non-Boers) in the Transvaal. In response, Ottawa decided to send an infantry regiment to assist the British. Equipped by the Dominion and commanded by Canadian officers, the unit was to be paid by Great Britain once it reached South Africa. Governor General the Earl of Minto (the former Lord Melgund) cabled to his Imperial masters: "My ministers hope that [the] Canadian contingent will be kept together as much as possible." English-speaking Canada's enthusiasm proved so great for the country's first foreign expedition that the entire contingent, numbering 1,000 men, might have been raised in only a few hours in any one of Canada's major cities. The government, however, wished every part of the Dominion to be represented. Companies were raised right across the country: in London, Toronto, Kingston, Ottawa, Montreal, Quebec, Saint John, and Halifax. Even sparsely populated Western Canada provided one company.

Earlier, Otter had been appointed regimental commander. With close to four decades of service in both militia and army, the fifty-six-year-old officer was indisputably the best choice. His hard and dour nature also appealed to the government, for cabinet members knew he could give and take orders. The unit's senior major was Lawrence Buchan, who like Otter had served in the Northwest Rebellion. Following it, both officers had proceeded to

England and taken instruction in the three arms of service — cavalry, infantry, and artillery. Their experience in the Canadian Northwest, especially, would be of the greatest assistance to them in the South African War, for the Boers of the Transvaal and Orange Free State employed tactics similar to those of the Métis and Indians of Manitoba and Saskatchewan. And the Canadian officers soon discovered upon reaching the Cape that they had to fight Boer commandoes who were even better shots and more adept at taking cover than the insurgents encountered earlier along the Saskatchewan.

As a political realist, Otter was aware of the need to mollify French Canada. Thus he himself suggested Oscar Pelletier, son of a Liberal senator, be appointed to one of the contingent's senior posts. He also chose to take 41 officers, instead of a battalion's standard strength of 31. The extra eight lieutenants and two captains allowed the Minister of Militia to make additional appointments. Additionally, they provided the contingent with the flexibility to be divided into two smaller battalions, should circumstance demand.

Officially, the unit was designated the 2nd (Special Service) Battalion of the Royal Canadian Regiment of Infantry. It would, however, be popularly known as the Royal Canadian Regiment (RCR). Organizationally, it was recruited around a nucleus of officers, NCOs and men from the Permanent Corps.

On October 30, the soldiers were issued equipment, but the process was marred by confusion and rampant theft. Moreover, although glad to be finally clad in regulation battle dress, Otter's command would come to despise the poor quality, brown serge uniforms. Stiff and uncomfortable at first, they would prove prone to rot following repeated wetting on the veldt. Other parts of the RCR's kit included a white pith helmet (ultimately stained brown), field service cap, two issues of boots, blue serge puttees, and leather leggings. Also, there was an abdominal bandage, to be employed if a soldier was wounded.

While the Citadel's minute-guns thundered, 50,000 men and women on shore waved and hurrahed — and prayed. Bands played "Auld Lang Syne," "The Maple Leaf Forever," and "God Save the Queen," as the 1,000 brave Canadian lads constituting the RCR departed for battle. They sailed aboard the *Sardinian,* a small, cramped, and dirty former cattle boat. As a reporter who was present recorded, the atmosphere was a mixture of rejoicing and overwhelming emotion. In these relatively innocent days, going off to war was still regarded as a great adventure. Certainly the emotions released by imperialism could easily deflect almost everyone from calculating the costs of battle, which could be terrible indeed.

Despite the rough and stormy passage, Otter made good use of time spent on board. Since even officers from the Permanent Active Militia, or professional corps, knew little of their drill manuals, training proceeded apace. Personnel also got to know one another. Under Otter's guidance, the contingent gradually became one family as the vessel steamed ahead in foul weather, between towering waves, on her 8,000-mile journey.

The *Sardinian* finally reached Cape Town, under Table Mountain, on November 30. By this time, Boer armies, equipped with modern Krupp and Creusot guns, had demonstrated their ability. Their mounted infantry were hard hitting, their riflemen every bit as fearsome as rumoured. Also, the enemy's generalship was impressive. General Redvers Buller's relieving force was making little progress to save besieged Ladysmith. To the west, at Kimberley, another similarly beleaguered garrison was attempting to protect millionaire diamond magnate Cecil Rhodes, South Africa's best-known English-speaking politician.

After it had departed Cape Town, the RCR's first assignment was the inglorious task of constructing a railway siding. Meanwhile, a Scottish battalion that had arrived at roughly the same time was slaughtered at Magersfontein by Boers firing from rifle pits. It was the first of a series of setbacks the British press dubbed "the Black Week." Following Buller's defeat, as well as that of two other British armies, the War Office named aged Field Marshal Lord Roberts — small, single-eyed, and much beloved — as supreme commander of British forces. (Earlier, his son had been killed at Ladysmith trying to recapture the ill-fated British guns.) "Bobs'" imposing Chief of Staff was Sir Herbert Kitchener, who earlier had defeated the Dervishes at Omdurman, in the Sudan, in 1898.

Spared the Highlanders' fate, the RCR moved up the line to Belmont, site of an earlier clash with the enemy. In his dual capacity as both camp and regimental commander, Otter desperately hurried to prepare his little command for real battle. Under his demanding supervision, the regiment practised parade-square drill, learned to take orders, and mastered the military art of outpost survival. A Canadian reporter noted that heavy enemy fire had necessitated a change in tactics. To counter the peril, the RCR was practising advancing in thinly extended "waves," so as to present a "minimum target." This, however, obliged the RCR to eliminate volley firing. Also, since the enemy invariably adhered to the unsporting practice of concentrating fire against officers and NCOs, officers were leaving their swords behind. Rank badges were also removed, and gold buttons were obscured with paint.

The rigorous training helped the Canadians get their ship-softened muscles back into shape. But Otter encountered another problem. It derived from his humourless personality and drive for perfection. It was plain such a style did not endear him to his troops. As J. L. Granatstein and David Bercuson, the authors of a modern study, perceptively observe, he "expected discipline, discipline, and discipline, and he disdained the little comforts that canteens could provide." Volunteer soldiers felt entitled to their tobacco, as well as some sweets, in addition to regular meals. But even providing the latter was a problem, for the British did not usually provide their men with anything at all between "tea," served at 4:00 p.m., and the following morning's breakfast.

Finally, an RCR company had the opportunity to "smell powder." On December 31, the British station Commander took a small mixed unit, consisting of the Canadians, Queenslanders and British, out of Belmont in search of a party of 400 Boers. At Sunnyside Kopje, the fleeing enemy came under fire from the pursuers. The Boers, in turn, returned their volleys. As T. G. Marquis, author of *Canada's Sons on Kopje and Veldt*, a popular history, wrote: "The fates were with them [the RCR], and although thousands of bullets splashed the brown dust of the veldt, in front, in rear, and sang overhead, no chance bullet found a victim." After enduring several hours of sniping, the Canadians and Australians charged the Boer position and took it. Most of the enemy had escaped. But at least the Canadians had experienced their first taste of battle.

Meanwhile, back at Belmont, Otter's rigid drill and discipline were gradually whipping the RCR into battle-fitness. And none too soon: Roberts, who had arrived at Cape Town in early January, now decided to mass his armies on the Orange River, to leave his base behind him, and commence a great turning movement directed against the Boer general Piet Cronje's communications. Summoned to confer with Roberts and Kitchener, Otter was pleased to learn that the RCR had been chosen to participate in the great crusade. On February 12, 1900, the advance began, with the Canadians assigned to Major-General Horace Smith-Dorrien's brigade. A young soldier, hitherto critical of his commander in letters sent to his father, noted: "We have good officers in Col. Otter down and we go forward with confidence." It was a good omen.

Breaking camp, leaving much of its equipment behind, the regiment set out. It travelled first by rail, then marched through excruciating heat. Even those who had served in India judged it unlike anything they had experienced. Their object was Magersfontein, where Cronje's forces were besieging the diamond mining town of Kimberley, situated on the border between Cape Colony and the Orange Free State.

Amazingly, Cronje, despite his experience, failed to realize the scope of the approaching net of British and Imperial troops until February 15. When he finally grasped the menace, Cronje and his forces attempted to escape northwards into the Orange Free State. Suddenly transformed into the hunted, the enemy army, encumbered by nearly 300 wagons and many wives, moved close to 30 miles in a single day's march. While British troops har-ried the Boer rearguard, Sir John French's cavalry dashed for-ward, swooping around the retreating foe's columns to seize the high ground that lay between the enemy commander and safety. With draft animals near exhaustion, the desperate Boers formed a laager (camp) on the north bank of the Modder River, at a place called Paardeberg Drift.

As part of the gigantic net pursuing the enemy, the RCR marched through the night of February 16. Clouds of dust raised by tramping British columns made the Canadian advance a diffi-cult struggle. The next night, the RCR provided the rearguard for the advance. As Otter noted: "[We] were choked with dust and parched for water, and it seemed as if daylight or the end of the march would never come." At last, tired and hungry, the Cana-dians crossed the brow of a low rise and found themselves in front of Paardeberg Drift. Halting the battalion, Otter took special pains to see that tea, biscuits and a half-tot of rum were distrib-uted to the men, many of whom were near the end of their en-durance. On their right, a British howitzer unit arced shells into a distant Boer stronghold. Troops, wagons, and guns were moving in every direction, accompanied by the clearly audible fire of rifles.

At last, the order came to attack. Crossing the swollen Modder was no easy task. But this was only the beginning. Scrambling up the far bank of the river, the Canadians found themselves on a barren, slightly undulating, dusty plain. The terrain was not un-like many parts of western Canada, the surface broken by occa-sional boulders, hills, and clumps of brush. The Boers had situ-ated their positions along a bend in the tree-bordered stream, directly to the right of Otter and his troops.

Smith-Dorrien, the brigadier, had disappeared along with the two other battalions of Imperial troops. Otter now swung his lead-ing companies eastward and ordered them to advance. The troops covered the first few hundred yards upright, then pushed forward in short rushes. The Canadians, however, soon found themselves obliged, due to increasing and accurate enemy fire, to seek shelter behind the few anthills and stones available. Casualties began to mount. By noon, under the sweltering heat, the Canadians had emptied their water bottles. Thirst, hunger, and exhaustion appeared as the new enemies. To the left, Boer marksmen, who had infiltrated a gully, commenced a sniping fire, spitting dirt around the besieged troops, and causing many casualties among the Canadians. Additionally, a relieving force of Boers under the able Christian De Wet had arrived, and consolidated a position atop the battlefield's highest vantage point, a height dubbed "Kitchener's Hill."

Kitchener, who wanted De Wet's men dislodged from their perch, issued the order for the Duke of Cornwall's Light Infantry to do the job. Later, from a vantage point a mile and a half to the north, General Smith-Dorrien witnessed what he thought to be a fatal tactical error on the part of the commander of the Canadians. As he recorded: "At 5:15 p.m. I was horrified in seeing our troops on the right of the line rise and charge forward with ringing cheers." But this was not Otter's doing. Instead, the Cornwalls' commander had rashly given his regulars the order to attack. He and his troops, who had risen and rushed forward with fixed bayonets, were mown down before they could cover the first 200 yards of 500 separating them from the enemy. Canadians, Black Watch and Seaforth Highlanders had been intermixed with the ill-fated troops. Sixty-three RCRs fell during the first minutes of the carnage, rendering the day's bloody toll 18 killed and 63 wounded, two mortally. As night fell, Otter withdrew his regiment, save those who remained to collect casualties, to the safety of a bivouac at the crossing point across the Modder.

During the next several days, hot and wet with cold nights, the slow pace of action continued. Boer morale was sagging, as both food and hope of relief dwindled. Still, the enemy was sustained by the fact that February 27 would be the anniversary of Majuba Hill, the defeat the Boers had inflicted on the British 19 years earlier. The British remembered Majuba Day too. Smith-Dorrien issued orders to attack. On the evening of February 26, Otter made his plans: six companies would participate in the assault at 2:00

the next morning. Otter himself would lead the attack in the centre. Buchan and Pelletier, his two majors, would command on left and right. The battalion would advance in two lines. The first, armed with rifles and bayonets, would charge home. The second, equipped with shovels, would be prepared to dig a new trench should the attack falter.

Fifteen minutes late, the RCR clambered over the parapets of their trenches, "going over the top" in an eerie preview of the Great War. Both lines moved forward with extreme care, advancing some 600 yards in the inky darkness. For about 30 minutes they were undetected. Then two Boer shots rang out. Most of the Canadians hit the dirt as a fusillade of fire from the enemy's Mauser and Martini rifles passed over them. Amid the confusion and casualties, the screams of the dead and dying, orders were forgotten. When a voice called out for the regiment to retire, many Canadians fell back to their original lines. Fortunately for Otter's command, however, not all of the RCR withdrew. "The brave Easterners," as a newspaper account termed the Maritimers, had not heard the order. Thus, they had stayed put, consolidating their first desperate scrapes in the earth into a serviceable trench, only 60 yards short of Cronje's front. At daybreak, Otter's troops were elated, for they discovered that their new position provided them unobstructed command of the Boer posts that lined the river's bank.

When they opened fire, a white flag appeared over one of the trenches within minutes, though firing continued. First one and then two or three defenders began to appear, brandishing pocket handkerchiefs in surrender. Once the surprised Boers had yielded to the Canadians, Paardeberg's cost would be calculated at eight Canadian lives, and 37 wounded, five mortally.

Despite confusion and panic, inevitable in a night attack, the RCRs had won their first battle laurels. After months of defeats and failures, the British could at last claim a solid victory. Otter had been initially humiliated by his men's precipitous withdrawal. Shortly, however, he was pleasantly surprised to find the RCR hailed as heroes in South Africa, Canada and throughout the Em-

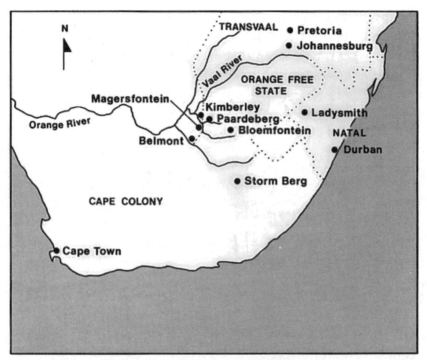

South Africa during the Boer War, 1899–1902

pire. Still, as he candidly confessed in a letter to his wife, the result "was not as satisfactory and complete as we had hoped for." But few shared his opinion. There was a romantic fitness that credit for the victory was awarded to colonial troops. After he had taken breakfast with the defeated Cronje, Roberts himself rode over to congratulate the Canadians personally. Later, the British House of Commons rose cheering at the brave Canadians' mention. Clearly, Paardeberg was a great triumph. Though largely forgotten today, it marked the Dominion's first overseas victory.

At home, Paardeberg was hailed as proof of the Dominion's rising star. The country had achieved a new maturity, both in the eyes of the Empire as well as in the estimate of the world. Coming on its heels, Ladysmith's relief, on February 28, and the capture of Storm Berg on March 5, only added to the euphoria.

By this time, a second Canadian contingent was on the high seas to South Africa. Consisting of mounted men and artillery, instead of infantry, of which the British already had enough, it proved a highly welcome addition. Ultimately, the four squadrons would form two battalions. Lieutenant-Colonel R. F. Lessard's battalion was formed around the nucleus provided by the permanent force's cavalry, the Royal Canadian Dragoons, and took that name in South Africa. The second battalion, commanded by Commissioner L. W. Herschmer of the Mounties, recruited mainly from the prairies and serving members of the North West Mounted Police, served in the Cape as the Canadian Mounted Rifles.

An additional cavalry unit was raised in the Dominion. Lord Strathcona's Horse was financed by Donald Smith, now in his eighties, an extraordinary figure who had made his fortune as a fur trader and director of the Hudson's Bay Company. He had also arranged the financial backing that made the CPR's construction possible. Strathcona's personal regiment consisted of a special corps of mounted riflemen. Like the Canadian Mounted Rifles, it was formed around a nucleus of North West Mounted Police officers and NCOs, and commanded by the now legendary Sam Steele, who had first made his name during the 1885 rebellion. The other half of its personnel were ranchers and farmers from the Northwest Territories and distant British Columbia.

Following Paardeberg's triumph, the tide began to turn against the Boers. Bloemfontein, capital of the Free State, fell to the Empire's troops, including the RCR, on March 15. At first, however, the British stayed put in and around the town, resting their forces and bringing up supplies. The respite gave the Boers time to restore their nerve and fighting capability. By this time, too, the war's nature was changing. Henceforth, there would be no set-piece battles. Instead, De Wet's mounted commandos would harass Roberts' huge army with lightning raids, or else would strike at other key objectives.

The Commander-in-Chief now decided to march on Pretoria, capital of the Transvaal, lying almost 500 miles to the north. The advance began on April 21, employing some 35,000 troops.

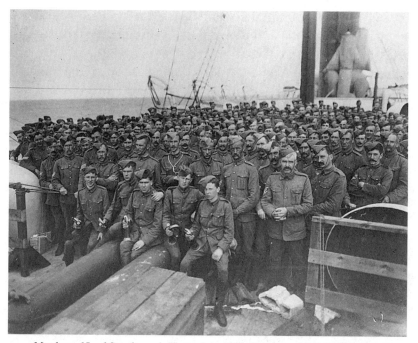

Members of Lord Strathcona's Horse aboard S.S. "Monterey." (NAC/C-000171)

Roberts led the main column across the desert-like veldt. The 9th (including Otter's Royal Canadians) and the 21st Infantry Brigade formed a second column on the left. Additionally, a third column, commanded by General John French, which included the mounted rifles of the Canadian Contingent, completed the strike force.

Otter was leading the forward companies of the RCR in person on April 25, when they ran into an ambush at Israel's Port. The Colonel was struck by a rifle bullet that penetrated the right side of his jaw. The wound would leave his leonine face with a distinctive cicatrix or scar for the rest of his days. Fortunately, though, the injury would not prove serious. After spending less than a month recuperating, Otter was back in command of his battalion. He was just in time to lead the Canadians across the Vaal River into the territory of the South African Republic.

As the correspondent accompanying the force noted, it was a good thing that "Black Bill" was back, leading the 500 remaining RCRs: "For Buchan is a coward, and Pelletier, while brave enough & particularly a fine fellow, loses his head & has no judgement." Such praise on the newspaperman's part was a marked and welcome change.

Now, as newspaper headlines tracked the triumphant progress, the public, both in England and Canada, sang: "We're marching to Pretoria." In fact, the trek to Johannesburg and the Boer capital was almost unopposed. After a brief clash at Doornekop, on May 29, in which Canadian mounted troops as well as the RCRs won new battle honours, the road to Johannesburg lay open. Shortly afterwards the city fell. A few days later, Pretoria, the "Golden City," ringed by impressive forts, surrendered without a shot. The RCR proudly entered the Boer capital as the infantry's advance guard. Next day, Otter and his Royal Canadian Regiment led the 19th Brigade (the "Fighting 19th") in the triumphant march past the saluting point. By this point they were a poor remnant of the fighting force that had departed Quebec eight months earlier. Only 27 officers and 411 men were on the unit's strength, despite the fact that a draft of 100 men had been added to the regiment. Although most participants regarded the victory ceremony as the high point of their lives, many were becoming concerned with how much longer they would have to spend in South Africa.

The Dominion's newspapers trumpeted the victory. The *Halifax Herald* shouted, "The Transvaal's Capital is Now Ours," set off with a sketch of the Union Jack and Queen Victoria. On its part, the RCR could take satisfaction concerning the manner in which Canadians had endured the prolonged campaign's many rigours. Still, there was no denying the cost. Otter himself captured the mood well when he privately confessed that it had been "blood and sand and everything that is disagreeable for a little bit of riband and silver." "Yes, we avenged Majuba," he wrote a relative, "and a d-d nasty job we had of it — not many of us are likely to forget that morning during the rest of our natural lives."

Many Boer leaders and commanders were close to capitulating. They took, however, new heart from the success of De Wet's commandos. Sweeping down, the daring mounted raiders wrecked the Pretoria-Bloemfontein railway and captured prisoners. Henceforth, the conflict would be a straight guerilla war, a preview of what the British would encounter in Malaya, and the French and Americans in Vietnam decades afterwards. As such, it would continue its bitter course for two more years, until the final surrender at Vereeniging, May 31, 1902.

During the time remaining, Otter's men served in a number of capacities. After garrisoning Pretoria, they became part of General Ian Hamilton's division and a reconstituted 19th Brigade. Then, as an independent force under Otter's command, they were charged with guarding a strategic railway line. Other assignments followed. By the time the battalion assisted in a ponderous and ultimately unsuccessful effort to capture Christian De Wet's commando force of 1,500 Boers, the RCR had brought its marching record since landing at the Cape up to an arch-wearying 1,000 miles.

At this time Roberts asked the Canadians to renew their terms of enlistment, and Otter felt he had no choice but to put the question to the men themselves. When the troops split between renewing — indeed 300 elected to stay — and returning home, the Colonel felt that he had betrayed the Field Marshal's trust, as he put it, on a question that seemed to be "the most important so far as the honour of Canada was concerned."

Soon, though, word arrived that the Dominion Government had amended the Militia Act in order to promote him to full colonel. (Australia already had three colonels in South Africa, to Otter's embarrassment.) Also, the much-anticipated order came for the Canadians to return home. Leaving the second contingent to fight the guerilla menace, the Royal Canadian Regiment began its own march to Pretoria. Shortly thereafter, it was on its way to Cape Town, bound for England and Halifax.

Back in Canada, Colonel Otter found many criticisms levelled against him. Realizing, however, that military professionalism precluded his answering his enemies, he chose to hold his peace. The most he admitted was that he may have annoyed the men by "harping that they must do the best for Canada and the Empire." And, he added, "the results speak for themselves." He concluded: "There never was a period in my life in which I was more satisfied with my work than I was with what we accomplished in South Africa."

Because of South Africa's lessons, the decade that followed Otter's and the RCR's return witnessed a major reform of the country's military establishment. The Earl of Dundonald, Canada's new commander of militia, was of much the same mind as Otter concerning the need for professionalism. He also actively promoted the grand design of creating a citizen army of 100,000 and eventually 229,000 men. In his mind, it would be commanded by a cadre of officers from both the Permanent Force and the militia. But its "flesh and blood" would be provided by the Dominion's numerous volunteer units and cadet corps.

Dundonald's program addressed a number of Otter's concerns. Meanwhile, in 1904, under the Militia Act amendment, Otter himself broke new ground by becoming the Dominion's first officer promoted to the rank of brigadier-general (although a Nova Scotia native, John Bradstreet, had risen to the rank of general in the 18th century).

Other changes continued to transform the face of Canada's forces: an Army Medical Corps, an Ordnance Stores Corps, and Army Pay Corps came into being. More important, the Permanent Corps' authorized strength was tripled when the Dominion assumed command of the Fortresses at Halifax, and Esquimalt, near Victoria. Otter's own Western Ontario Military District saw Camp Petawawa, near Pembroke, established to enable artillerymen to train in a realistic manner.

In July 1908, as Major-General Otter (who had become the first Canadian Chief of General Staff two years earlier) watched the great military spectacle marking Quebec's establishment three centuries earlier, he must have mused a little. Just as he had found himself rushed to organize the colourful martial review that showcased the Empire's might and Canada's proud place in it, he had been given little time to master the intricacies of his new position. But, in a sense, his busy lifetime, parallelling the growth and trials of the young Dominion's forces, had more than adequately prepared him for his new responsibilities and the challenges posed by a military budget now more than six times its former spending limit.

In addition to his pride in organizing the great review, Otter could also take satisfaction from a piece that appeared shortly afterwards in the *Canadian Military Gazette*. Of his eventful career, it editorialized: "A matter of detail and regulations; a good tactician, a severe disciplinarian; an upright and conscientious man whose motto was 'duty'; at times severe but always anxious to improve the conditions of his men." Even a perfectionist like Otter would have been hard pressed to improve on such a summation of the ideal qualities of a Victorian officer and the duties expected of him, qualities which Otter, during six decades of active soldiering, always demonstrated.

SELECTED READINGS

Farwell, Byron. *The Great Anglo-Boer War.* New York: Norton, 1976.

Granatstein, J. L. and David J. Bercuson. *War and Peacekeeping: From South Africa to the Gulf — Canada's Limited Wars.* Toronto: Key Porter, 1991.

Morton, Desmond. *The Canadian General: Sir William Otter.* Toronto: Hakkert, in co-operation with the Canadian War Museum, 1974.

Major A. Hamilton Gault, DSO, PPCLI.
Sketch by Richard George Mathews. (NAC/PA-007218)

13

PRINCESS PATRICIA'S
CANADIAN LIGHT INFANTRY

An Imperial Regiment Raised in Canada

The Princess Patricia's Canadian Light Infantry (PPCLI) was the brainchild of Montreal millionaire and militia major Andrew Hamilton Gault. At the outbreak of the Great War, in August 1914, Gault, a McGill-educated veteran of the South African conflict, offered $100,000 to raise a regiment. When Ottawa accepted the offer, it was probably the last military unit in the Empire to be mustered by a private individual for service under the Crown. Composed mainly of Imperial veterans resident in Canada, the Patricias actually fought for the first year under British command. The "Originals" action at Bellewaerde and Frezenberg Ridges, on May 8, part of the Second Battle of Ypres, was especially heroic. Later, artist W. B. Wollen would immortalize it in a famous painting: "Princess Patricias at Frezenberg." After joining the Canadian Corps, the rebuilt Patricias distinguished themselves at Vimy Ridge and Passchendaele. At war's end, a fighting patrol of the battalion had advanced to Mons' outskirts on the Armistice's eve. Today, along with the French-speaking Royal 22nd Regiment ("Van Doos"), organized in November 1914, and the Royal Canadian Regiment, the Princess Patricia's continues to exist as one of the Canadian Forces' permanent units.

On Sunday, August 23, 1914, the Princess Patricia's Canadian Light Infantry, which had been camped under bell tents at Ottawa's Lansdowne Park, held its first church parade. This done, its members marched in pouring rain to Parliament Hill, where the regiment received from Princess Patricia, the daughter of the Duke of Connaught, and granddaughter of Queen Victoria, its banner or camp colour. The flag she designed and embroidered with her own hands consisted of a square of blue and crimson, edged with gold, and bore at its centre Her Royal Highness's personal monogram worked in gold. After her father, the Duke of Connaught, Canada's Governor General, addressed the battalion, the Princess herself concluded the ceremony with a few prophetic words: "I have great pleasure in presenting you with this Colour, which I have worked myself. I hope it will be associated with what I believe will be a distinguished corps. I shall follow the fortunes of you all with the deepest interest and I heartily wish every man good luck and a safe return." Although the men of the regiment would nobly fulfill the Princess' desire for the new unit's success, its personnel would fare far less well. By the Great War's tragic end, only a broken handful of the splendid men present on this occasion would return from the artillery-shattered fields of France and Flanders.

A mere three weeks before the Ottawa ceremony, at midnight on August 4, Great Britain had declared war on Germany in response to Germany's mobilization to attack France by way of neutral Belgium. Shortly afterwards, the Government of Canada accepted a proposal from Major Andrew Hamilton Gault, a Montreal businessman, to provide the sum of $100,000 to equip a regiment for active service overseas. So eager were experienced soldiers residing in Canada to fight the Empire's battles once more that within seven days the ranks of the new unit were full, and the Princess Patricias had miraculously transformed itself into a living regiment.

The battalion's command was entrusted to Lieutenant-Colonel Francis D. Farquhar, DSO, Military Secretary to the Governor General. A better choice could hardly have been made.

Although he was only forty years old, Farquhar, a Coldstream Guards officer, possessed a wide range of military experience in both the theory and practice of war.

Superbly officered, the Patricias, as they soon came to be called, were a gift which one general history has described as being "much to the sovereign's taste." No similar body of soldiers had ever paraded under a single regiment's flag in the history of the British Empire. Hamilton Gault, thirty-three years old and founder of the regiment, was a militia officer, a Boer War veteran, and a millionaire. During the battalion's first decades of existence, the name of his wife would be perpetuated in the regiment's cap badge, a marguerite, or single daisy.

Among the unit's officers and other ranks were soldiers, lawyers, doctors, merchants, brokers, ranchers, trappers, miners, and businessmen. Nearly 90 percent were British veterans who had served throughout the Empire. The other 10 percent or so were Canadians who had fought in South Africa. Every British and Canadian regiment but one was represented. The Royal Navy, too, contributed its quota of seamen and marines. Later, it would be discovered that the men of the new battalion had participated in 27 British fighting campaigns. In retrospect, however, to structure a single regiment in such a fashion appears to have been a tragic mistake. Such personnel comprised a leaven which, more carefully employed, might have greatly assisted Sir Sam Hughes, Canada's colourful Militia Minister, in his herculean effort to create an effective Canadian Expeditionary Force.

Unlike other Dominion units, the PPCLI would actually fight under British command during its first year of existence. Thereafter, it joined 3rd Division of Canadian Corps. Initially proceeding to Winchester, England in 1914, the Patricias were brigaded as part of Brigadier-General Fortescue's 80th, a light brigade, attached to British 27th Division.

During almost six consecutive weeks of intense battle in early 1915, the Patricias demonstrated themselves to be the equal of their rival, the Canadian 1st Division. On the evening of February 28/29, a party of 100 Patricias under Major Gault's personal direc-

Princess Patricia reviewing the PPCLI at Bramshott before her marriage.
Department of National Defence. (NAC/PA-005990)

tion introduced a new type of warfare, the trench raid, on the St. Eloi front. Following this, the sector became notorious for attack and counterattack.

On March 20 Colonel Farquhar and his orderly were ushering the commanding officer of the Royal Rifles around the Patricias' communications trench when a bullet fired by an enemy sniper struck the unit's commander in the head. He died almost instantly, and was much grieved by every member of the regiment.

Under its new commander, Lieutenant-Colonel Buller, the Patricias were still mourning Farquhar's loss and 287 other casualties they had suffered in continuous and bloody combat, when they were ordered into the Ypres sector in early April. In a short time, the unit suffered an additional 80 casualties. Even more alarming was the news that 1st Canadian Division, which occupied lines not far to the north, had been attacked by poison gas on April 23. On April 24 news arrived that the enemy had employed gas again, this time against two Canadian brigades, Richard Turner's 3rd and Arthur Currie's 2nd.

At three o'clock on the morning of May 4, the Patricias, who had been withdrawn some two miles, were in the process of establishing a new position along Bellewaerde Ridge, a low ridge or rise of ground, just east of Ypres. The new line, consisting of little more than a shallow trench which the brigade had hurriedly dug, was a mere scratch. Additionally, its men occupied some gun pits in an abandoned artillery position, which the Patricias were in the process of turning into their battalion headquarters and an officers' dugout. No one was especially concerned about the weakness of the position, for, according to previous experience, they expected the Germans would not attack for three or four days. As a result, when dawn broke, the Patricias were engaged in the ordinary routine of sending out working parties and beginning their plan of trench improvement.

Suddenly, however, pioneers and others, some 900 yards in front of the line, saw a red-tinted cloud. It soon proved to be no sunrise or early morning mist. Coming through the woods on their side of the Polygon, a local landmark, were not groups, or even platoons, but entire battalions of red-shirted enemy. Having laid aside their tunics, the attackers, members of the Prussian Guard, were massing their numbers for the heavy fighting that lay ahead.

The German deployment proceeded in text-book manner. As the Patricias watched in disbelief, enemy scouts, followed by advance guard, then ultimately vanguard and flankers, moved toward them, advancing into full view over the rim of the opposing ridge. The official regimental history recorded: "all the men stood upon the parapet to see the show, some of them waving their arms and cheering [jeering] like mad, but the advance [guard] quickly lost interest in the spectacle, for the Germans pushed some machine guns within 200 yards and bullets were soon raking the parapets." The enemy's main force, including artillery, deployed in the open on the double as sheltering Patricias stared. Since friendly allied artillery could not be brought to bear, the Canadians could do little to check the enemy fire.

The severe bombardment that now commenced to fall on the Patricias' front would last all day, only occasionally slackening to permit enemy infantry forays. By ten o'clock that evening, when they were finally relieved by the arrival of the Shropshires, the Patricias had suffered another 122 casualties, mainly from the enfilade (flanking) fire of German heavy artillery.

Next day, May 5, Captain Buller, the battalion's acting Commanding Officer, was so severely wounded by a shell splinter that he subsequently lost an eye. He was invalided back to England for several months. Fortunately, the intrepid Major Gault, who himself had just returned to duty from hospital, was able to assume command at this critical juncture. But the battalion was already considerably reduced. Even counting the additional men Gault brought over from Battalion Depot, muster call indicated fewer than 650 rifles.

The fury of the German assault about to descend on the Patricias and their comrades-in-arms, the British 27th and 28th Divisions, was even more formidable than the green cloud of chlorine gas that earlier had been unleashed on Canadian 1st Division. For the coming battle, Duke Albrecht's 4th Army would throw three army corps, XXVI Reserve, XXVII Reserve and XV, from north to south, into battle between Mouse Trap Farm and Bellewaerde Ridge. Once again, Canadian infantrymen, this time the Princess Patricias, would show their mettle by thwarting the enemy's intentions.

The attack was preceded by the most intensive artillery bombardment the enemy could devise. Survivors afterwards claimed that they witnessed nothing to equal it in the whole course of the Great War.

There are many stories, fragmentary at best, concerning what happened between the evening of May 7, when the Patricias' battle roll stood at 635, and 6 p.m. on May 8, by which time its personnel had been reduced to but a fraction of that figure.

At 5:30 on the morning of May 8, dozens of enemy artillery of every conceivable calibre and type were called into action. The massed guns disregarded the solitary British field piece firing a running but inadequate protest somewhere in the rear. Soon, the concentrated fire reduced the elaborate telephone system connecting the Patricias' trenches and headquarters dug-outs to scrap wire. Expecting an enemy attack, Major Gault early on ordered grooms, orderlies and signallers, indeed every "unemployed" man in the battalion, up to the firing line. As dawn broke, the close-packed Germans attempted to carry the Canadian line at bayonet's point, but sharp, accurate fire, a Patricia hallmark, drove them back under cover.

By now, storms of shells and gas were descending like heavy thundershowers on the entire British line. From time to time, the rain of explosives would lift, but only momentarily, to allow the advance of several more ponderous but determined infantry assaults. These fell, with terrible effect, on 83rd Brigade, on 80th's left. The brigade, composed of stalwart North of England battalions, held its ground until reduced to a "mere torso." But when its relics were eventually pushed back, the 80th's left flank would be "in the air," leaving a mile-deep gash in the line. The task of holding it would devolve upon the Patricias.

At around 7 a.m. Major Gault, already slightly wounded but rallying his men with his personal courage and example, was struck a second time. Shell fragments, penetrating his arm and thigh, severely wounded him, making it impossible for him to continue to move about the firing-line positions. And, due to the fierce battle in progress, there was no chance to evacuate the Patricias' commander to the rear. All the soldiers could do was cover the trench in which he lay with fascines, or pieces of wood, to protect him from being further wounded. The battalion commander lay in this trench, alongside many other wounded, for more than ten hours. Although in great pain, Gault suffered in silence, without a single murmur. He grumbled, however, at his "bad luck" in being wounded so that he was unable to command the battalion. Finally the approach of darkness rendered it possible to move him to where he could receive medical assistance.

Around 8 a.m. the bombardment reached a new peak. From their lines on the Ridge's slope above, the Patricias watched the spectacle of the enemy ceremoniously deploying a six-gun battery, as if on parade. Once the guns were in position, its horses trotted off casually. That the enemy could execute such a difficult operation with the impunity he did spoke eloquently in itself. Soon, the effectiveness of both British and Canadian small-arms fire was being howled down by incoming waves of whiz-bangs and shrapnel. The very thought of a Patricias officer or enlisted man raising his head above the parapet to observe the enemy had become a futile, fatal exercise. So close was the enemy battery sited that its shells simply exploded without providing any warning sound.

Heavy howitzers combined with field guns directed a probing, searching bombardment on both the Patricias' fire and support trenches. On the right, screaming shells blew away the fire trench itself in several places. A lasting memory of the firing line's desperate holding would be Lieutenant Edwards standing on its parapet, blazing away with his revolver at advancing waves of Prussians. After passing to a captain, the battalion's command now devolved, in desperation, upon Lieutenant Hugh Niven. Before the war, young Niven had been a representative for an Edmonton-based mining company. Just a few months earlier, he had been a mere private in the ranks. Now the Patricias' very survival rested on his courage and judgement. By this time, the intensity of the barrage rendered it impossible to communicate with the rear by messenger. As a result, high command had no accurate knowledge of what the actual conditions were. Nor could Lieutenant Niven be informed of his brigadier's orders.

The situation appeared hopeless, even though shelling actually decreased in intensity. Clouds of poison gas were drifting across from the enemy lines, and a bayonet charge was bound to follow the intensive artillery preparation. Ammunition for both rifles and machine guns was perilously low. In addition, the Patricias had lost touch with their supporting regiments to both north and south. Clearly, Niven and the handful of survivors that re-

Vickers machine gun team on Western Front.
Courtesy Esprit de Corps.

mained faced a desperate situation. But no thought of surrender entered their minds. A determination to carry on, whatever might befall them, infused and united all ranks. Now the enemy attempted an infantry advance. The attack, however, was received with undiminished resolution. A storm of Canadian machine gun and rifle fire checked the assailants. But although the defenders accounted for a large number of Germans in the course of the attack, they continued to suffer casualties.

Around half-past nine, Lieutenant Niven managed to establish contact with the King's Own Yorkshire Light Infantry on the Patricias' left and with the Rifle Brigade on the right. But during

the recent bayonet assault, enemy marksmen had managed to secure firing positions in no-man's-land. Now, they were sniping
freely, causing heavy enfilade fire casualties to the Patricias. Their
cross fire also prevented the neighbouring British units from rendering effective assistance.

At this point, the enemy had taken the range of the Canadian
machine guns with extreme precision. Without exception, all four
would be buried at one time or another. Nonetheless the crews
serving with them continued to conduct themselves with remarkable coolness and bravery. Time after time, the guns would be
dug out, mounted, and used again. Some gun crews, only slightly
wounded, were buried alive. One weapon, operated by Corporal
Dover of No. 4 Company, was buried three times, gun and crew
disappearing altogether in the explosives that overwhelmed
trench, parapet and parados. Each time the game Corporal disin-
terred his gun, stripped it, cleaned it, and soon had it firing once
more. After being seriously wounded in a leg as well as an arm,
the heroic gunner extricated himself from the debris and painfully dragged his broken body back towards the unit's former support trench, which had now become its front, or firing, line. As
comrades were attempting to carry him to comparative safety, a
chance bullet passed through his head and ended his suffering.

From 12 noon until 1:30 p.m. Niven and his companions
attempted to hold onto the firing line trench under the most desperate difficulties. At last a Rifle Brigade detachment managed to
reach them. By this time, the left half of the trench had been
obliterated. Soon, a blast of high explosive shell would cause the
right to collapse as well.

Although the day had turned warm and sunny, the dwindling
ranks of Patricias scarcely had time to notice. With their front
trench gone, survivors were forced to make their painful way back
towards the support line. From the scant shelter it provided, they
could observe the methodical procedure employed by the enemy.
The Prussians planted a row of flags on the site of the Canadians'
former front line. The Patricias, who were not familiar with the
enemy's method of signalling their artillery, at first mistook the

pennants for battalion colours. The attackers, however, also erected shrapnel screens, nets of chain about six feet in height. Sheltered by the devices, the Germans now set about constructing a new parapet from what was left of the remaining parados, or elevations of earth that protected the front-line trench from attack from the rear.

With the full power of the German artillery barrage now falling on the Patricias' support trenches, everyone was pressed into the desperate struggle to hold them against waves of attackers. Captain Agar Adamson, who would later command the Patricias at Vimy Ridge, was assisting Sergeant-Major Fraser in distributing ammunition. Adamson, wounded and having lost his glasses, did not understand why his jokes, delivered with the drollery of the polished comedian he was, were being lost on the major. Suddenly, though, he realized why: Fraser, though still standing erect, had been struck and killed by an enemy sniper.

By the long day's end, only two of the Patricias' four machine guns remained in action, the other two and their crews having received direct hits from shells. The Patricias' fire, however, a steady 15 rounds' rapid drill, consistently drove the enemy attackers back. Later, Niven would recall: "We were getting off fifteen rounds a minute, and the Germans thought they were machine guns."

Fortunately, the Patricias were equipped with British-manufactured short Lee-Enfields with long bayonets, rather than the standard Ross rifle, which failed the Canadians so disastrously in the Salient. Corporal H. C. Hetherington remembered: "I fired rifle after rifle until they were actually too hot to hold." He also picked up weapons from dying comrades all around. "There was always a target to aim at," noted Hetherington. "They were coming in masses because I was aiming at Germans for hours."

As one might expect of a battalion of old regulars, cohesion prevailed. In particular, the officially unrecorded exploits of the Patricias' lieutenants, especially Niven, Talbot Papineau and Vandenberg, contributed to the heroic stand's ultimate success. Corporals, too, performed like commissioned officers. By 3 p.m. a detachment of Shropshires reached the Patricias' support line with a vital 20 boxes of small-arms ammunition. These were quickly distributed, and the party that brought them joined the line as reinforcement, occupying the left end of the support trench. By this point, however, some 80 percent of the Patricias were casualties. Only five officers remained. There was also a great gap in the Canadians' left flank, and holes and ditches the battalion's remnants occupied were under attack from three sides. At last, about 5 p.m., the final enemy bayonet attack was beaten back, and German artillery ceased to fire. The Royal Rifles relieved what was left of the regiment, a mere shadow of what the proud unit had been the day previously.

Moving along the line, astonished newcomers prodded numerous silent Canadians. Only then could they believe they were dead. Even men accustomed to warfare's horrors were shocked by the Patricias' casualties, which so far exceeded what might normally be found in a trench that was still held. When a pioneer, Leith, and his chum Bill Ashton finally completed collecting the identity disks of the dead and accounting for the bodies of their comrades, 98 corpses were laid out in rows of sixes in one trench alone.

Finally, at ten o'clock in the evening, Lieutenant Niven, under whose command the PPCLI came out of the line, assisted by Papineau, took a roll call. It disclosed a strength of 150 rifles and some stretcher bearers. At 11:30 p.m. the shattered battalion was officially relieved by the 3rd King's Royal Rifle Corps.

Next day, amidst the continuing German artillery cascade, survivors would toast their comrades in dry champagne recovered from the cellars of Ypres' abandoned big cafe, just off the town square. The defence of Bellewaerde and Frezenberg Ridges on May 8 cost the Patricias 392 men, killed, wounded, or missing. It also marked the effective end of the "Originals" as the core of the Regiment. When it entered the Ypres Salient in early April, the PPCLI was, as already noted, quite probably the most experienced unit in the entire British Expeditionary Force. But by the time it finally departed the Salient in late May, it had suffered close to

700 casualties. In compensation, it had won the respect, indeed admiration, of the entire British Army as well as the Empire. As Patricias survivors marched to the rear, the remainder of 80th Brigade lined the road, cheering wildly. "No regiment could have fought with greater determination or endurance," wrote General Snow, 27th Division's commander. He also added: "Many would have failed where they succeeded."

Ironically, the Patricias' Bellewaerde Ridge and Mousetrap Farm, pressed into action as the bullet-ridden headquarters of General Turner's battered Canadian 3rd Infantry Brigade, would fall to the Germans when they launched a gas attack on May 24. The enemy made few other gains, however, and both sides soon turned their attention elsewhere.

Reorganized, the Patricias would henceforth draw their recruits from Canada's universities, especially McGill. On more than one occasion, the unit would again come close to total destruction. By 1918, original survivors, after the battalion had seen service in all quarters of the British lines and had finally been absorbed into the Canadian Corps, numbered a couple of dozen. Not without reason does the proud name the Princess Patricia's Canadian Light Infantry deserve to rank among the greatest of Canada's and the Empire's regiments that fought in the Great War.

SELECTED READING

Dancocks, Daniel G. *Welcome to Flanders Fields; The First Canadian Battle of the Great War: Ypres, 1915.* Toronto: McClelland & Stewart, 1989.

Gwyn, Sandra. *Tapestry of War: A Private View of Canadians in the Great War.* Toronto: HarperCollins, 1992.

Hodder-Williams, Ralph Wilfred. *Princess Patricia's Canadian Light Infantry.* 3 vols. London: Hodder, 1928–[1958?].

Sutherland, Colonel William. "A. Hamilton Gault Honoured." *Esprit de Corps: Canadian Military Then and Now* 2:1 (June 1992): 10–14.

Williams, Jeffrey. *Princess Patricia's Canadian Light Infantry.* rev. 2nd ed. London: Leo Cooper in Association with Secker & Warburg, 1985.

Lieutenant-General Sir Julian Byng, GOC Canadians.
Department of National Defence. (NAC/PA-001356)

14

LIEUTENANT-GENERAL
SIR JULIAN BYNG

Canadian Infantry and Artillery Battle
for Vimy Ridge

*On Easter Monday, April 9, 1917, all four of Canadian Corps'
divisions in France, attacking together on a four-mile front, managed what neither the British nor French armies had been able to
accomplish in over two years of fighting. They assaulted, captured, and held the Germans' most formidable defensive position
on the entire Western Front, Vimy Ridge. The French, who had
earlier lost 150,000 men attempting to storm the ridge, hadn't
believed the Canucks could take it. Nor did the Germans; even the
British, our allies, were sceptical. But the Canadians triumphed,
largely due to the exceptional leadership and thorough planning
of their commander, Lieutenant-General Sir Julian Byng (1862–
1935), as well as Andy McNaughton's innovative use of artillery. Going over the top at dawn, and advancing behind a massive creeping barrage of shellfire, the Canadian infantry captured
most of the ridge by lunch time. The decisive victory cost 10,000
casualties, low by the standards of the time. The collective accomplishment would also bolster Canadians' growing confidence; not
least, it would inspire a new, enhanced sense of national con-
sciousness, even identity.*

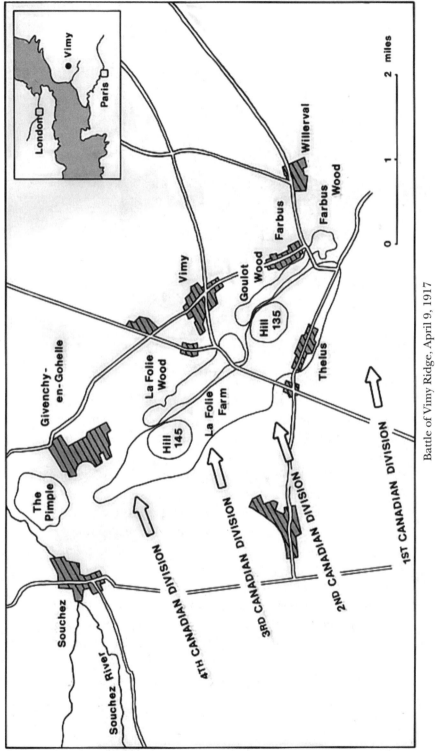

Battle of Vimy Ridge, April 9, 1917

In November 1916, Sir Julian Byng, called to a secret meeting with Lord Stamfordham, the King's secretary, stated that in his professional opinion the spirit of the Army remained excellent. His own command, the Canadian Corps, he spoke of with the highest praise, observing that if the present policy of "continued, persistent, determined wearing away of German strength was persisted in" that it "would be the quickest road to victory." Byng's view that the main forces of the enemy must be destroyed was one few officers would dispute. What he recognized but did not say, however, was that it was necessary to find new, less costly methods of accomplishing the task.

Shortly after returning to France, Byng was elated to learn that he was going to get a chance to fight the kind of intelligent, unorthodox war he envisioned. Summoned by Sir Henry Horne, the dapper commander of British First Army, to a conference on operations, he learned of the major offensive being planned for the summer of 1917. The main effort would be made by the French under General Nivelle. Large British forces would also play a part. On the left, the Canadians would form a strong defensive flank for Third Army's efforts by capturing the northern flank of Vimy Ridge. A British corps would be assigned the task of capturing the remainder. Shortly afterwards, on January 19, First Army informed Byng that his objective had been extended. The Canadians' task would include taking the entire four-mile crest of Vimy Ridge, except for The Pimple. Although an exact date still needed to be set, the timetable called for the operation to be completed by April 1. Byng and his staff had only two months to plan the massive operation, including its artillery component, and train the men who would be involved.

Now Byng's effort to improve the battle-effectiveness of the Canadians was directed to a specific task. This was the capture of what many experts conceded was quite possibly the most topographically impressive and tactically important feature of the entire Western Front. Already Byng knew it well. Situated between the River Scarpe on the south, and the smaller Souchez, lying to the north, Vimy formed what amounted to a nine-mile-long barrier of higher ground barring the western edge of the Douai plain. Its northern half rose above the village of Vimy, dominating the lower slopes pointing to Arras in the south. To the east, the commanding height overlooked the industrial cities of Lens and Douai.

The battle to control Vimy had already exacted a truly horrific toll. In October 1914 Vimy Ridge and Notre Dame de Lorette, its northern spur that extended across the Souchez River, had been seized by the Germans. During the spring and autumn of 1915, the French recaptured most of the Lorette Ridge — at a cost of 150,000 casualties. After attempting three times to take Vimy, they were halted on its western slopes. Joffre and French, the allied commanders, attributed their failure to insufficient and inadequate artillery preparation. Nonetheless, the expenditure on ammunition had been enormous. The assault and preliminary bombardment on September 25 had employed 147,500 rounds of heavy artillery ammunition. An incredible 565,000 rounds had been fired by field artillery as well.

The similarity between Vimy and the recent Canadian experience on the Somme was not lost on Byng. It was obvious that before the Ridge could be successfully stormed, radical improvements would have to be made in tactical methods. As we shall see, the artillery aspect would be the most difficult to solve.

Imposing as such technical difficulties would prove, Byng faced another problem, the solution of which required "faith, confidence, imagination, and knowledge of human nature." This was how to improve the tactics of the infantry. The infantry of 1916 continued to suffer the same horrendous losses as in the early months of the War. The skills of mobile warfare — fire, movement and flexibility, as well as independent action by platoons — had perished with the British Regular Army. In the period following there had been little need for such tactics because of the static condition of the Western Front, and little attention had been devoted to training the Empire's mass armies, including the Canadians. For them, the concept of attack remained an assault of a few hundred yards conducted in waves, the kind they had employed in the killing grounds of the Somme during the battles of

1916. Advancing in the centre of his platoon's line, a lieutenant, perhaps a few yards in advance, could do little but encourage his men by his brave example. At best, he could usually be seen only by those he led. There was no possibility of control by manoeuvre.

As a professional, Byng knew how pre-war infantry had been trained. In 1914, he had observed the skill with which small units had dealt with the Germans near Ypres. Admittedly, the Canadians who had been at St. Julien Wood (Ypres II, or the Second Battle of Ypres) or the Somme had learned something of war and discipline. But such newcomers could scarcely be described as "trained." Before they could be made into soldiers, the small-town Canadians would have to be drilled day after day, week after week. Scrapping the old assault machine, officers would have to teach them to advance at a steady pace, timed to the second, behind their own artillery barrage. In addition, they would have to be taught flexible methods of fighting. Such a transformation would require more than raw courage, which the troops already possessed in abundance. It would also require dedication and discipline. But as Byng was all too aware, the Canadians were notoriously undisciplined.

From the beginning, Byng realized that abandoning old battle methods, in which every soldier functioned as an automaton, involved training officers and NCOs as much as training men. Earlier, he had already made a start at improving the training of platoon commanders at the Corps school. In January, he sent Arthur Currie, the bright and able commander of 1st Division, to visit the French at Verdun to discover what they had learned. Currie's meticulous report confirmed that the infantry should advance in small groups, taking advantage of the lie of the battlefield, also that objectives should be natural features, not easily obliterated trench lines. Henceforth, platoon commanders and NCOs were trained to use their brains in addition to their courage. Even while the planning to capture Vimy proceeded, Byng found time to train both company and battalion commanders in such new techniques.

Despite the fact that Byng's method represented a radical

departure from orthodox military thought of the period, he appeared an unlikely choice to lead the rambunctious Canucks, who proudly boasted they carried their officers into battle "like mascots." On pedigree alone, Julian Byng, born in 1862, the 13th child and 7th son of a titled family, personified a stiff-necked aristocrat. His father was an earl; his mother, a peer's daughter and the bluest of blue bloods. In the 18th century his ancestor, Admiral John Byng, had been executed for dereliction of duty, or, as Voltaire sarcastically quipped, *pour encourager les autres*. Fortunately, though, it had not ended the family military tradition. Byng's grandfather had been a field marshal. "Bungo" himself, as Byng was christened during his schooldays by fellow aristocrats, was a product of Eton's playing fields and a friend from boyhood of the King.

Having grown up with horses, Byng was destined, initially at least, to join the cavalry, traditionally the most conservative of the army's branches. As a cavalry officer, he served in the outposts of Empire, including India and the Sudan, where the British lived by the old rules. Still, something of the innovator that was in his spirit was already hinted at in India, where he had given orders to alter the high collars of his men's jackets, so that they could wear them open in the sweltering heat. Although a minor decision, it was typical. To Byng, a soldier was never a mere digit or name on the casualty lists. Throughout his career, he never committed a patrol to battle without saying a prayer for its safe return.

Byng was no "Colonel Blimp," despite his professionalism and lineage. Far more than any other officer of comparable rank in His Majesty's service, he belied the image of the spit-and-polish Great War career officer. He was casual in dress, Spartan to the extreme in his habits, and invariably affable, even a favourite, with all ranks. Above all, he was an innovator. He possessed none of the stuffy formality and lack of imagination usually associated with his class of Briton. Even his senior Canadian commander, Arthur Currie, the subject of our next chapter, who was famous for his own strong interest in the ordinary soldier, was in fact considerably more aloof than Byng ever was.

The one quality Byng shared with Currie, as well as other Canadian divisional commanders, was flexibility of mind. Certainly he refused "to conform to outworn rules." This would be the key ingredient required to win at Vimy. Andrew Macphail, a physician and officer who hated politicians and stiff brass, was even more enthusiastic about Byng. Perhaps this was because he sensed in him the same qualities he so admired in Currie. Macphail graphically recorded in his diary the first sight he had of the new corps commander in July 1916. His unit, which was expecting the commander to arrive, as corps commanders usually did, escorted by troopers riding in advance and preceded by a cavalry orderly carrying the commander's pennant on a lance, was more than surprised. As he noted with approval: "He came into the horselines through a hedge, jumping the ditch as unaffectedly as a farmer would have come on a neighbour's place to look at his crops . . . this is a soldier — large, strong, lithe, with worn boots and frayed putties."

Byng looked at Macphail's men and their weapons. He also looked at their mess tins to ensure that every man had one and that they were clean. Such meticulous attention to the day-to-day welfare of the soldiers he commanded was typical of the man. Years earlier, he had even taught himself how meat was butchered, to ensure that his regiment was not cheated in the quantity or quality of rations purchased for its mess.

On Byng's part it should be mentioned that when he first learned that he was to command the Canadians, he was perplexed. Already a corps commander in the British Army, he did not on the face of it consider his new job a promotion. "Why am I sent to the Canadians?" he puzzled. "I don't know a Canadian. Why this stunt? I am sorry to leave the old Corps as we are fighting like hell and killing Boches. However, there it is. I am ordered to these people and will do my best but I don't know there is any congratulation about it."

Whether he realized it or not, Byng was well qualified for the command. Perhaps more than any other British officer he possessed extensive experience in commanding and working with

Empire troops. During the South African War he had established an excellent record commanding a pick-up force of loyal South African militia. More recently, during the disastrous Gallipoli Campaign of 1915, the object of which was to force the Dardanelles, Byng had commanded ANZAC forces. He had ultimately conducted the near-impossible night embarkation which brought the beleaguered troops off the beaches without suffering a single casualty.

Byng's new appointment would be one of the best-matched command decisions of the Great War. Indeed, he would be "the right man in the right place at the right time" to assume command of the Canadian Corps from General Alderson, its first commander. Even at this stage of the war it was a unique command, with a strong sense of its own identity. Unlike the British army, where a corps was little more than a skeleton headquarters in which divisions came and went, the four Canadian divisions were always kept up to strength. In addition, while a British division numbered about 15,000 men, at least at full strength, at Vimy the Canadian figure exceeded 21,000. In short, the Canadian Corps that Byng now found himself commanding was, in a sense, already a small army.

Byng exuded a personal manner ideally suited to his new command. Fifty-four years of age, he was a handsome man with knowing blue eyes. His lean face, brown as shoe leather, was set off by a large military moustache. In other Allied armies, the commander was more often than not some distant figure who seldom ventured from headquarters and was rarely seen by the private soldier. Such, however, was not Byng's style. From the beginning, he seemed to be everywhere, sometimes mounted, more usually on foot, his boots spattered with mud. Already famous for his informal habit of not bothering to take his hand out of his tunic to return a salute, he circulated freely with the soldiers — questioning, chatting, fraternizing with the ordinary private, both at work and at rest. Immediately warming to him, the rough, young Canadians soon began to call themselves "Byng Boys," the name of a popular London review of the period. Paradoxically, however, no two physical descriptions of the General would be quite the same. Some described him big, some tall; others describe him as lithe, still others charge that he was bulky. All say that he was strong, "with a strong jaw, strong hands, and a strong walk." Overall, the impression that emerges is of a powerful, even commanding presence, but also a commander who possessed the common touch.

During the time he was reforming the Corps, Byng was also busy formulating his plans to capture the Ridge. The operation was scheduled sometime after March 15, 1917. Byng's plans for taking Vimy were sent to his superior, Sir Henry Horne, on March 5. With only minor modifications to the artillery program, this Scheme of Operations would be the basis for the attack as it developed. In its essentials, it called for the four Canadian divisions, in numerical order from the right, to assault the obstacle together. The 5th British Division, in Corps reserve, would allocate its 13th Brigade to Canadian Division to participate in the attack on the final objective. Overall, the operation would consist of four distinct stages, each of which corresponded to an element in the German defences. Attaining the Black Line, some 750 yards from the Canadian trenches, would indicate the enemy forward positions had been captured. The next objective, the Red Line, ran to the north along a German trench called Zwischen-Stellung to the crest of the Ridge, and included La Folie Farm and Hill 145. For 3rd and 4th Divisions, attacking on the left, it would be the final objective. But the divisions attacking on the right would have farther to advance. Here, a third report line, the Blue Line, included Thelus village and Hill 135 as well as the woods above the village of Vimy. The Brown Line marked the final objective, the German Second Line and the guns situated in Farbus and Goulot Woods.

Operations called for all four Canadian Divisions to assault the Ridge together at 5:30 a.m. The timetable allowed them 35 minutes to reach the Black Line. Here, a pause of 40 minutes would allow both infantry and the creeping artillery barrage to resume the advance together. Twenty minutes later they were to attain the Red Line. This would bring 3rd and 4th Divisions to the far side of the Ridge by 7:05 a.m. First and 2nd Divisions, after halting for two and a half hours, would send forward their reserve brigades as well as 13th British brigade on the left to capture the Blue Line. Then the advance would pause for 96 minutes before moving beyond the Ridge to the Brown Line, the final objective, which the timetable stipulated should be attained by 1:18 p.m.

For once, Byng had sufficient artillery. For close support of the attacking infantry he could call on the guns of seven divisions plus eight independent field artillery brigades. This gave him a total of 480 18-pounders and 138 4.2-inch howitzers. Additionally, he could employ the immense firepower of 11 heavy artillery groups, consisting of 245 heavy guns and howitzers. The artillery of British 1st Corps provided a further 132 heavy and 10 field guns. To draw a simple comparison, at the Somme the ratio of artillery had been a heavy gun to each 57 yards of front. At Vimy the ratio would be one heavy gun to each 20 yards, as well as a field gun for every 10 yards of front. Overall, some 42,500 tons of ammunition were allocated to the operation, in addition to a daily quota of 2,465 tons.

But as Byng and his staff knew only too well, all the training and rehearsing in the world would not save the Canadian Corps if the enemy wire remained intact. The British High Command had been sobered by the Somme's tragedy, where, on the first day of the offensive, 20,000 British soldiers had been blown to bits. The stark reality was that the guns had not been able to cut the German wire, which formed an impenetrable barrier, 80 feet thick in places, with barbed rolls as high as a house. To deal with the problem, Byng and his brilliant chief gunner, Brigadier-General Edward "Dinky" Morrison, pressed hard through every possible channel for supplies of the new No. 106 fuse, which finally made it possible to clear barbed wire defences in advance of an infantry assault.

It had taken Allied commanders two years to learn that shrapnel, with its hundreds of steel balls per shell, was designed to kill men, not clear obstacles. Exploding in mid-air, it scarcely made a dent in the wire. The obvious solution to this problem was the development of the new fuse and the abandonment of shrapnel as a wire-clearing device. The fuse caused high-explosive shells to burst on contact, and to drive deep into the mass of wire. There, they tore it to shreds and ripped great gaps through which attacking troops could move. Once the new fuses began to reach the Vimy sector in mid-January, both Byng and Morrison breathed easier.

Nor had Byng any intention of repeating the folly of British and French commanders who sent massed men against massed enemy machine guns. To deal with the problem of enemy firepower, including both machine guns and artillery, Byng reached down and plucked the youngest brigade commander in France, requesting him to take charge of counterbattery work.

On January 27, Andrew McNaughton, only twenty-nine, a junior lieutenant-colonel, officially became Byng's counterbattery staff officer. He was given a blank cheque to focus his brilliant scientific mind on the twin problems of pinpoint intelligence and pinpoint accuracy. The position was a new one: there was simply no precedent. Thus McNaughton was faced with the challenge of developing counterbattery work from scratch. Before the Great War was finished, both the Allies and the Germans acknowledged him to be the best artillery officer the British Empire possessed.

The son of Scottish pioneers, a westerner born in what had been the Northwest Territories, McNaughton had already established a considerable reputation. Currie had spotted the McGill-trained engineer and noted him as a "comer." So had Morrison, Byng's chief gunner. A hard worker, McNaughton had put reveille back an hour, in order to gain more time for practice when he first arrived at his battery. The soldiers, who adored him, called him Andy. Now Byng sent him south, as he had with Currie, to see what the French had learned at Verdun and the British at the Somme.

In the end, McNaughton learned little from the French. At British 5th Corps, however, he encountered an unconventional gunner, Lieutenant-Colonel A. G. Haig, cousin of the British Commander-in-Chief. Haig, who had developed singular methods of fire power fighting in Burma's hill-country, told McNaughton of his experiments with flash spotting and sound ranging. In the weeks leading up to Vimy, McNaughton would develop and fine-tune these new techniques, right up to the eve of the attack itself.

While the foot soldiers carefully rehearsed their roles in the battle to come, McNaughton worked with his staff. Their self-assigned task was to nail down the position of every one of the German guns situated on the Ridge or hidden in the woods on its eastern slopes.

Old-line British gunners considered it radical nonsense — that one could actually pinpoint the position of an enemy gun, and then knock it out. Earlier, in 1915, Currie himself had questioningly noted, addressing his artillery adviser: "They fire at the opposing infantry but never at each other." A young Canadian, Harold Hemming, a McGill graduate, serving with British 3rd Army, had been experimenting with flash spotting, a method of locating a gun by triangulating its muzzle flashes. His General, however, was not impressed.

McNaughton, an old friend of Hemming, was eager to learn of his theories. He was also impressed by the ideas of a trio of bright young men he had persuaded to quit the British service and join his staff at Vimy: Lawrence Bragg, Charles Galton Darwin, and Lucien Bull. These men were experts in the new science of sound ranging, the companion to Hemming's flash spotting.

Flash spotting required a series of posts, located all along the front. Each was equipped with telephones and surveying gear, as well as a reporting system linked to a panel of lights at headquarters. So accurate did this system of lights and buzzers ultimately become, Canadian artillery would be able to locate a German gun position with an accuracy of within five yards.

Sound ranging was even more complicated. When an enemy gun began to fire miles away, it triggered a sequence of events. An observer at a listening post, often situated in no-man's-land, pressed a key that activated a recording device at McNaughton's headquarters. A series of microphones picked up the sound as it travelled. From the time-intervals between the microphones the enemy gun's exact location could be pinpointed. Similarly, the sound waves sent out by a shell's bursting on the Canadian side, picked up by a series of microphones, could locate exactly where it had landed and calculations could determine from where it had originated.

Despite the many problems involved, the scientific wizards who joined McNaughton's team were soon able to calculate not only the position of the enemy artillery piece, but also its type, its calibre and the target on which it was registered. Under optimal conditions, they could accomplish the process in three minutes, spotting its location within a 25-yard circle.

In addition to the two methods detailed, a steady flow of information from other sources constantly poured into Canadian headquarters. Especially important were the observation balloons, tethered to the ground and manned by spotters with strong field glasses, which overlooked the Ridge itself. From a mile up, observers in their flimsy baskets could see far behind the enemy lines.

Once hidden guns were located, McNaughton's and his gunners' task was to hit them and blow them up, forcing the enemy either to repair or move them. The Canadians would hit them again and again, even during the final assault, to make things so hot that enemy gunners couldn't operate. To accomplish this, of course, required stunning accuracy.

Similar accuracy was essential when the Canadian troops moved forward under a canopy of shrieking and flying steel, carefully calculated to explode only a few yards ahead of their advance. The term that soldiers commonly used to describe the procedure was "hugging the barrage." If the range were slightly off, or the shells faulty, infantrymen could die at the hands of their own gunners. Indeed, all generals in the Great War expected at least some casualties from friendly fire. It was the artillery's job to keep such wastage to a minimum. The French, it was reckoned, lost 50,000 men killed by their own shells. By discarding obsolete methods and faulty arithmetic, the Canadians employed science to assist the art of gunnery.

Trenches on Vimy Ridge. Photograph taken from a kite balloon.
Department of National Defence. (NAC/PA-002366)

Although they scarcely looked it, the huge artillery pieces were highly sensitive instruments. Of course the old hands had not treated them as such. Up until now, corrections for wind, weather, and barrel wear had been at best primitive. As McNaughton himself later noted, anyone who attempted to develop greater accuracy in shooting "was looked on as somebody who ought to have his head read — this wasn't war at all, this was some sort of fandango going on."

Still, Andy persisted. His meticulous experiments would be breathtaking. An example is his experiments into the problem of barrel wear. An 18-pounder, firing at a range of 8,000 yards, could lose 300 yards during its life. This was sufficient to kill all the troops moving behind the curtain of shells it was laying down. But this was only an average barrel; some guns wore out faster than others. Thanks to McNaughton's scientific background, and the fact that he employed an electrical chronograph to measure a gun's muzzle velocity, every key gun in the Vimy battle would be individually calibrated.

Old rules of thumb no longer applied. Falling air pressure, as recorded by a barometer, could make a difference of 300 yards on a 5,000 yard shot. A strong wind could push a large shell 15 yards off target. McNaughton and his counterbattery staff would change all this, adjusting range tables to account for weather, and revising dangerously inaccurate French maps of the battlefield. In this, air observation played a crucial role.

To prevent heavy casualties, such as those suffered by infantry in the Somme fighting, and to provide a covering route, Byng ordered 12 of the tunnels that had earlier been driven through the Ridge's chalky soil developed and extended. Adjoining chambers were excavated for headquarters, signals, dressing stations and ammunition storage. There were also large chambers in which troops could wait in safety. At the tunnels' ends, exits led to the front and support lines, as well as mortar and machine gun posts.

Byng's Scheme of Operations, which could only be called revolutionary, laid down measures to coordinate the advance of divisions. Flank units were trained to form defensive positions and to envelop "strong points or centres of resistance." Reserves were to be "pushed in behind those portions of the line that are successful rather than those which are held up." Units of every size, from platoons to divisions, repeatedly rehearsed their respective assignments on a full-scale replica of the battle area laid out in fields behind the lines. Everything possible was done to simulate realism. Mounted officers with flags led units forward anticipating the pace of the rolling barrage, soldiers carried everything they would require in battle, and every foreseeable stage of the advance was practised. This included climbing out of assault trenches, crossing broken ground, and reducing strong points. Almost daily Byng himself was there carefully watching.

A huge plasticine model of the Ridge was constructed at First Army HQ, reproducing in detail every enemy trench, dugout and

Canadian troops in trenches on Western Front.
Courtesy Esprit de Corps.

strong point. Subordinate officers and NCOs taking part in the attack were given ample time to study their unit's objectives in detail and to develop plans to deal with problems they faced. Often, the commander himself took part in the discussions, guiding, listening, attempting to discover weaknesses that remained to be solved.

Most importantly, Byng treated the Canadian soldier as an adult capable of thought. As such, he impressed the men as a straightforward chap who knew his work and had their best interests at heart. By taking the Canucks into his confidence, Byng "inspired them in a way which never could have been achieved by rhetoric or any other shallow device." Finally, Byng ordered a wide-scale issue of maps of the battlefield. This had a psychological impact on the ordinary soldiers quite over and above the men's satisfaction at having received a useful aid.

Only the date of the attack, set for April 9, remained secret. As it approached, everyone knew his specific role in the assault as well as those of both his commander and neighbours. The thoroughness of training was unprecedented in Allied armies. Nor had the raiding stopped while preparations were being made. Nightly, raiders, armed with truncheons, grenades and explosives, burst into some unlucky German position, blowing up dugouts and hustling a prisoner or two back across no-man's-land. Also, much information was gleaned by pilots of the Royal Flying Corps, acting as spotters, who directed the fire of both Canadian and British guns against hidden targets.

A week prior to the attack, the full weight of Andy McNaughton's counterbattery fury swept over the hapless garrison of the Vimy massif. Explosive shells collapsed trenches and blew gaping holes in the protective wire. The destruction of an area completed, the artillery switched its attention to other targets. Meanwhile, machine guns took over, laying down deadly streams of bullets under which the enemy could not move, let alone hope to repair his damaged lines. Even villages lying behind the Ridge were bombarded, as were roads and communications trenches. The intense barrage made the task of German ration parties, charged with bringing food up to the front line, immeasurably more dangerous and time-consuming. In many cases it proved impossible. As a result, frontline companies now found hunger and sleeplessness had been added to the other perils they routinely faced.

Byng and McNaughton dispensed with the intense heavy artillery bombardment that customarily announced an assault. At nightfall on April 8, assault battalions began to move to forward assembly areas. Not all sheltered in the protected subways. Above ground, lead companies, filing through gaps blown in the wire, took shelter in the shell holes of no-man's-land to await the signal to attack. They shivered somewhat as a bitter northwest wind drove snow and sleet across the battlefield. But the Canadians, best among the soldiers fighting on the Western Front, were accustomed to such conditions. Also, on Byng's orders, each man had been provided with a hot meal as well as a ration of rum before setting out. By 4 a.m. on this decisive day, 52 battalions, some 30,000 Canadians in all, had deployed in the darkness along the four-mile front. In many places, their lead companies already lay within 100 yards of enemy positions without giving alarm.

Byng had moved his headquarters up to Berthenual Farm in order to be near his troops. From here, he would be separated by only three miles from even the most distant divisional headquarters he commanded. During the night the farmhouse's bare wood floors echoed with the boots of dozens of officers coming and going, reporting the progress of the assembly for battle. At last, as dawn approached on April 9, there remained little that even the Corps Commander could do, save utter a prayer, as Byng invariably did.

Suddenly, at 5:30 a.m. the entire front lit up with a sheet of flame. Nearly 1,000 guns and mortars, under McNaughton's command, opened fire in support of the infantry. After descending on the enemy's main trenches and lingering for three minutes, the main barrage then continued. It proceeded to lift 100 yards every three minutes, rolling over the enemy's forward zones. Even before the barrage's first move, or lift forward, Canadian infantry were on their feet, advancing. The load each soldier bore as he sprang into battle was formidable. In addition to rifle and bayonet, he carried his haversack on his back, mess tin, and gas respirator. Under these he wore an overcoat; some of the troops had protective leather jerkins that served as a primitive flak-jacket. Every man carried either a pick or shovel, four hand grenades, two sandbags, two aeroplane flares, a Verey light, candles and a box of matches. Additionally, his back-breaking load included two days' rations, as well as an iron ration.

There are many detailed accounts of Vimy Ridge. None can convey the entire story in detail. Overall, the three Canadian divisions on the right succeeded marvellously, taking all their objectives on schedule. These included Thelus Village and Hill 135, La

Folie Farm, as well as the enemy guns in Farbus and Goulot Woods. Only on the extreme left did 4th Division run into difficulties. Thus, Hill 145 would not be taken until April 10. Two days later, on April 12, attackers succeeded in capturing The Pimple, leaving the whole of Vimy Ridge in Canadian hands.

At first, opposition was slight and enemy artillery fire particularly poor. Soon, though, advancing troops came under heavy machine gun and rifle fire. The massive bombardment, however, had obliterated German front trenches. Soldiers reaching them passed them by without recognition; only broken cupolas and traces of what had been observation posts remained. Underfoot, the badly drained earth had been pulverized into great puddles of clammy mud. Byng's careful planning had chosen zero hour at 5:30 to give infantry enough light to see their way through shell holes, shattered trenches, tangled remnants of wire obstacles and vast mine craters that required bypassing. But generally, conditions proved insufficient for the enemy to distinguish more distant attackers. Clouds, driving rain and sleet obscured the half-light before the dawn. So well rehearsed were the infantry that few became disoriented.

By 6:25 a.m. 1st, 2nd, and 3rd Divisions had overrun the entire German forward defence zone. At this point, fresh units moved through their lines to continue the assault. Now it was light enough for the Canadians to see where they were going. The German defenders were less fortunate. The wind, having shifted, now drove snow directly across the front line into their eyes. On the far right, on 1st Division's sector, the Bavarian defenders did not see the attack coming until the Canucks were almost on top of them, with lunging bayonets. Most were either captured or fled. Second Division, fighting hard, cleared the hamlet of Les Tilleuls, in the process capturing two enemy battalion headquarters, a pair of field guns, as well as 500 prisoners as it pressed forward to the Red Line.

Third Division reached the Red Line, on the crest of Vimy Ridge, at 7:30 a.m. The two divisions on its right, which had farther to advance, required half an hour longer. As planned, the Canadians bore two Vickers heavy machine guns forward with each battalion, to repel counterattacks. Two battalions with 1st Canadian Mounted Rifles, on the division's right, surprised a large party of the enemy on the slopes below, killing over 100 of the staff and men of a German battalion that was abandoning its headquarters situated at a tunnel entrance.

La Folie Farm fell to 2nd Canadian Mounted Rifles. Meanwhile, to the Royal Canadian Regiment's left, the Princess Patricia's Canadian Light Infantry made good use of Byng's new infantry tactics. Advancing by rushes, two leading companies closed on the enemy, reaching their final objective at the cost of only 50 casualties. After storming Zwischen-Stellung and La Folie Wood, 3rd Division dug in, sending forward patrols down the slopes towards Petit Vimy.

On the right, 1st and 2nd Divisions resumed their assault on the Blue Line, securing this objective shortly before 11 a.m. Mopping up, the Canadians took prisoner large numbers of enemy troops who had taken refuge in a series of caves, to escape the horrendous Allied shellfire. One lieutenant bagged over 100 enemy in a single cave, as attackers routed out Germans using a special smoke bomb designed to drive defenders from dugouts and caves.

As attackers reached Vimy's summit, the sun broke magnificently through the morning's menacing storm clouds. Suddenly the air was clean and clear, filled with spring sunshine. Ahead and below, the infantry could see red-roofed houses, set incongruously in green fields, untouched by war's ravages. The only enemy in sight were a few parties of grey-clad infantry straggling away to eastward.

Although the leading units reported the Germans to be on the run, Byng's orders were explicit. They called for him to capture Vimy and hold it as a bastion on the flank of the Arras offensive. Already the war had seen many initial successes ruined by successful German counterattacks. Byng's plan required time for each objective to be secured. If all restraints were removed now, such precautions would be abandoned, and the complex artillery plan that had ensured the infantry's success would also have to be scrapped. Quite correctly, Byng refused to do this.

Ninety minutes after the storming of the Blue Line, the assault on the final line, the Brown, commenced. On the right, Griesbach's 1st Brigade, advancing on Farbus Wood, found the guns that had been concealed in it abandoned. McNaughton's barrage having driven their gunners to seek safety, the artillery was taken without difficulty.

On the left, the German resistance was the hottest of the entire battle. Enemy artillery situated in the Bois de la Ville opened fire at point-blank range from concrete gun positions on 6th Brigade as it came over the slope. Nonetheless, the leading Canadians, charging downhill, bayoneted or captured the gunners. Eventually, the Canadians took 250 prisoner, including the commander and staff of 3rd Bavarian Reserve Regiment.

First and 2nd Divisions had taken their objectives, as planned. By early afternoon, 2nd Division's patrols were pushing through Farbus Village and beyond, and the Brigadier of the foremost troops was champing at the bit to continue the assault. Had it been possible to continue the pursuit in conjunction with the troops of other nearby divisions, the Canadians might well have swept through the line of villages beyond. Later, their defences would prove a formidable obstacle, and delay attackers for a considerable period. But the range of the protecting artillery had been reached. Slipping, slithering, fighting and swearing, gunners strove to force their horses on. But the guns were half buried in mud, and the wheels had nothing to grab. That evening 6th Brigade would attempt to seize the railway line and station situated east of Farbus Wood. But the enemy defended it strongly, employing machine guns.

On the left, or north, of the Corps, Major-General David Watson's 4th Division's attack on a front of 2,000 yards was not proceeding well. Its main objective, Hill 145, which afforded a commanding view, not only of Vimy itself, but also of the enemy rearguard defences situated on the Douai Plain beyond, was the most heavily defended position. As the Ridge's most important feature, the Germans realized that, were they to lose it, positions of defender and attacker would be dramatically reversed.

At 3 p.m. artillery had opened fire on the Hangstellung, or dugouts, lying below the crest. Fifteen minutes later, the 44th (Manitoba) and 50th (Calgary) Battalions charged down the slope, clearing them with bayonet and bomb. Within half an hour the formidable Hangstellung fortifications were taken. By late afternoon, the 44th had cleared the remainder of La Folie Wood. Finally, 12th Brigade was able to move its right flank forward to secure 11th Brigade's Red Line. By evening Brigadier-General Victor Odlum's 11th Brigade had pushed just short of the crest. Towards morning on April 10 the austere and teetotaller Odlum ("Old Lime Juice") would lead the last, desperate charge that surged over the hill's rim and occupied the trench that lay beyond, successfully holding it against a weak counterattack.

The "Southern Operation" was now complete. Vimy Ridge's main portion was safely in Canadian hands. On their right, British 51st Division had also secured its objectives. More than any other battle of the Great War, the assault had progressed exactly as planned. Except for the formidable obstacles 4th Division encountered, there had been little need for either Byng or his divisional commanders to intervene in the hour-to-hour direction of the battle.

On April 12, the final stage of the Vimy Battle commenced. A force consisting of 44th and 50th Battalions, as well as two companies of the 46th, crossed Zouhave Valley, then ascended the overlooking slopes to within 200 yards of the crest. Here, they waited in assembly trenches for another zero hour: this time to capture the northern end of Vimy Ridge, or The Pimple, as well as the spurs splaying out from it. As the attack began, a westerly gale was driving a blizzard of snow and sleet towards the enemy positions. It increased in force as the infantry began to advance at 5 a.m. through heavy, clinging mud. The enemy, not expecting a night attack, was completely surprised. Resistance was disorganized. The Saskatchewans, working steadily forward, established their Lewis guns above the Souchez. The Calgaries took their final objective by 5:45. Finally, at 6:45 the Manitobas secured The Pimple itself.

At daybreak the storm lifted. Bright sunshine enabled the three western battalions to view their accomplishment. To the south was the summit of Hill 145, cleared by them 36 hours earlier. Directly in front, stretching to the eastern horizon, lay the Douai plain. From the left, below them were Angres, Lievin and Avion, lying in front of Lens and its coal mines. On the flat ground below, German troops and transports could be seen hurrying towards the east.

The great victory won by the Canadians at Vimy was in large measure due to the artillery's effective contribution. Certainly Vimy set a new standard in the artillery's ability to safeguard such an infantry assault, employing counterblows. Even before the Canadian heavy artillery had moved forward, the arrival at the Ridge's crest of observation officers and signallers early in the battle had enabled the guns to take on many secondary targets. Not only had they broken up counterattacks, they had also shot up enemy guns and transport on the plain below. In addition, thanks to Andy McNaughton's meticulous planning, a number of German field pieces (in some cases with as many as 1,000 rounds of ammunition per gun) were soon pouring a heavy rain of fire on hostile trenches and enemy battery positions on the plain below, bombarding the enemy with his own gas shells.

Major credit, however, must go to Byng himself. (Or, as he would soon be known for his singular achievement, Field Marshal the Viscount Byng of Vimy.) Certainly, Canadians were sceptical about the idea that rank gave one an automatic right to lead. The ordinary soldier had volunteered for war, which he regarded as a horrendous business that should be finished as quickly as possible. All he asked of his officers was that they knew their jobs and how to accomplish them, and Byng fulfilled this role admirably.

Later, General McNaughton summed up the feelings Canadian soldiers had towards General Byng when he termed him the "wonderful commander who did so much to establish our identity, our unity of purpose and our general attitude towards life and our mission in it. He was in fact literally adored by the Canadians who were in France."

On June 9, 1917, Julian Byng took his final leave of his beloved Canadians. As Lieutenant T. A. Rowatt of the 39th Battalion noted in a letter sent to his parents, the General's departure typified the man:

> He came in quietly, walked up between the two lines [of officers], turned about and faced the château and without looking at anyone began to speak. It appeared he was afraid to look at anyone lest he become overwhelmed with emotion. After he had spoken, he walked away alone, head down and everyone could only stand and stare until one of the other Generals walked off with him. Then we all ran around to a road leading from the château to cheer him as he passed. He is a wonderfully solid looking man, with, I should say, a rather large head, not tall but rather stocky looking. Simple, unaffected and, of course, sad looking and mannered as was natural. He said when he started to speak that he had come to honour the saddest and hardest thing he had ever done.

SELECTED READINGS

Berton, Pierre. *Vimy*. Toronto: McClelland and Stewart, 1986.

McCulloch, Ian. "Bungo and the Byng Boys: General Sir Julian Byng on the road to Vimy Ridge." *The Beaver* 76:6 (Dec. 1996/ Jan. 1997): 20–27.

Nicholson, G. W. L. *Canadian Expeditionary Force, 1914–1919*. (Official History of the Canadian Army in the First World War.) Ottawa: Queen's Printer, 1962.

Reid, Brian A. "The Artillery Battle for Vimy." *Esprit de Corps: Canadian Military Then and Now* 1:11 (April 1992): 54–56.

"75 Years Ago . . . Dulce et Decorum Est." *Esprit de Corps: Canadian Military Then and Now* 1:11 (April 1992): 72–75.

Williams, Jeffrey. *Byng of Vimy: General and Governor General*. London: Leo Cooper in association with Secker and Warburg, 1983.

NOTE: CANADA'S ARTILLERYMEN

On the Western Front, the 18-pound field gun, which had been retained in the British Army by the narrowest of votes, would prove the artillery's workhorse. Indeed, for every shot fired by the lighter, more mobile 13-pound weapon, Byng and McNaughton's Canadians would fire 70 employing the heavier gun. The 4.2-inch howitzer, with its barrel slanting upward at a 45-degree angle, and firing a 35-pound shell, was its companion. Heavier models included the 6-inch, which hurled high-explosive shells more than six miles, also the 8-inch, which fired a 180-pound shell. The largest howitzer coming under Canadian command (the biggest howitzers and naval guns remained under British Army command) was the gigantic 9.2-inch howitzer, which hurled a 290-pound projectile capable of pulverizing enemy fortifications and batteries, and which had to be disassembled and transported in three sections.

To deploy such weapons and keep them firing required a small army of specialists. Two hundred men were needed to man a single battery of four 18-pounders. Although the gunner's lot was safer than that of the infantry man, the work was demanding. At Vimy, it would be the gunners, stripped bare to the waist, sweating despite rain and sleet, manhandling shells into their weapons' breeches, hour after hour, with little rest or respite, who proved the real victors in the battle to seize the Ridge. Canadians also demonstrated that the Vickers machine gun as well as the more portable Lewis, with its cylindrical drum-feed, could be used as a form of light artillery. The man behind the revolution was Brigadier-General Raymond Brutinel, father of the Canadian Motor Machine Gun Corps, whose unorthodox views had been honed, like McNaughton's, on Canada's northwest frontier.

Sir Arthur Currie as a young officer.
Glenbow Archives Collection. (NA-1715-1)

15

LIEUTENANT-GENERAL SIR ARTHUR CURRIE

The Canadian Corps and the Final Hundred Days

Sir Arthur Currie (1875–1933), a realtor from Victoria, distinguished himself by becoming the first native-born commander of the Canadian Corps during World War I. As a brigadier, he participated in 1st Canadian Division's battles at Ypres in 1915, and later commanded the Division. In June 1917, he succeeded Sir Julian Byng, a British officer, as Corps commander. A militiaman operating in the British Army, the bulky Currie was certainly an anomaly, nor did he conform to the stereotype of the typical officer. As detailed here, Currie's outstanding successes came, not at Passchendaele, but during the conflict's final hundred days, beginning August 8, 1918. During this epic period, his Canadians, one of two "star" British Empire army groups, engaged a quarter of the enemy on the Western Front. The Canadian Corps' attacks resulted in spectacular gains and inflicted heavy losses on the Germans. Appropriately, Currie and his troops would occupy historic Mons, the Belgian town where the war had commenced four years earlier, even as the Armistice took effect.

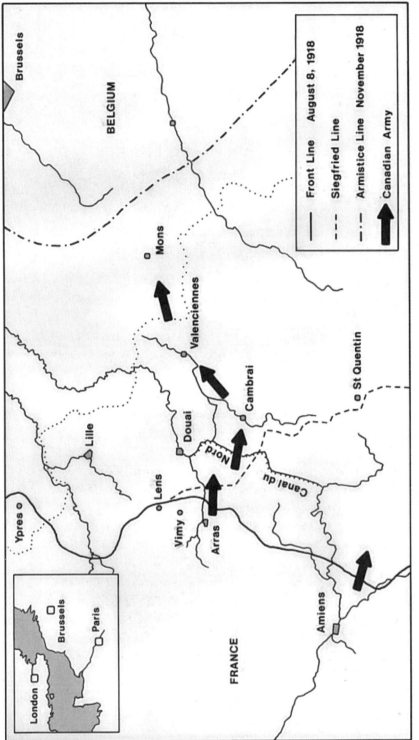

Canadian Army Corps' operations, Aug.–Nov. 1918

Legend:
Front Line August 8, 1918
Siegfried Line
Armistice Line November 1918
Canadian Army

Brussels

BELGIUM

Mons

Valenciennes

Cambrai

St Quentin

Douai

Lille

Nord

Canal du

Lens

Vimy

Arras

Ypres

Amiens

FRANCE

London

Brussels

Paris

By the Great War's heroic final year, Lieutenant-General Arthur Currie and his Canadians had certainly seen their share of war. In the course of the preceding four years he and his staff had forged a national fighting machine that stood second to none. By 1918 Currie's Canadians would be the single formation of the British Army that specialized in winning the attritional type of battle that has come to be associated with the Great War. Of this necessary but unenviable role, the General's biographer, Daniel G. Dancocks, has written: "This wearing-down process involved long, bloody campaigns, often in adverse weather conditions, and with millions of men taking part, the butcher's bill was grim." In such fighting, where death and stalemate were common currencies, the Dominion's force would number just over 100,000 men. Although this was small in terms of the overall strategic picture, it was of sufficient size to exert a significant impact on the Western Front's battles. The formation's name was the Canadian Army Corps.

Battle's perverse fortune is that it often causes hidden abilities to bubble to the surface. At least in certain men. Arthur Curry (he later changed the spelling to the more socially acceptable "Currie") was born, third of seven children, on a farm near Strathroy, Ontario, in 1875. However, there was little — either in his family background, or seemingly in the youth himself — to hint at his later distinguished military record. A tall, skinny youngster, he would later grow into an imposing young man, six-feet-four-inches tall, weighing nearly 200 pounds. As he matured, he would continue to fill out, eventually developing a truly impressive girth. From childhood onwards, young Arthur suffered stomach complaints. Later, the uncomplaining Currie would endure them on a daily basis during the course of the war, with all the stress they would engender.

After earning his Matriculation Certificate, the youth, seeking to better himself, moved west and taught school, in both Victoria and nearby Sidney. After marrying, he entered the more profitable insurance and real-estate businesses. He also joined the militia, as an avenue of social advancement in class-conscious Victoria. By 1909, Currie, aged thirty-three, was lieutenant-colonel, the highest rank the pre-Great War Militia had to offer. A newspaper photo of the period shows an authoritative-looking officer, in Highland dress uniform, plumed bonnet by his side, since he was the Commanding Officer of the 50th Gordon Highlanders. Currie's calm demeanour conveys a convincing sense of self-confidence. The image would be hauntingly prophetic. Transferring to the artillery, he was given command of the "Dandy 5th," which was acknowledged to be "the best gunnery unit in the Dominion," winning combined honours four years out of five running. During a visit by General Sir Ian Hamilton, the battery, personally commanded by the young battalion officer, achieved its finest moment, easily riddling the target, a canvas screen towed by a launch. When the British officer commended him and his men, the young Colonel replied, with a boyish grin, hazel eyes twinkling in the sun, "We haven't tried yet, sir." Then the gunners went to work once more. They fired four rounds, neatly severing the connecting rope.

Currie's singular accomplishment would see him rise past field rank, without benefit of professional military training, first to wear a major-general's red tabs and ultimately those of a lieutenant-general. It was an achievement that could not have been duplicated in the tradition-bound British Army of the period, where personal background and education counted far more than tactical competence. Neither would the Canadian commander's persona even remotely suggest a general. The stereotypical officer of the period resembled Sir John French: ramrod-erect, leanly fit, firm-eyed, chiselled face usually set off by a carefully clipped moustache. Currie, in contrast, remained clean-shaven. His broad face, with its open countenance, would retain an adolescent fleshiness well into middle life, and he sported a double chin. His intelligent eyes exuded a friendly, though intelligent glint, and his immense body was, as Pierre Berton has noted, "shaped like a gigantic pear." Aside from his immaculately kept uniform, there was nothing that could remotely be described as "dapper" about the towering, bulky Currie. Indeed, men who served under him loved to allude to their chief as "Guts and Gaiters."

Although he fell well short of the image of the perfect British officer, it did not take Currie long to establish his reputation as one of the ablest commanders the Western Front would produce. A grateful Prime Minister Robert Borden considered him the equivalent of any corps commander in the war. In his meteoric rise, the young officer would vault over two other officers, both senior in age and experience: Louis James Lipsett and Henry Burstall, a regular army officer. Field Marshal Lord Byng, vetting a list of potential Chiefs of Staff, is purported to have placed his thumb alongside Currie's name and said: "Of him, there are no 'ifs.'" In his mastery of himself, Currie reminded one British war correspondent of Oliver Cromwell, Lord Protector. David Lloyd George, Britain's prime minister, whose loathing of Sir Douglas Haig was pathological, had no problem with Currie. If anything, he praised the Canadian's "great ability and strength of purpose." Although Empire and world would thankfully be spared the experience, had the grim struggle continued beyond 1918, very likely Currie would have succeeded to command all British forces. The talented Australian general Sir John Monash would have been his able chief of staff.

Currie's greatest strength was that he suffered from no illusions concerning the kind of war that was being fought. The human cost of such a "war of attrition," as he wrote, was staggering. Even today, the Great War's tragedy continues both to fascinate and horrify historians. Ralph Allen, a Canadian journalist and author, has likened generalship of the period to "two near-sighted men caught in a revolving door." The main problem was that the majority of military professionals, particularly on the Allied side, had prepared for a Napoleonic style of conflict — armies marching into battle with banners flying, with a surfeit of cavalry to support the infantry. But technological advances, also the sheer and unprecedented size of the armies involved, now conspired against such generals.

Currie's clearly perceived views of how to wage war, gained from observing the French and others, would be adopted into the Canadian Corps, some immediately, others more gradually, and would reshape it into the superb fighting force it became. And the General's vision would prove to be remarkably durable. Tac-

Under Currie, static warfare would soon become mobile.
Courtesy Esprit de Corps.

tical and technological advances, including the employment of massed tank formations and the revolutionary 106 Fuse for efficient wire-cutting, rendered lengthy preliminary bombardments obsolete by 1918. This would enable the Allies to achieve genuine surprise attacks. But Currie's many other ideas — such as stressing the necessity of tactical manoeuvre, preparation, careful rehearsal, proper training and adequate military intelligence — would remain valid for the remainder of the war, indeed, the next conflict as well.

By early 1917 it seemed a turning point in the war had been reached. As military historian John Swettenham has observed, it was "significant that no later Corps attack when planned by Currie was ever unsuccessful." As already detailed, the truth of this axiom would be demonstrated during the battle for Vimy Ridge. Additionally, as Andy McNaughton later stated, in an even larger sense, Currie would stand out "as the individual who made the Canadian Corps." During the winter of 1917 he staunchly resisted the hard-pressed British Army's attempts to reduce, not only its own, but also Canada's divisions, from twelve to nine battalions each, in order to deal with the glaring manpower shortage. Not only would the proposed reorganization have been extremely cumbersome; it would have diluted the excellent staff already in existence. Popular as the so-called expansion in the number of divisions might have been with politicians, most of the new officers created would have been incompetent hangers-on. To his credit, Currie prevailed, after going head-to-head with both British brass and Canadian politicians. His down-to-earth solution was to break up the "useless" Canadian 5th Division and add 100 soldiers to each Canadian battalion. This actually put more bayonets into the field.

When General Erich Ludendorff's offensive in the spring and summer of 1918 sent Allied armies reeling back in disarray, Currie again proved a rock of solidity. He invoked his "cold," even "ruthless" manner to thwart General Headquarters' plan to strip 1st and 2nd Divisions, then 3rd and 4th, from his control, and place them directly under British command. When Currie complained that it was not the way to maximize the contribution Canadians were capable of making, Sir Douglas Haig, the Commander-in-Chief, wondered aloud whether "some people in Canada regard themselves as 'allies' [rather] than as fellow citizens of Empire." It was his way of commenting on, what appeared to him at least, the Canadians' lack of team spirit. Shortly afterwards, though, the Dominion's sons returned to their own service. Along with Sir John Monash's Australian Corps, they commenced to prepare themselves for the big push they hoped would finally win the war.

Intentionally held back during the savage enemy-imposed

Emperor's Battle, the object of which was to break through and win the war on the Western Front, the two star army groups of the British Empire team remained ready. Now that the enemy offensive had failed and expended its momentum, the four divisions of Currie's Canadian Corps and Monash's five-division Australian Corps were preparing to take the field.

Retrained by Field Marshal Byng, reorganized under Currie's direction, early in August the Canadian Corps headed south from the Arras front. A printed note that was pasted in soldiers' pay-books ordered: "Keep your mouth shut." The Canadians moved at night, in trucks, past the Somme battlefields where they had fought. A handful moved north to Flanders where signallers employed wireless messages to convince German monitors that an offensive was impending. Meanwhile, the motors of low-flying air-

Tanks advancing down Amiens-Roye Road. Battle of Amiens, August 1914.
Department of National Defence. (NAC/PA-002969)

craft masked the sound of troops, artillery, and tanks moving into forests situated west of Amiens.

At 4:20 a.m., August 8, 1918, at Amiens, the coiled spring that was the Canadian Corps struck the enemy with overwhelming force. Covered by the fire of 900 guns, troops of four Canadian brigades moved forward into dawn's thick mist to attack. Tanks plunged across the landscape and, for the first time in any strength, British aircraft supported a major ground offensive by making strafing attacks against the enemy. Nonetheless, it was guns and infantry that smashed the German defences. By night-fall, the Allies were celebrating their most successful day of the great struggle, which had lasted almost exactly four years. Currie's Canadians had advanced an unheard-of eight miles. On their left, the Australians had pushed forward seven. Fourth Army casualties numbered 9,000. However, the grim cost to the Germans was 27,000 men, 400 artillery pieces and countless mortars and machine guns. Afterwards, General Ludendorff would call it "the blackest day of the German Army in the history of this war." For the enemy, who several months earlier still entertained high hopes of winning the war in the West, it marked the "beginning of the end." Or, as Canadian schoolchildren would shortly be obliged to learn by rote, "a tale of five cities": Amiens, Arras, Cambrai, Valenciennes, and Mons.

Currie himself modestly described the day's work as "a fine success, surpassing anything we have ever done before." In truth, it had been remarkably easy. As 42nd Battalion's war diary recorded, the Canadian advance "was more or less a route march enlivened by the sight of panic-stricken enemy running in every direction" — so unsuspected had been the very speed and depth of the Canadian thrust. The decisive results of the Battle of Amiens underscored the effectiveness of Currie's elaborate methods of deception. His favourite story was that of a captured German medical officer. Congratulating his Canadian counterparts on the success with which wounded had been evacuated, he wryly concluded: "I wish I could congratulate our intelligence service with the same pleasure . . . we thought you were at Mount

Kemmel." To Currie's unconcealed amusement, the enemy had misplaced the Canadian Corps' location by an incredible 70 miles. The Canadians even fooled their own Allies. Currie, who loved a good joke, was clearly delighted when Albert, King of the Belgians, wrote to Marshal Foch, Supreme Commander, to complain that the Canadians were about to launch an assault on Belgium, and he had not been informed!

So unexpected had the scope of the Canadian and Australian advance been that senior officers hurried up to GHQ to see Currie. When they asked what he thought should be done, the Canadian Corps commander could only reply in the vernacular: "The going seems good: let's go on!" So the drive continued. Next day the Canadians managed a further four miles. But now the going was much tougher. Still, as Currie noted, the advance had brought our troops within the area of trenches and defences occupied prior to the Somme operations of 1916. "These trenches, while not in a good state of repair, were . . . protected by a considerable amount of wire, and lent themselves readily to very stubborn machine gun defence."

Currie maintained a high profile. On the first day of the attack, mounted on his favourite charger Brock, "followed by his banner and his orderlies," he galloped toward the front. The spectacle moved one correspondent to note: "In the early afternoon, we saw him riding over the battlefield, a soldierly figure of Canada in action as he rode resolutely forward." To keep up with the rapid advance, he was obliged to move his headquarters frequently. On August 9, he established his headquarters under canvas in a quarry near the village of Demuin. Several staff officers complained about the location, contending that Demuin itself, which had been the site of an enemy divisional headquarters, would be more comfortable. A few hours later German shells flattened the village. Henceforth there was no further griping about the quarry.

By the attack's third day, August 10, the advance had slowed considerably. To rest the weary Canucks, British 32nd Division was placed under Currie's command. When it failed to capture Parvillers, a fortified village on the edge of the Somme offensive belt, Currie replaced it with 3rd Division, commanded by Louis Lipsett, a former British officer serving with the Canadians. Two days later, following painstaking preparations, the 3rd stormed and seized Parvillers, at the cost of only five casualties. The incident was but another example of the stark difference that prevailed between the Canadian and British style of fighting at this decisive stage of the struggle.

As already detailed, four years of intense battle had schooled Currie and his Canadians in how to wage war. One of the qualities that rendered him an outstanding commander was that he knew when to fight. And when not to. On August 13 he recommended that the Amiens battle be halted. Characteristically, Currie noted: "Four years of war has taught us that troops cannot cross uncut barbed wire without suffering enormous casualties, and I am not going to have a good operation spoiled by over-zealousness."

Instead, he offered Britisher Sir Henry Rawlinson a daring alternative: "I suggest that rather than expose the Canadian Corps to losses without adequate results against the old [Somme] trench system . . . the corps should be redrawn and used in another surprise attack." Rawlinson liked the idea; he took it to Sir Douglas Haig. Two days later, Haig convinced France's Marshal Ferdinand Foch to end the Amiens offensive. The Canadians would now be shifted north to Arras, to mount a new attack.

On August 12, King George had named Currie a Knight Commander of the Bath (KCB). On his part, however, a stubborn Currie felt it was important that the entire Corps should receive recognition for its superb efforts at Amiens. Eventually, his protestations prevailed. On August 27, *The Times,* voice of British public opinion, conceded that Amiens had been, as it put it, "chiefly a Canadian battle."

In the meantime, in characteristic manner, Currie had taken matters into his own hands. Recalling the warm response his earlier March "special order" had evoked, he issued another on August 13, trusting that it, too, would be reprinted. "The Canadian Corps," the General's confident message read, "has every right to feel proud of the part it played. To move the Corps from the Arras front and in less than a week to launch it into battle so many miles distant was itself a splendid performance." The Corps had exceeded even this remarkable achievement in the actual fighting. The first day, after advancing 22,000 yards, it occupied a 10,000-yard frontage, and had completely routed four of the sixteen German divisions opposing it. In the fighting, as their Commander proudly noted, the Canadians had captured nearly 10,000 prisoners, 200 guns, and 25 communities had been "rescued from the clutch of the invader." "This magnificent victory," Currie was to note appreciatively, "has been won because your training was good, your discipline was good, your leadership was good. Given those three, success must always come."

Amiens dramatically confirmed Currie's reforms. No longer would fatigued Canadian infantry have to fight by day, repair roads by night. Henceforth, under Brigadier-General William Lindsay, specialized units of engineers and pioneers carried out such demanding chores. In addition, the effectiveness of Brigadier-General Raymond Brutinel's separate machine gun battalion, employing armoured cars to increase its efficiency and hitting power, had been demonstrated. So, too, had Lieutenant-Colonel Andy McNaughton's new methods of preparing artillery to engage the enemy in open field tactics.

On August 20, the Canadian Corps, destined to proceed "as if by magic" from success to success, prepared to withdraw from the stiffening Amiens front. Relaxed and confident, Currie supervised the move back northward in person. His impressive figure loomed out of nowhere, surprising Lieutenant-Colonel Bertram Hooper's decimated and tired battalion on the road. While the troops rested, the General, stern reproof in his eye and rebuke in his voice, ordered the unit's commander: "Let 'em rest." As recorded by Hooper, "the Chief spent the next half hour going from one reclining group to another, smiling down at the men, the warmth and praise in his voice and his human interest reviving them at every step."

Currie opened his new HQ near Arras on August 23. Shortly

thereafter, he was engaged in putting the finishing touches to plans for what would be his most brilliant campaign. The Germans had made the strategic decision to retreat to the Hindenburg — they called it the Siegfried Line — while fighting a series of stubborn rearguard actions designed to inflict as many casualties as possible. This great defensive position ran from the vicinity of Arras 100 miles south to Soissons. Northwest of Cambrai, it was connected to the enemy's defences by still another imposing series of defences known as the Drocourt-Quéant (D-Q) Line. As Currie observed, the Hindenburg Line "was the chief obstacle. In it the Germans had placed their trust, they would hold it until the end of the war, and before they would think of defeat that line had first to be broken. If we could break it, victory might yet come in 1918."

The Canadian Corps' formidable task would be to strike eastward, astride the Arras-Cambrai Road, smash the Drocourt-Quéant Line, and outflank the Hindenburg Line itself. To accomplish this, the Canadians would have to overcome a veritable maze of defences, situated in territory admirably suited to attritional warfare. The immediate objective would be the old British trench system centring on Orange Hill and Monchy-le-Preux. Beyond this lay the forbidding Fresnes-Rouvroy Line. Then came the first major objective, the formidable D-Q Line. Behind it again lay the partially constructed Canal du Nord, as well as several support systems in front of Cambrai. As Currie soberly noted, the positions were "without doubt among the strongest defensively on the Western Front." Broad glaces, or earthen berms, studded with machine gun nests, defended the immediate approaches to these lines, "requiring in each case heavy fighting to gain a suitable jumping-off line before assaulting the main position."

Currie and the Canadian Corps would have to fight the "hardest battle in its history" with only three days' notice. Fortunately, extensive reconnaissance and plans had already been made, as a diversion to the earlier Arras battle. The importance of the operation to Allied plans was indicated by the presence of Sir Douglas Haig himself at Currie's headquarters on four successive days prior to the battle: August 24 through 27. "Do you think it can be done, Currie?" asked the visibly nervous and excited Commander-in-Chief. Confident as ever, Currie reassured the Field Marshal: "Yes, we will break it."

On the evening of August 23/24, after aggressive Canadian patrols reconnoitred defences near Neuville-Vitasse, the Germans decided to abandon the village. As such, it conceded a bloodless victory to the Canadian storm troopers. Continuing onwards, attacking at 3:00 a.m. on the 25th, instead of the normal dawn hour, they were in Monchy before breakfast. By suppertime, the advancing Canadian Corps had crushed the two outer defensive lines. In the process, it advanced some three miles and captured 2,000 prisoners.

But the Fresnes-Rouvroy line proved harder to crack. Currie hammered at it for two days. While Lipsett's 2nd Division, on the left, managed to break through, Burstall's 3rd Division, unable to gain a firm jumping-off line, suffered heavy casualties. That evening, Currie replaced the latter with the 4th, temporarily under his command, while the 2nd was relieved by Archie Macdonell's 1st. On August 31, employing a single brigade group, Macdonnell's 1st overran the remaining segment of the Fresnes-Rouvroy Line.

Now, at last, the Canadians were face-to-face with their main objective: the Drocourt-Quéant Line. Its imposing defences consisted of "four distinct lines of trenches . . . all linked up with tunnels and communications trenches and bound by mile upon mile of barbed wire." Topography also favoured the enemy, leading the Germans to believe the D-Q line was, indeed, impenetrable. Currie and his stalwart Canadians were about to prove them wrong.

On September 2, following hectic preparations, Currie attacked at dawn. All three of the Corps' assault divisions — the British 4th on the left, David Watson's newly arrived 4th in the middle, and Macdonell's 1st on the right — punched through the much-vaunted defences. Currie was especially pleased with the "quite remarkable" performance of Macdonell's division. Not only had it broken through the D-Q Line, but it continued on to crush the main support position, the Buissy Switch, lying beyond. By nightfall, the battered enemy, having had enough, elected to with-draw across the Canal du Nord.

In Currie's words, crushing the D-Q Line ranked as "one of the finest feats in our history." Its defenders had enjoyed every advantage, and occupied an old defensive system as strong as he possessed anywhere. His guns were echeloned in great depth and brought the Canadian attackers under constant artillery fire. The Corps had also been obliged to meet and defeat 14 German divisions in the course of a single week's battle.

As a reward, Haig now planned to give the victorious Dominion troops a long-deserved break. But he soon realized that he needed the Corps if the war were to be brought to an end in 1918. Thus, a mere 13 days after the Canadians had overrun the D-Q Line, Currie received new instructions: ordering the Corps to cross the formidable Canal du Nord and strike at Cambrai.

For possibly the first time, Currie was visibly worried. The canal appeared to be an impossible barrier. The enemy had also flooded most of the vicinity. And, if this did not create a sufficient obstacle, the far side of the canal was embroidered with multiple lines of trenches protected by barbed wire and machine gun posts. To cross it as instructed, First Army would require a full-scale amphibious operation. However, the technology and techniques of such lay another 25 years in the future. Clearly, Currie believed, another solution had to be found.

In typical Currie fashion, the Commander quickly determined on an alternative. Much better conditions prevailed in front of neighbouring British XVII Corps, on the Canadians' right. At the outbreak of war, construction of the Canal du Nord had been interrupted. As Currie observed, in this sector "the canal was dry and its bottom was at the natural ground level . . . the sides of the canal consisting of high earth and brick banks." This dry section was only 2,600 yards, or about a mile and a half long, but the prospect it presented was good enough for the Canadian Commander to hazard all to fortune.

Currie's bold plan was to "side-step," or shift the Canadians, then reassemble them on this narrow front. It would be a classic employment of concentration of force at a decisive point. Once the attackers punched their way across the obstacle of the canal, his intention was that the force would "expand fanwise in a north-easterly direction to a front exceeding 15,000 yards." Coming as it did on the heels of four years of fruitless, bloody trench warfare, such a concept was startling. It would also require coordination, preparation, as well as leadership of the highest order.

The Commander himself conceded it would be a gamble "fraught with difficulties." The great danger involved assembling 10,000 Canadians, as well as artillery and support services, on so restricted a front. If the enemy had any suspicion of the Canadian attack, he could order down a devastating artillery barrage of high explosive and poison-gas shells. The Canadian Corps would be severely crippled, if not destroyed. Still, Currie calculated that the risk was worth taking. At least it gave his men a chance of success, in contrast to the British option of a frontal assault which provided no chance whatsoever.

When he announced his idea at First Army Headquarters, Sir Henry Horne was appalled. As he told his chief of staff: "I don't believe I ought to let them do it." And, knowing the close relationship Sir Julian Byng, the Corps' former commander, enjoyed with the burly Canadian Commander, Horne called on him to intercede with Currie.

A few days later, Byng came straight to the point: "Currie, I have read over your plans, and I know they are as good as they can be made, but can you do it?"

"Yes," responded Currie.

"Do you realize," continued Byng in his fatherly manner, "that you are attempting the most difficult operation of the war? If anyone can do it, the Canadians can do it, but if you fail it means home for you."

Currie realized that much more than his career was at stake. The lives of thousands of his young countrymen rode on the success or failure of the venture. Still, he adamantly reassured Byng that the Canadian Corps could, indeed, pull off the tricky operation.

Despite his outward show of confidence, Currie remained concerned as zero hour approached on September 27. Each flash and crash of German artillery only heightened his apprehension. Had the enemy detected the operation? Had he committed his troops to an overwhelming disaster? Should he have heeded the advice of Byng and Horne, who were professionals, while Currie himself had risen from being a humble militia officer at the war's beginning? It was, as Currie later observed, "a night of anxiety, but apart from the usual harassing fire and the night bombing nothing untoward happened."

At 5:20 a.m. hundreds of Canadian guns commenced bombarding the enemy positions, shattering the silence. With 1st and 4th Divisions leading, infantry pushed across the dry canal bed. Afterwards, prisoners recounted how "the attacking troops followed the barrage so closely that they were upon them before they could man their trenches." Swarming forward, the Cana-

Lieutenant-General Sir Arthur Currie, commanding Canadian Forces, July 1917.
Department of National Defence. (PAC/PA-001564)

dians quickly overran two trench systems bordering the canal. As Currie noted in his diary: "During the day nearly a hundred officers and three thousand prisoners were reported captured." He also recorded that a captured nobleman who commanded a cavalry brigade "was given lunch at headquarters, where he paid a great tribute to the attack as carried out this morning and stated further that in the German Army everyone agreed that the Canadian troops were most to be feared in all the Allies' Armies."

Canal du Nord was the greatest victory yet, considering the difficulty of the operation. Currie was, naturally, elated at the Corps' triumph. Most importantly, for him, casualties had been exceptionally light. The Canadians were possibly the only corps on the Western Front that could have pulled off such a manoeuvre. Next day, Sir Douglas Haig, as well as Horne, visited Currie to offer congratulations. Later, Sir Henry Rawlinson told Currie that he considered the Canadian capture of the canal to be "a marvellous feat."

Victors they might be, but the troops were given little time to dwell on their success. The next four days witnessed "attack and counter-attack every day," as the Commander recorded. The slow progress of Byng's Third Army, which was frontally engaging the Hindenburg Line on the Canadian right, allowed the desperate enemy to employ disproportionate numbers of troops and guns against the Canadians. The General later calculated that "on our front of 5 1/2 miles the enemy used 13 divisions and 13 independent machine-gun units. In the same operation, on a front of 10 miles to the South of us, he used six divisions. That shows the importance he attaches to stopping the Canadian Corps. He acts as if he thought that if he succeeded in stopping us, he stopped everything." But another reason would come to light later. A captured enemy intelligence appraisal revealed that the Germans believed there were "at least twelve Canadian divisions in action." In reality, there were but four.

The battle's climax came October 1. Sensing it, Currie committed all four of his already-tired divisions in a final bid to drive the Germans from the high ground they occupied north of Cambrai. But in doing so, Currie had stirred up a nest of hornets. Outnumbered, the attackers found each of their thrusts forward contained by a counterattack. Currie noted: "These counter-attacks were the most violent in character, with the consequence that little ground was gained. Today we met nine German divisions and have inflicted heavy casualties on the Boche. The Artillery never fired as much ammunition — 7,000 tons — as today and many of the targets were fired over open sights."

Heavy Canadian losses obliged Currie, wisely, to terminate the attack. As he observed, "To continue to throw tired troops against such opposition, without giving them an opportunity to refit and recuperate, was obviously inviting failure, and I accordingly elected to break off the engagement." The General also wryly noted: "I have never known the Boche to fight harder. He is like a cornered rat, and I believe will fight most desperately until beaten absolutely and totally." Even Currie could be momentarily dispirited, as the following remark in the same letter indicated: "I do not think he can be finished this year."

To buoy up his troops' spirits, Currie now issued a special order, congratulating the men, and noting the magnitude of the effort. A portion reads as follows:

> Every evidence confirms the fact the enemy suffered enormous casualties. He fought stubbornly and well and for that reason your victory is the more creditable. You have taken in this battle over 7,000 prisoners and 200 field and heavy guns, thus bringing the total captured by the Canadian Corps since the 8th of August of this year to 28,000 prisoners, 500 guns, over 3,000 machine-guns, and a large amount of stores of all kinds.

In two months of battle, the Corps had encountered and decisively defeated 47 German divisions. That is, nearly a quarter of the total enemy forces on the Western Front!

Still, it must be emphasized the Canadians were not alone in the heavy fighting that occupied September and early October 1918. Although they had been assigned an important and difficult task, the Canadians were only part of the general Allied offensive along the entire Western Front. The Americans were on their right, in the heavily wooded Meuse-Argonne region of north-central France; the French themselves occupied the middle, in Champagne; while the British on the left assaulted the forbidding Hindenburg Line. The massive and coordinated thrusts marked the beginning of the end. After an incredible and heroic struggle, the once-formidable German armies had lost their ability to endure the hammer blows directed against them on so broad a front.

On October 8–9, Cambrai fell to the Canadians. At the last moment, Currie decided not to wait for Byng's Third Army, and instead to go ahead on his own. According to Currie, the attack "was a brilliant success. The unusual hour of one-thirty was evidently a great surprise and an effective one as well." The Canadian thrust caught the enemy in the process of retreating. His rearguard was easily driven out. Currie was intensely angered, however, when he learned the Germans had made plans to raze the town. As he noted: "This beautiful city had been wilfully set on fire by the Boche. We are doing our best to confine the damage, but much destruction has already been wrought." Despite the vandalism, the Corps Commander was relieved. "The Germans," he recorded afterwards, "have at last learned and understand that they are beaten." Now, he "felt we would defeat Germany" before year's end.

The cost of the prolonged six-and-a-half-week battle for Cambrai, which had commenced on August 26, had been considerable. Canadian casualties exceeded 30,000: 4,367 killed, 24,509 wounded, 1,930 missing in action. Still, Currie was satisfied that they had not been excessive. Especially, as he put it, "when the extent and severity of the operation are considered; you cannot meet and defeat in battle a quarter of the German Army without suffering casualties." (Currie was particularly proud of this feat. In a letter sent to Robert Borden, the Canadian Prime Minister, the General wrote: "It was as if we said to the American Army, to the French Army, to the Belgian Army, and to the rest of the British Army, 'You look after three-quarters of the German Army, and we will take care of the rest.'")

Following our countrymen's success at Cambrai, the enemy

withdrew with the Canadian pursuers hard on their heels. The Germans, falling back on a large scale, allowed the Canadians to cross still another watercourse, the Canal de la Sensée, without serious opposition. Now the chase was on: as the Canadians and British pursued the retreating foe towards Valenciennes. The Dominion engineers, particularly, worked miracles to keep the advance rolling forward. They constructed bridges as required, built roads and cleared booby traps from the path of the advancing troops. Revelling in his new role as liberator, Currie recorded that during the first three days, passing through towns in which almost every house had been draped with a French flag by delirious inhabitants, the Canadians freed an estimated 40,000 civilians. By month's end, the total had swollen to 70,000.

Ahead, Valenciennes offered a strong position. Since it was protected by the Canal de l'Escaut, the enemy intended to make a stand here. The Germans had blasted holes in the dikes, and the only dry approach to the town was from the south. Thus, Sir Henry Horne suggested that Sir Alexander Godley's XXII Corps should capture Mount Houy, which blocked the southern approach. Meanwhile, the Canadian Corps would proceed across the canal and secure the city. However, after the British failed to storm and hold the heavily defended hill, Currie made his own plans.

To begin the assault, Currie assigned a single brigade to do what an entire division had been unable to achieve. Having been trained as an artillery officer, he had a card up his sleeve. He counted on massive artillery support to assist the planned attack. Counter-Battery Staff Officer Andy McNaughton's barrage was "a good one." Indeed, the last of the war as it turned out. Assaulting Mount Houy at 5:15 a.m. on November 1, 1918, 10th Brigade encountered little resistance from the shell-shocked enemy defenders. As Currie recorded: "In that operation we captured 1,800 prisoners, buried over 800 Boshes [sic] afterwards on the field, and sustained less than 400 casualties ourselves, of whom only 80 were killed; thus causing over 2,600 permanent casualties to the enemy with 80 permanent casualties to ourselves."

Currie's often tart relationship with the British would be further exacerbated when Sir Henry Horne insisted that he personally receive the address and the flag in the official ceremonies celebrating Valenciennes' liberation. If this were not enough, he also reversed the order of march-past. Thus British troops led the parade past the starting point, while the victorious Canadians were relegated to bringing up the rear. Still, such fraternal rivalries would shortly be forgotten as the Canucks continued hotly to pursue the retreating enemy.

On November 6, the Canadians crossed into Belgium. It was little scarred by the German occupation, since the enemy had planned to keep it after the war had ended. By November 9, the Corps had advanced to within a mile of historic Mons. In Allied eyes, especially the British, the town had a major significance, for it was here, on August 22, 1914, that the British Expeditionary Force had begun the war. Currie was well aware of the "Old Contemptibles," as the Kaiser had derisively termed the little British Army, whose riflemen's disciplined and orderly fighting retreat had delayed the German Army's triumphant advance through Belgium. Certainly, he appreciated the national pride the Canadians would feel "if they finished the war with the old battlefield in our possession." Still, he did not wish to suffer many casualties to do so.

Riding forward on Brock, his grey mount, to survey the situation personally, Currie kept in close touch with the advance. At the hour designated for the cessation of hostilities, the 116th Canadian Infantry Battalion received the order to stand fast at a point but 20 yards across the road from where Trooper Thomas of the British cavalry had fired his initial rifle shot. Thus, the war ended exactly where it had begun 51 months before. At the moment of cease-fire the Empire's most forward troops were two and a half miles beyond Mons. The Royal Canadian Regiment and the Black Watch had cleared the town only five hours previously. Later, Currie would proudly write "that not a single Canadian had lost his life" in capturing the town.

In Mons, after the 42nd Battalion had earlier sent its pipe band to play through the city, General Loomis invited Currie to stage a triumphant entry to coincide with the official armistice at 11:00 a.m. As Currie rode into the town, accompanied by an escort of the British 5th Lancers, he was proud that this time, unlike Valenciennes a week earlier, the 1,500 troops assembled in the Grand Place were all Canadians. He also showed that he had not lost his well-known sense of humour. When George Farmar, one of his British staff officers, remarked that the last time he had been in the town was on August 23, 1914, Currie turned to him, and, genially remarked: "Well, George, it's taken a damned long time to get you back here!"

Following the official ceremonies, Currie would be especially moved when he received a handwritten note from Sir Henry Horne, his sometimes antagonist, who had also fought in the 1914 retreat. Breaking the ice that had recently frozen relations between the two commanders, it generously stated that the Canadian capture of Mons was "just about the best thing that could have happened."

Viewed in retrospect, Canada's war record was truly one of a kind. It began at the Second Battle of Ypres, or Ypres II, when the raw, young Canucks had bravely — even foolishly — refused to flee history's first gas attack. From this point forward, our troops had never given ground or yielded. "In no battle," Currie would later write, "did the corps fail to take its objective; nor did it lose an inch of ground once that ground was consolidated. . . . The Canadian Corps never lost a single [field] gun." Of the Final Hundred Days, he would later conclude: "No force of equal size ever accomplished so much."

Currie's own personal record stands without equal in the history of Canadian arms. Although he started his military career as a militia soldier, he would not emulate professional military officers of other countries, who continually applied outdated 19th-century principles in the first modern great war. In marked contrast, he adopted "techniques and strategies to meet the new realities of [the] conflict." Although he had been a good brigade commander, Currie continued to grow in terms of personal capacity. Throughout the struggle, he remained a keen student of his craft, never allowing himself to become stale or complacent in his thinking; he actually seemed to perform better with each new challenge he faced. As Dancocks, his biographer, has observed, the picture of Sir Arthur Currie that emerges can be summarized as "persuasive, self-confident, clever, common-sensical, sincere, sympathetic, sensitive, sometimes stubborn."

Tragically, however, Currie's achievements are neither understood nor appreciated by many modern Canadians. In large measure this is the result of the campaign of innuendo and character-smear that was directed against the General from 1916 onwards. The most pressing problem concerned Richard Turner, whom both Prime Minister Borden and Militia and Defence Minister Sam Hughes favoured to head the Canadian Corps when General Byng moved on. Ultimately, both Currie and Turner would be promoted lieutenant-generals and peace restored. But Currie's problems were not over. When he appointed Archie Macdonell commander of 1st Division, instead of Garnet Hughes, son of the former minister, the die was cast. From this time forward, "a sinister, nebulous campaign" followed, the purpose of which was to remove Currie and tarnish his reputation. Overnight, creditors in Canada demanded settlements of debts arising from real estate losses prior to the war, threatening legal proceedings if their claims were not met. Even before this, knowledge of his obligation caused Currie's hypersensitive stomach to turn; the scant sleep that came his way in the field of battle was riddled with nightmares. And the trauma would continue throughout the war. Ultimately, the generosity of two brother officers allowed Currie to meet his debts and to continue to head Canada's war effort. The storm was not over, however. In 1928, it again emerged in a celebrated court case Currie brought (and won) against Frederick W. Wilson, owner and editor of the Port Hope, Ontario *Evening Guide*. Earlier, the newspaper had published an article alleging the General's "useless waste of human life" during the advance on Mons.

Ironically, Arthur Currie's accomplishments and reputation were best recognized elsewhere in the Western World. No less a figure than South Africa's Field Marshal Jan Christian Smuts wrote that probably there was no army commander whose place Currie could not have taken. And Smuts concludes in words that might well serve as our great countryman's ultimate epitaph:

> Men like Currie are rare and their story is the enrichment of their country and the human record as a whole and should not be allowed to pass into oblivion. . . . Single-minded at his great job, he kept his personal integrity. He moved unsullied through a world of political and military intrigue. He trained himself, he trained the practically untrained lives sent to him and trained them into finished soldiers. He studied his moves and rehearsed them in advance with his officers and men until the corps moved with clocklike regularity. He gave his division and corps a soul, which is the real task of a commander.

SELECTED READINGS

Dancocks, Daniel G. *Sir Arthur Currie: A Biography*. Toronto: Methuen, 1985.

Morton, Desmond and J. L. Granatstein. *Marching to Armageddon: Canadians and the Great War 1914–1919*. Toronto: Lester & Orpen Dennys, 1989.

Shannon, Norman. "Arthur Currie's Longest Battle." *Esprit de Corps: Canadian Military Then and Now* 5:11 (May 1997): 21, 26.

Sutherland, W. B. S. "Canada's Most Famous Forgotten Military Hero." *Esprit de Corps: Canadian Military Then and Now* 1:11 (April 1992): 30–32.

Canadian nurse, May 1917.
Department of National Defence. (NAC/PA-001355)

16

CANADA'S
NURSING SISTERS

We Went in Uniform

*Canada's women have always nursed our sick and wounded.
The Canadian nurses first actively employed in a military campaign served in the Northwest Rebellion. The creation of an official Canadian Army Nursing Service, however, would not be proposed until 1899. Shortly thereafter, four nurses accompanied the
first contingent to the South African War. In 1901 the nursing
service was inaugurated. In 1904, when the Army Medical Service was reorganized, the nursing reserve establishment was increased to 25, and in 1906 the first two sisters joined the Permanent Force. Soon after the Great War's outbreak, there were 113 PF
nurses, and 80 reserves. The ongoing conflict would prove the
making of the Canadian Army Nursing Service, or "Bluebirds":
by 1917 there would be 2,030 on strength, and a reserve of 203.
Hostilities would see 6 nurses killed on service, 6 wounded, as
well as 15 who lost their lives due to drowning as a result of
enemy action. Following the war, nurses would do much to advance peacetime nursing as a profession in Canada. In World
War II and actions since, the nursing service has been an inte-
grated part of the Royal Canadian Army Medical Corps.*

Even today, Montreal artist G. W. Hill's sculptured memorial panel, in Parliament's Hall of Fame, dedicated to Canada's pioneer Nursing Sisters who gave their lives in the Great War, continues to speak eloquently of their dedication. Its design embraces the history of nurses in Canada from their earliest days to the First World War. The right-hand side of the bas relief represents the contribution made by religious sisters who came to Canada during *l'ancien régime*. To the left, two nursing sisters in uniform tend a wounded soldier, symbolizing the courage and self-sacrifice of Canadian nurses who served in the war. In the centre, "Humanity" stands with arms outstretched. In her right hand, she grasps the caduceus, emblem of healing; and with the other hand she indicates the courage and devotion of nurses throughout the ages. In the background, "History" holds the book of records containing the deeds of heroism of our country's nurses during 300 years of faithful service.

An exceptional story lies behind this moving memorial.

Beginning with the establishment of the first New World settlements, Canada's women have cared for our sick and wounded. Three centuries ago, Jeanne Mance and the Sisters of St. Joseph de la Fléché dressed arrow wounds in Ville Marie, or Montreal. During the battles for New France, other nuns ministered both to French and British wounded. In the 1780s and during the War of 1812, nurses from the colonies helped in British military hospitals along the St. Lawrence. Military nursing, as a distinct profession, traces its origins to Florence Nightingale, "the Lady with the Lamp," who revolutionized Army practice by recruiting British women for British field hospitals, and ministering to the battlefield needs of England's soldiers during the Crimean War in the 1850s. Still, another 34 years would pass before Canada's women officially nursed military patients.

The first Canadian nurses to be employed in a military campaign were the handful who served in the 1885 Northwest Rebellion. Not only did they staff Battleford's little hospital, but they also provided personnel for two field hospitals, one at Saskatoon, the other at Moose Jaw. But with the emergency's end, the nurses were no longer needed, and the last was struck off strength two weeks later. All, however, were awarded the "North West Canada — 1885" campaign medal. It marked the first time women were honoured by the Canadian military.

During the Yukon's gold rush of 1898–99, 200 volunteers from the Permanent Force journeyed north to reinforce the North West Mounted Police. At the suggestion of Lady Aberdeen, wife of the Governor General, four nurses from the Victorian Order were included. Although the group's leader, Miss Georgea Powell, and her companions were not officially members of Canada's military service, they effectively carried out the many tasks allotted them in the north.

At last, in June 1899, the Army Medical Department was established. Among other duties, its commander was authorized to investigate the possibility of starting a Canadian Nursing Service "in the near future."

When the South African War broke out three months later, one Medical Officer and four nursing sisters embarked with the Royal Canadian Regiment, becoming the first Canadian military nurses to serve overseas. Georgina Pope, who became the first Canadian awarded the coveted Red Cross decoration, and her three colleagues were initially posted to a British hospital outside Cape Town. Four more nurses arrived with the second Canadian contingent, although shortly afterwards one would be invalided home. Through the overwhelming dust, heat and rampant cholera, our nurses performed creditably.

The Boer War clearly demonstrated the benefits of a permanent nursing department. On August 1, 1901, the Canadian Nursing Service was officially established. When the conflict took on new life under skilled Boer commando (guerilla) leaders, eight additional nurses would form part of the staff of No. 10 Stationary Hospital, located 6,000 feet above sea level at Harrismith in the Orange Free Colony.

By 1904, 25 commissioned Lieutenants (Nursing Sisters) were enrolled in the fledgling Canadian Army Medical Corps. Four years later, in 1908, Sister Pope became the service's first Matron.

She would hold the appointment during the next half-dozen formative years of the nursing service's history.

On Miss Pope's recommendation, the nurses' khaki uniforms dating from the Boer War period were now changed to blue. Dress regulations proclaimed in 1907 prescribed that full dress uniform would consist of a shirt-waist, or light jacket, and skirt of dark blue serge, a cape of scarlet cloth reaching to the elbow, white adjustable cuffs and collars, and a white cap. Gilt buttons were of Army Medical Corps pattern. In the field, nurses were to wear a shirt-waist and skirt of "pale butcher's linen," cuffs and collars as described, and a white apron. Winter wear consisted of a double-breasted overcoat of dark blue, as well as a headdress adapted from a sailor pattern. For very cold conditions, a Persian lamb coat, a fur cap with red brush, and fur gauntlets were provided.

So originated the famous "Bluebirds," the name by which our nursing sisters would be known by the Dominion's appreciative soldiers as well as the public during the course of the Great War.

Ironically, in the spring of 1914 the Permanent component of the Canadian Army Medical Corps stood at its lowest in four years. The outbreak of hostilities signalled the beginning of the real making of the Canadian Army Nursing Service. Within three weeks of the Empire's declaration of war on August 4, 1914, graduate nurses from every training school in the country as well as many U.S. institutions had volunteered "for the duration." Overnight, Matron Pope had under her command 113 nurses, 33 of them Permanent Force, and 80 reservists. In contrast to those who served in the armies of other nations, Canada's World War I nursing sisters held military rank. They were also under military orders.

On August 17, 1914, Matron Margaret C. Macdonald succeeded founder Georgina Pope as head of the Nursing Service. Her appointment as Matron-in-Chief, effective November 4, 1914, earned her the distinction of being the first woman in the British Empire to be granted a rank equivalent to major. Although Sister Pope, Macdonald's mentor and colleague, was now fifty-two years

old, it did not stop her from going overseas. After serving with
Canadian hospitals in the United Kingdom, she eventually took
over No. 8 Stationary Hospital in France.

Meanwhile, Miss Macdonald's first task, a formidable one, was
to supply staff for two hospitals scheduled to accompany the assembling Canadian Expeditionary Force to Britain. The first of
the "Bluebirds," comprising 101 nursing sisters and selected civilians, departed at the beginning of October 1914. As they struggled up the gangplank of the liner *Franconia,* the First Contingent's flagship, heroically labouring under their heavy kitbags,
the nurses were loudly cheered by personnel of the 90th Winnipeg Rifles, the "Little Black Devils," already aboard. A sister who
was there later observed: "It was the first tangible evidence of the
comradeship which united men and women as never before in
war, and especially the Sisters of the Dominion Forces and
their . . . 'Boys.'"

Once it became evident the war would not be over in a matter
of weeks, the British War Office requested that a Canadian hospital be placed at the disposal of the Royal Army Medical Corps for
immediate service in France. Hardly had Matron Ethel G. Ridley
and the 34 nursing sisters accompanying her prepared the Golf
Club Hotel at Le Touquet, a seaside resort, for admissions than
the first patients arrived. There were 115 of them, most of them
soldiers suffering from trench foot, frostbite, or minor gunshot
wounds. As they stumbled from ambulances or were carried in by
orderlies, the sick and injured soldiers were quickly stripped of
mud-caked uniforms and boots, bathed, and put to bed. Clean
dressings were shortly applied to their wounds.

In this manner, the first of Canada's nurses entered upon four
years of dedicated service. Curiously, their first patients were not
Canadian boys, but "Old Contemptibles" of Britain's brave but ill-
fated expeditionary force, who, as noted, had gallantly fought
their way back from Mons, in Belgium.

Twenty weeks passed before the world's first gas attack at Ypres
(Ypres II) produced a great flood of Canadian casualties. From
the heavy fighting that developed on April 22, 1915 and after,

long convoys of wounded were soon arriving at all hospitals in the area. Fortunately, just a month earlier, No. 2 General Hospital had been established on a high cliff outside Le Tréport, a fashionable watering place 50 miles south of Boulogne. In 19 hours it admitted 358 patients, many of them Canadians from 1st Division's heroic stand in the Ypres salient. The Battle of Festubert, on May 18, brought another rush of patients. On this day alone, the arrival of 537 casualties before breakfast brought the number under treatment to more than 1,000. Such numbers seriously strained the resources of No. 2 General, even though its capacity had been expanded to 615. As gassed and wounded countrymen arrived directly from the trenches by ambulance and Red Cross train, Canadian doctors and nurses temporarily transformed the facility into a casualty clearing station. The need to keep "walking cases" moving on down the line, as well as "stretchers" proceeding smoothly on their way back to England, kept the Dominion's first team of nurses at work: changing dressings, serving impromptu meals, as well as remaking beds several times a day until the emergency had passed.

Besides the 36 "Bluebirds" who initially staffed No. 2 Canadian Stationary Hospital, an additional 20 Canadian sisters would qualify for the 1914 Service Star. After arriving in France on November 23, members of this second group of early-comers were attached to British Stationary Hospitals.

Other Canadian nursing sisters were busy in the United Kingdom during the winter of 1914–15. By the time the first nurses arrived at the Canadian camp pitched on Salisbury Plain, the weather had broken. The abnormal winter brought heavy rain on 89 out of 123 days. Under the deluge, the thin soil that covered the impervious layer of chalk below quickly transformed into a quagmire. Meanwhile the number of sick in the ranks of the Canadian contingent increased in an alarming manner. As troops abandoned their tents and moved into huts, the crowded, poorly ventilated buildings led to serious outbreaks of influenza, cholera and meningitis. By Christmas, patients exceeded 1,000, and nursing sisters, although reinforced in numbers, found their hands full.

When 1st Canadian Division departed for the Continent in mid-February 1915, No. 1 General Hospital found itself handling a rapidly diminishing patient load. Many nursing sisters were transferred to assignments elsewhere. Some joined No. 2 General Hospital or No. 1 Casualty Clearing Station when the units prepared to cross the Channel. Others made up the vanguard of a great number of Canadian nurses scheduled to duty at Taplow, Buckinghamshire, where Major Waldorf Astor generously placed his fine estate of Cliveden at Canadian disposal as a hospital (later designated No. 15) for the duration.

Early in 1915, a second contingent numbering 72 Canadian nurses crossed the Atlantic. Soon they joined the initial group serving in both the UK and Europe. In addition to Le Touquet, three more major Canadian medical units were established in France. And in March, No. 1 Stationary opened a 300-bed tent hospital at Wimereux, on Boulogne's northern outskirts. The fields around the Canadian tents were red with thickly growing poppies, and patients loved to lie there after having their dressings changed. Towards the end of July, No. 1 Stationary prepared to strike its tents and move to Abbeville. Before personnel could do so, however, orders were countermanded. Instead, the Canadian hospital was ordered to proceed to the Mediterranean, by way of England.

After the commencement of the ill-fated 1915 Gallipoli campaign to force the Turkish Straits, the need for medical units in the Eastern Mediterranean suddenly became urgent. The only other group of Canadians who served in this frustrating theatre was a combat unit, the Newfoundland Regiment. The main hospitals in which Canadian nurses were stationed were located on the Greek island of Lemnos and at Salonika on the mainland. Some eight Canadian general and stationary hospitals would be established outside the UK during the Great War. While the majority ministered to troops fighting in France or Belgium, an honoured place in our country's collective memory belongs to the five units whose destiny took them to the Eastern Mediterranean.

By early 1916, units of the Canadian Army Medical Corps in

France or Belgium in which our country's nursing sisters were employed numbered nine. In addition to six hospitals operational at Boulogne, at Outreau (outside Boulogne), Etaples, Tréport, St. Cloud, and Troyes, No. 1 Casualty Clearing Station was at work at Aires. As well, Toronto's No. 2 C.C.S. and Winnipeg's No. 3 had set themselves up at Rémy Siding, Popringhe.

In addition to nurses, other groups of women were employed in France close to the battlefield. Based at Etaples, the huge military hospital complex situated ten miles south of the port of Boulogne, were about 100 young women who ferried soldiers back and forth between trains and hospitals and ships bound for England. Grace Evelyn Macpherson, who left an interesting diary record, was a native of Vancouver. Three other volunteers were also Canadian, and two were from Newfoundland, which was a separate colony. All wore the uniform of V.A.D. (Voluntary Aid Detachment) drivers, and served with the British Red Cross. Looking over faded photographs of such young women today, we are acutely aware of just how modern they are in a strangely haunting sort of way. For, as Sandra Gwyn eloquently notes, such images provide "a perfect metaphor of the emerging, self-confident new Canada."

A typical casualty clearing station received wounded who were sent back from field ambulance units farther forward. Early in the war, the main function of doctors and nurses was to accommodate patients for a few hours until their wounds could be suitably dressed and the injured placed aboard an ambulance train to take them back to a general hospital. Before long, though, casualty clearing stations would develop into advanced surgical hospitals and operating centres in their own right. Their main duties — to deal with serious wounds, particularly of the brain, chest, and abdomen — placed a demanding load on professionals if patients' lives were to be saved.

A wounded soldier commonly caught his first glimpse of a welcoming "Bluebird" in one of the Casualty Clearing Station's long operating huts, with its six to twelve surgical tables. Having overcome his initial surprise at being attended by a typical nurse

A Canadian V.A.D. ambulance driver at the Front, May 1917.
Department of National Defence. (NAC/PA-001249)

in white veil and apron, wearing on her shoulder the two brass pips of a lieutenant, an ailing man quickly came to admire and appreciate her skill and efficiency. One Medical Officer recorded his observations as follows:

> She is generally in a hurry, always busy, with a white veil flying in the wind and sleeves rolled up to her elbows doing dressings, taking temperatures, preparing patients for the theatre, looking after the fresh arrivals as the stretchers are brought in — in short, doing the hundred and one things that a nurse finds to do in a busy ward. And they are very grateful, the poor men, as they come in, wearing their dirty khaki and blood-stained bandages, with grey-lined faces that all the happiness of life seems to have left.

Situated as it was only seven miles from Ypres, less than ten miles in front of the famous Salient, Popringhe was virtually at the Front. On at least one occasion, an alarm was given that the enemy might break through. In response, worried sisters, packing up charges, prepared to evacuate. But not every moment was sombre. Admiring officers from a nearby Royal Flying Corps station often dropped into the mess for tea. A six-foot piece of coloured signal streamer provides an unusual souvenir and reminds us of such happy times. At its mid-point, a small pocket, weighted with lead, contains a note addressed to "Miss Murphy, No. 3 Canadian C.C.S.," which floated down to land near the Nurses' Mess:

> *In the Air*
> *Dear Miss Murphy,*
> *All sorts of airy greetings,*
> *We're coming round some day, Huns willing.*
> *Durham & McLung*

Most of the time, though, nurses were busy with their heavy round of duties. A surgeon serving with one such Casualty Clearing Station spoke highly of nurses selected for such difficult, hard work. He observed: "They deserve a great deal of praise for the very cheerful way in which they put up with the long fatiguing hours they were called upon to serve in the operating rooms and tents." And he noted, "Their steady nerves and calm demeanours were evident during the operations, even when the Fritzie planes were soaring overhead; the shriek of dropping bombs, the bursting of shells from our own Archies, did not seem to rattle them in any way."

Those nurses who could be spared from No. 1 Canadian General Hospital's staff in the great encampment at Etaples observed Dominion Day, 1916, in truly memorable fashion. A colourful sight in white veils, light blue uniforms, and dark blue capes, which swung open to reveal a lining of red, they carried bunches of flowers to the graves of 108 fallen Canadian soldiers. At the conclusion, they added a small silk Canadian red ensign to each marker. As the sisters marched back to headquarters from the simple yet poignant service, they remained blissfully unaware that, 50 miles inland, Allied armies had launched their opening attack of the bloody, doomed Somme offensive.

Next day, rumours of a great battle were confirmed when the first wounded arrived: a convoy of 393 soldiers. On July 3, No. 1 Canadian General increased its capacity to 1,350. Additionally, six nurses were rushed off to assist at three British clearing stations. By the end of the first week, the Hospital had admitted 1,909 wounded and discharged 1,543, most to England. Every available inch of floor space was soon covered with beds, and Australian troops arrived to level the ground for extra marquees.

A Canadian nursing sister assigned to No. 1 General as a reinforcement noted: "Usually half the patients were on the 'Seriously Ill list,' with a death every second night or so." She also recalled how "delirious cases . . . seemed to take turns pulling off their dressings or getting out of bed. We also had a number of gas gangrene cases . . . the infection travels so fast — and last, but not least, the haemorrhages."

During heavy fighting, all the hospital's lights would be flashed, then turned off, the signal that hostile aircraft were approaching. Nurses had to use shaded lanterns or possibly a rare flashlight even when undertaking a simple task. In France, nursing sisters might escape the constant torment of flies and mosquitoes common to the Mediterranean; they had to contend, however, with Flanders' rats. Not only did the monster rodents abound in frontline trenches and dugouts — where they frisked over the bodies of the living — but they also constituted a perpetual menace in hospitals to the rear. When an air raid alert sounded, a nurse would usually think twice before obeying the order to seek shelter on the floor or under a bed, where she might come face to face with one or more of the truly gigantic and terrifying pests.

Ultimately, the arrival of four general hospitals organized by Canadian universities brought the number of stationary hospitals on the continent to ten. During the war's last months, No. 98 (University of Saskatchewan) Stationary operated 250 miles inland, administering to the needs of the Royal Flying Corps. And in 1917 the last of four casualty clearing stations arrived in France. Moving forward with Sir Arthur Currie's Canadian Corps, this station, No. 4 C.C.S., was at Valenciennes when the Armistice was signed.

Canadian nursing sisters served in other capacities as well. In April 1915, twenty-two nurses recruited from various Dominion hospitals were mobilized in Montreal for volunteer service in Belgium. Four other nursing sisters of the Canadian Army Medical Corps (C.A.M.C.) had the interesting experience of serving at St. Petersburg, in Russia, under the charge of Lady Sybil Grey, daughter of the former Governor General of Canada. Between their numerous duties, the four witnessed some of the bloodiest events of the March revolution that overthrew the Romanovs.

On May 19, 1918, fifteen German aircraft attacked Etaples in a two-hour raid. One of the bombs fell on unprotected No. 1 Canadian General Hospital. Nursing Sister Katherine Macdonald died instantly, and seven other nurses were injured. Two more, Nursing Sister Gladys Wake and Nursing Sister Margaret Lowe, died within several days. Adding to the horror, at least one enemy aircraft took advantage of bright moonlight and the glare of burning huts to fly low and strafe those engaged in rescue activities. In addition to dozens of patients and staff killed and wounded at No. 1 Canadian General Hospital, No. 9 C.G.H. was also hit in the same raid. Fortunately, none of its nursing sisters was among the casualties suffered by patients and staff.

Before the end of May, the Etaples area was hit by four more raids. The Germans excused the bombing of the Etaples hospitals on grounds that they were located close to a busy railroad. But there was no justification for the attack the enemy carried out on another Canadian hospital situated at Doullens, 45 miles inland. About midnight on May 30/31, despite a large red cross painted on its roof, No. 3 Hospital took a direct hit when a bomb crashed through three floors. In the operating room, surgeon and patient, as well as two nurses, Nursing Sister Agnes Macpherson and Nursing Sister Edith Pringle, died instantly. Nursing Sister Dorothy Baldwin, on duty in the officers' ward, also died, along with a score of patients and orderlies. Another sister was wounded. For their heroic conduct in rescuing helpless patients from burning upper wards, Nursing Sisters Eleanor Jean Thompson and Mary Meta Hodge earned the Military Medal.

A Second World War nurse in steel helmet. Courtesy of Esprit de Corps.

Public opinion was further shocked a few weeks later by the enemy's torpedoing of the *Llandovery Castle*. The sinking of the ship, one of five Canadian ambulance transports, on the night of June 27, 1918, 116 miles off Ireland, cost 234 lives. Included in this number were the ship's entire complement of 14 nurses, headed by Matron Margaret Fraser. So outraged were Canadian troops that during the battle of Amiens they purportedly executed German soldiers who were attempting to surrender, an atrocity depicted in Canadian Charles Yale Harrison's controversial war novel *Generals Die in Bed* (1930).

In an attempt to destroy all evidence of this breaching of the Geneva Convention, the enemy submarine systematically shelled or tried to ram and sink lifeboats as well as wreckage on which survivors were floating. Only a single boat survived. One of the men it rescued was the sergeant who had taken charge of the lifeboat carrying the nursing sisters. As the boat was being lowered, all of its oars had broken against the vessel's side. As the lifeboat drifted helplessly towards the sinking ship's stern, Matron Fraser turned to him and asked: "Sergeant, do you think there is any hope for us?"

His forced reply was: "No."

In the report he later wrote, the sergeant praised the courage of the 14 sisters, who "unflinchingly and calmly, as steady and collected as if on parade . . . faced the ordeal of certain death . . . a matter of minutes — as our lifeboat neared the mad whirlpool of water where all human power was helpless." When the hospital ship went down, the suction capsized the lifeboat. As the report notes, "it was the last I saw of the sisters, and though they all wore lifebelts, it is doubtful if any came to the surface." The sergeant survived only by battling his way upwards through the sea's enclosing depths.

In addition to Canadian-staffed hospitals in the United Kingdom already mentioned, six other British military hospitals were taken over by the C.A.M.C. Ultimately, the Dominion's nursing sisters numbered 2,030, with 27 matrons and a reserve of 203. To many Canadian nurses, names such as Moore Barracks, Shorncliffe, Orpington, Bramshott, and Eastbourne summoned up for decades to come memories of wards filled with patients who had "bought a Blighty."

On a happier note, nurses also brought back pleasant memories of the kindness and generosity of Lady Nancy Astor. Most importantly, she welcomed Canadian nurses to Cliveden and her other residences, both to rest and recuperate. She had, however, strict orders forbidding alcohol being served at parties organized for nurses. Male guests often "spiked" bowls of fruit punch. Sisters also remember how on one occasion a difference of opinion rose between Lady Astor and Matron-in-Chief Macdonald. The hostess wanted nurses to come in evening dress. The Matron said no. Even when Lady Astor proposed making the affair a fancy dress ball, and generously purchased colourful kimonos for all the sisters, Miss Macdonald still said no.

As one of those who attended recalled: "We went in uniform."

Once fighting was over, the work of nurses did not end.

Patients still had to be evacuated from hospitals on the continent. In addition, doctors and nurses found themselves involved in the tremendous task of processing each Dominion soldier before he returned to Canada. The movement across the Atlantic of 253,000 troops and their families would keep nurses busy staffing trains, carrying passengers to points of embarkation, and accompanying soldiers and dependants aboard troopships travelling to Canada.

Ultimately, a total of 3,141 nursing sisters proudly wore the badge and uniform of the Canadian Army Medical Corps during the Great War. A total of 2,504 served in the Overseas Medical Forces of the Dominion. 46 sacrificed their lives; 6 were killed or mortally wounded on land; 15 met their death from enemy action at sea. In addition, 18 died of disease while overseas, as did seven more in Canada.

A bevy of honours was bestowed on members of Canada's nursing sisters during the course of the Great War. The special contribution and noble precedent such brave women established would inspire future generations of Canadian nurses. Not least, nursing has grown in importance in today's army, and this has paved the way for women to serve in many other areas of the Canadian Forces.

SELECTED READINGS

Gwyn, Sandra. *Tapestry of War: A Private View of Canadians in the Great War.* Toronto: HarperCollins, 1992.

Harrison, Charles Yale. *Generals Die in Bed.* New York: W. Morrow & Co., 1939.

Moxley, Andrew. "Angels of Mercy." *Esprit de Corps: Canadian Military Then and Now* 2:8 (January 1993): 39–41.

Landells, E. A., ed. *The Military Nurses of Canada: Recollections of Canadian Military Nurses.* White Rock, B.C.: Co-Publishing, 1995.

Nicholson, (Col.) G. W. L. *Canada's Nursing Sisters.* Toronto: S. Stevens, Hakkert, 1975.

Captain Cameron D. Brant, Killed in Action.

17

CANADA'S
INDIAN WARRIORS

Volunteers to a Man

Just three decades after the last war drum throbbed on Saskatchewan's Plains, the Dominion's Natives were at war once again. This time, they would support the Crown in a truly impressive manner. Although largely neglected, the story of Canada's aboriginal peoples' contribution to the Great War and the Empire's cause is both an inspiring and fascinating tale. In comparison with Canada's total population, the number of Natives who served in the Canadian Expeditionary Force between 1914 and 1918 was small, and they did not go into battle as a distinct unit. Nonetheless, all were volunteers, and their allegiance set a powerful example for others. As individual soldiers, they not only strengthened the offensive, but added to the daring and innovation for which Canadians would become famous. Not least, Indian warriors provided an effective precedent for Native participation in other 20th-century conflicts including World War II and Korea.

The importance the enemy attached to the Dominion's aboriginal warriors was born out by the picture his propaganda painted of them. At the War's beginning, German publicity tended to caricature the Native soldier depicting him in war paint and feathers, armed only with a scalping knife and tomahawk. After they had experienced the reality of the Native warrior, however, Germans adopted a healthy respect for the effectiveness of his methods of fighting. Certainly the patience and deadly accuracy of Canada's Indian sharpshooters gave the enemy pause for thought, as did the sudden violent onslaught of the trench raid, which quickly became a Canadian specialty.

By the time the Great War broke out, the Indian warrior's loyalty to the Crown went back a long way. During the American Revolution, Joseph Brant and his tribesmen of the Six Nations Confederacy allied themselves with the British. Later, during the war of 1812, Tecumseh and other Native warriors participated in virtually every engagement. During the 1837 Rebellions, Britain's Iroquois supporters assisted Sir John Colborne's forces. Traditions of loyalty such as these were still close to the typical Indian of Canada in 1914.

Indian Affairs' records indicate that between the beginning and end of the struggle, more than 3,500 Indians enlisted in the Canadian Expeditionary Force. Although the number may seem small to us today, it assumes major meaning when one realizes that Canada's Native population was far fewer at this time than it is today — so much had disease reduced Native numbers. Calculations indicate that an astonishing 35 percent, more than one in three, of aboriginal males of military age resident in the nine provinces of the Dominion, volunteered to go to war. Nor does this surprising figure include a number of Indian enlistments of which the Department of Indian Affairs was unaware at the time, which would doubtlessly boost the overall proportion even more.

The story of Canada's modern warriors remains largely untold and missing from the tapestry of proud deeds done by us as a people. Because the Native soldier was not formed into a distinct fighting force, but enrolled as individuals throughout the many battalions of Canada's divisions, their contribution to the story of the war tends to be a series of disconnected anecdotes, rather than a single continuous narrative.

At the beginning of the Great War, William Hamilton Merritt, honorary chief of the Six Nations, offered $25,000 to raise and equip an Indian regiment. After a lengthy discussion, however, the tribal council declined the offer, arguing that only permanent war chiefs, or sachems, possessed the power to assist the Crown. Authorities in Ottawa also seriously considered raising one or two Indian battalions, but this too was shelved. Later, when conscription was introduced under the terms of the Military Services Act (1917), Canada's Natives were excluded, unless they abandoned their Indian status, because they were effectively wards of the government.

Thus, Indian participation in the war would be entirely voluntary. The average enlistment among Ontario's Ojibways and Chippewas, who enjoyed closer ties to the British than did Natives elsewhere, was exceptional. Typically, many bands sent all their eligible men to the front. The majority of recruits from the Nipigon district enlisted with the 52nd Battalion, popularly dubbed the "Bullmoose Battalion," or "Currie's Pets." Among the 52nd's Nipigons, Sergeant Leo Bouchard would ultimately win the Distinguished Conduct Medal (DCM), a decoration awarded to army enlisted ranks for "distinguished service and gallant conduct in the field," rather than the Distinguished Service Order or Victoria Cross. More importantly, Bouchard was recommended for the decoration on seven different occasions, surely a record that speaks for itself! Another otherwise unidentified Native serving with the 52nd, and who was eventually returned to Canada, suffered no fewer than twelve wounds to the body during two years' service at the front.

Francis Pegahmagabow, an Ojibway from the Parry Island Band, was the most highly decorated Indian during the Great War. While training at Valcartier, "Peg," as he was called by fellow recruits, decorated his tent with traditional symbols which included a deer, his clan's symbol. After he won the confidence of his fellows, he told them that a medicine bag presented to him by an elder would guard him from danger and guarantee him a safe existence in the trenches. His exploits ultimately earned him the Military Medal, as well as two bars, for bravery in action. A rugged individualist, he successfully adapted Native hunting and field-craft skills to the fighting, with results detailed below.

Given their well-established military credentials, it comes as no surprise that Six Nations Indians of Ontario's Brant and Haldimand counties played a notable part in the Great War. Indeed, the closest Canada came to raising a distinctive Indian unit would be the 114th Battalion. Lieutenant-Colonel Andrew T. Thompson's appointment as the unit's commanding officer did much to stimulate the interest of the Iroquois and win their confidence. When the 114th organized a recruiting league on the Six Nations reserve, some 287 Natives enlisted. Additionally, many Indians from other reservations flocked to join the battalion's colours, including a substantial number from Quebec's Caughnawaga (Kahnawake) and St. Regis bands. Eventually, two entire Indian companies were formed, commanded by Indian officers. The battalion proudly dubbed itself "Brock's Rangers," commemorating the fact that many of its personnel descended from warriors who had fought alongside Sir Isaac Brock in the decisive battle of Queenston Heights. Appropriately, the regiment's crest consisted of crossed tomahawks, surmounted by an Indian head.

The Six Nations Women's Patriotic League created a unique and singularly beautiful regimental banner for the Rangers. Embroidered with figures that symbolized various legends prevailing among the tribes, it was officially authorized to be carried along with the King's colours and the unit's regular regimental colours. Thus the 114th, contrary to prevailing practice, had the distinction of carrying a third banner.

But to the great disappointment of its personnel, the 114th Battalion would be ordered broken up once it arrived in England. The decision was especially dispiriting to members of its Indian companies, who had eagerly anticipated going into battle as a Native fighting force. Today, one of the few existing memories that remains of the distinctive aboriginal fighting force is a period photograph of its unique flag.

Despite this setback, other Six Nations Natives distinguished themselves as individuals. Captain A. G. E. Smith, son of a Six

Nations chief, won the Military Cross for distinguished gallantry in action. While serving in the 20th Battalion, he was wounded three times. Invalided home, he served as adjutant to a Polish battalion stationed at Camp Niagara. Tragically, Cameron D. Brant, great-great grandson of Joseph Brant, became the first Brant county soldier to fall in action. While serving with 4th Battalion, he was killed repulsing the German gas attack during the Second Battle of Ypres, in 1915, gallantly leading his men in the heroic charge in which Colonel Birchall, the unit's commanding officer, and other brave officers also met their deaths. Earlier, as a result of his well-developed Native talent in scouting, Brant had established a reputation for reconnoitring no-man's-land by night. Additionally, two other descendants of Joseph Brant, Corporal Albert W. L. Crain, also of 4th Battalion, and Private Nathan Montoure, subsequently promoted captain, were severely wounded in the fighting at Ypres.

Two other Ontario Iroquois bands, the Bay of Quinte's Mohawks and the Thames' Oneidas, established exceptionally high enlistment records. The first sent 82 men from a total male population of 353; the latter, 48 from a total male population of 220. Additionally, Private Corby, of the Bay of Quinte Mohawks, was awarded the Military Medal.

Quebec's Indians, too, would establish an outstanding record serving with the Canadian Expeditionary Force. Delphis Theberge, a Huron from Jeune Lorette, won the Military Medal. Sergeant Joe Clear Sky, a Caughnawaga originally with Brock's Rangers, also won the Military Medal. When he saw that the gas mask of a wounded comrade, who was lying in no-man's-land during a heavy gas attack, had been rendered useless, he crawled to him through poisonous fumes. Removing his own respirator, Clear Sky placed it on the wounded soldier, saving his life, although he himself was severely gassed in the operation.

Prairie Indians as well sent a disproportionate number of their men to fight in the Great War. The participation rates of northern Natives, including the Peguis Band, the Pas Band, as well as the St. Peter's Band, proved exceptionally high. Possibly, this was due to the opportunities the conflict presented for both travel and pay, for few of these relatively isolated Native groups were able to follow news of the fortunes of the great European struggle. Less surprising, perhaps, was the appearance in battle costume, this time modern khaki, of Sioux warriors such as those from Griswold, Manitoba. During the 1870s and 1880s, their ancestors had fought in the famous Sioux wars against Custer and the American government before seeking sanctuary in Canada. Although the majority were eventually returned to the U.S., a few remained in Canada. Still, the warrior tradition remained strong among such aboriginals.

The File Hills Colony, a Native agricultural community, sent two-thirds of its males to war. Alexander Bass, a father of seven, won the Military Medal. The Coté Band, near Port Pelly, one of the earliest HBC posts, sent practically all its young men to war. Despite historic differences with Ottawa, numerous Métis also signed recruitment rolls and loyally supported the Crown during its time of peril, as they would two decades later when the conflict resumed.

Joe Thunder, a Saskatchewan Native, serving with the 128th Battalion, and who later transferred to the 50th, deserves special mention for his heroism. Finding himself surrounded by six Germans, he bayoneted them all, a feat for which he received the Military Medal.

In Alberta, the declaration of war struck a resonant note among grandsons of famous Blood, Blackfoot, and Piegan warriors who, only decades earlier, had roamed the plains hunting buffalo. That the warrior spirit still existed in such Natives was borne out by their numbers on the rolls of the Canadian Expeditionary Force, as well as by such ringing names as Mountain Horse, Coming Singing, White Bull, and Strangling Wolf.

The Indians of British Columbia contributed several hundred quality soldiers to Canada's Expeditionary Force. Private George MacLean, an Okanagan Indian, armed with a dozen bombs, killed 19 enemy, and captured 14, before himself being severely wounded. For this accomplishment, he earned the Distinguished

Conduct Medal. Edwin Victor Cook from Alert Bay also won the DCM. Twice wounded in action, he was eventually killed in the last months of the struggle.

Canada's northern Indians deserve special mention. Although Senai, a full-blooded Native from Osnaburg in the Patricia district, spoke no English, he journeyed to Port Arthur to enlist after a group of tourists had told him about the war. Crossing the ocean, he spent seven months in the trenches, participated in the great battle of Passchendaele, and was severely wounded. Another Native, John Campbell, of Hershell Island, learning of the struggle, travelled 3,000 miles by foot, train, canoe, and river steamer to enlist. By the time he reached Vancouver, however, hostilities had terminated, ending his chance of experiencing the Western Front's trenches.

Since most Native recruits spent their lives hunting, they were excellent marksmen. The record of a handful of these Indian riflemen is worth noting. Sniper Lance-Corporal Johnson Paudash of the 21st Battalion established an exceptional record, even for a Native: his sights claimed 88 enemy. A Mississauga from Rice Lake, he was awarded the Military Medal for saving life during a particularly heavy bombardment, and for passing on information that the enemy was massing near Hill 70 for a counterattack. One of the original "Firsts," as members of our country's first contingent to go overseas were dubbed, Paudash was also recommended for the Distinguished Conduct Medal for saving an officer's life during the Somme battle.

Another Mississauga, Sampson Comego of the Alnwick Band, was officially credited with 28 enemy "kills." One of the "Firsts" as well, he was tragically killed in action in November 1915. His brother Peter who also enlisted in 1914 survived four years of service in the trenches. Twice wounded, he, too, ran up a distinguished record as a sniper.

Private Philip MacDonald, a Quebec Native serving with 8th Battalion, Winnipeg's famous "Little Black Devils," also distinguished himself as a sharpshooter. Ultimately he claimed 40 dead Germans to his credit before himself being killed. Two other

Indian members of the same unit established notable records. "Paddy" Riel, from Port Arthur, a grandson of the famous rebel leader Louis Riel, had 38 notches on the stock of his rifle when he died. More fortunate was a Native named Ballendine. The trio's third member, he survived his tour of sniping in no-man's-land. When he finally returned home to wife and family, 50 notches on his gun eloquently recorded the story of his service to King and Country.

Among the most legendary and effective snipers of the Canadian Forces and entire British Army was Lance-Corporal Norwest, a full-blooded Indian from near Edmonton, serving in Calgary's 50th Battalion. Short and powerfully built, with a pleasant face and remarkable eye, he possessed a calmness of manner that never deserted him in an emergency or when dealing with high-ranking officers. Employing a rifle fitted with a telescopic sight, and famed for his patience in stalking his quarry, he claimed the highest sharpshooting record in the entire British Army: 115 observed kills. Tragically, he himself would be shot through the head by an enemy sniper, August 18, 1918, while he and two companions were attempting to locate a nest of German snipers. Although his record stands at 115, it does not represent the ultimate number of casualties he caused since he did not claim a "hit" without an officer being present to confirm his accuracy. Ironically, just prior to the Allies' final drive that led to the armistice, Norwest was specifically detailed to remain in the support lines, since he had been in continuous action during his entire two years in France. Nonetheless, in response to his constant pleading, he was allowed to go forward with the attack, rendering invaluable service destroying enemy snipers and putting enemy machine gun posts out of action. For his outstanding battle record, Norwest was ultimately awarded the Military Medal and Bar. On his grave, sorrowing comrades wrote, with the coarse understated humour of the Canadian infantryman, but also a sense of profound respect: "It must have been a damned good sniper that got Norwest."

Challenging Norwest for top sniping honours was Francis Pegahmagabow, the Ojibway from Parry Island Band mentioned earlier. Like his rival, he possessed the patience and skill that enabled him to blend into surrounding terrain so successfully that it was next to impossible to detect his movements as he crept slowly across no-man's-land. Iron nerves, patience, and adroit marksmanship rendered him a superb sniper. Accounts vary, but most credit him with an incredible 378 hits. Unofficial though this score appears to be, it is the best overall record of any sniper on the Western Front. Thankfully, "Peg" survived the conflict. Afterwards, he returned to live on Parry Island serving as Band Councillor and Chief. His experiences overseas renewed his concern for Native culture, and as chief he encouraged the preservation of traditional beliefs, customs, and skills. When he died in 1952, he was buried with full military honours.

Indian soldiers laboured in less glamorous roles as well. Special mention must be made of the 107th Pioneer (Engineering) Battalion, commanded by Lieutenant-Colonel Glen Campbell of Winnipeg, who prior to the war had been Chief Inspector of Indian Agencies for the Department of Indian Affairs. No other regiment in the Imperial Forces boasted such a wide representation of tribes: Crees, Salteaux, and Sioux from the North and West, Mohawks, Onondagas, Oneidas, Tuscaroras, Delawares, and Chippewas from Ontario and Quebec, as well as Micmacs from the Maritimes. Only Natives from B.C. appear not to have been included for some reason, although, as noted above, they served in other capacities. Campbell, who spoke a number of Native tongues, often issued orders and sometimes even held orderly-room, or informal, trials in the aboriginals' own languages. Invariably, though, he praised the courage, discipline and intelligence of Native soldiers in the highest terms. In particular, he stressed their ability and patience in adapting themselves, without complaint, to difficult conditions and bad weather. These attributes rendered Native efficiency far above the average.

Close to the war's end, at Hill 70 in the vicinity of Lens, Indian companies of the 107th were assigned the unenviable and perilous task of digging communications trenches between the Canadian and German front lines. Modern readers can only wonder whether they were considered expendable by the standards of the period, although none can question their dogged courage. While the work went ahead, the enemy was conducting an offensive and casualties were heavy. Oblivious to shells dropping on every side, the stoic Natives continued working without stopping, amid the roar and storm of steel. The scene caused one of the officers who was present to comment that the men seemed as calm as if "they were digging a potato plot." Despite the exhausting ordeal and terrible losses suffered by their battalion, the Natives recommenced work following only a brief stop to rest their tired muscles. None uttered the slightest complaint. Three of the very same Indians, Tom Longboat, Joe Keeper, and A. Jamieson, who earlier had won fame at home as long-distance runners, also distinguished themselves as dispatch runners on the Western Front.

Despite the discrimination their race continued to face at home, loyal Indians who had volunteered to assist Canada to fight the Great War forged one more important link in their proud tradition of supporting the Crown, whatever the personal cost. Two decades later, this straight path or chain of loyalty would be renewed with the outbreak of World War II. It has been estimated that 30,000 Natives and persons with some Indian ancestry served in this conflict.

If a single Native deserves mention it is Tommy Prince, for his outstanding record of achievement in this second struggle. As one commentator has recently noted: "More than just a rugged individualist, he was unique — the ultimate Native warrior." Great-great grandson of the legendary Chief Peguis, Thomas Prince was born on October 25, 1915 at Scanterbury, Manitoba. After enlisting in the Royal Canadian Engineers, he was transferred to 1st Canadian Parachute Battalion. A month following this, he joined the combined Canadian-American First Special Service Force, the so-called Devil's Brigade.

Tommy won his first decoration in the Anzio bridgehead, south of Rome, Italy, in early February 1944. On this occasion, he went tank-hunting equipped with a field-telephone: in a sense

Elders and Indian soldiers in the uniform of the Canadian Expeditionary Force.
Department of the Interior. (NAC/PA-041366)

sniping, but on a much grander scale. Crossing a canal and slipping into a deserted farmhouse, he patiently waited till morning.
Then, when he spotted a pair of tanks, he called down accurate
artillery fire that destroyed both. When enemy mortar shells inad-
vertently severed his field line, Sergeant Prince, donning a peas-
ant's black hat and jacket he found, rushed outside, doing "a little
dervish dance" to confuse any enemy who might be watching.
After repairing the line, and going back inside the house, he
called down shell fire that destroyed two more enemy tanks
before evening. For his day's work, Prince was awarded the
Military Medal. Afterwards, he maintained that, had he not been
an Indian, he would likely have won the VC. Such criticism indicates the bitterness Native soldiers often carried with them, even
on the battlefield, and perhaps also explains why so many brave
natives who performed exceptional deeds during the Great War
won the Distinguished Conduct Medal, or DCM, but never
achieved the much-coveted Victoria Cross.

Sergeant Tommy Prince (R), MM, 1st Canadian Parachute Battalion,
with his brother, Private Morris Prince, at an investiture at Buckingham Palace.
Photograph: C.L. Woods. (NAC/PA-142289)

Six months later in Southern France, Prince would add the American Silver Star to his medal collection. On this occasion, the sergeant led a two-man patrol deep into enemy territory consisting of rugged mountains to gain information concerning enemy outposts, guns and even a bivouac. The scouting mission, an operation requiring both highly developed observation skills and stealth, ultimately enabled Prince's battalion to move forward and wipe out the enemy camp.

The former lumberjack survived the war and later served with the Princess Patricias in Korea. His postwar years, though, were not easy. Crippled from arthritis, Tommy Prince died in poverty on November 25, 1977, age sixty-two. Today, a barracks at Camp Petawawa commemorates his memory. A statue unveiled in 1989 in Winnipeg also keeps alive the story of this "wonderful scout."

Native Canadians who served Canada in the wars of this century looked back, and continue to look back, with pride. They often harbour, however, a deep resentment, for, when they returned home, they frequently found their lot had not improved; but had worsened. This was especially true if they had resigned their Indian status.

Major "Big Jim" Stone (later a lieutenant-colonel) noted this sense of betrayal in the response Sergeant J. G. St. Germain, a Métis, made to a compliment Stone paid him during the bitter Christmas 1943 fighting at Ortona in Italy: "That's fine, Sir, but I hope I get killed before it's all over. Here, I lead a platoon and the boys all call me 'the Saint,' but if I get back to Canada, I'll be treated just like another poor goddamn Indian." Ironically, St. Germain later would be granted his wish, leading his platoon across the Naviglio's muddy banks near Rapallo.

On a brilliant August morning in 1990, a band of First Nations warriors, old men now, but proud of their Legion blazers and berets, campaign medals polished, formed up at Kanesatake, the Mohawk settlement just west of Montreal, whose residents had erected barriers at nearby Oka to protect an Indian burial ground they claimed from being bulldozed. Then they marched down the road towards the barricades which divided aboriginals and whites, to show their support for their people. Marching with them, in spirit, were the ghosts of Norwest, Francis Pegahmagabow, Tommy Prince, Joe St. Germain, as well as the fond memories of Canadians of all races who have proudly served alongside such superb warriors.

SELECTED READINGS

Gaffen, Fred. *Forgotten Soldiers.* Penticton, B.C.: Theytus, 1985.

Peate, Les. "The Korean War . . . The Amazing Tommy Prince." *Esprit de Corps: Canadian Military Then and Now* 4:6 (November 1994): 37–38.

Summerby, Janice. *Native Soldiers, Foreign Battlefields.* Ottawa: Veterans Affairs Canada, 1993.

Twatio, Bill. "Native Warriors." *Esprit de Corps: Canadian Military Then and Now* 4:4 (September 1994): 9–11.

(Visit of W.L.M. King) General McNaughton and the Prime Minister, Aldershot, England. (NAC/C-018246)

18

GENERAL ANDY MCNAUGHTON AND GENERAL HARRY CRERAR

Senior Commanders: World War II

Two senior officers with very different styles commanded Canada's Army during World War II. Under General Andrew G. L. "Andy" McNaughton (1887–1966), the country's newly constituted overseas army, a successor to the Great War's Canadian Corps, evolved from a single division to a corps, and finally to First Canadian Army. But McNaughton was not a good enough tactician nor sufficiently skilled to achieve his dream of field command. After British General Bernard L. Montgomery prevailed upon Ottawa to remove McNaughton, he was succeeded by General Henry D. G. "Harry" Crerar (1888–1965), a graduate of Royal Military College. In contrast to his charismatic predecessor, the quiet, pipe-smoking Crerar, with his studious and capable manner, managed the country's rapidly expanding military with adroitness. In addition to keeping his mercurial subordinate Lieutenant-General Guy Simonds in check, and dealing with Monty's demands, he had to satisfy Ottawa's politicians. More importantly, during the war's final operations, he would do an excellent job of commanding a huge army, comprising not only Canadian, but also British, American and other troops.

Andrew McNaughton was born in 1887 at Moosomin, in the Northwest Territories, as Saskatchewan was then called. Growing up on the Dominion's remote northwest frontier far removed from society's constraints and conventions encouraged his keen mind to develop its own unorthodox, and questioning character. His background also gave McNaughton the common, down-to-earth manner and concern for others that was his hallmark.

After attending Bishop's College School, in Quebec's Eastern Townships, and McGill, where he completed a master's degree in electrical engineering, young Andy joined the university's teaching staff. When war broke out in 1914, as a result of Germany's invading neutral Belgium, McNaughton, who soldiered in his spare time, was already a major in the 3rd Battery, Canadian Field Artillery. Soon, he put theory to test by taking a battery overseas with Canada's First Contingent. By 1916, the precocious gunnery officer had attained the rank of a lieutenant-colonel. By 1917 Andy's exceptional talents had made him Counter-Battery Staff Officer of the entire Canadian Corps. At the battle of Vimy Ridge, McNaughton's pinpoint counterbattery fire played an essential, even major, role. It is estimated that his gunners destroyed an incredible 83 percent of the enemy's artillery capacity. One military expert would later praise McNaughton as "probably the best and the most scientific gunner of any army in the world." It was not an overstatement.

Sir Arthur Currie, impressed by McNaughton's "strong common sense [and] aggressive mind," encouraged him to remain in the army at war's end. By 1923, thanks to his brilliant mind, he had risen to Deputy Chief of Staff, following attendance at British Staff College. In 1927 McNaughton was off to Britain once again, this time attending Imperial Defence College. Once more, he drew glowing praise for his "ability, knowledge, experience & enthusiasm." Back home again, McNaughton assumed command of the West Coast's No. 11 Military District. In typical fashion, he promptly constructed a swimming pool which tides filled and emptied in Victoria's new Work Point Barracks — an innovation for the period.

Lieutenant-General Andrew G. L. McNaughton.
Department of National Defence. (NAC/PA-132648)

Succeeding as Chief of Staff of Canada's interwar army, Mc-Naughton led the force during the early years of the Depression. Always, his fertile mind managed to find ways to obtain more funding for his soldiers. When Prime Minister R. B. Bennett's government could find no funds to construct military bases or airfields, McNaughton devised a scheme that utilized unemployed men, many demobilized veterans, to build such needed facilities. "The Royal Twenty Centers," as they were called, turned radical, however. It caused an embarrassment to Bennett, whose Conservatives faced an election in 1935. Clearly, McNaughton had to go.

As a compromise, the General reluctantly accepted an appointment to the National Research Council, becoming its president. He continued to insist, though, that he had been "merely seconded" from his first love, National Defence.

During his interlude at NRC in the late 1930s, McNaughton indulged his natural bent for scientific innovation. He developed and patented a cathode-ray direction finder (a forerunner of radar), worked on problems of aircraft location for coastal artillery, and developed a trajectory chart for crest clearance and air burst ranging. He also pioneered automatic sights for coastal guns. In 1939, with war clouds darkening, the General led a delegation from the Canadian Manufacturers Association to Britain, seeking munitions contracts.

Even after war broke out in September 1939, as a result of Germany's attack on Poland, whose security both Britain and France had guaranteed, the exact nature of what Canada's military role should be in the conflict remained unclear. Prime Minister Mackenzie King remembered how the Conscription Crisis had split the country in 1917, threatening national unity. Ever cautious, he feared heavy casualties would again promote demands for conscription and split the Liberals into warring factions. To forestall this scenario, he needed a charismatic general to head the Dominion's army, one who commanded not only politicians' respect but also the public's. McNaughton appeared to be his kind of officer. As King confessed to his now-famous diary: "I thought no better man could be selected, certainly not one whose appointment would meet with more general approval."

In many respects — although not all, given his perpetually dishevelled appearance and battle dress that never quite seemed to fit — McNaughton seemed a modern version of military leadership. In his memoirs, military historian Colonel C. P. Stacey paints a vivid portrait of the Canadian commander as he appeared in January 1941:

> McNaughton at this time was at the height of his personal powers, and the impact of his personality was extraordinary. Meet-

ing him was like shaking hands with a dynamo. He seemed to radiate energy. This sense, combined with the bright eyes, shaggy hair and eyebrows, the "rather melancholy" expression which I remember an English newspaperman noting, left an indelible feeling of contact with a most remarkable and unusual human being. It was not surprising that the British press should sometimes speculate about McNaughton as a possible Supreme Commander for the future Allied invading forces, though such speculation was highly naive, disregarding as it did the basic fact that the great powers were certain to reserve the appointment for one of their own.

Certainly when he and the almost totally untrained Canadian division he commanded arrived in the United Kingdom in December 1939, McNaughton seemed made for the job. Part soldier, part scientist, as well as a natural politician, he possessed a magnetic personality which impressed virtually everyone he encountered in both Canada and England.

McNaughton's "damn the red tape" approach to the myriad problems that beset the recently arrived and poorly equipped Canadians only fed the legend. Unable to draw boots for his unit from Ordnance, the C.O. of the Royal Montreal Regiment purchased them from Eaton's. Ottawa refused to pay. The General, however, cut through the Gordian knot by approving the purchase on the spot. Eight months later, a junior staff officer, charged with obtaining winter kit for 1,500 troops bound for Norway, discovered that none was available. Acting on his own initiative, he called a British sporting goods firm. He arranged for the well-known establishment to supply fleece-lined jackets. When the War Office cancelled the questionable military operation, and the sheepskin jackets turned up on the backs of sweethearts across England's southern counties, the captain was summoned by McNaughton. Pointing to the bills, the General told the officer he was going to make him responsible for them. The young man's face whitened. Suddenly, though, the Commander's tone changed: "To hell with rules, get it done, that's the kind of young officer we want." The army paid the bills. And the officer went off to Staff College. Afterwards, every time the officer was promoted, Andy, who loved a good joke, would call him on the telephone asking for him by his new rank. He loved the resulting confusion.

Stories such as these confirmed that the General would always choose to solve problems in a logical manner. Also, that "Andy" always put the welfare of the officers and men he commanded first. All this enhanced McNaughton's growing reputation as the most brilliant and best-known personality, bar none, of the conflict's early, or "phoney war," period.

Prior to taking up his appointment overseas in 1940, as General Officer commanding the Canadian Army, McNaughton had gone on official record, stating that our country's contribution to any European conflict should consist of a division, complete in all respects. His reasoning was clear. As he put it, the public "demanded that Canada should be represented by a fighting unit in the line of battle and that public opinion would be satisfied with nothing less." But such a statement struck a sensitive note with the cost-conscious government. It also caused the Prime Minister to have second thoughts about McNaughton — especially concerning his capacity to subordinate himself to civilian authority — and there was the problem, overlooked before, of his age. But the General soldiered on. Despite his advancing years (he was fifty-three) McNaughton assumed personal command of newly formed 1st Canadian Infantry Division. And the General's self-promoted popularity continued to grow. During this "honeymoon" period, an admiring newspaperman began the campaign of concerted adulation, bordering on deification, which ultimately converted his personage into that of the Dominion's "Super Soldier." Nevertheless, the General had yet to demonstrate his capacity to conduct a modern war.

McNaughton's military judgement remained open to doubt. Touring the Maginot Line's hedgehog-like defences, he declared he was "greatly impressed by the morale of the French Army." In February 1940, he sent a distinct chill of alarm through Ottawa by hinting that a Canadian Corps would shortly be sent overseas.

This was much more of a commitment than our government was willing to concede at this point in the war. In April, when the British War Office requested a Canadian brigade be included for special service in Norway, the General again enthusiastically concurred. Although the government honoured the commitment, Mackenzie King's cabinet was beginning to question both McNaughton's political and military expertise.

Despite misgivings, it was only natural that, as senior Canadian officer in Britain, McNaughton would continue to command the evolving Canadian army. Certainly he was innovative in the uses of new technology, especially with respect to artillery, and he was exceptionally well-liked by the troops.

The *Blitzkrieg,* or "Lightning War," that overwhelmed Allied Armies in France and the Low Countries thrust McNaughton into a new prominence. Ten days after he went to France to assess the situation, Canadians would once again be on their way to Brest, as part of the hastily assembled British Expeditionary Force, under Lieutenant-General Sir Alan Brooke. But after entraining and moving inland, they were promptly ordered returned to the coast. Despite the "Big Bust of Brest," as some christened it, and the fact they had left some of their equipment in France, the evacuated Canadians henceforward constituted the most battle-ready division in a beleaguered Britain, bracing itself to resist Nazi invasion.

Promoted Lieutenant-General, McNaughton was placed in command of VII Corps, composed of Canadians, a British formation, and New Zealanders, which was responsible for defending a major portion of southeast England's coastline. Such recognition played well back home in Canada, which, weak though it was, formed the United Kingdom's principal ally. In both England and at home, the General's doings continued to dominate the press. Likely, even he himself found the attention and adulation pleasant, if not entirely convincing.

Nor did McNaughton limit his powers to those of mere military commander. Like his mentor Sir Arthur Currie, a quarter of a century earlier, he was acutely aware that, as commander of Canada's army, he represented the country itself, and was ultimately responsible for employing her soldiers. In contrast, Sir Alan Brooke regarded McNaughton's Canadians, despite the substantially enlarged responsibilities given their General, as British colonial forces to be deployed at will. After further scrutiny, Brooke also recorded that he was "depressed at the standard of training and efficiency of Canadian Divisional and Brigade Commanders." It was "a great pity to see such excellent material as the Canadian men controlled by indifferent commanders." Concluding that the over-aged, and out-of-date McNaughton "was no judge of the qualities required by a commander," the British officer added that the General "[has] not got the required qualities to make a success of commanding a Corp[s]."

Two Canadian officers, members of Monty's "Young Turks," or ambitious young senior officers, were even more damning of the senior Canadian commander. They were Brigadier E. L. M. Burns, and his successor at General Staff, Brigadier Guy Simonds. Simonds, brilliant officer and tactician that he proved, told one of Montgomery's staff officers that he worried about the Canadian Corps' training. Problems were evident at all officer ranks, but the greatest deficiency remained at the crucial battalion and brigade commander level. Bolstering this stark assessment, Simonds noted that very few battalion officers were capable of effectively commanding their units in battle, and that only four of nine brigadiers were capable of training their battalion officers. General Bernard L. Montgomery regarded Simonds highly. And, since Monty's new broom was sweeping clean through the ranks of South-Eastern command, the British Commander now set out with a will to rectify such problems.

McNaughton, showing signs of nervous stress, fell ill and went on sick leave. His departure now afforded Monty the opportunity to act. Even Crerar, temporarily replacing McNaughton as acting commander, later owned, "McNaughton had sadly neglected training," leaving the force in a "hell of a state when he [Crerar] came to take over from Canada." Monty, on his part, personally imposed systematic training on the Corps. He also assessed virtually every officer and senior NCO for fitness to command. In a short time, impressive results were evident on the training front.

Rigorous and realistic exercises such as "Operation Tiger" tested troops' fighting qualities by putting participants through gruelling trials.

Monty also personally saw to it that sweeping changes were forced on the Corps at division, brigade, and even battalion level. Major-Generals C. B. Price and George Pearkes, as well as several brigadiers, were either replaced or returned to posts at home, and heads rolled at the battalion level as well. Still, not all such problems could be traced to McNaughton's role. The reality remained that the small Permanent Force contained within its ranks few generals capable of assuming senior posts. Nor had years of tight budgets and inadequate training properly prepared militia counterparts. True, McNaughton had spotted "comers" such as Simonds, Charles Foulkes, D. C. Spry, and Bruce Mathews, and had brought these young officers along. But senior officers were weak and remained so.

McNaughton's real Achilles heel, though, was that he thought in technical and political, rather than strategic and tactical terms. Additionally, he was burdened with having to defend the interests of the army at large. He grew increasingly distant from the troops, who scarcely saw him, and he paid little attention to the important process of training. In his mind, training remained the responsibility of staff officers and divisional commanders. The meticulous Simonds, whose own role in the war is detailed in a later chapter, correctly identified the problem, recalling how the General "would not focus his mind on training and operational problems, and for a long time we were adrift." Decades afterwards, officers would remember McNaughton climbing under a truck to check its transmission, leaning over engines on inspections, crawling under tanks, testing gun sights, or working on an artillery breechblock. Or he might even have a machine gun stripped down on a table in his office, his hands coated in protective grease. The interest was human. Doubtlessly it produced better weapons for the boys, as well as saved lives. But a general's job specifications did not call for him to be a technician, no matter how much it might awe American visitors.

McNaughton's tragic demise began with "Spartan," the great

exercise in March 1943 to test "the problems arising in an advance from an established beachhead." During two weeks, it pitted McNaughton's army composed of two corps and a third British corps against an "enemy" army of two corps. The manoeuvres, involving in excess of a quarter of a million soldiers as well as 72,000 vehicles strung out across a large swatch of southern England, clearly indicated the General was not capable of coping with the task. If anything, he tied up his force in what proved an incredible traffic jam.

The General was also hampered by the difficult task of dealing with the complex politico-military questions that flowed daily between Ottawa and London. He had to press Ottawa to keep the formations flowing that he required to build his division into a corps, and his corps into an army. Most importantly, he had constantly to act as a watchdog to ensure the War Office did not commit his beloved troops piecemeal to operations for which they were either unready, unsuited, or ill-equipped. During an interview in 1941, McNaughton coined the soon-famous phrase that the Canadian Army was a "dagger pointed at the heart of Berlin." If he had his way, it would be kept together until the invasion of Europe. Still, the danger remained that the much-vaunted dagger might turn out to be all handle, with very little blade evident.

Meanwhile pressures to employ the Canadians were building. Thanks to oversights and errors in British planning, the only battles employing Dominion troops had proven to be disasters: the ignominious surrender of Hong Kong in December 1941 and the bloodbath of Dieppe in August 1942. Canada — including most soldiers under the General's command — wanted another taste of battle, to show what our boys really could achieve.

In early 1943 Mackenzie King's government finally prevailed upon the War Office to utilize Canadians in the upcoming Mediterranean campaign. The forces committed to the as-of-yet unidentified landing would be 1st Canadian Infantry Division and a tank brigade. Eventually, Canada's contribution consisted of I Canadian Corps, composed of 1st Canadian Infantry Division, the armoured brigade, as well as 5th Canadian Armoured Division.

McNaughton agreed, reluctantly, to participate in what became the Sicily campaign, if 1st Division returned to the UK afterwards. He also initially opposed dispatching I Canadian Corps, since by reducing First Canadian Army to a single corps its independent existence was threatened. Despite his reluctance, however, McNaughton calculated — falsely as it turned out — that his position as GOC was so strong that the government dared not oppose him. In reaching this judgement, he was likely lulled by the fact that the Governor General had termed him "an idol in the eyes of his countrymen."

McNaughton further compromised his position by attempting to visit the operations in Sicily once they were underway. Although the War Office had given its approval for him to observe 1st Canadian Division in action, Montgomery, Eighth Army's Commander, refused to permit the General to set foot on the island. His superior, General Harold Alexander, seconded Monty's stand, observing that McNaughton was "rather snotty" about the rebuff. For Alexander, it was sufficient that Monty wanted no visitors at all for the moment, and he added, "these incidents are very upsetting when we are trying to win battles." In his memoirs Monty noted the reason for this decision: "For God's sake keep him away," Simonds had pleaded when told of his own GOC's imminent descent. It appears the intense young Canadian general was too busy learning how to fight the Germans. The last thing he wished at this point was to have his concentration diverted from this task by the niceties of having to entertain his superior.

When the blow came in the winter of 1943, it was almost anticlimactic. An extraordinary flurry of telegrams, as well as a series of hasty meetings, negotiations, and secret talks made it appear McNaughton was the monarch of an independent nation rather than a mere soldier at his government's beck and call. But in the end the General was dismissed. The official reason provided was that he was in "poor health." On the day he was fired, McNaughton ("The God Who Failed," as J. L. Granatstein has colourfully dubbed him) was riding with one of his former personal assistants beside him in an automobile. He is reported to have stated: "I hope there won't be mutiny in the army, Eliot." No such uprising took place. In fact, there was scarcely a ripple.

Given the proud Highland blood that coursed in his veins, McNaughton did not plan, as old generals must, to "fade away quietly into the night." Even before departing England, he plotted revenge against those who had done him in. He planned to denounce Allied policy, also Monty himself, and "add some scalps to his belt when he got back to Canada." More importantly, he plotted to disprove any perception on the public's part that he was unfit to lead his countrymen into battle. Indeed, he dreamed he "might [yet] be able to command the Canadian Army."

McNaughton clearly underrated the politicians who had carefully laid plans to deal with such a loose cannon. Press and parliamentary statements were drafted and redrafted, emphasizing the former commander's ill-health. Additionally, the Prime Minister now belatedly showed opposition leaders the labyrinthine correspondence on the matter. This shrewd device quickly defused the General's attack. After McNaughton and James Ralston, the minister, met in June 1944, the General's leave was extended for a further three months. By this time, all attention was focussed on Normandy. The McNaughton affair had been transformed into little more than a damp squib.

For a brief period, the dethroned chieftain threatened to join the Progressive Conservatives. To end this new threat, King turned to the General as the one man who he felt might assist him to find a way out of the rapidly growing conscription crisis that was confronting the country. Although the General accepted, replacing the colourless Ralston as Defence Minister, he would fail in his larger purpose. Popular as he remained with the ordinary soldier, he proved incapable of inspiring sufficient numbers of "Zombies" (the name given conscripts who refused to go overseas) to agree to such service. Nonetheless, McNaughton's partnership with King during this critical period likely helped preserve the country's unity. Later, following the war, McNaughton twice failed to gain election to the House of Commons. Still, he continued to serve his nation magnificently elsewhere: at the United Nations and on the Joint Board of Defence. Not least, he would serve for more than a decade as Canadian chairman of the International Joint Commission on continental water resources.

As Professor Granatstein states: "If the trio of McNaughton, Crerar and Simonds dominated the Canadian army during the Second World War, the key figure was not Andy McNaughton. It was General H. D. G. Crerar, who truly might be said to have modelled Canada's army in his own image and fashion."

The two senior commanders were quite different types. McNaughton, as we have seen, was rumpled and magnetic and colourful. Crerar, anything but a warlike figure of the standard model, was immaculate and precise, not least in dress. The new commander of 1st Canadian Corps would coin no dramatic phrases, nor would he capture imaginations like "Andy." Still, despite his lack of battle experience there existed no doubt, even from the beginning, that he was "a general's general." In time, he would win the affection, even deep respect, of officers who worked under him and came to know him well. Of Crerar, critics liked to say: "he'll never make a bad mistake." On the surface, his proficiency and respect for regulations made him appear cold, even aloof. He wasn't really; it just seemed that way. Despite his quiet manner, which belied his inner strength, Crerar would make his mark as "the most important Canadian soldier of the war."

Henry ("Harry") Crerar was born in the steel-making city of Hamilton in 1888. Like many of the Dominion's officers-to-be, he attended Upper Canada College. Here, one of his mentors was Stephen Leacock. During World War II, Canada's greatest humorist would author an amusing piece entitled "Generals I Have Trained." Touching on half a dozen senior officers he had taught at the prestigious boys school, he painted a sympathetic portrait of Crerar as a youngster. As Leacock's humanistic eye observed, Crerar was essentially an emotional man who cared deeply about people. Nonetheless, few outside his close family circle would ever really sense the fact, so rigid would be the officer's self-control.

At Royal Military College, the slight youngster, only five-feet-eight-inches tall, was no academic star. Coming in, he stood 27th, although going out he had moved up to 13th. During the Great War, the young officer indicated his potential, establishing a distinguished record. After serving in Canadian Division's first action fought at Ypres, he became a junior staff officer. By 1915 he rose to command an artillery battery. By 1917 he had become an acting lieutenant-colonel, commanding 3rd Brigade, Canadian Field Artillery. Following a further staff course in England, he joined 5th Canadian Divisional Artillery as brigade major. In the process, he also came in contact with McNaughton.

The war over, Crerar briefly returned to civilian life, then joined the Permanent Force Artillery as a major. His decision was aided by the annual income provided by a substantial inheritance from his mother, who died in 1919. In fact this private income would prove more benefit than he could possibly realize. Given the small size of the Dominion's army during the interwar period, he would find himself frozen in rank for almost 15 years. This circumstance frustrated the ambitious Crerar beyond measure. Indeed, the young officer remained acutely conscious of his rank, his place on the army graduation list, as well as his pay allowances, especially given the fact he now had a wife and family to support.

Despite such difficulties, his career postings were the correct ones, providing both exposure and experience. Activities included a tour of Staff College, Camberley, England, in 1925, where he excelled. Crerar also contributed occasional articles to the *Canadian Defence Quarterly*, and lectured whenever he could.

Most importantly both for his own career and the future of his country, Crerar continued to grow and change during the interwar years. Repeatedly he demonstrated he was a political soldier in the best meaning of the term. Certainly, he was an officer who understood that in Canada, as elsewhere, military questions are usually linked to domestic and international politics. Today, this seems obvious. In the interwar Permanent Force, however, Crerar was one of perhaps only two or three officers who were capable of "taking their imaginations out and doing some serious thinking." Superiors also noted that he was invariably careful, methodical, and precise in word and action. In fact, he carefully cultivated a file of stories and jokes for speeches. Such attention to detail only increased his worth.

After attending the Imperial Defence College in London, where he again studied with his friend Alan Brooke, Crerar was ready for a critical new appointment. In the capacity of Director of Military Operations and Intelligence at National Staff Headquarters, he was now the army's senior staff planner. Still, for a recognized "comer," and one of the army's brightest luminaries, his progress up the promotional ladder was glacial. On one occasion, when an officer standing junior to him was promoted, a con-

General H. D. G. Crerar.
Department of National Defence. (NAC/PA-166584)

cerned Crerar wrote the Chief of Staff to protest. He noted: "I am in my fiftieth year. The time during which I can apply the knowledge I have gained through the somewhat exceptional military education which has come my way cannot be long." Within a year, he was raised to the position of temporary brigadier, upon being appointed Commander of Royal Military College.

Crerar spent only a short period as commander of RMC. Briefly recalled to Ottawa in 1939, he helped put the finishing touches on the army's mobilization plans. He also immediately started to lobby for an overseas appointment. But he was not destined to spend much time in England. The *Blitzkrieg* and stunning Nazi victories of May and June 1940, which brought about France's surrender and drove Britain from the continent, forced wholesale changes on a reluctant Ottawa. The clear-thinking Crerar would arrive back in Canada just in time for Ralston, the new defence minister, to appoint him Chief of General Staff.

At Defence Headquarters, Crerar's greatest accomplishment would be to bring order out of chaos as quickly as possible. Alarmed that everyone was working so intensely, often foregoing sleep, he ordered officers to take one day's rest per week, to labour no more than three evenings, and to take a long weekend each month. Crerar was fond of saying that the staff officer was "the servant of the troops, not the master." Nonetheless, he realized officers couldn't do their jobs if they were overtired or burnt out. Meanwhile, Crerar himself and E. L. M. Burns prepared a major paper. Entitled "The Canadian Army," it called for highly mechanized forces, and for radical changes in the use and training of National Resources Mobilization Act soldiers. Specifically, it proposed ending the 30-day training period and replacing it with a 4-month scheme. By early 1941 this new plan had been implemented.

During this critical period, plans were circulating around NDHQ for a truly "big army": composed of six infantry divisions and two armoured divisions, all commanded by headquarters. After studying the slapdash studies on manpower that were available, Crerar concluded that there were insufficient men to maintain a national army of six divisions, two of which would be kept in Canada. Instead, he eventually convinced McNaughton to consider "the pros and cons of a Canadian army comprised of two corps each of 2 divisions and an Armoured Division." Crerar's ambitious blueprint, with the deletion of one infantry division, and an additional two armoured brigades, would eventually be accepted by the government in 1942. Of course, it required more than a volunteer system of recruitment to maintain its manpower. But that was primarily left to the politicians to solve.

In Crerar's mind, being a general was a serious, often lonely, full-time job, yet he never felt sorry for himself. One of his favourite sayings was: "A commander should lead always and drive seldom — but when he does drive, drive hard." Certainly, he was serious about "lead always." Despite his earlier order, referred to above, that officers at National Defence Headquarters take the occasional weekend off, he drove himself. Officers around him in Britain and Europe soon learned that it meant "24 hours a day." An aide recounted how, "regardless of traffic conditions or blackout or anything else, he expected to be brought to every meeting never one second late and within one minute of the time appointed. He was acutely aware that a tardy general is a pain in the neck. He respected his troops and I think he felt that keeping them standing around was something you simply did not do."

Certainly Crerar was one of the best staff officers produced by the Canadian Army. "A real professional," is how one officer described him. "He knew his job cold." Another noted: "he did not tolerate weaklings, negative personalities, or officers who explained too much. To him a good officer was one who knew his profession and could express himself concisely and briefly."

Surprisingly, to officers who knew him, there smouldered in Harry Crerar's ascetic and academic soul the ambition actually to command in the field. When he returned to Ottawa from England in July 1941, the General made it clear he wanted to command a division. Accordingly, in December, 1941, he assumed command of 2nd Canadian Infantry Division, replacing Major-General Victor Odlum. Shortly after being made a lieutenant-general, he would take over command of Canadian Corps from McNaughton on April 6, 1942.

When the quiet, pipe-smoking Crerar doffed his dress uniform and donned the standard Canadian battledress worn overseas for the first time, he cut anything but a warlike figure, despite his reputation for immaculate uniforms. Battle dress would not prove flattering to the middle-aged general — especially an officer like himself who was not blessed with a trim figure. Although he continued to look academic in appearance, he quickly mastered the art of combing theory with practical soldiering. For example, it did not take him long to discover that, as charged, the Canadian soldiers' training had been sadly neglected. He also concluded that many senior Canadian commanders were less than adequate.

After the August 19, 1942 attack on Dieppe turned into a debacle, not a triumph, Crerar's innate political instinct did not fail him. In justification, he adopted the positive line that (according to Simonds) "although the raid had been costly, it had been well worthwhile because of what we had learned from it." This has been the standard justification of Dieppe ever since and may even possibly be correct. On his part, McNaughton confessed he had "examined the plans carefully," and took "full responsibility for the Canadians taking part." Such a response was honest. On his part, Crerar managed to avoid either responsibility or blame attaching to himself, at the time or afterwards. Clearly, the General led a charmed life. His boss, McNaughton, in contrast, did not.

As noted earlier, "Exercise Spartan" in March 1943 would finally bring differences to a head between the two senior Canadian generals concerning the preparation and training of troops. Crerar, commanding I Canadian Corps, performed well. After watching McNaughton in action, however, the British were actively interested in seeing him replaced. Likely as well, Crerar privately supported complaints against his chief. Despite Crerar's protests that he was innocent, he severely wounded his superior.

When Crerar went to Italy in the autumn of 1943, the tough, battle-tested 1st Division led by Major-General Chris Vokes came under his 1st Corps command. "We no longer stressed the spit and polish habitual to soldiering in the United Kingdom," Vokes later noted. "Frankly I couldn't have cared less what a man wore so long as he did his job in action. In this Crerar and I differed. He demanded the standards which pertained in the U.K. I found it no use to argue. He was a stubborn man and the 1st Division had to conform."

Italy's poor weather prevented Crerar from launching any offensive that winter. When the General was recalled to Britain in March 1944 to command the First Canadian Army, he still had no experience in directing offensive operations. His later success in northwest Europe, Vokes observed, "confounded all those who predicted he'd fail because he lacked experience in the lower echelons of field command. He proved himself an exception to a rule which should rarely be ignored in war. In this he was like General Eisenhower."

Much of Crerar's brilliance derived from his careful planning and his capacity to handle his officers and employ them to full advantage. Vokes caught the basic essence of the general's command style when he claimed, "His forte as an army commander was his willingness to decentralize responsibility to his brilliant corps commanders like Guy Simonds and British generals like Brian Horrocks who served under him." Often it was Simonds who did the actual battle planning and saw to its execution, despite the fact Crerar and he possessed such opposite personalities. Major-General Churchill Mann, Crerar's chief of staff, also proved a key subordinate whom the Canadian commander knew he could trust and to whom he frequently delegated command decisions. Mann always knew he had his superior's full authority to act, whether moving a brigade, or even, as on one notable occasion, an entire army corps.

Crerar went to France on June 18, just 12 days after the Normandy landings. His army headquarters became operational a month later on July 23, taking over the Allied front's extreme "long left flank." Following the successful drive to capture Falaise in August, Crerar would spearhead the clearing of the Channel

Ports, oversee the capture of enemy flying bomb sites, and supervise the commencement of the drawn-out campaign to clear the approaches to the Scheldt Estuary and open the vital Belgian port of Antwerp. When he became ill, however, the army would fight the brutal Scheldt battle under Crerar's II Corps commander, Lieutenant-General Guy Simonds.

During the General's absence, Canadians earned the title "Water Rats," a name that echoes the World War II "Desert Rats" of El Alamein fame. It originated from the fact that they had crossed so many rivers and fought in so many flooded areas. Third Division, proud of the symbol, painted a rat on its bridging and road signs. When he returned, the meticulous Crerar was unimpressed. "Take that lousy rodent down," he is reported to have ordered. But the Division, proud of its new name, continued to use it, at least unofficially

Despite his temporary absence, Crerar's war was not yet finished. On November 16, 1944, he was promoted full general. In February 1945, following a long recuperation after the costly Scheldt campaign, First Canadian Army moved into action once again with Crerar in command. Its task was the great battle for the Reichswald: Operations "Veritable" and "Blockbuster." Conditions were extremely difficult. The enemy, desperate to defend the Reich's approaches, breached the Roer River dams, transforming the battlefield into a horrid quagmire. Yet, Veritable proved Crerar's finest hour. The operation showcased Crerar's strategic talents and his tactical ability to direct his overall plan. As military historian Bill McAndrew has said, this battle, especially, was "the epitome of the Canadian way of war: large scale orderly preparation, accumulation of massive resources, and meticulous planning. It was another Vimy Ridge." The army Crerar commanded was now 450,000 strong. In fact, it was the first time a Canadian officer ever led a full army into battle.

Speaking of Crerar, Sir Brian Horrocks, who led XXX British Corps under Canadian command, recorded: "He was always very well-informed because, in spite of the weather, he made constant flights over the battlefield in a small observation aircraft." Although such flights were dangerous, Crerar did not hesitate to run the risk, for he appreciated that he was possibly sending men to their death. The Canadian General also employed the aircraft, which he occasionally flew in person, to maintain his personally imposed schedule, enabling him to make daily visits to corps and divisional commanders when it would be difficult to do so by staff car.

Although Crerar enjoyed good relations with most of his headquarters staff and with British commanders, he remained an enigma to some. "He was not the kind of man one gets to know easily," noted General Sir Miles Dempsey, whose British Second Army fought alongside Crerar's forces under Montgomery. "I liked Harry very much but he didn't expand easily." Horrocks, who as already mentioned served under Crerar during the month-long Rhine battle, observed: "He was very patient with me because I found myself getting rather irritable toward the end of the battle. I think he suffered a bit from having Montgomery as his boss — not in a tactical sense but because Montgomery was such a personality it was difficult for his army commanders to show any personality of their own."

Crerar has been somewhat misunderstood, chiefly because of his aloofness. But his distancing himself in order to have time to think was not really intended to be anti-humanitarian. His care for his men showed in many ways, such as the personal notes he sent to the next of kin of men he knew who had become casualties in the Dieppe raid in 1942. Also in his habit of detailing an officer accompanying him to quietly question troops in a unit he was visiting about their concerns. His humanitarianism showed in other ways, too. In mid-April 1945, Intelligence reported that a concentration camp in the Canadian line of advance was populated entirely by Polish women. General Crerar immediately ordered that 1st Polish Armoured Division be directed to liberate the camp. A few days later, the Poles liberated it, and many found wives and sweethearts they had not seen since Poland fell in 1939.

Despite the fact he was an exponent of military orthodoxy, Crerar could, when the situation demanded, go head-to-head with authority to make a point. Aware of what General Sir Arthur Currie had put up with during the Great War to establish an independent Canadian Corps and a national identity, Crerar proved himself a match for the exceedingly opinionated Monty. For example, when Montgomery thought 2nd Division shouldn't "waste time" in marching into Dieppe after it had been liberated, Crerar determined that the Division would — in order to pay tribute to brave countrymen who had died there. This was because Crerar thought it was the Canadian thing to do.

Overall, though, the General's strongest suit was the finesse with which he handled pressure. Part soldier, part politician, he was able to balance and adjust the many demands made upon him. Indeed, one officer who witnessed his adroit performance marvelled how he kept "8 balls in the air at once." Not only did he have to get along with Eisenhower and the staff at Supreme Headquarters Allied Expeditionary Force, but also with Monty and Twenty-First Army Group. Additionally, he had to keep both Ottawa and the War Office content. Moreover, he had to factor into the equation allowance for all the different nationalities he commanded under First Canadian Army: Canadians, Britons, Belgians, Poles, Dutch, Norwegians, Czechoslovakians and Americans. As the officer concluded: "He wasn't a popular figure, not an egocentric bird like Montgomery, but he was a very good diplomat and he never got his just due for what he did." In fact, not being like McNaughton or Monty was actually Crerar's strength, and proved a good thing, because usually it meant he got the task done in his own quiet, and effective manner.

Despite the outstanding job he did in commanding Canada's army in its greatest battles ever, Crerar would die in 1965 at the age of seventy-seven, largely a forgotten figure. Sole among Eisenhower's senior commanders, he is the only one whose life and career has not been treated in a major biography (although as this is written one is about to be published). His countrymen should not forget Harry Crerar's contributions in shaping the Canadian army in our nation's greatest time of peril. He built up its overseas headquarters, established an efficient training organization at home, and began the process of transforming Canadian Corps into an effective military organization. During the campaign in Northwest Europe, the General led the army cautiously, yet effectively. In the difficult, often savage combat, Crerar more than proved his potential as a field commander. Despite his lack of military charisma and traditional leadership qualities, he was humane in dealing with both junior officers and ordinary soldiers. Overall, he proved that he was a superb choice to head his country's forces in an Allied war effort in which the Dominion remained a junior partner.

SELECTED READINGS

"Closeup: A general 24 hours a day." In *Reader's Digest The Canadians at War 1939/45*, 434–435. 2nd ed. Westmount, Que.: Reader's Digest (Canada), 1986.

Foster, Tony. *Meeting of Generals*. Toronto: Methuen, 1986.

Granatstein, J. L. *The Generals: The Canadian Army's Senior Commanders in the Second World War*. Toronto: Stoddart, 1993.

Horrocks, Sir Brian. *Corps Commander*. Toronto: Griffin House, 1977.

Montgomery, B. L. *The Memoirs of Field Marshal the Viscount Montgomery of Alamein*. Cleveland: World Pub. Co., 1958.

Swettenham, John Alexander. *McNaughton*. 3 vols. Toronto: Ryerson, 1968–69.

Whitaker, Brigadier-General Denis and Shelagh Whitaker. *Dieppe: Tragedy to Triumph*. Toronto: McGraw-Hill Ryerson, 1992.

Soldier of Calgary Regiment on tank overlooking city of Potenza, Italy, September 20, 1943.
Photograph: A. M. Starton. Department of National Defence. (NAC/PA-136197)

19

CANADIANS
IN ITALY

"D-Day Dodgers"

On July 10, 1943, 1st Canadian Infantry Division, commanded by General Guy Simonds, and 1st Canadian Army Tank Brigade (later 1st Armoured Brigade) stormed ashore on Sicily's south coast as part of British General Bernard L. Montgomery's Eighth Army. After the successful conquest of the island during the summer, the Allies crossed the strait into Italy, with intentions of forcing dictator Benito Mussolini's capitulation and tying down large numbers of the German army. These limited aims were also intended to assist the Russians fighting in the east and to weaken enemy resources in Northwest Europe prior to a cross-Channel attack, but the Italian campaign proved much more difficult than expected. The mainland's terrain, much like Sicily's, favoured the defenders, and the cumbrous Allied forces advanced only slowly and at great cost up the Boot. The price to Canada of what many regarded as a "sideshow campaign" was high. Recently, near Rimini in northern Italy where the bloody fighting finally ended, the newest memorial honouring Canadian valour in the Second World War was officially dedicated; today, it and a series of military cemeteries remind us of the sacrifices Canadians made to defeat Mussolini's Fascism more than half a century ago.

As early as the initial combat in Sicily, German soldiers came to respect their hard-fighting Canadian opponents, dubbing them "Red Patch Devils" after the badge they wore: the same shoulder patch made famous by the Canadian Corps' 1st Division during the Great War. But in Britain, Lady Nancy Astor, the first female member of parliament, coined the name "D-Day Dodgers" for troops fighting in the peninsula. The derisive term implied such soldiers had deliberately chosen to avoid the more serious fighting in Northwest Europe. In critics' eyes, the troops were "living it up" in Italy, with its sunshine and abundant wine. In mockery, troops coined and sang the "D-Day Dodgers Song." Sung to the tune of "Lili Marlene," the famous German marching song, as a defiant challenge to the enemy, it derisively chronicled the "life of luxury" the Canadians never led: "Always on the vino, always on the spree."

Those who were there, however, know the harsh truth. With only a minimum of men and material, the Italian campaigners managed to engage and fight more than 20 crack German divisions for over a year-and-a-half, from the summer of 1943 until the final surrender of 1945. They also paid a bloody price to do it.

When Canadian troop convoys sailed from England in June, they carried with them every conceivable item needed to sustain the Division and Tank Brigade. It was calculated that supplies for the troops, totalling 1,851 officers and 24,835 other ranks, would have to last a minimum of three weeks following the invasion. No detail was overlooked. The 30,000 tons of supplies included everything from camouflage paint to mosquito netting.

The trip was a grand voyage. Food was wonderful, the Mediterranean's sunshine searing. The only setback was provided by German dive bombers. They sank three of the Slow Assault Convoy's merchantmen, costing Canadian Divisional HQ 22 of its 26 specially equipped vehicles. Ironically, the three vessels had been intentionally loaded with vehicles and equipment in equal proportions, so that if one ship were sunk headquarters could still function smoothly. The chances of all three becoming casualties, out of the sizable convoy, was, as General George Kitching later observed "a million to one."

When orders were opened, the Canadians learned the target of the assault was Sicily. Although scarcely remembered today, the Sicily invasion was the largest amphibious invasion of the war. The Normandy Campaign would be larger in terms of ships and aircraft, but more troops participated in the landings in Sicily. "Operation Husky's" statistics are indeed overwhelming. In round numbers 180,000 troops took part. Also, nearly 15,000 vehicles (including 600 tanks), and 1,800 guns. They were transported in more than 3,000 vessels of every size and description. Above them, 2,500 aircraft provided a protective umbrella.

On Saturday, July 10, 1943, Allied invasion forces stormed ashore, more or less simultaneously, over nearly 125 miles of coastline. U.S. troops landed in the southwest, near Gela and Licata. Meanwhile, on the east coast south of Syracuse, British and Canadians went ashore in five separate landings. 1st and 2nd Canadian Infantry Brigades waded ashore on the southernmost tip of the Island near Pachino, which possessed an important airport.

Italian troops opposing the Canadians put up a light resistance in most places, almost none in others. This was fortunate, for the landing process was complicated by unexpectedly deep water that lay between the offshore sandbar and the beach itself. Lieutenant Farley Mowat (today well-known as a writer), of the Hastings and Prince Edward Regiment (the "Hasty Ps"), who was shorter than most, recorded his anticlimactic exit from the landing craft:

> Revolver in hand, Tommy gun slung over my shoulder, web equipment bulging with grenades and ammo, tin hat pulled down over my ears, I sprinted to the edge of the ramp shouting, "Follow me, men!" — and leapt off into eight feet of water.

> Weighted as I was, I went down like a stone, striking the bottom feet first. So astounded was I by this unexpected descent into the depths that I made no attempt to thrash my way back to the surface. I simply walked straight on until my head emerged.

Soon, Italians were surrendering to the Canadians in droves. This imparted a comical atmosphere to the Allied invasion, at least during the first few days. Driving inland, the invaders' advance was met by the surrender of thousands of Fascist dictator Benito Mussolini's finest troops. Among them was General Achille d'Havet, a protocol-conscious divisional commander, who surrendered only on the understanding it would be to an officer of equal rank. In the end, Major-General Guy Simonds, commander of 1st Canadian Infantry Division, accepted his capitulation.

But the Canadians were about to be introduced to "real warfare." It was provided by determined German troops, a week after the invaders had landed, at Leonforte, Nissoria, and Agira. It took five days of fighting to seize the latter. Stanley Mullins of Manitoulin Island, Ontario, later a platoon commander of the Irish Regiment of Canada, recalls the difficulties involved in taking the medieval town: "They [our boys] did it the way porcupines make love — with great difficulty."

The heat was as formidable an enemy as were the Germans. Tourist manuals counselled against travelling in Sicily in July. Soon, invaders found out the reason. On July 19, the temperature rose to a sweltering 114°F (45.5°C) in the shade — at least when shade could be found. CBC war correspondent Peter Stursberg recorded that "the scorchingly hot" sun "was frying the skin on my face." So he sought shelter in an Italian pillbox, unpacked his typewriter, and wrote his first invasion story. Even though troops quickly adjusted to the heat by wearing only shorts, everyone was soaked in sweat. An innovative truck driver, ever aware of protocol, though stark naked but for a looted top hat and issue boots, greeted army commander Bernard Montgomery. He doffed his hat, saluted, and cheerfully said, "Good day, boss." Marching soldiers found themselves enveloped in clouds of fine, white dust whipped up by their boots.

Malaria and jaundice also attacked the Canadians as they climbed, marched, and fought through summer dust and ravenous insects around Mount Etna. Mules burdened with mortars, guns, ammunition, ever-present water bottles, and supplies accompanied the troops as they trekked through rugged and mountainous countryside.

The advancing Canadians received a lukewarm reception from Sicily's civilians. The khaki-clad soldiers were but the latest in a long line of conquerors that islanders had watched come and go. Invaders included Byzantine Greeks, Carthaginians, Romans, Saracens, Normans, Spaniards, and Moors. Still, no one had ever conquered Italy from the south — "from the bottom up" — since the Byzantine general Belisarius, in the sixth century. The Canadian troops gained a poor impression of the Sicilians. This spawned its own dynamic. As Mowat has observed: "[It] seemed to sanction making these people's meagre possessions fair game. In any event, many of their pitiful little orchards (a handful of fig trees, pears or pomegranates) and garden plots (mostly melons or gourds) were casually looted. The disturbingly commonplace practice was rendered easier by the fact the island was not being liberated but conquered."

The first real battle, the brief, furious one for Grammichele, gave our boys a sobering preview of the real cost of fighting enemy troops such as the crack Hermann Goerings they encountered. Although just a mere skirmish, it cost 25 Canadian casualties. During the battle, a Hastings and Prince Edward Regiment private bearing the famous Canadian name of Huron Brant, a Mohawk from Deseronto, Ontario, proved a one-man wrecking squad. Single-handedly, he attacked a group of 30 Germans, either killing or wounding every last one. For his bravery, Brant won the Military Medal. By noon, the town had been cleared of the hard-fighting enemy.

The battle for Valguarnera, or "Valcartier" as the Canadians called it, on July 20, was won at a high price: 140 casualties, including 40 dead; the Germans, too, paid dearly for slowing 1st Division's advance: 240 wounded or dead, and 250 taken prisoner. "Near Valguarnera troops trained for fighting in the mountains have been mentioned," *Generalfeldmarschall* Albert Kesselring himself reported in a message communicated to Berlin. "They are called Mountain Boys and probably belong to the 1st Canadian Division."

More was going to be heard from these Mountain Boys. The

next day, July 21, the Hasty Ps achieved one of the most stirring exploits of the entire campaign by capturing the hilltop town of Assoro. To pull off the incredible feat, members of the battalion scaled a 1,000-foot cliff to gain access to the naturally fortified position. No decorations were awarded for Assoro. But the battle for Leonforte by the Loyal Edmonton Regiment and Princess Patricia's Light Infantry which raged simultaneously would garner no fewer than 21 awards for bravery. By Thursday, July 22, 1st Canadian Division could be well pleased with its efforts. Brilliant manoeuvre and hard fighting had deprived the enemy of two key defensive positions, Assoro and Leonforte. But the price of three days' combat had been high. Overall, the Division suffered 275 casualties, the highest toll to this point. Two-thirds had been incurred by 2nd Brigade in the fighting for Leonforte.

The battles indicated that the "make believe war" preceding the actions was over, for Grammichele, Piazza Armerina, even Valguarnera had been contested against enemy rearguards engaged in the operation of falling back. In contrast, Assoro-Leonforte brought the Canadians head-to-head against a large, first-class German formation (in fact, all three battalions of the 104th Panzer Grenadier Regiment), which had been ordered to hold its strong defensive positions as long as possible.

At Nissoria which followed, Guy Simonds, commanding Canadian troops, committed the "supreme military sin" of reinforcing failure. Ironically, as the young artillery Captain had written in 1939: "Several independent company and battalion battles launched on a divisional front will meet with the repulses that lack of coordination and concentration always deserve." Now, he threw such forces into battle not only once, but twice. His shortcomings also included employing World War I-style artillery tactics. At this point, however, Simonds had been a major-general for only four months. As Strome Galloway, a company commander during the campaign, has observed: "Often cited as Canada's most brilliant field commander, which he probably was, Simonds had much to learn about his job while in Sicily."

On July 27, at Monte Fronte, a company of Seaforths, reduced to a mere 50 by casualties, scaled the square-topped hill. Opposing them was a full company of Germans. "By fire, movement, and plenty of guts" — in Colonel Bert Hoffmeister's words — the outnumbered Highlanders ultimately prevailed in the day-long battle. Major Henry "Budge" Bell-Irving considered the losses of his company — only two dead, five wounded — "particularly remarkable." This was especially true, considering that, just before midnight, the enemy had made the only bayonet charge that would be mounted against the Seaforths in the course of the entire war. By dawn, July 28, Monte Fronte was firmly in the hands of the weary Seaforths, who had fought and marched more than eight miles to overcome the commanding landmark. Appropriately, both Hoffmeister, the unit's commanding officer, as well as the hard-working Bell-Irving were rewarded with Distinguished Service Orders.

Meanwhile, the "Loyal Eddies," or Loyal Edmonton Regiment, were running into action of their own. One company stormed Monte Crapuzza, which turned out to be undefended. Two other companies attacked a nearby hill, appropriately dubbed Cemetery Hill, crowned by a "walled cemetery characteristically bordered by tall, sombre, cypress trees." Given the fact that "the tombstones bristled with machine and anti-tank guns," and defenders outnumbered attackers by a ratio of four to one, this second position proved a much harder nut to crack.

The hilltop town of Agira was captured the following day, July 28. Thus ended 1st Division's biggest battle of the Sicilian campaign. Although originally planned to be a one-day operation, the prolonged struggle for Agira had occupied five full days of fighting, and cost 438 Canadian casualties. By employing a skilful defence in favourable terrain, and by taking advantage of questionable Canadian tactics, the enemy had bought valuable time. But, they paid a high price for it. The 104 Panzer Grenadier Regiment lost an estimated 200 killed. Its successor, the 15th, suffered 125 dead. Both units lost an additional 30 men taken prisoner by the victorious Canadian attackers.

Surprisingly, a warm welcome awaited the Canadians in Agira.

Its citizens, like most Sicilians, were in a mood to celebrate, given that Italian dictator Benito Mussolini had been deposed on July 25. Reaction in Germany, however, was considerably different. An infuriated Adolf Hitler denounced his successor, King Victor Emmanuel III, as a "weakling" and plotted revenge. Within 49 hours of *Il Duce's* fall, the Germans were hard at work on plans to occupy Italy should their erstwhile ally either collapse or surrender. Such an eventuality had been expected since May.

While General George S. Patton Jr. launched his American army north of Etna, Eighth Army commenced its own operation. Spearheaded by Lieutenant-General Sir Oliver Leese's XXX Corps and code-named "Hardgate," it commenced its drive on Regalbuto the night of July 30/31. It required five days of bitter battle by the balance of Canadian Division and the 231st Brigade to capture the town, for the Germans, who regarded the town as an important outpost, moved up fresh troops to defend it. For the first

The Three Rivers Regiment in Regalbuto, Sicily. Courtesy Esprit de Corps.

time since the fighting at Grammichele, Canadian soldiers found themselves grappling face-to-face with elements of the Hermann Goering Division. The engineer battalion, reinforced with tanks and artillery, were superb soldiers. In Tunisia, 40 such combat engineers had routed an entire battalion. And, at Regalbuto, they had been given instructions to hold the town "at all costs."

Following Regalbuto's fall, our troops unknowingly entered the final phase of operations in the battle for Sicily. At this point, Guy Simonds launched a plan worthy of his later reputation as "Canada's foremost tactician." Ascending a hill at Centuripe that offered a panoramic view of the battlefield, he saw what proved one of the few opportunities to employ tanks in the entire campaign. Thursday, August 5, proved to be one of the most propitious days for Canadian troops in Sicily. Hastily assembled, "Booth Force" surged down the valley at 1000 hours. Following a half hour's pleasant drive through orange and lemon groves, the attackers were practically on top of their objective. Despite the fact it was defended by fanatical enemy machine gunners of the 3rd Parachute Regiment, the fighting was over by early afternoon. One military historian, Reginald Roy, quite rightly describes it as "a classic example of exploitation, speed, and co-operation." For his leadership Lieutenant-Colonel Leslie Booth, commander of the Three Rivers Regiment, would be awarded the DSO.

Next day, the Edmonton Regiment captured Monte Revisotto, while the PPCLI took Monte Seggio. When the "Van Doos" (Royal 22nd Regiment) established a bridgehead over the Simeto River on the morning of August 6, and subsequently sent patrols into Adrano, Canadian Division's operations in Sicily drew to a close. The five-day drive along the Salo Valley cost 2nd Brigade "more than 150 casualties," close to two-thirds of them among the Loyal Eddies, who had fought stubborn struggles for Hill 736 and Monte Revisotto.

With the capture of Adrano at Mount Etna's foot, 1st Division was now squeezed out of battle, as the Allied front surged forward. Catania had fallen to the British on August 5, and the Americans had captured Tooina, northwest of Adrano, on the 6th. The rapidly constricting front of the advancing armies meant that some formations could be rested. Monty, envisioning the as-yet-unauthorized invasion of the Italian mainland to follow, appropriately chose the Canadian division for the honour.

Our troops were veterans and they knew it. In the first prolonged campaign against the enemy, they had proven themselves worthy successors to the enormous reputation their fathers and uncles had established on the battlefields of France and Flanders in 1914–18. But the basis of such professionalism had not been established overnight. The majority had enlisted in 1939, and for four ensuing years had done little else but train for the demanding task of defeating Germans. Afterwards, General Geoff Walsh, the Canadian engineering chief, would recall how 1st Division was "extremely well trained, when I look back on it, far better trained than the divisions we put into Normandy [in the summer of 1944]."

Thankfully, losses during four weeks of fighting in the hot and arid island were not as high as anticipated. Nonetheless, the cost was heavy enough. Canadian troops suffered 2,310 casualties, including 562 dead, 1,664 wounded, and 84 taken prisoner. Many critics refer to such losses as "light." The harsh reality, however, remains that losses of such magnitude foreshadowed Canadian casualties that lay ahead in the vicious fighting around Ortona, on the Adriatic, during December. Four hundred and ninety graves in the lonely hilltop cemetery east of Agira, the only entirely Canadian war cemetery in Italy, stand as testimony to the stark cost of conquering the island. Here, buried side by side, rest the commanding officer of the Royal Canadian Regiment, Lieutenant-Colonel Ralph Crowe, and the second-in-command, Major Billy Pope.

Incredibly, the Germans escaped. While the publicity-conscious Patton was plotting how to beat the British into Messina, one-armed German corps commander Panzer-General Hans Hube created his own miracle of sorts by pulling back across the Messina Strait with the remainder of his rearguard. As such, the enemy had brought off one of the most spectacular escapes from disaster in military history. During the first 15 days of August, the desperate Germans moved 39,951 troops, 94 guns, 47 tanks, 9,605 vehicles, and 17,000 tons of ammunition, fuel, and miscellaneous equipment across the narrows. Additionally, the Germans ferried 62,000 Italians to Italy's mainland.

Back in London, General Andy McNaughton was under the impression 1st Division and the Armoured Brigade would be returned to the UK for operations against Northwest Europe. But the Commander-in-Chief's political and military masters in Ottawa had different plans. Soon, the army's chief of staff, General Ken Stuart, telegraphed McNaughton, advising him that Allied high command had been authorized "to use Canadians in extension of operations to Italy." Not only were the Dominion's forces going to extend their odyssey to Italy, they were actually going to spearhead the invasion!

The last two weeks of August, which the Canadians spent in reserve, seemed to many more penance than reward for their victories. To the troops' disgust, spit and polish were resurrected, since the Canadians had picked up many of Eighth Army's informal habits. Training resumed as well. Recreation was provided in the form of a vigorous sports program ("ah, the joys of the hundred-yard dash!") and swims in the sea, while entertainment took the form of two-hour concerts provided by military bands. Meanwhile all towns and villages were placed "out of bounds" to Canadian personnel who, as Farley Mowat charges, "were treated like inmates in a reform school."

Soon though the Canadians were back in action. At dusk on September 2, the first assault troops vacated hiding places in the hills, and moved down to board assault craft that would take them across the Messina Strait. The two-hour crossing to the mainland, on a dead calm sea illuminated by faint moonlight, went routinely, save for the tremendous covering bombardment, more show than substance, which exploded overhead when the invasion fleet was half-way across. When the first invaders splashed ashore at 0430 hours, on Friday, September 3, the more history-conscious among them noted that it marked the fourth anniversary of Britain's declaration of war.

Good luck prevailed, and the landing was unopposed, making the operation even easier than at Pachino two months previous. Beaches were deserted: no mines, no barbed wire, certainly no defenders. Miraculously, the Canadians had managed to land in Continental Europe — Hitler's formidable Fortress Europe — without being shot at or suffering a single casualty. Now that they were actually beginning to fight their way up the mainland, or "Boot," the Italian campaign would commonly be referred to as "the Spaghetti League." But there was nothing "minor league" about the opposition the invaders were taking on.

The "stiffest resistance of the day" was that experienced by General Roger Penhale, who had established his headquarters at Reggio di Calabria's zoo. Higher command was regaled with reports that the portly Brigadier had met a "loose wildcat" that had escaped its shell-torn cage and taken "a fancy to the brigade commander." Ultimately, the animal was driven off by small-arms fire.

As they pushed into the heart of Calabria during the next five or six days, Canadians met terrain that reminded war reporter Ross Munro "of the Laurentians or parts of the Rockies" at home. They christened the single, narrow road assigned them "Maple Leaf Highway." Soldiers even decorated the route with signs featuring a gold maple leaf on a red background, bearing the command: YOU ARE A CANADIAN — DRIVE LIKE ONE. Such countryside was ideal for delaying tactics, executed with a high degree of expertise by enemy demolition teams. Near the village of Straorini, Germans had blown the bridge, setting the pattern for what would follow: "craters, blown bridges, and more craters." Soon the engineers would be the unsung heroes of the Canadian advance.

On the mainland, Canadians were going to discover that the enemy would employ the same tactics he had used in Sicily, again and again. In a special message, Major-General Richard Heinrich, commander of newly arrived 1st Parachute Division, carefully outlined the procedure. Officers were to fight delaying actions on "lines of resistance" rather than "in a main defensive line." Located along "forward crests of ridges," such positions were only to be abandoned when the Allies prepared "a major attack." Heinrich calculated that such tactics would oblige attackers to move up artillery to cover each stage of the advance as they moved forward.

This delaying tactic failed, however, to bottle up the Allied advance, especially in Southern Italy. Canadian mobility and improvisation was going to teach the Germans a lesson about how to fight in mountainous and rugged country whose topography offered little opportunity for conventional armies to engage each other. In such combat, speed, a Canadian specialty, would carry the day.

Larger events now unfolding would also influence the tactics of the Allied thrust. On September 8, word arrived via the BBC that Italy had surrendered. Next day, it was followed by another major news story. An Anglo-American force had conducted coordinated landings in Salerno Bay, south of Naples. Because of it, the Canadians now found themselves obliged to advance as quickly as possible. A rapid thrust would enable Eighth Army to exert its expected impact on the operations that were fast developing to the north. Lieutenant-Colonel Cy Neroutsos, commanding the Calgary Tanks, organized a "Jock column" to race northeastward up the coastal highway which ran from Reggio around the southern and eastern coasts of Calabria. By night on September 7, "X Force" had demonstrated its value. It reached Locri, 64 miles from Reggio, following an uneventful drive, highlighted only by the sighting of a submarine. The few Italians encountered surrendered readily. By late afternoon of September 10, the Canadians had rolled forward another 60 miles, reaching Catanzaro, a town of 20,000. Its capture, as Nuroutsos noted, was "entirely a bloodless affair."

Still clad in tropical uniform, required in Sicily's sweltering summer, troops found themselves inadequately dressed for the mountainous mainland, with autumn commencing. Meanwhile, until the arrival of warmer battledress, the Canadians had to improvise by dressing in captured clothing. The result often proved hilarious. One PPCLI subaltern, Sydney Frost, described his weird appearance in a letter to his mother. His impromptu uniform consisted of "German pants, a summer drill shirt, home-knit sweater, German shirt, battle dress blouse, and a pair of Australian boots!" Frost noted: "I also carry a German pistol or my issue revolver. My head-dress is anything I happen to have at hand: a beret, skull cap, field service cap, or nothing at all. All in all, I am a peculiar-looking specimen."

The Canadians were soon back at work, putting on a dazzling display of mobile warfare. The drive into mainland Italy, which resumed on September 13, was a wild ride. Accidents were inevitable given the nature of the precarious coastal highway, portions of which were little more than "modified goat track." Still, by Friday evening, September 17, the division's lead elements had pushed through to Spezzano, Casano, and Villapiana, 100 miles from Catanzaro. The racing troops would soon be given a new and urgent assignment: the large town of Potenza. Lying 125 miles to the north, it was a key road and rail centre, and General Harold Alexander had chosen it as Eighth Army's objective during the next phase of operations.

Simonds now created a Jock column of his own, similar to "X Force" which had performed so spectacularly a week previous. In the early afternoon of September 17, "Boforce" — composed of Calgary Tanks, artillery, machine guns, and engineers, as well as the West Nova Scotia Regiment, its main element — set out on a 60-hour race to Potenza. By nightfall on the 19th, it managed to reach the town, situated on a 2,700 foot hill overlooking the River Basento. Next day, assisted by Van Doos, Boforce's tanks thrust into the town. The enemy, however, had slipped away overnight.

1st Division could be proud of the successes it achieved during September. Despite German resistance, the 375-mile advance from Reggio had been highlighted by a general absence of heavy combat. Casualties were 32 men killed, 146 wounded, and 3 prisoners of war. But the sickness toll, mainly from malaria and jaundice (infectious hepatitis), was proving alarming. Fifteen hundred troops were ill. The most notable case was the division's commander, Guy Simonds, who had to be evacuated to a British casualty clearing station at Bari.

Hitler had been undecided concerning what defensive strategy, if any, would be followed in Italy. But Mussolini's rescue by German commandos from his prison in the ski resort of Gran Sasso, as well as the fact that the Germans had come within an ace of crushing the Allied landing at Salerno, soon restored the German leader's morale and confidence. While the Führer waited to see whether the main objective of Allied operations would be either Italy or the Balkans (which he expected), Albert Kesselring's job, as commander, was to buy time. Since no reinforcements were available, he ordered General Heinrich von Vietinghoff's 10th Army to conduct a fighting retreat to the Bernhard Line, situated between Gaeta and Ortona, 85 miles apart. According to Kesselring's strategy the Bernhard Line (termed the Winter Line by the Allies) was "one of a series of defensive lines to be occupied . . . in the retrograde movement towards Rome." While it was only partly built at the time, the German commander hoped "to create an impregnable system of positions in depth, and so save German blood."

In the meantime, the Canadians were strengthened by the arrival of an additional infusion of their countrymen. In October, at Prime Minister King's insistence, the Canadian Armoured Division was ordered to Italy. The decision, however, which took General Alexander completely by surprise, only served to annoy him. "The proposed move of the Canadian Armoured Division has come as a complete surprise to me," he telegraphed. "We already have as much armour in the Mediterranean as we can usefully employ in Italy. I should have preferred another Canadian Infantry Division. . . . I do not want another Corps headquarters at this stage. I shall be grateful if I can be consulted in future before matters of such importance are agreed upon."

Campobasso, a picturesque city nestled in the Appenines' eastern foothills, the next Canadian objective, fell surprisingly without a battle, despite the fact the Germans had further continued to slow the Canadian advance along the few roads available. Bert Hoffmeister's 2nd Brigade captured nearby Vinchiatura, the next day, October 15, following a gruelling cross-country drive.

Now the Canadians at last got some well-earned "time off."

Despite the fact that the major recreational activities of Canadian troops were, as General Chris Vokes pointed out, "to get drunk" and "to get laid," Campobasso's delights in November were strictly limited. Winter was on the way and there were unmistakable signs of its approach as peasants tilled their fields, cut back vines, and collected firewood. Farley Mowat, the Hasty Ps intrepid intelligence officer, captured the sense of the country in exact fashion when he complained in a letter sent to a friend that Italy's climate was "the worst in the whole bloody world. It either burns the balls off you in summer, or freezes them off in winter. In between, it rots them off with endless rains. . . . The first travel agent I see when I get back home with a poster of sunny Italy in his window is going to get a damned big rock thrown right through the glass."

The Eighth Army's next objective was a major offensive. Its task was to cross the Sangro River, a natural barrier that helped anchor the formidable Bernhard, or Winter Line, the enemy's main defensive position below Rome. By November 22, new commander General Graeme Gibson and 3rd Brigade had done their jobs well. Aggressive patrolling and skilful shooting by artillery had managed to clear the enemy from the near side of the river, save for 20 or 30 paratroopers holed up in a monastery atop the rocky pinnacle towering over Castel di Sangro. Two days later, on November 25, two companies of the "West Novas" scaled the frowning cliffs, designated as Point 100, while mules brought up mortars and machine guns of the Saskatoon Light Infantry. Additionally, nine field regiments' Canadian and British guns blasted the peak. But it proved unnecessary. The paratroopers had withdrawn the previous evening.

Meanwhile, the rest of the Canadian division had left Campobasso for the Adriatic coast, to prepare for what would be one of the most legendary of Canadian battles, the battle for Ortona.

Monty's plan called for, as he put it, a "dash to the prize of Rome." By now it was becoming evident, however, that the advance risked being thrown drastically off schedule. It appeared the Allies faced a strenuous winter campaign in rough terrain. Indeed, the formidable nature of the upcoming battle was indicated by the alarming quantities of enemy troops and armour that were pouring into Italy. By the end of October, the 13 Allied divisions fighting in the peninsula found themselves facing nearly twice that number of German divisions.

On the eve of his offensive, Monty issued a message he ordered read to all troops: "The enemy had been outfought by better troops ever since we first landed in SICILY, and his men don't like what they have been getting. The Germans are in fact in the very condition in which we want them. WE WILL NOW HIT THE GERMANS A COLOSSAL CRACK." Much of such talk was sheer bravado. Instead of a breakthrough battle, the Eighth soon found itself in a slogging match. Not only were the attackers fighting determined Germans, but heavy rains had turned the normally sedate Sangro into a raging torrent.

On December 5 the Division struck. The Hasty Ps forced a crossing on the coast, while, four miles inland, the PPCLI managed to force their way across and assault San Leonardo in the centre. But the Seaforths were driven back in the face of heavy resistance. Nevertheless, an attack launched two days later by the 48th Highlanders and RCR, supported by armour, managed to expand the small bridgeheads. San Leonardo fell on December 9. The divisional war diarist celebrated the hard-fought victory, recording: "This day will be remembered by the 1st Canadians for a long, long time. We had our first real battle on the divisional level with the Germans."

The next stage, the battle for The Gully, opened on Saturday, December 11. Three miles in length, the feature served as a natural barrier running inland from the coast, until petering out in the vine-tangled muddy foothills. Here, C Company of the French-speaking Van Doos, reduced to nine men by the battle's end, supported by the Ontario Tanks, managed to reach Casa Berardi, a strongly-fortified group of buildings on the opposite side of The Gully. Under cover provided by massed artillery, Toronto's 48th Highlanders as well as the battered Royal Canadian Regiment fought their way across The Gully. By the time the RCR overran "Cider Crossroads," on the afternoon of December 19, it had been reduced to an effective fighting strength of only 178 officers and other ranks. But its heroic sacrifice had moved 1st Canadian Division another step towards its most famous battle — that for Ortona itself.

For his role, Captain Paul Triquet of the Royal 22nd Regiment won the first Victoria Cross awarded a Canadian in that theatre. The capture of the strongly fortified Casa made possible the turning of the German flank and opened the route forward.

Strange to say, no one expected a battle for Ortona, a picturesque town of 10,000 perched on a bluff overlooking the Adriatic. But it was here that the Canadians, among the allied troops, proved themselves unquestioned masters of street-fighting. A Canadian journalist captured the atmosphere when he noted that Ortona was a "carnival of fury. There was something different here, something heroic and almost superhuman, at the same time dark as night."

Two battalions of German paratroopers fighting as infantry defended Ortona with all the skill and determination for which they were famed. The town consisted of closely packed stone houses, with narrow alleys between them. Every so often one or more of the sturdiest structures had been strengthened, creating miniature fortresses, garrisoned by the enemy. Pummelled by mortars, the dazed and determined enemy "paras" hunkered down in the ruins and the infantry had to winkle them out. Block by block, the Germans were forced back, past the great church which had "been blown in half" as though cut right through its dome by "a giant cleaver," into the warren of medieval buildings clustering round the town's ancient castle overlooking the harbour.

Canadians paid a dear price indeed for this small corner of Italy. The Eddies lost 172, the Seaforths 103, killed or wounded. Although enemy losses were unknown, the Canadians recovered the bodies of over 100 paratroopers scattered among the shattered town. At last, following a week of fighting that raged over

Christmas, the Edmontons and Seaforths with justifiable pride posted a sign at the entrance to the town: THIS IS ORTONA, A WEST CANADIAN TOWN.

Ironically, Field Marshal Kesselring had complained that "we do not want to defend Ortona decisively, but the English have made it as important as Rome." Canadians would remember Ortona, too. December had been a grim month. In forcing the Moro and fighting their way past Ortona, they had taken heavy casualties. In fact, it had proven the "bloodiest month" of the entire campaign: 695 dead and 1,738 wounded, not to mention 1,773 sick, for a staggering total of 4,206. At Ortona, Canadian Medical Officers also met their first cases of battle exhaustion. It would take months to rebuild 1st Canadian Infantry Division.

Unlike Ortona, Rome had a tremendous moral and political significance. Across the deep gorge lying between the Matese and Aurenci mountains, German defenders had constructed the Gustav and Hitler Lines. In the spring of 1944 Eighth Army (with its Canadian Corps) moved to Italy's west coast. Its task was to punch its way north, following successive failures of the Americans, Indians, and New Zealanders to relieve the hard-pressed Anzio bridgehead which the Americans had established in mid-January. This would clear the way for Allied forces to press on to Rome.

After Canadian tanks had helped drive a gap through the Gustav Line, General E. L. M. "Tommy" Burns was given the further task of penetrating the formidable Hitler Line. Although one witness described the Liri Valley as "a green paradise," the image it presented was illusory. Hidden behind "orchards, olive groves, copses of small trees, undergrowth, and standing crops" were formidable defences. Extending nearly 800 yards in depth were weapons sites, concrete shelters, portable steel pillboxes and observation posts. Additionally, there were "Tobruck-style" pits (underground turrets mounting either an anti-tank weapon or machine gun) as well as 18 *Panzerturm,* consisting of a tank turret mounted atop a reinforced base. Eight of these were located in the Canadian sector alone.

On May 23 the attack went in, launched by I Canadian Corps, fighting as a unit for the first time in the war. Miraculously, a gap opened, and the tanks of 5th Armoured, dubbed "Hoffy's mighty maroon machine," poured through. The Germans broke, their defences crumbled, and the maple leaf troops followed hot on their heels.

For the pursuit, army commander Sir Oliver Leese launched I Canadian Corps and a British corps up the narrow valley, only three or four miles in width, which soon became a "Valley of Death." 5th Division and Corps headquarters, commanded by General "Tommy" Burns, soon found themselves snarled in a massive traffic jam. In the end, the snarl provided enemy defenders plenty of time to disengage and re-establish themselves as they withdrew up the 19-mile-long valley. Still, the Canadians had made it across the Melfa River, and the attack proved unquestionably to be one of the decisive battles of the Italian Campaign.

The fighting also demonstrated the ability of thirty-six-year-old Major-General Bert Hoffmeister. Indeed, some critics regard him as "arguably the most successful Canadian divisional commander of World War II." A native of Vancouver, he had gone overseas with his regiment, the Seaforth Highlanders, in 1939 as a major. By 1942, following a staff course, he was appointed the battalion's commander, and led it in Sicily. By November 1943, "Hoffy," who commanded from the front always, was a major-general in charge of 5th Canadian Armoured Division. Ultimately, he would win three DSOs and the high regard of troops he led in Italy, and later in the Netherlands.

Now, at last, the long-expected "Road to Rome" lay open. But the Canadians and Eighth Army would not realize their cherished dream of taking Rome before the Americans. On June 8, the city fell to U.S. Forces and the Free French. It was a bitter blow for the Canadians, who had shared in the bloody battles of the Cassino and Liri Valleys, that they would not be marching into the Eternal City as victors.

Still, Canadians could take a vicarious pride in the accomplishment of some of "their own." The first Allied unit to enter

Rome, the First Special Service Force, or "Devil's Brigade" as it was popularly known, was a joint U.S./Canadian formation created and trained for special operations. After being raised, it had served in operations at Kiska, in the Aleutians, in 1943. Later, it fought at Monte Cassino, and its paratroopers also saw action, the only Canadians to do so, at Anzio. Following this, it participated in the advance on Rome which had ended with the unit's capturing Italy's capital.

Ironically, a mere two days after Rome's liberation, Italy would become a forgotten theatre. On July 6, 1944, the Allies successfully staged "Overlord," the greatest combined operations in history. Under a grey, threatening sky, and after plunging their way through rolling seas, 5,000 ships reached the shores of Normandy

(L-R): Major-General C. Vokes, GOC, Brigadier Hoffmeister, Brigadier Wyman during operation on the Moro River, Italy, 1st C.A.T.B. Photograph: Lieutenant T. Row. Department of National Defence. (NAC/PA-131064)

to disembark 107,000 soldiers and 7,000 vehicles in a single day. Henceforth, the campaign in Northwest Europe would command top priority in Allied planning, manpower, and material. Nonetheless, the fighting up the Italian boot north of Rome was destined to continue for another nine bitter months.

The hard fought campaign also revealed the Canadian army's strengths and weaknesses. As Daniel G. Dancocks, who has written a book on the campaign, notes, our soldiers' militia roots and professional competence were admirably reflected in the consistent successes in platoon and company actions they fought, and frequently at the battalion level as well. But at the brigade, division, and corps level, battle performance was at best inconsistent. Historians W. A. B. Douglas and Brereton Greenhous have also commented on "the paucity of talent at the higher levels of command," stemming from the neglect of our country's military before the war. In their estimate, Canada produced only three "first-rate" battle generals: Guy Simonds, Chris Vokes, and Bert Hoffmeister, all of whom served in Italy and gained valuable experience commanding in the theatre.

Influenced by Michael Ondaatje's award-winning novel *The English Patient,* and the movie made from it, Canadians tend to think of the fighting in Italy, which brought about the collapse of Mussolini and Fascism, as something out of the ordinary, even strangely haunting, in a romantic sort of way. Reality, though, was much different. As D-Day dodger Duncan Fraser has observed: "The war in Italy was cruel and dirty. Under-equipped with everything but spirit, guts, and determination, the Canadians in Italy made a reputation as tough and courageous fighters. They slugged viciously north against an implacable, efficient, and seasoned enemy army, through the most difficult and heartbreaking terrain encountered by any army in the Second World War. . . ." They also faced one of the best German commanders in Kesselring. The cost would be high indeed: of 92,757 Canadians of all ranks who served in the Italian theatre, more than a quarter became casualties. The final toll includes 5,399 dead, 19,486 wounded, 1,335 captured. Our country's dead can be found in 17 major cemeteries from Agira, Sicily, to Argenta, in north Italy.

Some, such as Cassino at the foot of the rebuilt monastery, or Gradara guarded by its fairytale castle, are strikingly beautiful. Others are less so. All, however, provide testimony to the bitter, obdurate fighting that once convulsed this beautiful land, and the sacrifices young Canadians made. Today when the focus of World War II has shifted to the Normandy invasion, we as a nation should not forget the Canadians "who fought, bled, and died" in the struggle against Fascism in Italy.

SELECTED READINGS

Dancocks, Daniel G. *The D-Day Dodgers: The Canadians in Italy, 1943–1945.* Toronto: McClelland & Stewart, 1992.

Douglas, W. A. B. and Brereton Greenhous. *Out of the Shadows.* Toronto: Oxford University Press, 1977.

Galloway, Strome. "Remember the D-Day Dodgers." *Esprit de Corps: Canadian Military Then and Now* 4:1 (June 1994): 35–36.

———. *Bravely Into Battle: The Autobiography of a Canadian Soldier in World War Two.* Toronto: Stoddart, 1988.

Gilchrist, C. W. "This Show Started in Sicily." *Legion* 71:1 (June/July 1996): 9–11.

Nicolson, G. W. L. *The Canadians in Italy.* Ottawa: Queen's Printer, 1956.

Ondaatje, Michael. *The English Patient: a novel.* Toronto: McClelland & Stewart, 1992.

Officers of the 3rd Canadian Infantry Division landing in France on D-Day.

(L-R): Captains Charles Turton, MM, W. H. Seemark, Major-General R. F. L. Keller, Brigadier R. A. Wyman. Bernières-sur-Mer, France. Department of National Defence. (NAC/PA-115534)

20

3RD CANADIAN DIVISION, 2ND ARMOURED BRIGADE

A Day Called D

Half a century has passed since Canadian troops stormed ashore on "D-Day" (June 6, 1944), to begin the liberation of the continent from Hitler's yoke. Today few Canadians remember the discipline and bravery of those ordinary soldiers, many of whom were mere youths of nineteen or twenty, but it is important that we not forget their heroism. "Operation Overlord" and the ensuing Normandy Campaign rank among the most decisive battles of our age. One of the five Allied infantry divisions participating was 3rd Canadian Division, reinforced by 2nd Armoured Brigade. By June 12, despite savage counterattacks by Field Marshal Erwin Rommel's forces, the Canadians and their British and American allies had managed to unite their beachheads into a continuous front 60 miles long and 15 miles deep. During the next three months, 100,000 of our countrymen participated in the heavy combat. More than 11,000 of them never returned. Another 18,000 suffered crippling physical and mental wounds that shortened their lives. Yet as a result of these and similar sacrifices, Nazism and its horrors were defeated, victory achieved.

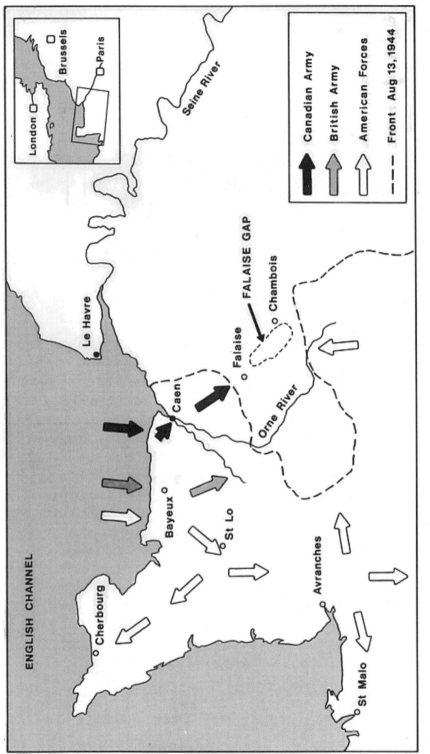

D-Day Invasion, June 6, 1944

On a Sunday in March 1944, Major-General R. F. L. "Rod" Keller broke the news to the Chaplains of his 3rd Canadian Infantry Division. "Gentlemen, I know that when anything serious is about to happen you want time to get the men ready," he said. "All I can say is: get ready. Good afternoon gentlemen." As a Catholic clergyman, Reverend R. M. Hickey, who was present, later recorded in his book *The Scarlet Dawn,* "As we drove back, we chaplains agreed that D-Day was near."

By early 1944, everyone was aware that training was intensifying and taking on a "special edge." In picturesque English villages, troops learned the deadly art of street-fighting and house-clearing, as well as how to blow apart barbed wire using hand explosives. Mechanics learned how to waterproof and de-waterproof jeep and lorry motors. Dwight Green, a sergeant with the 1st Canadian Parachute Battalion, and his buddies, found themselves making parachute jumps over Salisbury Plain at night. As he remembered, landings were always the worst. Extremely hard to execute in the darkness, they reminded him of when, as a youngster, he had jumped off the roof with his eyes closed. Just minutes past midnight on D-Day, C Company of the Parachute Battalion would be some of the first Allied troops to arrive in France. Their mission: to secure the drop zone near Varaville. An hour later Lieutenant-Colonel G. F. P. Broadbrooke and the rest of some 600 Canadians would jump as part of British 6th Airborne's daring *coup-de-main* to the invasion of Europe.

Meanwhile, Larry Lusk and fellow members of the Canadian Scots D Company spent the spring of 1944 attired in full battle gear. Orders called for them to pedal madly around the Isle of Wight. They had a "loverly time," although they didn't know exactly for what they were preparing.

Some Canadians had been in England five years, many of them three. During the long wait they had played at soldiering. They went on schemes, as they called it, practising storming English beaches. They marched until their feet bled. They also drank warm beer, which they liked, and endured an unchanging diet of "muck and vomit," mutton and overcooked veggies, which they didn't much appreciate.

The Canadians could only suspect they were being streamed towards something big. Each man felt that he was a piece, albeit extremely small, in some gigantic puzzle. But none could fathom the grand picture. Graffiti on latrine walls and the usual camp network of rumour and blind guesswork suggested an invasion was in the works. But no one had any concept when it was being mounted. Or where. Or even in what country it would strike.

Soon, though, the fog of rumour hardened into still-shapeless certainty. The Big Push was indeed in the works.

At the beginning of May the machine of which they were a part began to move. It was composed of infantry regiments, tank battalions, artillery batteries, engineers. Veritable rivers of men and material. "Along the roads to the south coast of England the convoys rolled day and night," Edward Meade would write in *Remember Me*. "Into the woods and towns, under the trees of old lanes, under camouflage nets, along hedges, in disused quarries, in the shade of houses, even in rock caves, the trucks disappeared and the earth gobbled them up and gave no clue. The allies stood ready to launch the greatest attack in history." In numbers of ships and aircraft involved, it would be the greatest amphibious operation ever mounted.

Journeying to their respective destinations, troops could not help but marvel at the planning. They passed depots full of thousands of neatly parked tanks and lorries. Or drove down hedgerows lined by stacks of camouflaged steel bays holding piles of artillery shells. Convoys of North American-built fighter aircraft, wings removed to provide clearance through town streets, were towed from Liverpool's docks to southern airfields. Thousands of ships of every size and type not only crowded, but clogged, Channel ports. In port towns, warehouses groaned with necessary munitions. And with more mundane needs of war: "grenades, powdered eggs, commando knives, canned Spam, flame throwers, condoms, mortars, morphine, underwear, gas masks, socks, brooms, motor oil, prefabricated bridges." One warehouse in Dorchester was rumoured to hold stacks of coffins, in this pre-body-bag age.

American troops concentrated in the West Country around

Plymouth and Dartmouth. The Canadian and British regiments eventually flooded into camps in the vicinity of Southampton, Portsmouth and Newhaven.

By late May and early June, over 30,000 Canadians were assembled in Britain for the expected assault, its destination still unknown. Thousands in the 3rd Division and the 2nd Armoured Brigade, hundreds in a parachute battalion of the 6th British Airborne Division. Thousands more of our countrymen were aboard Canadian Navy landing craft, or manning destroyers, corvettes, frigates, and torpedo boats. Not to mention the brave little minesweepers that would spearhead the attack. Additional thousands of Canadians crewed the bomber and fighter squadrons of both the Royal Canadian Air Force and Royal Air Force.

Now the men got the first glimpse of their objectives. Under the direction of officers, they studied finely detailed, room-sized "sand tables" that depicted every detail of the seaside towns and countryside they would be attacking. Scales were exact. Targets and objectives were updated and changed according to information supplied by daily air reconnaissance photos. If a defensive wall was being constructed, the wall on the table would grow brick by brick as the real wall was built. Platoons, companies, and battalions studied detailed photographs that showed every window, alleyway and machine gun position.

One veteran, Basil Robinson, remembers: "They were marvellous. In photos of our area, you could see the tracks in the dew between a German machine-gun emplacement and where its crew used to go to do its business in the morning."

On May 26, military police strung barbed wire round the perimeters of the camps, sealing them off. It was an unsettling feeling. Now no one could enter or leave without a special pass. If you were an ordinary soldier, it was as if you had renounced the world for the duration. You could not go to a movie, you could not go for a pint. This was finally it, men realized. Like iron atoms, everyone was in the force of the gravitational pull of war. Without exception, all were being inexorably drawn into the great crusade.

Each passed the time as he could. Some (the more adventurous) got Mohawk haircuts. Others of their fellows played soccer, held makeshift music revues, or merely ate incessantly out of boredom. The beautiful weather that prevailed conspired to render being penned-up all the more disquieting. For England, it was glorious: the warmest spring locals could remember.

An uneasy lassitude fell over the camps. British writer Alan Moorehead has written: "The feeling grew that one was cut off, that all the normal things would go on, the tramcars and the shops, but they were, for you, of no consequence any longer. . . . It simply drove the mind into a fixed apathy. It made you reluctant to walk, to talk, to eat, to sleep. . . . You were driven back into yourself to the point where you lacked even a normal companionship with the others. . . . It was not fear that oppressed you, but loneliness. You were without identity, a number projected in unrelated space among a million other numbers."

Like everyone else, the Canadians could do nothing but wait. Finally, however, they received a clue as to where the invasion would take place. At pay parade each man was given 10 shillings in silver and 200 francs in French currency.

The next few days passed even more slowly. Now, though, the mood had changed. Everyone was at fever pitch with anticipation. Only one's CO knew the exact place of attack. Nevertheless, men guessed and conjectured. No rumour proved outlandish enough to be discredited. Meanwhile, as tension mounted behind the barbed wire in the army camps, the Allied air forces went to work. They bombed rail lines, airfields, harbours, radar stations and factories throughout northwest Europe. German aircraft plants and other strategic industries were heavily damaged. Bridges and tunnels leading to the target area were immobilized. The Luftwaffe was outfought in the air, its replacement capability smashed in the factories. In a short time, it had become powerless to interfere with the invasion concentrations underway in southern Britain. Once the Allies had landed in France, German ground forces, to their credit, would have to fight bloody, dogged defensive battles, lacking effective air cover of any sort.

The evening prior to D-Day, the 418th, the RCAF's only night-intruder squadron, flying twin-engine Mosquito fighter-bombers, would be hard at work. Its task was to cover the landing eight miles behind the beaches, of paratroopers, and glider-borne infantry. In addition to targeting vital bridges and canals in advance of their descent, the squadron achieved an artistic touch by knocking out all of the German searchlight batteries in the jump zone. Enemy forces would be effectively blind as the Allied gliders and paratroopers came down.

Allied forces' preparation was based on the costly lessons learned at Dieppe, when a Canadian combined operations force attacked the heavily fortified Channel port on August 19, 1942. After the badly shocked survivors of that terrible morning had been recovered from the beaches and counted, only 2,110 of the 4,963 who had sailed the previous day could be accounted for. Later it became known that 1,874 were prisoners. Of these 568 were wounded, and 72 would die of their wounds. In total some 1,051 Canadians had died in the attack on the Channel port. In fact 65 percent of the Canadians engaged had become casualties — a total that could only be compared with that of July 1, 1916, the first day of the Battle of the Somme.

To avoid repeating Dieppe's errors, special equipment had been developed which would now be shortly employed. It included floating artillery and rocket batteries, amphibious tanks and the "funnies": bulldozer tanks to clear beach obstacles, and flail tanks to beat a path through minefields. There would also be massive fire support from both sea and air. Canadian troops not scheduled to go in until later had even been moved eastward to Kent. Here, they assisted in what was a successful attempt to make the enemy suspect that the attack would be targeted on the Pas de Calais, where France's coast was only 20 miles from Dover's white cliffs.

Whether they realized it or not, the tens of thousands who waited in England's ports were now about to make history, not unlike Henry V's "brave band of brothers" had centuries earlier at Agincourt. Although their numbers were superior this time to the enemy's, there lay ahead what Prime Minister Winston Churchill described as "the most difficult and complicated operation that has ever taken place." Called by its code name "Overlord," it had been decided upon by the Big Three during their meeting at

Quebec. Its commander would be Britain's celebrated General Sir Bernard Montgomery, who had fought the enemy in Africa and Italy. The operation itself would be an assault on a 70-mile portion of the Normandy coastline, bristling with guns, concrete emplacements, pillboxes, barbed wire and mines — indeed, all the vicious military paraphernalia of Hitler's much-vaunted "Atlantic Wall."

During May 1944, Supreme Headquarters fixed June 5 as D-Day. It was the date on which conditions of light, moon, and tide would prove most suitable for the perilous operation. The landing, however, could be postponed until June 6 or 7, if prevailing weather dictated. On May 30 troops began moving to the marshalling areas, and by June 3 the majority of 3rd Canadian Infantry Division's and 2nd Canadian Armoured Brigade's personnel had embarked on a variety of landing ships and craft in the vicinity of the Isle of Wight.

Bad weather, however, forced a one-day postponement. The storm and dark clouds continued to threaten operations. For a time, it seemed everything might be thwarted by the single factor that could not be harnessed to the master plan, the weather. But then, at 4:15 a.m. on June 5, Supreme Allied Commander General Dwight Eisenhower, after listening to his advisors, made the decision. After a slight pause, he uttered the fateful words: "Okay, We go." Thus would commence history's "Longest Day." For this was the order needed to activate the 5,300 ships and landing craft needed to put the massive invasion force ashore, as well as the armada of 12,000 aircraft that would fly support and screen the attack, and the 150,000 men and 1,500 tanks the schedule stipulated would go ashore during the initial 48 hours.

The operational plan called for them to assault the beaches of Normandy that lay between Ouisreham on the east and the base of the Cherbourg (Cotentin) Peninsula situated some 50 miles due west. Lieutenant-General Miles Dempsey's British Second Army would be responsible for the landings on the eastern half of the front (Sword, Juno, and Gold Beaches), while Lieutenant-General Omar Bradley's U.S. First Army would attack the western sector (Omaha and Utah Beaches).

The British-Canadian front was situated roughly between

Bayeux and the mouth of the Orne River. The Canadians would be responsible for the centre, that is, the five miles of beach lying between Courseulles and St. Aubin. After they had secured a bridgehead, their difficult task would be to push through the gap lying between Bayeux and Caen. Their final goal, to capture Carpiquet Airport located some 11 miles inland, would require the day's deepest penetration by any troops.

The Canadians' task was formidable. They and the British would land last, on the most exposed beaches, have the farthest to go, and would have to fight what was potentially the most formidable enemy defensive forces. Because of the tide and rocks, 3rd Canadian and 3rd British Divisions could not touch down until an hour and a half after dawn had broken. This provided the enemy ample opportunity to prepare in a sector where he could draw upon ample reserves. In addition, "outcrops of rock so divided this front that the only suitable beaches for these two divisions were five miles apart."

The afternoon of June 5, Padre Hickey said Mass and troops received Holy Communion. Protestant chaplains also conducted services and prayers. For many it would be the last. Evening came, and the wind calmed. At dusk the great expanse of the modern armada began to move. The English coast faded slowly, and the Canadians and their Allies sailed to meet a scarlet dawn.

The Queen's Own Rifles' war diary recorded: "The real maps are issued. Grenades are primed and a good many 'last' letters written. The spirit is very high. If the Hun could see our lads tonight it would shake him."

The minesweepers were far ahead of the armada. Sixteen were Canadian, with names like *Canso, Caraguet, Thunder, Vegreville*, and *Wasaga*. Their dangerous chore would be to sweep channels into the Americans' Utah and Omaha Beaches. Scores of other Canadian naval units were involved as well, such as the *Prince Henry* and *Prince David*, which would carry 14 assault landing craft to 3rd Division's Juno Beach. Next, came 26 Landing Craft Infantry (LCIs), which would deliver second-wave troops. Once the fleet was in position, destroyers *Algonquin* and *Sioux* would lead the way into Juno, bombarding the enemy's defences and keeping him pinned down. Meanwhile six Canadian motor torpedo boats would patrol off the Seine's estuary. In the Channel proper, dozens of brave corvettes and frigates would patrol the convoy routes as well as escort landing craft and barges.

Reveille sounded. Some soldiers ate breakfast, consisting of bully beef and hardtack. Many, though, opted not to. Most had spent the three days aboard ship in the Channel battling seasickness. Below, decks stank of vomit. Now, as the run-in to the beaches approached, they mechanically checked their gear one last time: Lee-Enfield .303-calibre rifle, grenades, bandoleer, rubber poncho, entrenching tool, field rations, field dressings (wrapped in the camouflage netting of their helmets), Commando knife. Last, but not least, cigarettes, secured safely inside their helmet webbings.

Once on deck, the Canadians were amazed to see ships everywhere. Of every shape and size, they seemed to extend to the horizon, both east and west. Others stretched back to England in lines so straight they seemed to be reeling off giant spools. Overhead,

Landing craft of Force 'J' off the coast of France on D-Day, English Channel.
Photograph: A. O. Tate. Department of National Defence. (NAC/PA-137007)

floating on tethers above the biggest ships — battleships, sleek cruisers, open assault ships carrying tanks and self-propelled guns — were big silver barrage balloons. Their purpose was to keep dive-bombers from attacking. Above the roily seas swarmed a sonorous and comforting blanket of thousands of fighters. White "invasion stripes" painted on the wings of these "little friends" denoted their status as members of the Allied air force. All the warships were firing as they approached the beach. Battleships lobbed 16-inch shells, weighing as much as jeeps, against unseen, inland gun batteries. To the Canadian troops on deck the rushing sounds of the big shells passing overhead sounded exactly like the chuffing sound made by a freight train. As a nearby British cruiser opened up, the flash of her guns illuminated the darkness and the blast bruised the air. Certainly it was hard to imagine anyone standing up after being on the delivery end of such a barrage.

Thirty-five miles east of the drop zones where American paratroopers had landed, and five hours after the paras had first touched earth, the North Shore (New Brunswick) Regiment of 3rd Canadian Division commenced to disembark. The first heart-stopping task that the troops had to surmount was the difficult trans-shipment between the ships that had brought them across the Channel and the Landing Craft Assaults (LCAs), hanging from davits, that would take them ashore. The lowliest class of vessels on the books of the Royal Navy, the assault craft were wood, flat-bottomed, with a steel ramp for a prow. Commanded by a petty officer coxswain, they could transport a platoon of 35 men, and their diesel motor was just powerful enough to push them ashore at 10 knots. To board them, infantrymen — straight-jacketed in 60 pounds of equipment — had to negotiate a dangerous descent down scrambling nets. Then they had to feel for footholds between the adjacent hulls and the chasm of space that lay between.

On the run-in to the beaches, order, rehearsed in a dozen prior exercises, now imposed some semblance of pattern on the confusion. The spectacle of the armada, as well as the naval bombardment and heavy bombing, was terrifying to the Germans. But it seemed to bring courage and resolve to the Canadian infantrymen peering over the gunwales of their respective LCAs. Still, it was difficult to take inspiration from the heavy sea conditions that the retreating bad weather inspired. The 15-knot wind and 4-foot waves pushed the assault craft toward beach obstacles that the ocean would have covered, had the earlier landing hour been possible. Some smaller craft found the choppy seas too much, due to their low freeboard, puny engines and heavy loads. Only a single craft of the first wave of LCAs (Hedgerows) found its way safely ashore. Worst of all, the commanders of Duplex Drive (DD) tanks in the second wave of landing craft judged conditions too rough to risk their barely-amphibious cargoes in the water. Thus the decision was made to ditch ten Landing Craft Tanks (LCTs) and to disembark the tanks they carried directly onto dry land. After passing the 7,000-yard mark, however, the Senior Officer of 7th Brigade's DD tank wave had a change of heart. Tanks had to "swim off" close inshore. They landed barely ahead of the infantry. On the other brigade front, tanks actually landed behind the assault troops whose landing they were to cover.

Fortunately, enemy fire from the beach was not only light, but poorly aimed. It proved a saving grace as the Canadians were making their last 4,000 yards of run-in to the beach. Coastal batteries were silenced temporarily by the fire from bombarding cruisers. German field batteries further inland were not hitting their targets because they could not follow the trajectory of their shells. The beach guns, too, remained mercifully silent. The design of their embrasures prevented them from aiming until the enemy was quite literally on the beach. Only mortars, hit or miss when directed against maritime targets, and small arms fire, incapable of carrying more than 2,000 yards, comprised the enemy's main defence.

At the last moment, incoming Canadian landing craft found themselves facing exactly the trap the Germans had planted for the enemy all up and down the Normandy coast. The landing hour had been intended to avoid this. But due to the rough sea and the ten-minute delay it caused landing craft in crossing the reef parallel to the beach, the attackers' carefully worked out schedule had been fatefully delayed. The enemy beach defences, which the now rapidly ebbing tide no longer totally covered, consisted of mines and booby traps attached to massive beams or stakes. In places where clearing teams had managed to blast passages through the obstacles, the nearest craft headed for such gaps. Elsewhere, the larger landing craft had little choice but simply to drive ashore despite the explosive obstructions. Smaller craft wormed their way through as best they could. Some of the landing craft did not make shore, either blowing up as they touched bottom amid the V-shaped pylons, or while pulling off for the return trip.

The vaunted Atlantic Wall filled each man's mind. Each experienced his own living hell of fear and self-doubt as he approached the shore. War correspondent Ralph Allen, who was there, graphically describes in his novel *Home Made Banners* how a soldier by the name of Mike Tully reacted as the forces reached the beach:

The boat jarred and a tremendous grinding shook its hull as it came to a stop on the shoreline. Mike heard the impatient clanking of the opening ramp and stumbled toward the square of daylight that had replaced the boat's flat bow, shoving the man ahead of him in his haste. He held himself at the crest of the ramp for an instant, then slithered into the sea, took a step on the edge of a sandbar and found himself waist-deep in water. Holding his rifle above his head, he half ran and half pushed straight ahead until he felt the heavy warm grip of the water drop from his waist to his hips and finally his knees. He saw several dead men, and a man using his arms like flippers to draw a mash of crushed legs and shredded battledress back from the shore into the water. He saw black mines and yellow shell cases bobbing in the water on wooden stakes. He saw concrete blocks and iron tank traps at the water's edge, some broken and twisted by bombing and shelling or by demolition parties, but many still intact.

Straight ahead and very close, he saw a straggling settlement of tall pillboxes and squat machine-gun turrets anchored to a high concrete breakwater. As his feet hit the sand he scarcely noticed the thwack-thwack-thwack of Bren guns quietly merging with the quick slurp of German Spandaus and Schmeissers from behind the breakwater. But then a rifle bullet sang above his shoulder, a heavy mortar broke nearby with a testy crump and a German 88-mm. shell fused its warning swish with the cruel smack of an explosion.

For Mike and the others, the next few hectic minutes seemed to lengthen into an eternity that a lifetime would not be long enough to erase from memory. After clearing the bullet- and shell-splashed surf, attackers faced the individual test of summoning from deep within themselves sufficient courage to dash across the beach, ultimately seeking shelter wherever each could find it. At this moment, there was little a soldier could do for his comrades, or his fellow soldier for him. Ironically, this was the moment for which they had so carefully trained for months, even years. Now, each man reacted automatically, carrying out the specialized task he had been assigned as part of an assault team, and had carefully rehearsed so many, many times, in preparation for this supreme occasion.

Even when landing craft were damaged or sunk, most of the Canadian infantry managed to survive the explosion and struggle ashore. Equally important, the Canadian attackers found the DD (swimming) tanks readily at hand, already landed or wading ashore close behind. The infantry struggled ashore, heavily laden, cold and wet, weak and nauseated. Nonetheless, they had made the beach. Almost everywhere tanks were immediately in action. The next few minutes would be crucial. For the attackers had now entered the deadly zone on which defensive fire had been arranged to bear. Enemy defenders knew that they had but a short time either to destroy the force of the Canadian attack or else themselves be killed.

The Regina Rifle Regiment, disembarking under Courseulles' defences, the strongest of the sector, had prepared with particular thoroughness. Proudly, the battalion's war diary records: "First Battalion The Regina Rifle Regiment, on Exercise Overlord, landed at Nan Green Beach, Courseulles-sur-Mer, Normandy, France, at 0805 hours, with 'A' company being first in, followed by 'B' company at 0815 hours. 'C' company at 0855 hours, Command group, with Lt. Col. F. M. Matheson, touched down at 0900 hours."

Upon landing, A Company immediately had been brought under attack by German artillery. Troops also continued to be fired at by German machine guns, which had been firing at them during the stage of the run-in to the beach. Fortunately B Squadron of the 1st Hussars got its tanks ashore ahead of them. Fourteen out of 19 of the machines made the beach, after electing to swim for it while 2,000 yards out. The Canadian armour now began to engage the German guns — an 88-mm., a 75-mm., and a 50-mm. — from about 200 yards out. In the spirited duel that ensued, no tanks were knocked out, but the 88-mm. gun beside the harbour exit and the 50-mm. behind it continued to fire until their protective shields were pierced by shells from the Shermans. On the right flank, the 75-mm. gun held out much longer. It managed to fire 200 rounds, its entire ammunition stock, before 1st Hussar tanks finally fired a lucky shell that pierced its embrasure.

The Regina's sister battalion, the Royal Winnipeg Rifles, experienced a landing that was almost a duplicate of the above. Its left-hand company, landing west of the strongpoint area, moved easily into open country, clearing a path through the minefields, and capturing the small village of Graye-sur-Mer lying beyond. But the other Winnipeg company, B, experienced a tragic ordeal. Coming under fire while still out to sea, it finally landed. Its personnel were shocked to find "the bombardment had failed to kill a single German or silence one weapon." Many incoming attackers were killed "while still chest high in water." Those who managed to reach the sand saw that their only hope of salvation lay in a direct charge at the enemy. After waiting under shelter for six long minutes for the Hussars' tanks to arrive, survivors moved forward from the obstacles they had initially found shelter behind on the beach. Casualties, however, came thick and fast. By the time the company reached Courseulles itself, only 26 of its number were still standing. Among the ruined houses of the small village, shadows of Dieppe seemed, indeed, close at hand.

The ill-fated landing of the Queen's Own Rifles at Bernières also had a Dieppe-like quality. Here, tide and wind conspired to carry B company's landing craft 200 yards east of their assigned landing place. Approaching the beach, infantry came into the zone of fire of two 50-mm. guns and seven machine guns defending the village. Since the tanks of the Fort Garry Horse had not yet swum off the LCTs, unprotected infantrymen could only shelter behind the beach obstacles. Meanwhile the withering fire from German guns dropped many into the surf. Sixty-five were killed or wounded before three of the Queen's Own broke for the seawall and worked their way along it until within range of the strongpoint. Employing grenades and Sten-guns, and firing through the gun slits, they destroyed the defenders within.

Farthest east of all, the North Shore Regiment touched down at Lion-sur-Mer, where the British 3rd Division was landing. Swimming tanks of the Fort Garrys, which thankfully arrived simultaneously with the infantry, brought a large concrete gun shelter, which had survived the naval bombardment, under attack. Still, the enemy managed to destroy two of the tanks in the surf. Defenders also fired some 70 rounds before being overwhelmed by the combined effort of shelling from a Royal Marine Centaur's 95-mm. gun, a concrete-breaking petard of an Armoured Vehicle of the Royal Engineers, as well as the high velocity shells of two Fort Garry Shermans.

After a two-hour fight all along the five miles of coast attacked by the Canadians, enemy defences started to give way. Many of the Assault Vehicles Royal Engineers (AVREs), Crab flail tanks, and Royal Marine Centaurs had either floundered or been forced back to English ports, but those that reached the beaches now broke their way through dry obstacles at the beach tops. With the way now cleared by such "funnies," as the modified obstacle-clearing armoured vehicles were dubbed, assault troops broke through the massed barbed wire and pillboxes. Moving in on the towns, they began to clear them, block by block. Behind them the reserve brigades and the artillery now came ashore. Larry Smeaton, driver-operator of a big self-propelled 105-mm. artillery gun, rumbled ashore. Built on a Sherman tank's chassis, such howitzers had open cockpits and a crew of five. In ironic derision, troops christened the strange vehicles, which lacked turrets, "Priests" because of their pulpit-like machine gun mount.

By this time the beach, pockmarked with craters and strewn

with dead bodies and debris, was a mess. German mortars continued to shell it from the fields behind the towns.

On the beach, Smeaton encountered the beachmaster, who yelled: "Get off the beach! Get that machine off the beach!"

In response, Smeaton and his crew drove through a gap in the seawall, followed by three more Priests. After rumbling through the town, they took up a defensive position at its back edge, where the wheatfields started.

Smeaton didn't hear the first shot that struck one of the machines, lined up four abreast, but suddenly there was a crack of metal, and one of the Priests "brewed up" in a spectacular explosion. Then a second Priest exploded. Then a third. Leaping from his vehicle, Smeaton flung himself head-first into a nearby ditch. His machine was the only one not hit. Instantly, it roared off into the field, leaving him behind. A camouflaged German "88," the most lethal anti-tank weapon of the war, had picked the three Canadian mobile guns off in less than a minute. Weighed down under loads of extra fuel, ammo, and shells, the machines had blown up only ten yards from Smeaton. Six men were dead, five wounded. Miraculously Smeaton himself was not even grazed. He would not, however, see his own gun crew until later that evening.

By now the Canadians had been on the beaches for more than two hours. But the going still was not easy. In Courseulles, B Company of the Winnipegs was finding Germans, still alive and fighting, in the ruined houses around the harbour. On the Regina side of the harbour, troops found themselves having to repeat the dangerous work of shooting and grenading to deal with enemy who filtered back into trenches and tunnels cleared by the first arrivals. At Bernières, fighting continued on the landward side of the village, and at St. Aubin the North Shore's reserves had blundered into booby-trapped houses. On the beach, the Canadian Scottish, the reserve for the Winnipegs and Reginas, held up by minefields lying inland, found itself heavily mortared. The Chaudières, the other reserve battalion, had all five landing craft sunk under its leading company by mines and mortar bombs. Fire from the Queen's Own rescued many of them from where they had swum ashore and taken shelter under Bernières' sea wall.

At St. Aubin, the North Shore Regiment would not finally overcome resistance until 6:00 p.m. By this time, however, the majority of the first two brigades were safely ashore, unimpeded by the enemy, and ready to push inland. Behind them, the reserve brigade, the 9th, commenced to land, accompanied by its supporting armour, the Sherbrooke Fusiliers. The beaches were still clogged with men and vehicles. Flail and engineer tanks continued to struggle to clear gaps in the minefields. (Indeed, 14,000 mines had been laid between Courseulles and Bernières.) Engineers and others also worked desperately to blow gaps through the seawall and dunes to enable wheeled vehicles to exit. Already, though, the first infantry companies to land were commencing to advance inland towards their objectives. The rest of the Canadian Division would follow hard on their heels as soon as troops were able.

Pushing inland, Canadians found civilians had almost disappeared from the countryside beyond. Some had been killed by the horrific sea and air bombardment. The rest had taken shelter in their cellars. But if the advancing Canadians encountered few French, equally important there were few Germans. Because the Germans had been short of men, their policy had been to place troops at the very forward edge of the defended area. Now there were almost no enemy left to hold the chain of inland villages beyond the beach. As their lead patrols advanced, the Reginas found none in Reviers, two miles south of Courseulles. And the Winnipegs found only a few half-hearted snipers in the neighbouring village of Banville. There were also some snipers in Columbières-sur-Seulles, west of Reviers, who commenced firing on the Canadian Scottish as they approached through cornfields in the late morning. The advance continued, however, once the enemy snipers had been cleared. The Queen's Own Rifles on the left flank, too, found that once they were out into open country, the worst was over. The Queen's met a little resistance in the village of Anguerny, but had advanced and taken possession of the hamlet by late afternoon.

Amidst the crackling death and confusion, small vivid details stood out. They provided those who experienced them with mem-

ories destined to last for decades, if not a lifetime. Lieutenant-
Colonel Allen Nickson, commander of C Company of the Queen's
Own, entering a farmyard near the beach, found a shell-shocked
cow so traumatized its eyes didn't even blink. He also found a
cage of bunnies, likewise frozen from fear. Ed Meredith, a mortar
car driver with the Reginas, turned off the beach and drove inland. Suddenly, he was approached by an old woman who offered
her liberators a basket of eggs and a bottle of wine. Today, he
remembers: "It settled my stomach down better than anything I
could have imagined." Basil Robertson, with the Canadian Scottish's assault company, came across mooing cows needing to be
milked. He and his companions obliged. It was the first fresh milk
they had tasted for months. The official diary of the Queen's Own
Rifles records: "0900 hours: Cafe 100 yards off the beach is open
and selling wine." Additionally, the Reginas received their first
formal welcome and thank-you when locals emerged from their
cellars. They applauded the grimly marching but smiling troops,
and tossed roses in their paths.

The battle continued to rage as the day advanced. Many of the
opposition, conscript troops from Poland or Russia, surrendered
almost immediately. Some died where they stood, or else simply
evaporated towards the enemy rear. Meanwhile, Larry Lusk and
his platoon of Canadian Scottish bicycled towards the small inland bridge that was their objective to capture. Although they
were sniped at once or twice, they soon concluded that they
looked ridiculous riding their folding bicycles through the quiet
countryside. They captured the bridge, which was deserted, without firing a shot. Strange as it seems, they also captured four
German officers in a park nearby. Attired in shiny boots and dress
uniforms, they were apparently having a picnic.

Some Canadians had a hotter time of it. Al McDonald, in the
vanguard of the battle, knocked out three German machine gun
nests in the wheatfields off the beach. Larry Smith, a 1st Hussars
tank commander, blew a track when he drove over a land mine on
the beach. He spent the next two hours desperately trying to
repair the damage. When he finally got underway again, he spent
a productive day blasting snipers in church steeples and machine

gun nests hidden in wheat fields. Larry Smeaton, the driver-operator of the "Priest" 105-mm. self-propelled artillery gun, whose story has been recounted above, was reunited with his crew. Just before midnight, he captured a dazed German officer at bayonet point, pocketing his much-prized Luger pistol as a trophy.

By the end of history's "Longest Day," enough details of Allied successes and setbacks had drifted back into Supreme Headquarters to relieve tensions. There, Eisenhower and Montgomery were able to follow, albeit a few hours delayed, the assault's progress all along the landing zone, extending from the American air beachhead at the Cotentin Peninsula's base to the British operations east of the Orne. Satisfactory reports had come in concerning British seaborne landings at Gold and Sword Beaches, west and east of Juno. There had been gratifying news that the American 4th Division had managed to get ashore quickly at Utah and rescue the paratroopers. There had been tragic news, too, of the sufferings and near failure (except in spirit) of the U.S. 1st Division at Omaha Beach. The unit had taken 2,000 casualties merely crossing the sand from surf to cliff foot. There was news as well of the daring Rangers who had scaled the cliffs.

But nothing in the day's drama brought as much satisfaction, indeed excitement, as the account of the daring Canadian landing. 3rd Division had not only saved Supreme Command from inflicting a second national tragedy on Canada, but had achieved an important and impressive victory. At day's end, its forward elements had advanced deeper into France than those of any of the other four Allied divisions. The North Nova Scotia Highlanders, who had arrived fresh on the beach at noon, now stood in Villon-les-Buissons, only three miles from Caen. In their advance they also took 19 German prisoners. Additionally, a tank squadron of the 1st Hussars had encountered little resistance along the beach. It had managed to drive ten miles inland and cross the Caen-Bayeux railway, thereby establishing its proud claim to be "the only unit of the Allied invasion force to reach its objective on D-Day."

Although the beachhead had been won, and Canadian forces had pushed farther inland than those of other armies, the heart-

Winnipeg Rifles moving through fields, south of Vaucelles and Cormelles, Normandy, France, July 22, 1944. Department of National Defence. (NAC/PA-132435)

breaking fact remained though that the break-out phase of the battle had stalled. The British-Canadian objective, to capture Caen, the transport and industrial hub of Normandy, had fallen short. Nonetheless, Canadian casualties, relatively speaking, were thankfully light: 340 killed, 574 wounded, 47 captured. D-Day's solemn planners had envisioned at least 2,000, including 600 drowned. As the Canadian survivors pressed onwards into Normandy's countryside, the nightmare that had haunted every man was finally over. It was the spectre of Dieppe, 22 months earlier, on the beaches 70 miles to the east. Their successful landing would also ease the anxieties of hundreds of thousands of Canadians listening at home — when the first full information concerning the assault was broadcast across the Dominion the following morning.

Ironically, D-Day, compared to the campaign that followed, would prove a cakewalk. During the next three months of battle, casualties among Allied troops fighting in Normandy exceeded even the worst of the Great War itself. Battle fatigue, the trauma of men losing their minds under the pressures of constant fire (the troops called it "shell happy"), would wreak its havoc in epidemic proportions. The enemy's casualties would prove even higher. Despite the overwhelming, even obscene, advantage the Allies enjoyed in material, they did not sweep the Germans aside. The Norman countryside, with its *bocage,* or hedgerows, provided perfect defensive positions for the enemy, especially for his outnumbered, but far-superior Panther and Tiger tanks, which were capable of destroying Canadian Shermans before they could come within effective range of their adversaries. In addition, the German "88s" were a highly effective anti-tank weapon. On the beachhead's western flank, where the enemy had few Panzer units, the Americans were able to make relatively rapid progress. But in the east, the British and Canadians, many of their men and armour going into battle for the first time against the full weight of experienced German Panzer divisions, would pay a heavy price indeed.

The battle for Caen, seven-and-a-half-miles inland, proved particularly expensive. Following five weeks of struggle, the Allies finally prevailed. The cathedral city fell to the Brits and Canadians and the enemy pulled back. Finally, 88 days after the initial landings in France, the Norman Summer officially ended with the Battle of the Falaise Gap. In this desperate action, detailed in the chapter that follows, two retreating German armies were trapped between British and Canadian units on the north and American forces on the south. The result was a killing ground. Attempting to run the gauntlet of Allied artillery and strafing fighter aircraft, the withdrawing enemy suffered 50,000 dead and 200,000 wounded or captured, within the confines of a 30-mile area. Wrecked equipment was so extensive it rendered roads temporarily impassable, holding up even the victors. Pilots flying high above the area smelt the sickening stench of death, and avoided it if possible. From this time onwards, virtually to the war's end, death would become routine, just part of the soldier's everyday existence.

By the end of August 1944 the Battle for Normandy was over.

According to General Eisenhower's official report: "By 25 August, the enemy had lost, in round numbers, 400,000 killed, wounded or captured, of which a total of 200,000 were prisoners of war. One hundred and thirty-five thousand of these prisoners had been taken since the beginning of the breakthrough on 25 July. Thirteen hundred tanks, 20,000 vehicles, 500 assault guns, and 1500 field guns and heavier artillery pieces had been captured or destroyed, apart from the destruction inflicted upon the Normandy coast defences."

General H. D. G. "Harry" Crerar's Canadians made a very great contribution to this final result. General Montgomery himself later acknowledged that no division under his command during the Normandy Campaign suffered more casualties than 3rd Canadian did. Nor would the Canadians' sacrifice stop in Normandy. The "second front" now underway would last until May 7, 1945, when the Nazi government of Germany headed by Admiral Karl Doenitz unconditionally surrendered. Between D-Day and that much-desired date, some 11,000 Canadian soldiers would die, or, about 1,000 brave Canadians a month, in order to bring an end to Hitler's tyranny.

SELECTED READINGS

Bishop, Arthur. *Canada's Glory: Battles that Forged a Nation.* Toronto: McGraw-Hill Ryerson, 1996.

Blackburn, George G. *The Guns of Normandy: A Soldier's Eye View, France 1944.* Toronto: McClelland & Stewart, 1995.

"D-Day." *Esprit de Corps: Canadian Military Then and Now* 4:1 (June 1994): 26–31.

Granatstein, J. L. and Desmond Morton. *Bloody Victory: Canadians and the D-Day Campaign 1944.* Toronto: Lester, 1994.

Hickey, R. M. *The Scarlet Dawn.* Campbellton, N.B.: Tribune Publishers, 1949.

Keegan, John. *Six Armies in Normandy: From D-Day to the Liberation of Paris.* London: Penguin, 1983.

Roy, Reginald H. *1944: The Canadians in Normandy.* Toronto: Macmillan of Canada in collaboration with the Canadian War Museum, 1984.

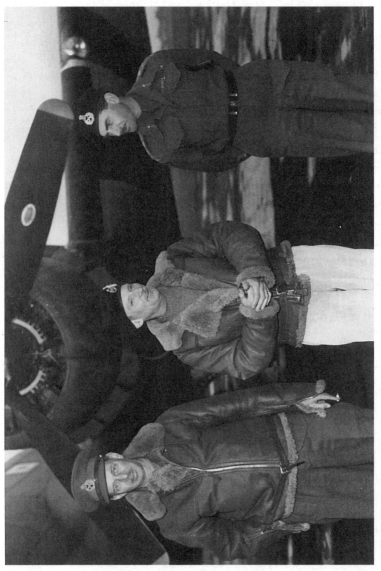

Field Marshal Montgomery (C) and General Dempsey (L) arrive to confer with General Simonds (R), Antwerp, Belgium, October 16, 1944. Photographer: Lieutenant M. M. Dean. National Defence Collection. (NAC/PA-131258)

21

LIEUTENANT-GENERAL GUY SIMONDS

*Mastering the Battlefield
at any Cost*

*Enigmatic and intense, Lieutenant-General Guy Simonds (1903–
1974) proved himself one of World War II's most imaginative
strategists, earning the respect of British generals Bernard
Montgomery and Alan Brooke. After observing the British Eighth
Army in action in Africa, and commanding Canadian infantry
and armour in Italy, Simonds was brought back to England and
placed in charge of II Canadian Corps, in preparation for the D-
Day landings. In Normandy, Simonds planned "Operation
Totalize," which opened the way to Falaise after the fall of Caen.
He also invented the Kangaroo, the world's first armoured personnel carrier. During the battle to open the Scheldt so that the Allies
could use Antwerp's vital port facilities, he "sank" the strategic
island of Walcheren by ordering its dikes bombed. This campaign
resulted in Canada's most important victory of World War II.
Later, Simonds spearheaded the successful Canadian march into
the Rhineland. Often hamstrung by troop and equipment short-
ages and the lack of imagination of his superiors, Simonds overcame such difficulties. In the process, however, he made enemies.
After war's end, he received the bureaucratic cold shoulder. But*

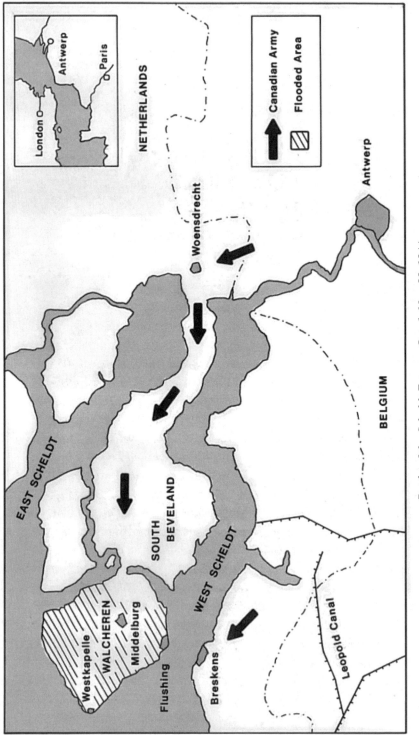

Battle of the Scheldt Estuary, Oct. 1–Nov. 28, 1944

just as he had always mastered combat's blackest moments, he would triumph again. In 1951 his superlative abilities were finally acknowledged when he was appointed Chief of the General Staff.

Only a few officers of Canada's minuscule inter-war Permanent Force were destined to achieve high command during the Second World War. In part, at least, this was because the Permanent Force during the 1920s and 1930s remained a mere twenty-fifth the size of its counterpart, the U.S. Regular Army. Nonetheless one officer in particular among the 400 officers of the regular corps stood out as an obvious comer. This was the enigmatic, driven Guy Simonds. Despite the constrained inactivity the army faced during the peaceful inter-war interlude, photographs of Simonds indicate the sense of serious purpose, flair, and obvious panache, or style, that would carry this young officer to the very top of his profession during World War II.

Indeed, Guy Simonds' career trajectory possessed a "comet-like" quality all its own. Officers such as Harry Crerar or Tommy Burns, both of whom would become generals, were respected for their intellects. Other future generals, including Rod Keller, Chris Vokes, Harry Foster, and Dan Spry, ranked strong in leadership potential. Guy, however, possessed both qualities. Most importantly, he stood out as "driven to succeed at almost any cost." Such ambition, coupled with a ruthless drive for perfection, would cost him many close friends. It would even cost him his marriage. But he calculated this was the natural "price of command." His ambition would take him to the very apex of Canada's military pyramid. A mere battalion commander a short time earlier, he was destined to be a divisional commander in Sicily and Italy, a corps commander in Northwest Europe, and acting army commander in the same theatre during the autumn of 1944. In addition, he was the very exemplification of military professionalism. Following the war, he would be the first Canadian ever appointed to Britain's Imperial Defence College. He would also serve a term as Canadian Chief of General Staff. His appointments are part of the country's history as well as his own.

Born in England in 1903, Simonds knew instinctively that he wished to pursue a military career. As a youngster, he took special pride in the fact that his family included a long line of soldiers who had served the British Empire. His great-grandfather had soldiered in India under the East India Company. His grandfather had retired from the Imperial Indian Army with the rank of major-general. Guy's own father, Cecil, commissioned in the Royal Artillery, had served in the South African War.

In 1911, however, Guy's father suddenly left the army and emigrated to Victoria, British Columbia. Guy strongly resented his father's precipitate decision, since in his mind the Simonds were a military family. Indeed, as his biographer Dominick Graham notes, the driving force that fuelled Simonds' own burning ambition was the conviction that his father had "broken the mould." In his mind, no cost was too high to pay in order to restore the family's honour and record of service. From the age of nine, when he won a set of lead soldiers displayed in the window of a Victoria recruiting office for an essay on the military, Guy was single-minded about joining the army. Sent east along with his brother to a private school, Ashbury College, he shone in all activities. When the results of entrance exams for Royal Military College were announced, young Simonds stood second in merit in all Canada.

Guy's career at RMC merely confirmed his superb leadership potential. Exceptionally mature from an early age, he did not chase after popularity. Still, he was noticed. His aloof, super-efficient style soon established itself as the role model for his peers, as rivals watched the handsome youth excel without apparent effort. Even though Guy's school career was affected by his family's financial problems, the brilliant cadet managed to graduate from RMC with the prestigious Sword of Merit. He also won the Governor General's Silver Medal for ranking second in his class academically. Both at RMC and during his subsequent 18 years of peacetime service with the Canadian army, Simonds would be called, appropriately or not, "The Count." The nickname was a slightly sardonic allusion to his immaculate appearance and anglicized accent and manner. As W. Denis and Shelagh Whitaker note: "Just under six feet tall, straight of stance and spare of build, dark hair combed back behind a carefully coiffed widow's peak, moustache meticulously trimmed, uniform impeccably tailored, Simonds was 'the compleat officer,' as one senior officer termed him." Also, "his dark good looks were not lost on the ladies, who found the renowned icy blue eyes somewhat more melting in effect."

Those who slowly worked their way up through the ranks in Guy's turbulent wake recall his perseverance in mastering his profession — how he put aside all else to concentrate his full effort on achieving his chosen objective. Such single-mindedness was the key to his future career. In 1936 he was one of a handful of Canadians selected to attend Staff College in England. Here he performed brilliantly. He responded especially to the college's stress on the "thinking approach" to solving problems of modern warfare. At the end, his assessment by the Commandant was nothing short of superb, an appraisal full of genuine commendation. It was evident Simonds had not received one of the "courtesy passes" that were often given to visiting Dominion officers. When he was posted back to RMC Kingston in the late 1930s Guy did not leave the important lessons of Staff College behind. He continued to think about military problems systematically, constantly organizing and testing out his ideas on both colleagues and students. And, though he was an artillery officer, he would publish three seminal articles in the *Canadian Defence Quarterly* dealing with the organization and deployment of infantry in order to deal with the demands of armoured warfare.

Once the Second World War began, Simonds' commitment intensified. One of his first assignments in Britain was to establish the Canadian Junior War Staff College. The institution helped fill the gaping need to train staff officers. Later, as General Andy McNaughton's principal staff officer, Guy was placed in charge of the important task of planning Canadian Corps' training and possible operational roles. Fortunately, he was not associated with the Dieppe raid. Instead, he prepared an appreciation of the possibilities of an attack on Norway. But in September 1942 Simonds' staff duties came to an end when he assumed command of 1st Canadian Infantry Brigade in 1st Division. In April 1943, at the age of forty, he was promoted to major-general, commanding 2nd Canadian Infantry Division, which was still recuperating from the mauling it had received at Dieppe. Simonds' climb had been spectacular. He had risen from a mere major to major-general in three-and-a-half short years. It was a record that no other officer, in either the Permanent Force or the Non Permanent Active Militia, had achieved.

Like General E. L. M. ("Tommy") Burns, another officer who possessed a brilliant intellect, and who would likewise make his mark during World War II and after, Simonds had established a reputation as being "austere, cold, a no-nonsense, business-first planner." When Major-General Harry Salmon, 1st Canadian Infantry Division's GOC, died in a tragic air crash, General Andy McNaughton immediately nominated Guy to succeed him. In the spring of 1943, when the Allies invaded Sicily, Simonds would become the first Canadian officer to lead troops into battle in a sustained campaign.

A news photo taken on the occasion of the Sicily landings shows the dapper Simonds, martially erect and slenderly fit, dressed in khaki fatigue shorts, wading ashore on the landing beach near Pachino airport. Appropriately, he is wearing the famous black beret that would, like his mentor Monty's, become his hallmark. After more than two decades, the "Old Red Patch" worn by 1st Division of the Canadian Corps was going into battle once again! Overall, the Sicily Campaign would serve as the "blooding" Guy and the Canadians so badly needed. An easy landing slowly escalated into bitter fighting against a resourceful German rearguard. By the time the Canadians reached the Straits of Messina on August 6, they had become, as we have earlier seen, aggressive, battle-hardened fighters. Guy, too, had more than proven himself in Montgomery's highly critical judgement. Indeed, no other Canadian would so satisfy the controversial and opinionated Monty's demanding standards.

Later, when 5th Armoured Division arrived in Italy dangerously unprepared for battle, Guy would be given the challenging task of commanding it. His determination and vigour soon transformed the unit into a battle-effective one that would distinguish itself in the bitterly contested fighting as the enemy countered the Allied advance up the boot of Italy. The Canadian effort, however, would be temporarily diverted when McNaughton's replacement, General Harry Crerar, arrived in person. There was a celebrated altercation between Simonds, ill and exhausted, and his superior. From this time onwards, the gap between the two could not be bridged. Having served under General Currie in the Great War, Crerar believed that his main goal was to keep Canada's army united. In contrast, Simonds and the young officers serving in Italy had adapted to the British battle environment, and stressed battlefield performance at all costs. They believed that it was the "McNaughton-Crerar gang," still fighting the earlier war, who were badly out of step.

While Simonds still had much to learn as a battle commander, his experience in Italy would do much to redress the neglect of Canada's military and its outdated thinking and training. Although a "paucity of talent" continued to characterize the Canadian army in the field, this charge could not be levelled against generals such as Simonds, Chris Vokes, or Bert Hoffmeister. All received, as we have noted, sufficient battle experience in the "Spaghetti League" to become first-rate commanders. Once Guy was posted back to the UK to assist in the preparation for D-Day, he would execute his own ruthless purge of ineffective commanders, replacing them with officers under forty who had learned their trade in Italy.

Even in Italy, Simonds' implacable command style spawned a raft of colourful stories. Conducting a field inspection of the Calgary Tanks, he purportedly emerged from the turret of one of the machines, pointedly remarking: "Peanuts!" The single word, forcibly uttered, indicated his marked displeasure at having found peanut shells and candy wrappers on the floor. Simonds also attempted to emulate Monty's impromptu "chats" with groups of soldiers encountered on the battlefield. But the overall impression was that such forced efforts left much to be desired. Despite possessing a similar prima donna complex, Guy enjoyed none of the British general's common touch and "dash of pixy" that rendered his talks so popular with participants.

Italy, however, was a mere prelude to the role Simonds was destined to assume as commander in Northwest Europe. Promoted to lieutenant-general, Guy was given the command of II Canadian Corps in the invasion of Normandy in June 1944. The Canadians' demanding task would be to spearhead the decisive "breakout" phase of Overlord, once the Allied beachhead had been secured. Here, in the constantly shifting, fluid battle situations provided by difficult terrain and a fiercely determined opponent, Simonds would quickly come into his own. His uncanny ability to improvise flexibly, as well as an instinctive imagination for combat, would be noticed by the senior commanders of all the major countries involved.

During the Norman Summer's protracted combat, Simonds, who was still somewhat inexperienced in the subtleties of executing large-scale armoured attacks, would grapple with a number of problems that would cost the divisions he commanded a heavy price in executing Monty's strategy. Most importantly, Allied failure to capture Caen, Normandy's strategic port, rail, and road centre, until late June, would dramatically alter the course of the battle. Instead of provoking the Germans into counterattacking at heavy cost, as originally planned, British and Canadians were obliged to go over to the attack themselves. Their new goal was to hold elite German panzer grenadier and panzer divisions on their front, and to "write [or wear] them down," as Monty described the bloody process. The sacrifice involved was intended to render it possible for General Omar Bradley's Americans to break through farther south in "Operation Cobra."

During his first five weeks in operations with II Corps, Simonds directed four separate major attacks on the Germans. His corps would also play a major role in helping close the Falaise Gap, through which the enemy was retreating. The first two battles, Operations "Atlantic" and "Spring," would be attritional. The

A Sherman tank: the standard Allied tank in WW II. Courtesy of Esprit de Corps.

last two, "Totalize" and Tractable," fought two weeks later, would be classic breakout battles, coordinated with the U.S. breakthrough in the west.

The Canadian Corps would fight some of its bloodiest encounters in the gently rolling countryside south of Caen. Here, fields of fire were very long. German "88s" and special 75-mm. guns, either mounted on Panther and Tiger tanks, or else on wheels, often destroyed half or more of an armoured regiment's 60 tanks before they could engage the enemy. In fact, as claimed in a new book entitled *Time to Kill,* edited by Paul Addison and Angus Calder, 60 percent of Allied tank losses in Normandy were the result of a *single* shot from such vastly superior weapons and two-thirds of all tanks "brewed up" when hit, that is, their fuel and ammunition ignited immediately, virtually incinerating any crew members not fortunate enough to be blown out a hatch. An even greater shortcoming was both the British and Canadian infantry's lack of preparation. During the six months preceding D-Day, the major emphasis had been placed on the amphibious phase of the battle, not the dogfight and breakout phases to follow. As

Dominick Graham, Simonds' biographer, notes, Allied infantry frequently suffered from "tank fear" and "88-mm. phobia." Compounding the effect were the Allies' inferior Churchill and Sherman tanks, the poor handling of anti-tank guns, and the troops' marked inability to defend themselves in the open.

Indeed, the casualty rate — killed, wounded, missing — among foot soldiers in Europe 1939–1945 would be virtually the same as it had been for their fathers' and uncles' generation in the slaughter fields of France during the Great War. A single, rough comparison for Normandy confirms this fact. During 105 days in 1917, British and Canadian soldiers fought the bitter battle known as 3rd Ypres, including the struggle for Passchendaele, at a cost of 244,000 casualties, roughly 2,121 a day. Normandy would cost the allies more than 200,000, or 2,354 a day. Seventy percent of such casualties were from the tiny minority of men in infantry rifle companies. Such figures advance our understanding of the problems that a senior Canadian field commander such as Simonds faced on a day-to-day basis, and help us understand his and other commanders' often somewhat erratic battle performances. But they do not totally absolve such officers of all blame for such a high casualty rate.

In "Operation Atlantic," July 18–19, Simonds' II Corps was to support British VIII Corps' right flank and capture various suburbs of Caen and nearby villages on the Orne. The 8th Brigade's infantry kicked off the Canadian attack on the town's built-up areas, behind an intensely concentrated barrage 45 minutes after British armour started to roll. General Harry Foster's 7th Brigade followed later, crossing the river from the centre of Caen, and occupying the twin city of Vancelles. Meanwhile, 2nd Division waited as a follow-up reserve, its special tasks allotted by the flint-eyed Simonds to General Charles Foulke's various brigade commanders.

Characteristically, Simonds' personal Staghound armoured command car was never far from the front lines. In Normandy, the fighting's intensity quickly tested the unique mix of physical and mental attributes required of a top-notch battle commander.

Guy's were not found to be wanting. As Harry Foster, who later commanded the 1st Canadian Division in the fighting in the Netherlands, wrote, "When others fell asleep after two or three days on their feet, Guy could keep on going, his brain still working at top speed. He had an amazing ability to be able to analyze a given situation quickly and accurately, cutting through irrelevancies to the heart of the problem, then quickly making up his mind. His orders were always clear, concise, and straight to the point. But he was a hard man to work for."

Although some categorized Simonds as a "cold fish," he quickly established both a reputation and respect, due to his ability to conserve manpower and minimize battle casualties. When necessary, though, he was quite capable of ordering an attack through its own artillery cover, if he judged the result would actually minimize deaths. On one notable occasion during the Normandy fighting, a group of Canadians had been cut off and surrounded by the enemy. Rather than order their immediate relief, which he calculated would have produced heavier casualties, Guy pointedly ordered them to hold on till morning. In Normandy, Simonds also enhanced his growing reputation as a demanding commander who would not hesitate to remove subordinates he judged were not performing competently. In the course of a single day, he fired a brigade commander as well as two of his battalion COs.

Some officers strongly resented Guy's seemingly insatiable drive to attain perfection, as well as his highly aloof manner. Of a chance encounter with Simonds in Normandy, one senior officer later graphically recalled: "I was sitting in a jeep by the side of the road, having just done a recce to find our next battalion headquarters, when Simonds came up. He was in that Staghound armoured car of his, complete with dispatch riders, and he asked me (we had been friends for years), 'Where is the headquarters of 4th Armoured Division?' I said, 'Sir, I don't even know where the headquarters of 3 Division is and I'm in 3 Division.' He said, 'That's why you're still a major. Drive on!'"

In the fighting beyond Caen, in "Operation Spring," British

and Canadian troops faced more open country. It looked decep-
tively inviting to tank battle. But the lurking reality was that every
village and forest was a ready-made fortress for German troops,
tanks and their formidable 88-mm. anti-tank weapons. The only
asset the Allies enjoyed was air superiority. Even this did not provide much help at night or in overcast weather. Throughout the
hot weeks of July, both the Canadian armour and infantry kept up
the pressure. But at a bloody cost. At Verrières Ridge, on the 25th,
a battle that one surviving officer compared to the Charge of the
Light Brigade, 300 men of the Black Watch, a Montreal-based
militia regiment, were almost all cut down while advancing
through cornfields, without adequate tank cover, towards the village of May-sur-Orne. Only 13 attackers survived the long, hopeless assault. The incident was reminiscent of the fate British
infantry had met during the Somme battles in the Great War. As
one private later told military historian Colonel C. P. Stacey: "We
just pushed on, sir; we had been told that was the Black Watch
way." Except for Dieppe, more Canadians died on this single day
than on any other in World War II. The stubborn, even mindless
attack against dug-in German tanks cost in total 1,965 men,
mostly 2nd Division.

After his death during the battle for Verrières Ridge, twenty-
four-year-old Major Phillip Griffin, who found himself in command of the regiment, after both the commanding officer and
the next-in-command had been killed by machine gun fire, was
blamed for the attack's failure. But it was really a combination of
bad generalship and bad luck that resulted in Griffin being
forced to lead his command in a suicidal advance.

Although Simonds himself was not to blame — rather errors
had been made by both brigade and division commanders — the
disaster showed his unique ability to learn quickly and to profit
from mistakes. His coldly objective analysis of the Operation
found there had, indeed, been shortcomings at every level of
command. A short two weeks later, in "Operation Totalize," he
would demonstrate a revolutionary method of setting up the battles that his units, especially infantry, would have to fight.

This attack, designed to pierce the German defences astride the Caen-Falaise road and cut off the retreating enemy, was ground-breaking in conception. Armour attacking at night would play the leading role. Meanwhile, infantry, realizing a vision that came to Simonds in North Africa, would "leap frog" forward in improvised armoured carriers. These were hastily fabricated from mobile howitzers, or Priests, whose guns had been temporarily removed, transforming such vehicles into "de-frocked Priests," or Kangaroos. Simonds' brilliantly innovative plan also employed a creeping barrage, laid down by some 360 guns, that began once the attack commenced. To guide the attackers and vehicles, searchlights were bounced off low cloud cover, creating a form of artificial moonlight. Simultaneously, on the advance's flanks, Royal Air Force heavy bombers laid down a curtain of high explosives to screen the attackers. The battle marked the first appear-

Infantry riding into battle in Priest tanks, 4th Infantry BDE (Brigade) —
2nd Canadian Division, France, August 7, 1944.
Photograph: R. Barnett. Canadian Army Film Unit Collection. (NAC/PA-129172)

ance of the armoured personnel carrier (APC) on any battlefield. Today, of course, every modern army employs such vehicles.

At 2300 hours on August 7, 1944, "Totalize's" first phase commenced. As conceived by Simonds, its primary objective was to break through German positions south and east of Caen. If successful, the operation would expedite the Canadian drive towards Falaise, a critical road junction lying behind enemy lines. Although not fully realized initially, ensuing operations were going to develop into a major turning point in the Normandy fighting. Two miles distant, tents shuddered as 1,000 aircraft dropped 3,000 tons of bombs on targets on the flank of the axis of advance. Witnesses would record the barrage "going full blast," intermittently lighting up the sky. Also, on either flank, streams of tracer shells fired from Bofors guns as a means of guiding the troops in the darkness flew "leisurely through the air." The Canadians roared forward in two massive columns, each composed of eight lines of tracked vehicles "almost nose to tail." Flail Shermans (mine destroyers), developed as we have seen for the D-Day invasion, headed up each column. "Kangaroos" with turrets full of infantry and Bren-gun carriers occupied the middle. More tanks, rumbling along in the rear, provided additional protection and back-up.

Viewed through attackers' observation slits, the scene was one of controlled chaos. Drivers, confused in the noise and dust, swerved abruptly across the paths of others as they dodged bomb craters and other obstacles, or as they took sudden evasive action. In the confusion, vehicles hit by German anti-tank gunners burned "alarmingly brightly." Despite the "hades-like" aspect of this new form of battle, the Canadian columns succeeded. Morning's light revealed they had punched through close to three miles of the enemy's defences. An added bonus was that they had suffered relatively little loss while capturing most of their objectives. These included the village of Tilly-la-Campagne, which earlier attacks had failed to gain.

Unfortunately, "Totalize's" second phase (August 8) was dogged by misfortune. When heavy bombers of the U.S. Air Force were called on to substitute for Royal Air Force bombers at the last moment, many bombs fell nowhere near specified targets. Some 20 bombers, mistaking yellow signal smoke, actually dropped their bomb loads on Canadians and Poles just outside Caen. The three divisions Simonds employed in the attack were relatively green. And, as Major-General George Kitching, one of Guy's protégés, has observed, chaos resulted from "putting some 50,000 soldiers into an area approximately 2 miles by 4 miles . . . particularly when there was a battle going on in the middle of it!!"

Other factors as well contributed to the difficulties. Primary among these was the stout resistance put up by SS General Kurt Meyer's outnumbered, but superbly led troops. Also, considerable casualties were suffered by senior Canadian officers, in addition to heavy losses inflicted on the attackers by shelling and mortaring on their flanks. Although Simonds' force consisted of hundreds of tanks and the Germans had been reduced by August 10 to only 35 still operational, the advance ground to a halt.

By this time, Field Marshal Gunther von Kluge, the enemy commander, was becoming increasingly anxious for the safety of all German troops west of the Seine. He made a crucial decision to extricate them and remove them to safety. To accomplish this, the retreating enemy would have to channel all his troops and equipment through a 15-mile-wide gap that existed between Falaise and Argentan, and fall back in a northeasterly direction towards Rouen. Should German forces fail to do so, they would be left trapped in an embryo pocket that was fast developing.

Simonds' cancellation of "Totalize," on August 11, would necessitate a second Canadian thrust towards Falaise. Code-named "Tractable," the operation was intended to sever the east-west road link running out of the town, and trap the withdrawing Germans. In broad daylight, on August 14, Simonds attacked with two armoured brigades, followed by a further two infantry brigades. Their flanks were protected by a thick blanket of artillery smoke. The thrust was supported in addition by massed medium artillery, and the RAF contributed the full weight of Bomber Command. "Tractable," however, would also suffer from problems. The bombers' second wave dumped its bomb load in error on 2nd Division's forces. The mistake cost 50 Canadian and Polish lives, in addition to leaving another 250 wounded. Another piece of bad luck ensued when the enemy captured battle orders from an Allied officer, who had mistakenly driven into enemy territory. German defenders were able to make their dispositions accordingly.

Despite such lapses, the attack made substantial gains. Kurt Meyer, commanding 12th SS Panzer Division, would later note that the Canadian attack was "so rapid that I could not withdraw my Infantry and the Canadian Infantry completely passed all of my Infantry Battalions, and when they held up they were halfway between my infantry and the Armoured Columns. It took my infantry two days to rabbit-leap back to my armour." As the desperate SS troops fought for survival, they employed a new trick they had developed on the Eastern Front. This was to deploy personnel in a manner that forced Allied formations to face in two directions. The task of such troops facing westward was to stem the tide of Germans trying to escape. Those continuing to face eastward were kept busy fending off the counterattacks of the enemy breaking back to save those who were trapped.

After vicious fighting, elements of the Polish Armoured and 4th Canadian Armoured finally closed the Falaise Gap. By the evening of August 17, the area had shrunk to a strip barely seven miles long and six miles wide. By August 19, German forces trapped within it were being relentlessly assaulted from the air as well as by 3,000 Allied guns. By now, however, friend and foe were so closely intermixed that there were major problems for both artillery and air support. Despite their tactical advantage, the Canadians were unable to prevent sizable numbers of enemy, especially fanatical SS units, from breaking out. By August 21, the worst of the battle of the Falaise Pocket was over. As a Canadian officer recorded: "A host of white flags appeared and hundreds of the enemy crowded in to surrender." In the horrendous combat and bombardment, two German armies had been savagely mauled. Their casualties amounted to 60,000 men and most of their equipment. Nonetheless, a third of the German Seventh Army had managed to cheat the encircling prongs of the Allied armies closing round them. The Canadians also paid a high price. Simonds' three divisions suffered 1,479 killed, 4,023 wounded, and 177 taken prisoner from the beginning of "Operation Totalize" until the day the Falaise Gap was closed.

American critics, and some later historians, would charge that the Allies had allowed a quarter of a million enemy to escape, mainly because Simonds failed to press home his attack against Falaise sufficiently. Because of such failings, Simonds would subsequently conduct a major shake-up of his command, relieving his friend George Kitching, who headed 4th Canadian Armoured Division. Other officers who he thought had failed the severe test of battle were also replaced. When viewed in a larger context, though, many of "Tractable's" difficulties stemmed from decisions made by the Americans. It seems very few enemy would have escaped had General Bradley not prematurely halted General George S. Patton's northern thrust. The effect was comparable to a giant nutcracker, or pair of slip-pliers, whose lower jaw suddenly loses much of its force. Studied objectively, the Battle of the Falaise Gap, and Canada's role in it, continues to impress and intrigue us. Terry Copp, a military historian who recently revisited the battle evidence, has concluded that — judged on its merits rather than errors — the action qualifies to stand alongside Stalingrad as a great Allied victory.

In spite of Simonds' obvious successes, his tactical decisions in Normandy have been criticized. But the basic question remains: just what more might have been accomplished, given prevailing conditions, which presented him with few alternatives? The majority of battles fought were indeed costly, and offered few, if any, "bargains." The question also remains whether Monty simply demanded too much of his gifted protégé, given the enemy's superior battle experience and distinctive advantages in both armour and anti-tank weapons.

The Normandy campaign was over, thanks to the Allied superiority in numbers alone. But there would be scant respite for

Guy, his commanders, or the Canadian troops. The advancing Canadians now employed their momentum to pursue the retreating Germans across the Seine. As Simonds reported, it was like "cutting through cheese." When he came across an abandoned enemy 88-mm. gun, in perfect working order, with its ammunition neatly stacked beside it, he noted: "I knew that we would win. It was the first time I had ever seen a German gun position abandoned without a fight." By September 5, rapidly advancing British forces had captured the great Belgian port of Antwerp, although not the seaward approaches. Indeed, at this euphoric point in the advance, it even seemed possible that the war might soon be over.

This hope caused Montgomery to launch "Operation Market Garden," in mid-September. The huge airborne assault's objective was to capture the bridges that spanned the lower Rhine at Nijmegen and Arnhem. Tragically the attack failed. And with it went the Allies' dream of achieving a speedy victory in 1944. The fact that the Allies had neglected to clear the Scheldt River approaches to Antwerp, in Belgium, now became critical. Without access to the great port city's dock facilities, the herculean task of supplying the massive Anglo-American armies in their drive northeastward into the German heartland was at best problematic. As General Eisenhower himself acknowledged, "Right now our prospects are tied up so closely with our success in capturing the approaches to Antwerp . . . if we can only get to using Antwerp it will have the effect of a blood transfusion."

Until this point, First Canadian Army had been the Cinderella, or poor step-sister, of Eisenhower's force. It had spent September slogging up the Allies' "long left flank," clearing the Channel ports. Now Montgomery gave it the important, even vital, task of clearing the Scheldt approaches, so shipping could reach Antwerp's facilities. On the operation's eve, the army's commander, Lieutenant-General Harry Crerar, was invalided back to England and hospitalized for persistent dysentery. Simonds now became acting army commander. Charles Foulkes, in turn, replaced him as II Corps' acting commander. Of this event, the Whitakers note: "For Simonds the command opportunity was like opening up the

*Major-General H. W. Foster and Lieutenant-General Guy G. Simonds, Eekloo, Belgium,
October 10, 1944.* Photograph: R. H. C. Angelo.
Canadian Army Film Unit Collection. (NAC/PA-142097)

door of a smouldering furnace. His feverishly active mind exploded in flashes of brilliance that marked him, even in the first few weeks, as the most tactically innovative general ever to emerge from a Canadian army."

The battle to open Antwerp's approaches would develop into an undertaking that stands only second to the Normandy landings themselves. Relatively unknown to the public today, it is considered to be Canada's most important contribution to the Second World War. At its height, the army that Simonds commanded would consist of five infantry and two armoured divisions, two Commando brigades, as well as several smaller formations. A large proportion of Twenty-First Army Group's medium and heavy regiments would be involved. So were a monitor ship and two battleships. Additional parts of the force included scores of naval amphibious craft and hundreds of aircraft of all types, employed in bombing and strafing. Despite such massive Allied force, the highly complex operation was destined to occupy seven weeks. Also, terrible weather conditions, as well as the water-logged terrain, conspired to make it a very "messy" battle indeed.

With justifiable pride, infantrymen who fought in the campaign referred to themselves as "Water Rats." The dead-flat sodden ground, interspersed with 15-foot dikes, offered man-made barricades easily defended by the enemy. Either flooded or liable to be flooded by defenders, the fields, or *polders*, were virtually useless for tank warfare. As one soldier put it, it was a battleground "for men with web feet and waterproof skins." Colonel C. P. Stacey has said: "No written record can do justice to the situation." Suffice to say that the Canadian infantrymen, or "grunts," who were engaged in the assaults in such country were destined to "become bearded, hungry, sleepless, muddied forms. There remained to them only the knowledge that they were part of something, a section, platoon, company, regiment, and that it all held together."

When he took over command of First Army, Simonds, in typical fashion, had already studied the appreciation, or draft assessment, that Plans Section had worked up. He soon shredded it. In his estimate, Walcheren Island, which dominated the Scheldt's seaward approaches, was a formidable obstacle. As he noted, the Germans had fortified its nearly diamond-shaped perimeter with some 60 heavy guns, each deeply embedded in concrete. Nowhere on the Atlantic Wall, even in Normandy, at Dieppe, or in the Pas de Calais region defending the Channel crossing, were so many heavy and casemated guns trained on the seaward approaches. To take the objective, Simonds stated, a combined operation across water would likely be required. He ordered the necessary military and naval forces to be readied and trained for such an eventuality.

The key to opening Walcheren's locked door came to Simonds' fertile mind like a flash. It was to bomb the island's dikes, to flood the land, and to deny the enemy the advantages provided by dry ground. Earlier, Crerar's planners had considered such an idea, but the RAF rejected it because Prime Minister Winston Churchill wished to avoid further bombing of Dutch and Belgian towns. Bomber Command also wanted to concentrate on targets in Germany. Additionally, the Chief Engineer of First Army had rejected the concept due to "technical objections" as to whether the dikes could indeed be breached.

Even decades later, officers who had been present and witnessed the evolution of Simonds' daring concept would remember the scene. How, looking up from map overlays of Walcheren's formidable defences, which could withstand even the most vigorous conventional bombardment, Guy suddenly said: "If we've got to do this, there's only one way. We've got to have an element that isn't orthodox or we'll never make it. We have to let in the sea." The unconventional proposal electrified army and corps headquarters. Opinions ranged from "this is a brainstorm," to "this is a wild idea." Others thought: "He'll never persuade bomber command to go in by day." Technical types in particular tended to be negative, arguing: "They won't be able to breach the dikes: the whole thing is half-baked, it will never work."

The Americans and the air force declined to help. But Guy persisted, invoking his new status as Canada's acting Commander-in-Chief to press his innovative scenario forward. When Bomber Command remained a major obstacle, he fixed them in characteristic manner with his steely blue eyes and bluntly said, "Well gentlemen, that's pretty disappointing. Had you been able to take that on as a task it would undoubtedly have saved many lives in the assault." After conferring again, the airmen came back and said that, though they couldn't guarantee the operation's success, "by God they'd try."

Fighting in the Scheldt estuary was the worst that Canadians engaged in during the entire war. Inching forward in dreadful conditions of water, mud and cold, the troops encountered their first obstacle: the Breskens Pocket. Also known as "Scheldt Fortress South," it measured about 25 miles from east to west, and 12 from north to south. It was defended by 14,000 troops and supported by heavy guns on Walcheren Island to the north; it also possessed over 500 machine guns and mortars of its own, in addition to 300 other guns. The hard-slogging battle occupied all of October. By month's end, Simonds' troops, including the Canadian Scottish and Regina Rifles, managed to attack across the Leopold Canal. Under a searing wall of fire from 27 WASPs (flame-throwing Bren-gun carriers) they cleared the pocket. Attacking the dikes of Woensdrecht (the village guarding the narrow "peninsula" leading to South Beveland), every man in the rifle companies of the Black Watch was wounded. At last, however, units of the Royal Hamilton Light Infantry won a foothold in the hamlet and cleared it. This opened the way for more vicious fighting over the narrow causeway beyond, which connected the mainland to Walcheren's eastern end. Now three of four major obstacles blocking the approaches to Antwerp had been removed. The battle for control was poised to enter its final stage: that for Walcheren Island itself.

On October 30, 247 four-engine Lancasters delivered 1,270 tons of high explosives on the 100-yard-wide dikes, in the form of 4,000, 2,000, and 500-pound armour-piercing bombs. As the planes departed, the ocean rushed in to flood the land through a breach already over 100 yards long that every wave quickly enlarged. Ultimately a total of four successful raids — two at Flushing in the south, one on the east coast at Veere, and one at Westkapelle (West Cape) — would smash Walcheren's formidable belt of dikes. Air reconnaissance now reported that most of the island was flooded. Only perimeter dikes and dunes, as well as the town of Middleburg and a portion of Flushing, were still above water.

"D-Day" for "Operation Infatuate" was scheduled for November 1. The attack, however, actually began a day earlier when Canadian troops opened the offensive from the east. The thrust of their assault was the 12,000-yard-long causeway that linked Walcheren to the South Beveland Peninsula. When the operation bogged down, it was diverted two miles south. Here, assault craft would be employed to carry attackers across successfully. But not until November 3.

Elsewhere, as planned, at 0445 on November 1, motors of 20 assault craft of the No. 4 British Army Commandos rose to a full roar. Their objective was Flushing, at the island's southeast corner. Although technically this was the second phase of the battle, in actuality it constituted the main operation of the attack on Walcheren. Five minutes later, the leading Commandos had landed. They swiftly overran enemy pillboxes and anti-tank guns. As visibility improved, rocket-firing single-engined Typhoon fighter-bombers of 84 Group came in to support the infantry.

Four hours later, the third attack, "Infatuate II," kicked off. The most hazardous, dramatic and costly, it was directed at Westkapelle on the island's western tip. Heavy guns of the battleship *Warspite* and the monitor vessels *Roberts* and *Erebus* engaged the main German batteries. To reduce losses to the more vulnerable landing craft carrying the attacking brigade, the support squadron split into two groups. They also intentionally exposed themselves to enemy defensive fire to draw it away from the assault craft. The gamble proved successful. Two hours later, the village had been taken. So had the nearby battery, consisting of 150-mm. guns. They had run out of ammunition just as the first of the assault troops were landing.

Next morning Commando groups captured Zouteland. They also assaulted the four 150-mm. guns located west of Flushing, which would be captured early the following day. Meanwhile 47 Commando pushed on south, until it reached the gap in the dike near Flushing. Although street fighting continued in the town itself, enemy resistance was fast ebbing. The last main enemy force on Walcheren, at Middleburg in the island's centre, would surrender early on November 19.

In the end, Simonds' much-celebrated sinking of Walcheren had proved successful. The tactic had isolated the defenders' batteries, damaged ammunition, broken communications, and immobilized enemy garrisons. As well, the ploy actually assisted the attackers by enabling them to use amphibious vehicles. This was in marked contrast to the earlier Beveland and Breskens Pocket combat, in which infantry had no option but to struggle bloodily forward on foot. The final balance sheet on the Scheldt Battle shows that the Canadian Army captured 22,000 prisoners. Also, it is estimated the Germans suffered 30,000 casualties. Nonetheless, the price paid by First Canadian Army was high, amounting to 13,000 casualties, half of them Canadian. On the balance's positive side, Simonds' insistence on flooding Walcheren had resulted in Antwerp's docks being opened at least two weeks earlier than they would otherwise have been. The crucial importance of the great port with its miles of docks would be dramatically demonstrated very shortly when the Germans, counterattacking through the Ardennes Forest, overran massive stocks of Allied supplies in the Battle of the Bulge.

Simonds' performance as First Canadian Army's commander during the Scheldt battles marked the very pinnacle of his outstanding career. It also demonstrated that he had emerged as a truly international commander — one who, despite his earlier shortcomings in launching Canadians and Poles into battle in Normandy, could be trusted with the command of British, Polish, Czech, and even U.S. troops as well as Canadians.

Upon Crerar's recovery and return to duty, Simonds resumed command of II Canadian Corps. In this post, he was going to see much additional combat during the bitter Rhineland fighting in Holland that lasted until the end of the war. During the massive early 1945 struggle to force a crossing of the lower Rhine, involving some 50,000 Allied troops overall, he would again demonstrate why he was our country's "irreplaceable battle general." Simonds' most classic battle, fought and re-fought many times since by military experts, would be that of the Hochwald Gap, a prominent, wooded ridge whose topography resembled a sickle handle. Appropriately christened "Blockbuster," Simonds' advance was, in customary fashion, designed to "lull" the enemy into thinking that the Canadian attack was proceeding on a southwestern axis. At the last moment, however, as planned, Chris Vokes pivoted and struck eastward through the rail gap that traversed the massif, or ridge, with his 4th Armoured Division. To the enemy's astonishment and confusion, the clanking Canadian tanks ground noisily by in the dark, infantry on their backs, as they thrust up the rail corridor. Ultimately, though, the daring spearhead ran out of steam, stalling for several days when it met savage German resistance.

True to form, it would be Simonds himself who broke the impasse. Driving forward in the early morning's light in his Staghound to check the "Stickiness" of 2nd Division's infantry, he discovered what had happened. The effects of the Canadian fighting on the left and right of the gap had made the German commanders pull back. Suddenly no one was firing at the Canadians. Clearly the enemy had gone. Returning, the Commander shouted at the forward company to follow him: "Come on you bastards, there's no one there!" The impassable Hochwald Gap had been captured, and the forest cleared. By the end of March 4, II Corps was less than two miles from Xanten. The front on the right had broken open as Thirtieth and Sixteenth Corps of Ninth U.S. Army made contact at Geldern, and swung in towards Wesel. The way was now clear for the subsequent push by the Canadians and the other Allies to cross the Rhine and invade Germany itself. Even today, however, the Dutch remain eternally grateful to Canada for liberating them from over four years of enemy occupation at the hands of the Germans.

Any evaluation must concede that, erratic as he was on occasion, Simonds was the nearest our country came to producing a military genius during the Second World War. What made him one of a kind was his superb natural aptitude for battle, both armoured and otherwise — not only on land, but also in the air and on the sea. He also grasped how ancillary forces could be employed to influence the outcome of costly and difficult land battles. Most importantly, he was never far from what soldiers call "the sharp end." And it produced results. One of his staff noted in his diary: "I will say this for the Old Man. He believes in getting his own HQ as far forward as possible, and frequently he is in advance of the Divisional HQs. This really burns them up." As a corollary of "leading from the front always," Simonds rightly prided himself on the fact that, throughout the war, he never asked Canadians to go into battle under an officer who did not command his (and indirectly their own) explicit trust. A British expert has observed that, although Simonds was "young, ruthless, and aggressively intolerant . . . his educated approach to battle made use of every possible modern aid to reduce casualties and still achieve striking penetrations of the enemy line." He was prepared to see casualties suffered, if, by taking an objective, it saved lives in the long run. Because of his cold ambition, neither officers nor men loved him, but at all levels no one doubted his competence. In the troops' judgement, Guy had proven himself a worthy successor to "The Old Red Patch's" Arthur Currie.

At war's end, after Hitler's suicide and the collapse of Nazi Germany, as senior corps commander, Guy Simonds would be deeply hurt when he was passed over to succeed Harry Crerar as Canada's next Chief of General Staff. Instead, the highly political General Charles Foulkes was chosen for the job. In response, Simonds is reported to have asked for an appointment in the British Army. All that Monty, who had to look after his own, could offer him, however, was the rank of major-general. Certainly, it was no prize for a lieutenant-general with a long and brilliant record as a corps commander. Thus, Simonds chose to remain in the Canadian Army. His sensitive pride was healed somewhat when he was offered, and he accepted, a senior appointment to the Imperial Defence College, London.

When Foulkes was elevated to Chairman of the Chiefs of Staff Committee in 1951, Simonds finally attained the job he aspired to, and felt he had deserved all along. Both he and our country were exceedingly fortunate that his tenure as Chief of Defence Staff, as the position was now termed, coincided with the Korean War and the beginning of re-arming under the supervision of the newly formed North Atlantic Treaty Organization, which commenced a period of sustained Canadian military expansion. In a short four years Simonds would employ his professionalism to create, from virtually nothing — so far had we allowed our post-war forces to decline — a powerful Canadian regular army. Ultimately it would number more than 50,000 troops. Backed up by such manpower, the Canadian Brigade in West Germany would be much respected by our NATO Allies. Only today are we learning the important role it played, over and beyond atomic weapons, in helping prevent war in Europe. Simonds, however, whose temperament put military matters first, and seldom if ever considered political questions, was going to get into difficulties one more time with his political masters. It is rumoured that when he retired in 1955 Montgomery asked for him to be named to a senior NATO position in Europe. Ottawa, however, refused. Tragically, as Colonel Stacey notes, Simonds was destined to "[leave] the service in a very bitter mood."

Servicemen, thankfully, do not forget as easily as countries. At Simonds' funeral in 1974, an unexpectedly large number of veterans turned out to honour the General's memory. It was mute testimony to the unspoken esteem both colleagues and the men he commanded truly held for this aloof, demanding, talented professional officer.

SELECTED READINGS

Addison, Paul and Angus Calder, eds. *Time to Kill: The Soldier's Experience of War in the West, 1939–1945*. London: Pimlico, 1997.

Blackburn, George G. *The Guns of Victory: A Soldier's Eye View, Belgium, Holland, and Germany, 1944–45*. Toronto: McClelland & Stewart, 1996.

Graham, Dominick. *The Price of Command: A Biography of General Guy Simonds*. Toronto: Stoddart, 1993.

Whitaker, W. Denis and Shelagh. *Tug of War: The Canadian Victory that Opened Antwerp*. Toronto: Stoddart, 1984.

Williams, Jeffrey. *The Long Left Flank: The Hard Fought Way to the Reich, 1944–1945*. Toronto: Stoddart, 1988.

Charlie Chung. Courtesy Charlie Chung.

22

CANADIAN CHINESE

Behind Enemy Lines
in Sarawak and Malaya

*During World War II, a number of Canadians served behind
enemy lines as special agents. Recruited and trained by two top-
secret British organizations, Special Operations Executive (S.O.E.)
and Force 136 (in Asia), they volunteered to go on hazardous assignments. This chapter recounts the little known story of Chinese-
Canadians such as Roger Cheng, Victor Louie, and Charlie
Chung, who, after undergoing rigorous training, were dropped
into Burma, Sarawak, and Malaya at the end of the war. Although they fought for Britain under truly testing conditions, they
were never commissioned. Nonetheless, this handful of brave men
used their linguistic and technical capabilities to sabotage important communications facilities, report on enemy operations,
supervise the surrender of Japanese troops and effectively assist
the restoration of civil government in such regions. Additionally,
their contribution helped Canada's Chinese attain full rights as
citizens shortly after the Second World War's conclusion.*

Situated on British Columbia's beautiful Lake Okanagan, the
camp where the dozen volunteers trained seemed about as far
away from war as one could possibly get. The top secret location
which Major-General George R. Pearkes, general officer in charge

of Pacific Command, had helped set up, was no resort, however. The dozen, including Roger Cheng, a brilliant McGill electrical engineering graduate, who earlier had become the first Canadian commissioned into the Royal Canadian Corps of Signals, was divided into two groups for the four months' training in special warfare. Four received instruction in wireless. The remainder became experts in the art of sabotage and small arms, practising on secluded bench lands overlooking the lake. They also spent long hours in boat work on the placid blue waters. Finally, on September 6, 1944, the candidates, all promoted sergeants, literally packed up their tents and departed. Cheng and four radio operators flew to New Delhi, via Gander, in Newfoundland. Once in India, they learned message coding and decoding at Meerut's Special Operations school.

Despite the fact that Canada's Chinese had contributed money and volunteers during World War I, as had the Japanese, and that many Chinese had enlisted in the Canadian Army, Prime Minister Mackenzie King's government had originally rejected repeated offers by both Chinese- and Japanese-Canadians to serve as volunteers for special operations overseas. When Major Mike Kendall, a thirty-six-year-old engineer and British recruiting officer from B.C., first arrived in Ottawa, he had to fight his own battle to alter such racist-inspired policy. Finally, in March 1944, he prevailed, gaining both the government's sanction and the cooperation of Army Headquarters to help him search for candidates.

Ultimately, Major Kendall crossed Canada by rail, interviewing possible volunteers. From the pool of young Canadian Chinese already short-listed by army staff officers, he selected the dozen candidates he desired. The major took special pains not to spell out to potential volunteers just where such hazardous special duty might take them, although the original plan called for a Cantonese-speaking team to land by submarine near Hong Kong. All candidates were bright enough. As authorities soon discovered, however, only four spoke fluent Cantonese. All save Roger Cheng were in their late teens or early twenties, and had joined up as privates. Each was enthusiastic at the prospect of becoming a special agent fighting against the Japanese invader of their ancestors' homeland and enemy of their own.

There was another reason why they volunteered so eagerly. Prior to the war, Canadian Chinese could not be professionals, hold office, or vote. They hoped that, as a result of their efforts, the Chinese in B.C. would achieve equal status, and at war's end would be accepted with complete equality.

The original team from Camp Okanagan completed its preoperational training at Camp Martha, near Melbourne, Australia. Training consisted of exercises conducted under Kendall himself, another officer, as well as Cheng. They were designed partly to test equipment which would be taken on the mission, partly of boat and beach work, including simulated attack scenarios. By mid-December 1944, the arduous preparation had been completed and stores assembled. As a Special Operations Executive (S.O.E.) summary report noted: "A distressing long period of waiting followed. The team continued training, every effort being made to maintain the men's morale." Parachute training was also part of the final preparation, although no one was sure why. Even at this stage, volunteers continued to believe the plan called for them to be sent to China.

The reality was that the overall strategic picture was changing rapidly. Following the Anglo-American decision to allocate the Chinese theatre to the United States, "Oblivion," the British plan of which the agents were a part, would be put off before it got going.

Fortunately, for Cheng and four others, the conflict was far from ended. They had the wireless skills urgently required in Sarawak, into which several S.O.E. teams had been dispatched only a few months earlier.

Sarawak, part of northern Borneo in the East Indies, had been seized by the Japanese early in the war. Much of it consisted of low-lying swamps. The interior of the jungle island was dense and humid, with alternating heavy rainfall and hot, hazy, sunshine. Because of the formidable climate and environment, Britain's first major operation there did not take place until March 25, 1944, the third year of Japanese occupation.

Drifting along in his tree-trunk canoe on a river in Sarawak, a Canadian agent who had just learned that more of his country-men were on the way, cryptically recorded: "Cat arrives tomorrow bringing Cheng and his party of Chinese-Canadians." At last, on August 6, 1945, a Royal Australian Air Force Catalina flying boat landed Cheng and four wireless sergeants, Jimmy Shiu, Norman Lowe, Roy Chan, and Lewis King, on the Rejang River. Their mission was to join a small British team operating about 30 miles from Sibu, Sarawak's second largest town.

The team members' initial encounter with the tropical jungle was indeed a memorable experience. Dense green forest, giving way to shadowy black woodland depths, came right down to the water's edge. The river itself was treacherous, complete with dangerous rapids, shallows, as well as poisonous fish and crocodiles. Thanks to local Iban tribesmen's knowledge of Japanese movements, the team was able to move safely along the river by day. Still, the canoes themselves were not entirely reassuring. An account notes: "They were slight craft, each hollowed from a single tree trunk, and usually . . . [with] only an inch of freeboard . . . above water. . . . The danger was all the greater because a hungry crocodile might be swimming below. Yet the catastrophe never occurred. The oarsmen's strokes were deft, the passengers sat with calm nonchalance on their frail seats, and the canoe skimmed smoothly and safely forward."

One of the major things that would stick with team members afterwards was the "three Ms": Monsoon, Mosquitoes, and Malaria. They had been taught: "If you can survive these, you'll live." Otherwise the group's major task was to assist in gathering, collating and evaluating information concerning Japanese strength and intentions. By the time the Canadian Chinese went into action, however, radioing information to the Australians at Labuan, the fate of the war itself had been decided. Ironically, the morning after Cheng's team touched shore, a U.S. Superfortress bomber (B-29) dropped an atomic weapon on Hiroshima. The planned assault on Sibu was now unnecessary. Still, despite the new scenario, Cheng and his colleagues would play an important role: assisting with the transfer of emaciated prisoners to the care of Australian forces, recovering arms and equipment and organizing Japanese units for repatriation.

Cheng's team was not the only Canadian Chinese employed by S.O.E., or Force 136, as it was termed in Asia. Six more groups were hard on their heels in Australia, more were being trained in India. Back home, the recruitment of Canadian Chinese had been speeded up dramatically. By early 1945 several hundred volunteers had been accepted by Canadian authorities and were undergoing basic training as wireless operators and guerilla instructors.

Ultimately, a total of 143 Canadian Chinese would serve in Australia and India. Official records of their enlistments remain sketchy. Also photos of volunteers are almost non-existent. It appears, however, that in mid- or late-1944, S.O.E. requested Ottawa to recruit them. Like Cheng and the initial dozen agents, they were to be lent to the British for operations in Southeast Asia. As events transpired, though, none would see combat service, except for a small handful that served in Malaya's steamy jungles.

Several volunteers who made the cut would see action in the state of Selangor, which includes Kuala Lumpur, Malaysia's present capital. Nineteen-year-old Henry Fung of Vancouver would be the first Canadian Chinese parachuted into the region. He jumped from a Royal Air Force Liberator bomber on June 22, 1945. Fung and his companions were one of four such patrol liaison teams serving under one of the most intrepid S.O.E. colonels in Malaya. Assisted by communist guerillas, members of the Malayan Peoples' Anti-Japanese Army (M.P.A.J.A.), Fung and his companions made their way for four days and four nights through the hot, humid jungle to a camp near the town of Kajang, south of Kuala Lumpur. Once the Force 136 team established its small base, air drops brought in badly needed arms, food, clothing, and medicines for both them and the guerillas. As a rare photo indicates, the youthful Fung soon took to wearing the M.P.A.J.A. tiger-headed cap badge on his military-issue beret. Still, he found most

Henry Fung. Courtesy Mrs. Henry Fung.

of the guerillas extremely young and green. Fung's group assisted in the blowing up of a railway bridge and tracks and destroying telephone lines. By day they harassed Japanese truck convoys.

Upon Japan's sudden surrender, the team of which Fung was a member entered Kajang. Its goal was to take over the local Japanese command. Fearing the guerillas, however, the enemy garrison refused to surrender its arms until the British arrived in force.

Fung's and other members' experiences were typical of those faced by Force 136 teams throughout Malaya. Japanese cooperation was uneven at best. Also the attitude of the M.P.A.J.A. was unpredictable, although the guerillas remained mainly in their own camps. During the next few weeks, the S.O.E. team would have to survive such confusion. Members also attempted to prevent the beating, or worse, of collaborators. Once substantial British forces arrived in the Kajang region, Fung and other members moved into Kuala Lumpur itself, where several other Canadian Chinese agents had already congregated.

Two other Canadian Chinese, Bing Lee and Ted Wong, both of Vancouver, had parachuted into Selangor from a four-engine Liberator in July as part of another team. In the dense jungles, Lee and Wong collaborated with guerilla patrols, shooting up truck convoys and trains, then "beating it." Team members survived on sacks of rice augmented by Australian canned food dropped to them. To relieve such boring rations, they also shot monkey and wild boar. During this period Lee contracted malaria. Indeed, he would suffer intermittently from the disease until he eventually returned to India.

The highlight of Lee's service would be accompanying the local Special Operations commander, Lieutenant-Colonel "Duggie" Broadhurst, into Kuala Lumpur itself. Commandeering a Japanese officer's staff car, the duo drove into the future capital of Malaysia. Next morning, the pair were received by the Japanese officer commanding the city. To their evident relief, he politely informed them that he had issued orders for his troops to remain where they were, until the Japanese could arrange to turn Kuala Lumpur over to the British.

Still suffering from a bout of severe malaria acquired during training in Ceylon, Bob Lew, a native of Nippissing, Ontario, parachuted on a July night onto a dry riverbed. The team's jump zone was situated about 25 miles from Kuala Lumpur. The sole casualty was the team's trained dog, which unfortunately was killed in jumping. Once team members had safely landed, their guerilla reception committee led them for the next five days through

A Canadian trainee learns how to jump from a DC-3 Dakota aircraft. (NAC)

dense jungles to a bush camp near Serendah. Here, the Force 136 team trained guerillas in small arms and explosives dropped to them. Action was not all in one direction. Lew participated in a visit to Japanese-occupied Serendah to collect information on its enemy garrison. Dressed in a borrowed shirt and trousers of local design, he accompanied several guerillas. His job was to report in person on the state of the local rail yard and the size and appearance of the Japanese unit stationed in the town. His training in Ceylon, which had included instruction on how to walk like a

Chinese or Malay rather than a Canadian, assisted him in carrying out the mission. Not long after, Lew and his Australian team leader drove into town to accept the reluctant surrender of its garrison.

George Chin, another Canadian Chinese, was sent into Kuala Lumpur just as war was winding down. His team contained two Nationalist Chinese radio operators. Chin was never quite certain just why they were along, and they didn't last long. Shortly after the group established itself, the pair were murdered by communist guerillas while setting up their radio on a nearby hilltop. The incident was a graphic reminder of the dangers special agents lived with on a daily basis. All Force 136 volunteers in Malaya had been warned before leaving base in Ceylon to avoid any political discussions or plots. Following the execution of the two Nationalist Chinese, the team's leader again warned remaining members: "Keep your bloody mouths shut or you won't be alive! And don't be too tough with the guerillas."

Overall, however, Chin, himself a demolition specialist, was not impressed by the calibre of the guerilla trainees. Generally, he found them "inflexible" and "unimaginative." On one occasion, the team and its guerillas prepared to ambush an enemy truck convoy, employing explosives delivered by several air drops. After laying wire-triggered charges across the road, they also drove bamboo spikes into the road's shoulders. This was to prevent the enemy from seeking shelter, so that he would remain exposed. Chin and his colleagues repeatedly admonished the guerillas "to fire for three minutes and get the hell out of there." The native attackers, however, remained in place firing at the convoy long beyond the agreed-upon time. The Japanese troops were able to recover from their initial surprise. Two guerillas were killed in the encounter and two wounded, due to the enemy's superior discipline.

One of the last Chinese-Canadians to be dropped into Malaya with Force 136, and the last to come out, was the large, irrepressibly cheerful twenty-six-year-old Victor Louie, a Vancouver resident. As a boy he had accompanied his merchant father on a 12-

year sojourn to Southern China. When he finally returned home, young Louie spoke Cantonese fluently. Thus, unlike most of the volunteers, he would not have to learn its basics during training.

Louie had originally been trained with the main body of Canadian Chinese. His cousin Ernie was also part of the group. Victor was not dropped into the steamy Malay jungles until the first week of September 1945, a mere week prior to the enemy's surrender. Originally, the task of Louie's small group had been to support "Operation Zipper," the amphibious landings the British had planned to drive the Japanese from Malaya. Now, however, they were diverted to the dangerous, often bewildering task of convincing Japanese units to obey the surrender order, as well as helping restore the outlines of civil government. The group parachuted to a guerilla camp located in the mountainous Selangor region, northeast of Kuala Lumpur. On occasion, team members and their companion M.P.A.J.A. patrol encountered Japanese units that were still full of fight, despite the ravages of disease and isolation. Even at this late date, the enemy fought back fiercely. On their part, guerillas, in need of food themselves, often raided Japanese camps. During such a raid, Louie was captured. Fortunately, after being held prisoner for two days, he managed to escape, wearing clothes guerilla supporters smuggled to him.

The Malayan guerillas' effectiveness, also their raids, would be enhanced by the S.O.E. team's instructing them how to use small arms, including both Bren- and Sten-guns, also the much-admired U.S. carbine. Louie and his companions also provided guerilla leaders with binoculars as well as .45 calibre revolvers. Clothing and medicines were organized employing an "S-phone," which allowed ground-to-air communications during a drop aircraft's crucial final approach. Louie would later recall how one such flight delivered a Bing Crosby recording of "Don't Fence Me In." Entranced guerillas played it endlessly on an ancient gramophone, while Louie and others yearned for the jungle's peace. One of the highlights of Louie's mission would be to accompany his chief southward by car to the adjoining state of Malacca. Here, they convinced the local Japanese commander to surrender.

Following this, Louie and team members would be kept busy through early 1946 providing assistance to civil authorities in and around Kuala Lumpur itself. In particular, they arranged for the disbanding of the 1st M.P.A.J.A. regiment.

Charlie Chung and Harry Ho, both native British Columbians, were members of still another team that parachuted into Malaya's torrid jungle. A second team accompanied them. The target was Alor Seta, the tiny capital of the northern state of Kedah. Clad in their jungle-green uniforms, the agents were on a dangerous mission.

Today, Rambo, a movie warrior who snubs or defies the odds and employs the jungle's cover to strike deadly blows against opponents, has become an icon for the young. But Chung, who still resides in his hometown of Chilliwack, in B.C.'s Fraser Valley, thinks Rambo is little more than a U.S. myth. Certainly Chung knows what he is talking about when you ask him what it really was like to participate in clandestine missions behind enemy lines in the jungle of Southeast Asia over half a century ago.

Early in 1945, Chung volunteered to serve with Special Operations Executive Force 136. After undergoing the usual training, he and fellow trainees were posted to Southeast Asia. At last, after being shelled by Japanese naval craft on their 1,200-odd-mile flight from Ceylon (today's Sri Lanka), his team arrived over its destination. Twenty-two-year-old Chung and seven other agents parachuted into the dense, steaming jungle of Kedah state on July 14, 1945. The operation called for the agents and their equipment to land in a dry riverbed. The mission got off to a bad start, however, when the parachute of one of Chung's superiors, Captain Derek Burr, a British officer, became entangled in a tall tree. He struggled throughout the night, before the two teams and the guerilla reception committee that met them finally managed to lower him to the ground, using the 12-yard ropes parachutists carried for such emergencies.

Composed of British, Canadian and Chinese-Canadian personnel, the motley team of secret agents was commissioned by Lord Louis Mountbatten to march northwards through Kedah's dense jungles. Their mission was to carry out sabotage against the Japanese and to gather intelligence about enemy activities. Chung and Ho's team continued the long, difficult trek that would ultimately take them to the small sultanate of Perlis, situated on the border of Thailand. Two weeks of toilsome, tension-ridden travel ensued. Team members often made no more than six miles a day through the thick foliage, for the Japanese still controlled the rivers. "I got used to the jungle very fast. Up to that point, I had worked all my life in the bush [of British Columbia]," Chung recently told a reporter. Others in the group, however, had a hard time with the hot and humid climate, the dense rain-forests and the leeches and mosquitoes that transformed their existence into a green hell.

Even though the team had orders to sabotage enemy installations and supply routes, the group did not cause much damage. "How much damage can you do in the jungle?" Chung would ask rhetorically decades later.

"You just do the job, you don't invade or start something, you just keep as quiet as possible," he recalls.

In addition to transmitting intelligence reports back to the home front, Chung and his companions, like other teams, instructed and trained the communist guerillas of the M.P.A.J.A., a task they would continue to do throughout the operation. As Chung remembers, most were small farmers, fighting for their freedom and independence.

"I wouldn't say they were communists, they were just fighting the Japanese invaders," he notes.

According to Chung, the soldiers of the M.P.A.J.A. were ready to run immense risks. "These guerillas would strip to the waist and sneak into Japanese army camps at night. There, if they felt a person with clothes on, they would kill him silently," Chung reports of a M.P.A.J.A. tactic "that did a lot of damage to the Japanese."

Chung, who spoke Cantonese, was able to converse with the guerillas in their own language, although some were well educated, able to speak fluent English.

Finally, Chung and his companions reached Perlis and their

principal objective: the crucial roads that connected Malaya with Thailand. These, the enemy was prepared to defend at all costs as he fell back eastward. With Japanese patrols searching for them, the team kept on the move through Perlis and northern Kedah. During this period, Chung and his companions endured the dysentery, sores and monsoon rains that plagued Europeans and other newcomers who attempted to live in the jungle. Although suffering from extreme exhaustion, the agents continued ambushing convoys and sabotaging bridges. For more than a month, team members evaded Japanese patrols, existing in part upon rations from occasional air drops.

After the Japanese capitulated in late August, Calcutta, the base for British operations, ordered the team leader, Major Pierre Chassé (a French Canadian who following the war would command the famed "Van Doos," or Royal 22nd Regiment) and his four haggard companions, including Chung and Ho, to Kangar, Perlis' little capital. Here, the task of restoring civil government proved a formidable one for a young officer, with only a four-man team to support him. Many fanatical Japanese refused to believe that their homeland had surrendered, despite frequent broadcasts from Calcutta repeating the Emperor's order for them to lay down their arms. Additionally, team members had to deal with Thai marauders, and work to restore Perlis' young rajah to power. Finally, with Gurkha assistance, the Japanese were returned home. Also, a number of disgruntled Chinese guerillas were put on warning by Chassé and his companions to remain across the border in Thailand. In such fashion, civil government was gradually restored.

Eventually, Chung was able to fight off a flare-up of malaria and return home to Canada relatively unharmed. He would, however, experience a tragic loss when one of his wartime buddies, Sergeant Danny Dutton, died a few years after war's end. Dutton had married a Malayan girl and remained behind to administer a prison. "He got the prisoners to remove the fences and tried to establish a modern prison. But one day they [the prisoners] got him and burned him at the cross," Chung hesitantly notes.

Today, Charlie Chung's khaki battle jacket, with its medals, occupies a glass display case in the Canadian War Museum in Ottawa. The honoured relic symbolizes the hundreds of brave agents who parachuted behind enemy lines in both Southeast Asia and Europe. In Chung's hometown of Chilliwack, however, most persons know him only as a friendly, elderly Chinese-Canadian, and are not aware of his tour of duty in Malaysia's green hell.

"You just don't talk about it," Chung says, shrugging his shoulders. "If you talk too much, you might offend somebody."

On August 8, the day before the U.S. dropped an atomic bomb on Hiroshima, an all-Canadian team of Force 136 participated in "Operation Tideway Green." In addition to its two Caucasian officers, Major Joe Benoit and Captain John Hanna, the third Canadian on the mission was sergeant-interpreter Ernie Louie, the cousin of Victor Louie. A fourth member would arrive two days later, having been delayed by a training injury.

Louie's and the others' task was to collect information concerning Japanese movements in northern Johore. They were also to instruct and supply local guerilla groups and to block three major roads when planned Zipper landings occurred. The Japanese surrender changed all this. Fortunately, three weeks later, Tideway Green was reinforced by the arrival of several Australians. They were a welcome addition, given mounting tensions between local Chinese guerillas and Malays, who feared postwar domination by the Chinese.

In the report he later wrote, Tideway Green's commander noted that both Louie and Hannah, the officer who served as second-in-command, "showed much courage in carrying out their task of setting out alone on unknown jungle trails, marching to compass." Once reinforced, the team moved to Batu Pahat, where 900 near-starving, diseased Commonwealth prisoners were held in a nearby camp. After arranging for food and medical drops, completed on September 13 and 14, Louie and team members began arrangements to ship the emaciated internees home.

Even then, Tideway Green's perils were far from over. Although hostilities had officially ceased, the six members faced the same hazards confronting all S.O.E. groups emerging from the jungle. In Batu Pahat a state of panic reigned. Malays had allegedly executed some 200 Chinese a few days earlier. When Louie's team leader learned that Chinese were still being executed, he radioed for assistance to nearby Singapore. Soon, a company of Punjabi troops helped restore order.

Eventually, the operation's members, including Louie, who won an enthusiastic commendation from the group's commander, completed their Malayan tour on November 12.

Overall, the handful of Canadian Chinese employed in Sarawak and Malaya performed exceptionally. All had gone into war as light-hearted young soldiers, eager to make the best of their unique and dangerous assignments. Despite the fact that British authorities denied such volunteers commissions, they laboured bravely and capably under horrendous conditions. In our country's military history, Sarawak and Malaya served as exotic way stations on such soldiers' route to full equality as Canadian citizens. When Canada's Chinese received the right to vote in 1947, it was in large part as a result of their efforts.

SELECTED READINGS

Beamish, John. *Burma Drop*. London: Elek, 1958.

Bowen, John. *Undercover in the Jungle*. London: William Kimber, 1978.

McLaren, Roy. *Canadians Behind Enemy Lines, 1939–1945*. Vancouver: UBC Press, 1981.

Roy, Patricia E. "The Soldiers Canada Didn't Want: Her Chinese and Japanese Citizens." *Canadian Historical Review* 59:3 (September 1978): 341–358.

Brigadier J. M. Rockingham briefs platoon and company commanders of 1st Battalion PPCLI on arrival in Korea, October 7, 1951. Photograph: Paul E. Tomelin. Department of National Defence. (NAC/PA-128875)

23

THE CANADIAN ARMY
SPECIAL FORCE IN KOREA

Rocky's Army:
Canada's Forgotten War

Australian-born Brigadier John M. Rockingham (1911–1988) would command the Canadian Army's contribution in the early stages of the United Nations' bitterly fought intervention in Korea between 1950 and 1953. During World War II, "Rocky" established a distinguished record, eventually commanding 9th Canadian Infantry Brigade ("the Highland Brigade") in the fighting in Northwest Europe. After the war he returned to civilian life. In response to a call from Ottawa, however, he agreed to organize 25th Canadian Infantry Brigade Group (Canadian Army Special Force) that the Canadian government was sending to Korea. After personally supervising the training of "Rocky's Army" at Fort Lewis in Washington State, he commanded "his boys" until the end of their first rotation in 1952. Thereafter, he headed 3rd Canadian Infantry Brigade. The story of ordinary Canadians who fought and died in the conflict is important. Although Korea remains our country's "forgotten war," it marked a major turning point in Canada's foreign policy and thinking. The UN action established a precedent for our country's subsequent peacekeeping operations, which fortunately have been of an entirely different order.

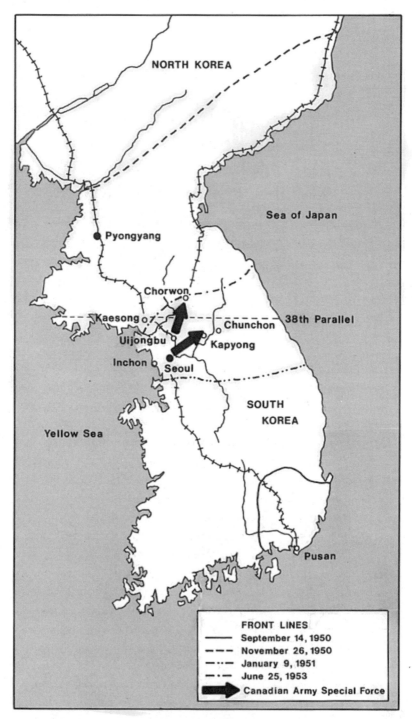

NORTH KOREA

Sea of Japan

Pyongyang

Chorwon

Kaesong   Chunchon   38th Parallel

Uijongbu   Kapyong

Inchon   Seoul

SOUTH
KOREA

Yellow Sea

Pusan

FRONT LINES
———— September 14, 1950
– – – – November 26, 1950
–··–··– January 9, 1951
–·–·– June 25, 1953
➤ Canadian Army Special Force

Korean War, 1950–1953

When his phone rang at 6:30 p.m. on August 7, 1950, the tall, dark, burly man who answered was busy in heated discussion. John Rockingham, a former brigadier, now head of Pacific Stage Lines in Vancouver, was occupied in a troubled negotiation session with the bus drivers' union. The last thing he wished for was an additional interruption to his already over-occupied mind.

"Rocky" rebuked his secretary for allowing the call through. Then he took the phone. It was Brooke Claxton, the Minister of National Defence, calling from Ottawa. He was making an urgent call to inform the former General that cabinet had decided to send Canadian forces to fight in Korea. Would Rockingham lead them? After five years in civie street, Rocky would be putting on a uniform once again. Also, he would take his trusted Tommy gun, veteran boots, survivors of World War II, as well as his former batman, or military servant, with him.

Earlier, on June 25, 1950, Communist North Korea's troops had crossed the 38th Parallel and attacked the South, or Republic of Korea. In the aftermath of World War II, the North had been occupied by the Soviet Union, the South by the United States. The Korean conflict, therefore, was immediately interpreted as a major test of the growing Cold War, one involving high principle and the global balance of power. The Americans led and shaped the West's response. Ironically, due to the fact the Soviets were boycotting the United Nation's Security Council, the U.S. soon won agreement that the UN would respond to the North's aggression in what was called officially a "police action." But it was already evident that it was in danger of rapidly escalating into a major conventional conflict. Led by U.S. General Douglas Mac-Arthur, the UN put an army into the field, slowly and hesitantly. Soon, however, it became apparent that South Korea's army was disintegrating in the face of the invasion, and the Americans, with only garrison troops from Japan immediately available, were managing little better. Clearly, the United Nations needed help from friendly nations, including Canada, if it was going to survive the test it faced.

One would have been hard-pressed to find a better commander than Rockingham. Rocky was a soldier's soldier, a strapping giant, six-feet-four-inches tall, darkly handsome, wide-shouldered, and trim waisted. He also possessed a parade-square bellow that could be heard half a dozen blocks away. After coming to Canada to play rugby in 1930, the young Australian had joined the Canadian Scottish Regiment in Victoria in 1933. Starting World War II as a lieutenant, by 1943 he was a lieutenant-colonel commanding the Royal Hamilton Light Infantry. A month after going into action in Italy, he had won a Distinguished Service Order, and had been appointed to command 9th Brigade, the Highland Brigade of 3rd Canadian Infantry Division. By war's end he had earned the Order of the British Empire, and also gained a bar to his DSO. Not least, he had risen to the confirmed rank of brigadier.

Rockingham, "a magnificent fighting soldier," personified bravery, combined with tough, sometimes unconventional leadership. On one occasion, he disciplined a delinquent soldier with his fists. Still, he was a good tactician, possessed an unerring eye for detail, and a justified hatred of red-tape. Such credentials explain why he was selected to head the brigade group Canada was now placing at the disposal of the United Nations in its moment of need. The Special Force would eventually consist of three regiments: the Princess Patricia's Canadian Light Infantry and its long-time comrades in arms, the Royal Canadian Regiment, as well as the French-speaking Royal 22nd Regiment, with supporting arms and reinforcements. In total, they would bring its strength to close to 10,000 men.

The Brigadier's Tommy gun had seen lots of action. He had used it to kill a lurking German sniper who creased the bridge of his nose with a bullet. Later, during the Scheldt campaign, he had also employed the weapon to kill two members of an enemy Spandau crew that had continued to fire, and taken another three prisoners. On another occasion, he used it as a club to knock out a German who had taken him prisoner, and to escape. Still another time, after getting lost in the confusion of battle, he helped two companies of his men attack a chateau, by personally leading the attack with his trusted burp gun.

The old tank suit, one arm torn by mortar shrapnel, which Rocky would wear at Fort Lewis in Washington State during the Canadians' initial winter training, and later in Korea, was also an old friend that evoked adventurous memories and made him feel once again at home. He had worn it on V-E Day, while personally taking the surrender of the big German submarine base at Emden. Sitting in the turret of his scout car with a Bren gun in his hands, in characteristic fashion, he had ordered the crew to drive, in pouring rain, through thousands of well-armed enemy troops. When the German commander, taken aback by such audacity, advised him to put up a white flag, or he could not be responsible for his safety, Rocky replied: "Go to hell. You drive up ahead and if any man raises a weapon I'll empty a whole Bren gun mag in the back of your neck."

One thing was sure: Rocky never ordered a man to do what he himself would not attempt. Soldiers he commanded knew this, and respected him for it. They also accorded him their undivided loyalty.

"He was hard on his men, but a lot harder on himself," Jacques Dextraze, the ascetic general who later became Canada's Chief of Staff, recalls, "Rockingham drove his men until they dropped, but he was a magnificent soldier."

Brigadier-General Joe Cardy remembered Rockingham's command style, too. As he recounted to John Melady, author of *Korea: Canada's Forgotten War:* "I remember seeing him chew a guy out until he cried. He was hard on his men, but he always backed them. If he had a major fault, it was his tendency to get too close to the lines, to put himself in danger. He was too valuable to lose. He was a first-class leader of men."

Another officer who served under Rocky told the same author: "He was tough, but tough on himself as well as the rest of us. He worked hard and he played hard. . . . He never spared himself, but the next morning he was the first man on the job."

Now Rockingham was to take on the biggest challenge of his already busy career.

The debate concerning just what military forces Canada

would contribute to Korea had been heating up for days. For awhile, the departure of destroyers HMCS *Cayuga,* HMCS *Athabaska,* and HMCS *Sioux,* dispatched to Far Eastern waters in July, was enough to ease expectations. Yet many outspoken Canadians continued to think that the country was not doing enough. After all, North Korea had committed naked aggression by unleashing its army against the South. Once Royal Canadian Air Force's No. 426 Thunderbird Squadron and its North Stars started ferrying supplies from the West Coast to Japan, the protests died down. Still, the expectation remained that Canada should commit units of her army, small though it was.

Two days after External Affairs informed the UN it was sending the destroyers, which had actually sailed from Esquimalt a week earlier, the international organization renewed its call for added assistance, especially ground troops. In Ottawa, the request was carefully studied, both by the Cabinet Defence Committee, as well as by Lieutenant-General Charles Foulkes, Chief of Defence Staff, and senior officers. After a good deal of mental wrestling the decision was made. Neither group thought that Canada could spare any troops from her existing strength. The limited size of the Active Force in particular, a mere 20,369 all ranks, meant that even if the country sent a modest regular force to the campaign, it would require "almost every soldier in the army." It would also seriously weaken home defence.

Still, the clamour for Canada to make a major contribution to the UN's intervention in Korea continued, both in the press and among the public at large. In the U.S. as well, the press and politicians were voicing their "disappointment" concerning our country's intentions.

At last, on August 7, Prime Minister Louis St. Laurent, acting on Foulkes' suggestion that a special force be raised for employment by the UN, announced on national CBC radio that Canada would recruit a 5,000-man brigade for service in Korea. The day following the Prime Minister's speech, recruiting offices were busier than they had been for years. Times were good, however, and the economy prospering, and this meant that the quality of recruit initially signed up by a dozen or more recruiting offices from Halifax to Vancouver was marginal at best.

Volunteers included fourteen-year-old boys who tried to look old enough; also sixty-year-olds who attempted to pass themselves off as being in their forties. As at the beginning of all wars throughout history, many were on the run from debts, wives, or the law. Some signed on because they needed work. A number of volunteers wanted to "relive" their earlier experiences of World War II. Some came simply because friends joined. A substantial number signed up because they craved excitement and wanted to escape their humdrum civilian existence. Also, a large number opted to join on the spur of the moment, with little real consideration of what they were doing.

Decades later, Colonel Stone noted of the enlistment process: "They were recruiting anybody who could breathe or walk. Brooke Claxton pushed the enlistment along because he was a politician at heart and really didn't give a damn about what else was happening. He was recruiting an army in order to fight. We had to show some of those guys how to put their shoes on."

Fortunately, the war also attracted a leavening of veterans possessing real combat experience. Most notable was James Stone, who, within weeks of quitting his job running a summer resort, was leading Canada's first contingent to the Far East. Even today, "Big Jim" Stone continues to be regarded by many ex-Pats as the "greatest Canadian soldier who ever fought." Jacques Dextraze, a former officer, who would shortly command the 2nd Battalion Royal 22nd Regiment in Korea and later go on to serve as Chief of the Defence Staff, was employed by a sewing machine company in Quebec. Ed Haslip, who was working for Dow Chemical in Sarnia, drove to Windsor to enlist. In Montreal, Andy Mackenzie, a World War II veteran who was busy forming the RCAF's No. 4341 fighter squadron at St. Hubert, Quebec, persuaded his superiors to second him to fly slot position with the United States Air Force in the peninsula.

With enlistment underway, recruiting depots were soon authorized to accept up to 10,000 additional men to serve as replacement personnel for the 5,000 troops originally designated. During the first weeks, training proceeded at several places throughout the country. Units of the Special Force received their basic training either from active force or regular force counterparts. Autumn, however, was fast approaching, and the weather becoming decidedly colder. Defence Headquarters in Ottawa sought an alternative site. Eventually, Fort Lewis, the sprawling American base situated in Washington State, would be chosen as the major winter training venue for the Canadians.

Decades later, men who were there would still remember Fort Lewis with mixed emotions: the incessant rains which drenched them to the bone; the often sloppy dress of the Americans; and the immense size of the 90,000-acre reserve itself.

But their most vivid memory continued (and continues) to be Rocky himself. Appearing to be everywhere at once, the big Brigadier was constantly on the move, supervising training in person. When he was not driving his own jeep, he sat on the edge of the turret of his armoured car; on other occasions he employed a powerful motorcycle to zip in "dare-devil" fashion around the acreage. Often he would cover 70 miles a day, over the range's bumpy and rough terrain, observing various units of the 25th Canadian Infantry Brigade in action. Indeed, officers who had served with Rocky in World War II reminisced how he had burned up the road in his scout car, costumed in the same Balmoral cap, red tabs and battledress as he presently wore, his burly frame halfway out of the turret.

Visiting an anti-tank platoon, the brigadier perused their position critically. "How about the muzzle flash?" "Would it give the position away after a couple of shots?" "Why not move the gun back a couple of feet?" Then, moving to another corps who were digging in two more guns, he asked: "Pretty close together, aren't they? I don't like the looks of it too much. The lead tank could lob HE [High Explosive] in there and pin both your crews down."

Afterwards, he inspected the bivouacs of an armoured carrier platoon. Rocky was told the men were not sleeping on the groundsheets because it wouldn't be fair to the other troops who didn't possess any. The expression of such altruism caused a smile to creep over Rocky's face. Then he told the young recruits that, personally, he had never heard of a carrier platoon that didn't succeed in making itself "at least twice as comfortable" as any other type of unit.

As the scout car moved on, a slight drizzle had begun to fall. On the sharp December wind echoes of a familiar song carried along:

> *Why don't you join up?*
> *Why don't you join up?*
> *Why don't you join Rocky's*
> *army?*
>
> *Plenty of sleep*
> *Nothing to eat*
> *Great big shoes and . . .*
> *Blisters on your feet.*

The Brigadier grinned. He remembered how his old battalion, the Hamilton Light Infantry, had sung the ditty, racing through the Channel Ports and helping to clear the Scheldt Estuary. They also sang it as they breasted the Rhine, the first Canadians to cross the river:

> *Why don't you join up?*
> *Why don't you join up*
> *Rocky, you bastard, why don't you*
> *join up?*

As Rocky listened to the song's irreverent final verse, he recalled they hadn't lost an inch of ground to the enemy during the ten months he had led the unit.

The Brigadier was still smiling as the car sped on to the winding gully where the Royal 22nd Regiment, the "Van Doos," were practising platoon drills. "They attack with live ammunition!" concerned U.S. officers had complained. Rocky was hardly out of his car before the wiry French Canadians, coming under fire, began to deploy rapidly, if not exactly smoothly. For the next half hour, Rockingham himself hardly stopped running, as he watched the deployment.

"Fire and movement," the Brigadier shouted: "The whole basis of infantry tactics."

Surveying the troops rushing in, bayonets fixed, firing from the hip, he was quite obviously delighted. Rocky rushed along behind them. Alongside trotted the lithe figure of Lieutenant-Colonel Jimmy Dextraze, the Van Doos' Commanding Officer.

"They're bunching a little in the centre, Jimmy," Rockingham observed.

"Yes, they are," the Colonel conceded. In explanation, he noted the men "were watching the damned safety angle" the Americans insisted on. "They thought we were crazy for using live ammunition anyway."

After a brief lunch, Rocky was off again, speeding to the artillery observation post in time to capture the afternoon's shoot. All at once he was among the officers, compass to eye, checking bearings and distances, map references, and correcting the officers' radio telephone procedure. The day previous he had caught a couple of his staff using the word "repeat" instead of "say again." It was a deadly sin. "Repeat" is an artillery term capable of bringing 25-pounder shrapnel down on you in short order.

Later, Rocky watched a dozen M-10 tanks as they manoeuvred, churning a green meadow into a sea of mud. On the return trip, it began raining hard. Crossing the river, the Brigadier was quickly out on the new U.S.-style aluminum pontoon bridge, asking questions. Before departing, he challenged the captain and crew to see "if they couldn't do it [erect the structure] a little faster than the Americans tomorrow."

Such painstaking tutelage achieved its goal. In short order, Rockingham would create a truly outstanding force from the mainly citizen soldiers with which he started. Decades later, an American who served in Korea with the U.S. Marine Corps, itself a formidable service, noted of the Canadians that not only did they have better food than their U.S. cousins, but they were also better trained. As he remembered: "I was never fortunate enough to see them in action, but their reputation among us, at least, inspired considerable respect — on the level with our own airborne and special forces people."

Meanwhile, in the Far East, it seemed the war was coming to a successful conclusion without any assistance from the Canadians. While Rocky's 25th Infantry Brigade was training at Fort Lewis, UN forces were achieving more and more success in Korea. Summer's horrible retreats and the near-disasters in the face of the North Korean onslaught, which had swept everything before it, ended. General Douglas MacArthur's brilliant amphibious assault at Inchon, on Korea's west coast, which sent troops driving inland to liberate Seoul, South Korea's capital, and threaten the enemy's supply lines, made it possible for UN troops to advance northward again. So rapid was the UN offensive that for a time at least it was feared that Canada's ground forces would not even get to Korea in time to engage the invader.

The politicians decided one battalion should be rushed to the theatre. This would ensure Canada would at least have troops on the ground when hostilities ceased. The unit chosen would be Lieutenant-Colonel Jim Stone's 2nd Battalion Princess Patricia's Canadian Light Infantry. Preceded by an advance party of 350, which left in October, the battalion departed Seattle for Pusan, sailing aboard the crowded American troopship *Private Joe P. Martinez*, November 25.

After a short shore leave in Yokohama, the contingent was soon back aboard ship, heading across the strait that separates Japan and Korea. Many of the men had not heard of the Land of the Morning Calm. Nor did they know where it was. Many of the volunteers, mere youngsters, had little concept of why they were fighting, or who the enemy was.

By the end of the first week of October 1950, almost all the North Koreans had been pushed north of the 38th Parallel, dividing line between north and south. Bitter debates raged for a time in western capitals concerning whether MacArthur should be given authority to move into North Korea. When the UN finally supported a British resolution to do so, MacArthur's armies struck across the 38th Parallel. In less than 75 hours, the North Korean capital, Pyongyang, had been captured. Soon, the port of Wonsan, on the east coast, was captured by Republic of Korea (ROK) troops. Buoyed by the successes, the commander predicted many of the boys would be home before Christmas.

But the General's optimistic prediction was not to be. Two weeks later, China entered the conflict. The massive assault took UN forces completely by surprise, due to the effectiveness with which Communist Chinese troops had masked their infiltration from air reconnaissance. Soon, the UN troops were reeling backwards. With UN forces withdrawn to a position 38 miles south of Seoul, the war MacArthur thought was over was entering a new and desperate phase.

When the Patricias landed at Pusan, U.S. Lieutenant-General Walton H. Walker wanted to deploy them immediately. But Colonel Stone intervened personally. He went to see General Walker at staff headquarters. Stone argued successfully that his battalion needed more preparation. Shortly afterwards, the Patricias packed up their gear and moved northward to Miryang, for training camp.

Training was both thorough and tough. In the end it was completed in six rather than eight weeks, as originally planned. "Big Jim" lived up to his task-master reputation. The troops both cursed and feared him. Stone even constructed his own punishment camp. A tent surrounded by rows of barbed wire, it was known as Stone's Stockade. After two days in this field camp, even the hardest cases wanted out and agreed to the Colonel's conditions. Moreover, the Miryang training paid off: 2nd Battalion's soldiers soon felt themselves to be part of a well-functioning, disciplined unit. Complaints turned to praise for the Colonel.

Finally, on February 15, 1951, seven months and 21 days after North Korea had launched its invasion, the Canadians were ready for action. Combined with the 27th Commonwealth Brigade, composed of English and Scottish troops, Australians, New Zea-

*Troops of B Company, 2nd Battalion, Princess Patricia's Canadian Light Infantry cross-
ing log bridge, North Korea, ca. February 1951.* Photograph: Paul E. Tomelin.
Department of National Defence. (NAC/PA-115034)

landers, and Indians (the latter in the form of a field hospital
unit), the Canadians felt at home. Throughout the war, the Patricias and other Canadians believed "that the Commonwealth Division was far superior to any other Allied formation in Korea."

As the Patricias motored northward through the mountainous Korean countryside (80 percent of the peninsula is mountainous), they began to realize the kind of war they faced. It would
involve 24 hours a day, 7 days a week, in hastily dug trenches,
sloshing around in soggy snow, and managing just to survive as
the icy rains of winter poured down their necks.

In an article he wrote for *Maclean's* (June 1, 1951) Pierre Berton noted: "The trenches, waist high, two and a half feet wide,
were dug in deep snow and frozen soil. The section was barely
dug in before rain mixed with sleet began to fall. . . . The men's

parkas, battledress, and underwear became soaked and frozen. They crouched in a foot of icy water. . . . Blankets turned into sopping rags."

The hills themselves were transformed into the foe. As Korean war historian John Melady observes: "[They were] monotonous, endless, nameless, generally identified only by their height in metres. One ridge looked like every other ridge, and beyond each ridge was another, and another, and another." Initial objectives for the Pats were Hills 404, 444 and 419. Meanwhile, Australian and British troops fought for Hills 523, 614, 494 and 450. And, if soldiers ever fought and bled, and died, for apparently pathetic objectives, it had to be in Korea. Major J. H. B. George, commanding C Company, lost four men in an attack on Hill 444. Shortly afterwards, when the Patricias overran Hill 419, they would find the bodies of another four of their comrades who had been killed in an earlier assault, stripped of weapons and clothing. On occasion, this discovery of their friends brutally treated in death seriously demoralized some of the Canadian troops.

On March 7, two companies of Patricias found themselves engaged in another fierce engagement, the attack on Hill 532, supported by mortar fire, bombardment from the New Zealanders, U.S. tanks and air strikes near the summit. Since the terrain was steep and treacherous, the men moved in a crouched position. At times, Chinese machine guns would open up from camouflaged dugouts, ripping into the attackers, and sending them bleeding and in pain, retreating down the face of the precipitous slopes.

By early afternoon, snow began to fall. Big, sloppy flakes that, paradoxically, transformed the strange battle ground into a scene of stark beauty — save for the bloody battle for survival the two armies were waging on the slopes. At day's end someone counted 50 enemy bodies. No one knows for sure how many Chinese died. But six young Canadians lost their lives that day in bloody snow halfway up a Korean hill that wasn't considered important enough even to have a name. In the engagement, Private L. Barton of D Company, later awarded the Military Medal, became the first

Canadian decorated in Korea. After his Commander and several others in the platoon were hit, the young batman, or military orderly, had rallied the survivors. Under his direction, the wounded plunged forward towards their objective. Hit several times, half dead from loss of blood, spent adrenalin and fatigue, the young soldier could at last go no farther, and was ordered down the slope.

Near Kapyong, a sprawling country town in central Korea situated northeast of Seoul, the Canadians would play a major role in one of the crucial battles of the Korean War, fought between April 23 and April 25, 1951. On the night of April 22/23, massing Chinese and North Korean forces struck in the western and west-central sectors, obliging U.S. and South Korean troops to withdraw. Overwhelmed and forced to retreat, the panicked Koreans were in danger of being cut off and completely destroyed. Fortunately, the location of the Commonwealth Brigade, then in corps reserve, offered an ideal escape route along which the routed troops could withdraw. Here, where the Kapyong valley narrowed and curved, dominated by surrounding hills that controlled its entrances, Commonwealth forces dug in. The 3rd Royal Australian Regiment defended Hill 504, the 2nd PPCLI held Hill 677, while the British 1st Middlesex Regiment assumed a position south of the Patricias.

On the evening of April 23, the Chinese, following on the heels of the retreating ROK troops, attacked the Australians. Wave after wave of the enemy surged forward in darkness, threatening their lines. After standing their ground all night and well into the day, the Aussies finally withdrew under tremendous pressure. Even after firing point blank into the mass of attacking enemy, two U.S. tanks had been unable to blunt the ferocious assault — now the Patricias stood alone.

According to the official history, the Canadians were deployed "to cover the north face of Hill 677, with 'A' Company on the right, 'C' Company in the centre, and 'D' Company on the left. 'B' Company occupied a salient in front of 'D' Company."

Suddenly, the Chinese signalled their first attack on the Canadians. "They started blowing bugles and whistles," recalled one former PPCLI member. "Then there was screaming, shouting, and they were coming through the bush towards us."

The next few terrible hours would meld into a complete blur for the men who were there. The attackers moved forward in human waves. Many became casualties, but there were always others who continued to come on. Slipping through the darkness, they moved "softly, stealthily, deadly," like panthers through trees. A Canadian defender, busy firing on shadows in the bush in front of him, would suddenly find himself having to fend off a bayonet attack from the rear. All that most survivors would remember of the battle was the overall hell of "curses, screams, Bren gun chatter, half-sobbed prayers, acrid smoke, flashes of flame, bursts of fire, shouted warnings."

Corporal S. Douglas lost his hand grabbing and throwing a live grenade out of the way. For saving the lives of others, he would be awarded the Military Medal. Wayne Mitchell, the number one Bren-Gunner, had his position overrun and was hit by shrapnel. His wound dressed, he would go back to fight. Wounded a second time and losing blood, he would continue at his post. Finally, an American helicopter evacuated him. (Later, in a ceremony attended by those whose lives he saved, Private Mitchell would have the Distinguished Conduct Medal pinned to his jacket by Brigadier Rockingham himself.)

When D Company's commander, Captain Wally Mills, found his position overrun by Chinese, he courageously requested artillery fire be brought down right on top of the hill his men were defending. Artillery and mortars fired right into the wooded area. Mills, who won the Military Cross, was lucky. He was dug out. Nor did he have a single man wounded. But the fire drove back the surrounding enemy attackers.

Private Ken Barwise, a twenty-two-year-old, six-foot-four Patricia, also won the Military Medal. He dispatched half a dozen enemy in vicious hand-to-hand combat: two he killed with their own grenades, two others with their own guns, one with a machine gun recovered from the enemy, and a sixth with his own rifle.

Although the Patricias fought valiantly, they were surrounded by the enemy, who controlled their supply route. With ammo and rations almost depleted, Lieutenant-Colonel Stone requested air supply. The parachute drop, delivered by American "flying box-cars," was made within six hours. By 2 p.m. the Middlesex Regiment had managed to clear enemy troops from the rear, and the road to the PPCLI was re-opened.

For their collective gallantry at Kapyong, the American government later awarded the Princess Pats, as well as the Australians and a U.S. tank battalion, the Presidential Citation for "outstanding heroism and exceptionally meritorious conduct in the performance of outstanding services." At present, it stands as the first and only time Canadians have ever won the award. Appropriately, the 2nd Battalion of the PPCLI is authorized to decorate its regimental colours with the blue ribbon denoting the United States Presidential Distinguished Unit Citation. Of the battle, the unit's colonel, Jim Stone, observed, possibly with undue modesty: "Kapyong was not a great battle. But it was well planned and well fought. We were surrounded by the enemy. We could have run, panicked in some way, or surrendered. We stayed, fought, and withdrew in soldierly fashion. In such circumstances, the Presidential Citation was earned."

Fortunately, the cost to the Pats was only 10 killed, 23 wounded. Even today, no one is certain about the price the Chinese paid. When the guns ceased firing, however, one section of Hill 677 alone was littered with over 50 shredded corpses. Later, many more would be removed from the battlefield's slopes.

Meanwhile, back in Canada, the Minister of National Defence announced the 25th Brigade would be sent to Korea after all, to join the Patricia's 2nd Battalion. While the Brigade completed its training, Brigadier Rockingham, its commander, flew to the Far East to confer with both MacArthur and General Horace Robertson, Commander-in-Chief of the Commonwealth Division. For some reason or other, Rocky did not see eye-to-eye with Robertson, a fellow Aussie. On the other hand, he and American General Matthew Ridgeway got along well and readily understood one another. Decades later, Rockingham told John Melady: "I thought a good deal of him. I was always a bit amused by the fact he wore a shell dressing though. [The kind that World War II troops carried with them in the field to serve as a wound dressing, if required.] That seemed a bit melodramatic to me — particularly for a man of that rank. You never saw anyone else wearing that kind of thing. I guess he thought it made him look like a combat soldier to his troops."

A special highlight of Rocky's visit to the front came when the Commanding Officer of the Van Doos contacted him, and asked permission to shell an enemy ammo dump. One of his soldiers, who understood Chinese, had learned about it from enemy radio messages. Although he initially doubted the story, Rocky ordered a "shoot" just to be certain. As the Brigadier loved to tell the story afterwards: "The artillery was told the location of the target and they fired a few rounds. There was a most wonderful display of fireworks and we knew they had destroyed the dump. The guy in the forward post had been right after all. I was amazed."

While the 25th Brigade was winding up its training at Fort Lewis, events elsewhere were moving ahead. On April 11, 1951, President Harry S. Truman took the momentous and controversial step of removing the revered MacArthur from command. The General's sin was that he wanted to widen the war to include China and dispose of the "Chinese Communist Question." But the peppery seventy-seven year old Truman really fired the General because he wouldn't respect the authority of the President. By the time the Canadians reached Korea, their new commander was Matt Ridgeway. As the UN's senior officer in the Far East, he could be trusted to do as he was told.

Having arrived before the Brigade's main body, Rocky himself assisted with the unloading at dockside. He personally drove a two-and-a-half-ton truck for two days, towing four or five of the non-running vehicles on each trip. Soldiers who witnessed "Old Rocky" driving trucks thought it was "great." One of them who, as a headquarters dispatch rider, would later get to know the Brigadier well, commented, "He was a beautiful man, every inch a soldier."

In less than two weeks, the Canadians were in action with the Commonwealth Brigade, firing their first shots in battle on May 17, in an action north of the Han River. By May 20 the rest of 25th Brigade had made the difficult trip northward through the central part of Korea, moving by tracked vehicle, truck and train.

At six o'clock on the morning of May 30, the Canadians attempted to capture Chail-li, a small village immediately north of the 38th Parallel. A driving wind and rain storm not only obscured the intended objectives, but also denied the four companies any possibility of air support. Although the attack captured the village itself and two adjacent small hills, the assault eventually ran out of momentum on the rugged, misty slopes of nearby Kakul-Bong, vital to the enemy's supply lines and communications.

The deep salient the Canadians occupied left the brigade's flanks without protection. When it appeared that the Royal Canadian Regiment could not continue to hold Chail-li or capture Kakul-Bong, Rockingham ordered a withdrawal so a defensive position could be formed. With Chinese troops pressing them closely, the regiment now fought its way back to the new position. Still, in this, its first serious action, the brigade acquitted itself well. Casualties were remarkably light, just 6 killed and 54 wounded, a testimony in itself to the skill with which the action had been fought.

Meanwhile, on May 27, the 2nd Battalion of the Patricias, which had earlier been in action, and which remained with 28th Commonwealth Brigade, moved south to rejoin the Canadian command it had left more than six months earlier at Fort Lewis.

During the summer of 1951, two significant events occurred. Early in July, at Communist request, cease-fire talks began (although the enemy likely never intended them to produce a lasting peace, but counted on using them to advantage). Also, on July 25, Canadian Brigade became part of the newly formed Commonwealth Division, commanded by Major-General J. H. Cassells.

From this juncture onwards, until the war's end, almost all fighting engaged in by Canadians in Korea would be centred on a small area north of Seoul. Its perimeter was formed by the 38th Parallel on the south, the Sami-Chon River on the north, and extended from the Sami-Chon east to Chail-li. At its widest point, the area was about 30 miles across. The bulk of the Canadian fighting, however, would take place within an even more limited position, extending along the UN's front, approximately six miles in length. Here, some Canadians would die, many more would be wounded, some would be captured. Most, though, would complete their rotation unharmed. Indeed, a few would even become heroes.

On the night of December 13, 1951, Private Doug Carley, a signaller with D Company, 2nd RCR (Royal Canadian Regiment), found himself involved in a fighting patrol near Hill 166. The patrol, consisting of 25 soldiers, faces blackened and advancing silently, suddenly came under fire from enemy machine guns point-blank in front of them. In the initial action, Carley's short radio antenna was shot off. Scrambling backwards with his companions through waist-deep water, Carley, crouching down, pushed up the longer ten-foot antenna, which had not been damaged, and called for artillery support. All the time, he was exposed to steady and increasing enemy fire. For his courage and "example to all signallers," Carley was awarded the Military Medal. What the citation neglected to mention, however, was that he saved the lives of 20 companions.

On March 19, 1952, Corporal Ken McOrmond, C Company, 2nd Battalion RCR, a sergeant and eight men were detailed to destroy an enemy machine gun post. Suddenly they ran into a large number of enemy. McOrmond, in charge of number two group and lying in a rice-paddy swamp, sensed a threatening presence in the darkness to his left. Slowly, he crept forward to within five feet of the dim figure. Seeing a squat, thick-set man in a heavy coat, with a burp gun, he immediately started firing. He killed his target. But several other machine guns immediately opened up. When his sergeant was wounded, McOrmond assumed command of the patrol, enabling it to fight its way clear of the numerically superior foe. For his quick thinking and bravery in leading his

Reconciliation: "The Peacekeepers" memorial, Ottawa.
Photograph: Carol Andrews.

men safely through the night, McOrmond also received the Military Medal.

Other Canadians who served in "Rocky's Army" performed bravely, too. Although they never won medals, they exhibited behaviour that comrades would consider outstanding. Many were too modest to mention what they had done. Some performed with great courage, but their actions were overlooked by those in command. Private Emerson Patterson (PPCLI) died just a few days before he was due to be rotated home, attempting to carry ammo to three comrades who had run out of it while repulsing an enemy attack that threatened to overrun their position.

The memory of his friend Private Pat O'Connor, a twenty-seven-year-old stretcher-bearer with the RCR, would be written indelibly on the mind of Ed Haslip. On the second-last day of May 1951, O'Connor's company was overrun by the enemy. Ignoring his own exposed position, O'Connor moved through dead and dying, comforting men, bandaging wounds, occasionally praying with them. He told other wounded they would be "okay." Finally, medical supplies were running out. O'Connor told Haslip he was going to get help. "I watched him run back," Haslip later bitterly recounted, "but before he'd gone fifty yards a Chinese machine gun cut him down. He died trying to save the lives of the men with him. In my opinion, he should have received the Victoria Cross. He was a completely selfless and dedicated soldier, as well as a wonderful human being."

A few hours later, gathering up O'Connor's personal belongings, comrades found a poem he had written on the evening before the action in which he was killed. Passing the piece of paper around the bunker, the misty-eyed soldiers read the poignant words. They might well serve not only for Pat O'Connor, but also for all the other brave young men who died in Korea, fighting Canada's forgotten war:

KOREA

There is blood on the hills of Korea
The blood of the brave and the true

Where the 25th Brigade battled together
Under the banner of the Red, White and Blue
As they marched over the fields of Korea
To the hills where the enemy lay
They remembered the Brigadier's order:
These hills must be taken today
Forward they marched into battle
With faces unsmiling and stern
They knew as they charged the hillside
There were some who would never return
Some thought of their wives and mothers
Some thought of their sweethearts so fair
And some as they plodded and stumbled
Were reverentially whispering a prayer
There is blood in the hills of Korea
It's the gift of the freedom they love
May their names live in glory forever
And their souls rest in Heaven above.

With the signing of the armistice on July 27, 1953, the guns finally fell silent. The survivors of Rocky's hastily raised volunteer legion came back to a homecoming that, in most cases, was far quieter than their departure. Fortunately, Korea had not been as long, or indeed as horrible, as the Great War, the Second World War, or the war already underway in Vietnam would ultimately prove. Nonetheless, it is part of our country's history. As the Korean war's chronicler, John Melady, argues, "We cannot continue to regard Korea as simply Canada's forgotten war. It is too important for that."

The cost to Canada of this action was the lives of 516 brave countrymen, 312 of whom died in the shooting war itself. The rest perished either in training, in transit, or during subsequent peacekeeping activities along the Demilitarized Zone, which the peace talks at Panmujon had established, between 1953 and 1956. Overall, some 25,000 of our soldiers served during the course of the struggle. Canada's contribution was larger in proportion than that of most of the other countries that provided ground troops for the international force. The brigade group sent from Canada was almost equivalent to four of the divisions sent to Korea from the United States, which possessed 11 times our population. And, as the record indicates, our contribution was excellent.

One must ask, was the price worth it? At present, North Korea remains what is likely the world's most repressive remaining Communist dictatorship. Its populace is on the brink of starvation. In contrast, South Korea, which was almost overrun by North Korea, is prospering economically. Although democracy and freedom have sometimes been suspended, the country's populace and political system have obviously benefited from its association with the west.

Odd as it may seem, the Republic of Korea, the United Nations and countries which fought under its banner, including Canada, are still officially at war with the North. This is because a formal peace treaty to end the conflict has never been concluded between the two sides. Even today, a state of tension and suspicion continues to divide the two Koreas, and incidents continue along the 38th Parallel. Will the future change this? Will the two peoples become unified as happened with Germany? Only time will provide an answer.

Korea was indeed a "strange battleground," and a very odd sort of peacekeeping. In reality it was a war situation. It convinced Canadians of the need to maintain strong conventional forces in Europe to contain Communism globally. From 1951 to 1993, as part of Western Europe's defence, our country would maintain a NATO Brigade Group in Germany, which played a major though often unappreciated role in maintaining the peace during four decades. At present, however, especially since the thawing of the Cold War, memories of Korea are fading rapidly into history.

Not least, Korea was the first occasion our nation was called upon to honour our obligation under the UN Charter. During the past five decades, our concern for the international community has transformed our foreign policy and image as we have become involved in dozens of peacekeeping operations. To some degree, this has meant that our army is no longer seen as part of our defence, but as a peace-keeping operation for troubled parts of the world, and this change in national direction certainly needs further consideration. Nevertheless, policy matters do not deter us from remembering our brave countrymen who sacrificed their lives in Korea's hard-fought struggle. The ancient Romans used to say, *dulce et decorum est pro patria mori:* "It is sweet and fitting to die for one's country." It is perhaps even more fitting to die for mankind's future.

SELECTED READINGS

Granatstein, J. L. and David Bercuson. *War and Peacekeeping: From South Africa to the Gulf — Canada's Limited Wars.* Toronto: Key Porter, 1991.

Halliday, Jon. *Korea: The Unknown War.* London, England: Markham, Ont.: Viking, 1988.

Melady, John. *Korea: Canada's Forgotten War.* Toronto: Macmillan of Canada, 1983.

Wood, Lieutenant-Colonel Herbert Fairlie. *Strange Battleground: The Operations in Korea and Their Effects on the Defence Policy of Canada.* Ottawa: Queen's Printer, 1966.

Major-General Lewis MacKenzie.
Photograph: *Time Magazine.* Courtesy Lewis MacKenzie.

24

MAJOR-GENERAL
LEWIS MACKENZIE

*The World's Best-Known
Peacekeeper*

*When in early 1992 Lewis MacKenzie (1940–   ) was cho-
sen chief of staff of the 14,000-man United Nations Protection Force (UNPROFOR) in Yugoslavia, little did he realize
the challenge he would face. The General's outstanding and
unorthodox leadership would see him both promoted Major-
General and given a UN Security Council mandate to secure
and command Sector Sarajevo. Leading a 30-nation international force, he successfully liberated the city's airport,
turning it into a UN facility to receive desperately needed food
and medicine. By the time he resigned his posting, he had
brought renewed hope to the strife-torn region and substantially assisted the process that eventually resulted in a Bosnian peace accord. Also, due to the manner in which he used
the global media, MacKenzie became, virtually overnight, the
world's best-known Peacekeeper and our country's most popular soldier. Now retired from the military, the General continues to be an eloquent spokesman for improving the effectiveness of UN peacekeeping.*

On February 26, 1992, before going in to dinner, veteran Canadian officer Brigadier-General Lewis MacKenzie, who was a guest at a celebration hosted by the Toronto-based Institute of Strategic Studies, told Alex Morrison, the organization's executive director, that he would not be part of the 1,200-member Canadian contingent the UN was sending to war-torn Yugoslavia. Instead, the veteran peacekeeper told his host that he expected to move to Ottawa in the summer to assume a new posting at National Defence Headquarters. A short time later, half way through his dinner, the General was called from the room to accept an urgent phone call. Returning a few minutes later, the stern-faced MacKenzie, with his knitted brows, square, jutting jaw, and intense blue eyes, walked over to his old buddy Morrison, and quietly whispered in his ear: "Now, I'm going to Yugoslavia."

A few days later, on March 2, "The General," as his troops liked to call him, was aboard an aircraft on his way to New York to be briefed concerning the new responsibilities he would be assuming as chief of staff for the United Nations Protection Force in Yugoslavia. It would include 14,000 personnel — and he had a mere 48 hours to come up with an organizational plan for its deployment. On the flight across the Atlantic from New York, the General, "smoke-free" for 12 years, turned to his Danish second-in-command and asked him, "Svend, what are you smoking?" He replied: "About three packs a day." MacKenzie said: "Gimme one."

Although the unexpected orders had caught both the General and his family unprepared, friends and colleagues were not surprised that "Lew" had been chosen for the appointment. He was a born leader, a good-humoured professional officer, who not only attracted the fierce loyalty and respect of the men he commanded, but also possessed an uncanny ability to mediate disputes and defuse problems under the most dangerous conditions.

Lewis MacKenzie, born in Princeport, Nova Scotia, comes from a military family. When he was twelve, the Korean war broke out, and his father, "Connie" MacKenzie, who would become a Regimental Sergeant-Major, re-enlisted and was posted to Chilliwack, British Columbia. The same year, Lew joined the base's cadet corps, beginning his long involvement in the military. Four years later, the family was transferred again: back to Sydney, Nova Scotia, where MacKenzie finished grade 11 at Sydney Academy. Rather than attend grade 12 there, he followed friends to Sydney's Xavier Junior College.

At Xavier, MacKenzie joined the Canadian Officer Training Corps (COTC). He also met Morrison, adding him to his closely knit group of friends, who were destined to become life-long buddies. Although he had joined the Corps, selecting "Engineers" for his occupation, young Lewis thought of the commitment as "simply a one-summer deal to get a free trip to B.C."

The decision enabled him to be in Chilliwack to witness his old high-school class's graduation. Additionally, he enjoyed his summer training. But it was more short-term thinking that would lead him to join the permanent force upon graduation: very simply he wanted money to buy a car. Within a year of being commissioned he was sent to Germany, then to England to take a "jock-strapping course." As a young sports officer, MacKenzie already showed signs of his canny combination of strategic thinking and humour. When he was sent to supervise the athletic requirements of 1,200 Canadians stuck in the middle of the desert in the Gaza Strip, the junior officer promised a month's leave and a flight back to Canada for anyone who hit a baseball through the hole he put in the ballpark fence he had constructed in the sand. Overnight, the number of teams jumped from two to twelve. In addition, attendance soared when he gave paying spectators the opportunity to pair themselves with a player. The proceeds enabled the Canadians to build two re-hydration hospitals in the Gaza Strip. And as one might expect, in two years, no one ever put the ball through the hole.

Following his initial Mid-East posting, MacKenzie's own career and postings would graphically illustrate the importance of Canada as an international peacekeeper. From Gaza, he proceeded straight to Cyprus as a platoon commander with Canada's UN peacekeeping force. When some trigger-happy Greeks began firing at UN peacekeepers, MacKenzie made a formal request to meet their commanding officer. First, he told him to get his men

Canadian UN soldier mans armoured vehicle at Sarajevo Airport. Courtesy of the
Department of National Defence, Director-General Public Affairs. (ISC92-5340)

under control. When this did not achieve any results, he decked
him to make sure he got the point. The sniping did not occur
again. In 1967, MacKenzie left for Germany, accompanied by his
new wife, Dora, to participate in a two-year exchange program
with the British Army. He was promoted captain the same year. By
1969 he was back in Canada taking a year of advanced strategic
and tactical studies at Kingston's Staff College.

Despite his many hijinks and escapades, MacKenzie was a serious soldier, an officer who was developing growing experience in
conflict resolution. After completing the course at Kingston, he
was back in Cyprus as operations officer with the Princess Pats.

MacKenzie's next posting was Vietnam. Joining the International Commission for Control and Supervision, he commanded
a team supervising the peace accords. Following this, he returned
to the Middle East, as a company commander with UN troops in
Cairo.

During the next two decades, MacKenzie's career directors
ensured that the promising young officer was exposed to a multi-

plicity of assignments. Generally, his time was divided between tours of duty with Canadian forces at home and abroad and additional training. In 1977 he spent six months at the NATO Defence College in Rome. Later in the same year, he took command of 1st Battalion Princess Patricia's Canadian Light Infantry and took them to Cyprus in 1978 — his third UN tour on the island. In 1982, he attended the United States Army War College in Carlisle, Pennsylvania. Five years later, in 1987, MacKenzie was appointed brigadier and placed in charge of introducing women into the Combat units of the Canadian Forces.

On occasion, MacKenzie's family would also be called on to absorb the cost of his success. Prior to the Yugoslavia posting, for example, while MacKenzie and his 300 unarmed UN observers were brokering the shaky armistice between the Contras and Sandinistas in Central America, his wife Dora would be robbed three times in their official residence.

When MacKenzie was suddenly whipped away in the winter of 1992, and posted to Yugoslavia, it was because of his great experience. Despite his 32-year military career and eight former peace-keeping postings, however, Bosnia was going to be something else again.

Even before he departed, it was evident to MacKenzie that the UN operation he would be heading up in Bosnia, a former republic or part of Yugoslavia, was going to stretch the very definition of peacekeeping as our country had practised it during the four decades since Korea. To begin with, there was no peace to keep.

MacKenzie and troops from 30 nations including Canada arrived in Croatia in March 1992. Initially, their task was an extremely limited one: to effect a cease-fire between the Croatians and the Serbian-dominated Yugoslav army, and to monitor the withdrawal of Serb forces from certain portions of the Croatian Republic. In order to monitor the process, MacKenzie established the UN's headquarters in the lovely old city of Sarajevo, site of the 1986 Winter Olympics. Seemingly tranquil and civilized, it possessed good restaurants and live theatre. MacKenzie dubbed the garishly painted hotel in the middle of the city in which he installed his troops "The Rainbow Hotel." This was because it reminded him of a motel in Canada where he and his wife had stayed in the past. Little did the General guess that the hotel would shortly be smack-dab in the centre of artillery and other fire exchanged between Bosnian Serbs and Bosnian government forces. Or that it would provide a superb, although somewhat scary observation post.

A short four weeks after the mission's arrival in Sarajevo, fighting erupted among Muslims, Croats and Serbs. Soon rebel Bosnian Serb forces began to shell Sarajevo. Representatives of other international organizations, among them the UN High Commission for Refugees and the Red Cross, beat a hasty retreat. Only MacKenzie's UN troops remained, pinned down by sniper fire.

The decision had earlier been made in New York to locate the majority of Canadian personnel serving with the UN operation at Daruvar, in neighbouring Croatia, to the north. Here, they were under the command of General Satish Nambiar of India, who was in overall command of the operation, and MacKenzie's UN superior. Now, in response to the firepower being unleashed in Sarajevo itself — and without a UN mandate for the newly reorganized country of Bosnia — Nambiar and MacKenzie and his staff of 200 were ordered out of Sarajevo to the relative safety of Belgrade, situated within Serb territory. While the General met with his UN colleagues in the Serb capital to consider how to halt the violence escalating in Sarajevo, the death toll in the Bosnian capital began to mount as Muslim and Serbian forces battled for control. Given the tiny staff at his disposal and his limited mandate, the General would be repeatedly frustrated. As he later observed, "I kept telling each side: 'I understand where you're coming from, gentlemen. All I'm trying to do is get a cease-fire so you can sit down and talk.' But after seventeen shattered cease-fires, I eliminated the word 'optimism' from my vocabulary."

By this juncture, UN negotiators had almost persuaded the opposing forces to allow UN troops to take over the airport. This would enable badly needed humanitarian aid to reach Sarajevo's 300,000 besieged and starving civilians. Eager to act, MacKenzie was determined that the soldiers who opened the airport for such mercy flights should be Canadians. As he argued forcibly to General Nambiar, the Canadians were the only battalion possessing sufficient tracked vehicles and firepower to carry out the task. As MacKenzie later admitted: "This was because we cheated." Originally, the UN had calculated that the Canadians would need 10 to 15 armoured personnel carriers for their mission. But the Canadians, convinced that they would require more, had arrived in Belgrade with over 80. As their excuse, they argued, "We didn't have time to unload them [the extra vehicles] from the train in Germany." As it turned out, the extra vehicles would prove invaluable.

After Nambiar agreed that the Canadians should open Sarajevo's airport, MacKenzie travelled back to the beleaguered city to establish his new command, Sector Sarajevo. With a mere skeleton UN contingent, the General set out to prepare the ground. To accomplish this, he convinced the Serbs that their international image was deteriorating. To save face and to make a conciliatory gesture, they should abandon their position, which

At Sarajevo's Airport. Courtesy of the Department of National Defence, Director-General Public Affairs. (NAC/PA-115034)

threatened the airport. Gradually the Serbs began to depart. But it would take a dramatic six-hour personal visit by France's President François Mitterand, on June 28, finally to convince the outside world that the airport was really open for business. Mitterand's surprise visit was a welcome shot in the arm to the process of taking over the airport but also a security nightmare for Mac-Kenzie's modest force. As the General noted: "It was one of the happiest days of my life when I saw his aircraft become a small black dot on the horizon." MacKenzie's hobby came to the rescue as well. As it worked out, the General's men had to make emergency repairs to the wing of the jet aircraft that had originally flown the President in. They did so using military duct tape to repair the gash a drunken Serb fork-lift driver had made in its wing. This done, the aircraft was ready to be flown back to Split on the Croatian coast. The trick, which the General had often used to secure temporary repairs to his race cars, proved equally successful on this occasion.

On his part, Mitterand was visibly impressed by MacKenzie and both the Canadian and French troops under his command. He promised two French plane loads of food and medicine, plus French marines to unload their cargoes and help secure the airport. When the aircraft arrived the following day, it sent the message to the world that mercy flights could now land in the besieged city.

At this point, MacKenzie ordered the impatient Canadian troops under the command of Lieutenant-Colonel Michael Jones to leave their base in Daruvar, where they had been standing by, and to start for Sarajevo. During the 300-kilometre journey, which lasted for three days, they would have to stare down a drunken Serbian militia commander whose bodyguards waved Kalashnikov assault rifles at the Canadians. When they finally arrived at Sarajevo on July 2, MacKenzie issued orders to "Dig in." Of his men on this occasion, the General would proudly note: "In my entire career as a grunt, I've never seen the dirt fly like that. We couldn't see the sun for nine hours. I tell you, it's something else to watch a bunch of soldiers pumped up with adrenalin, risking their lives to assist a population that didn't particularly appreciate them." Yet thanks to the combined effort of both Canadian and French soldiers in the Sarajevo contingent, the airport remained open for the next 30 days.

As MacKenzie and his staff soon found, running a "UN Airport" was not an easy task. On July 3, just a day after the main body of Canadians arrived, heavy shelling by what appeared to be both the Croatians and Bosnian Serbs started all around the city and its outskirts. As everyone dived into bunkers for protection, they wondered if the Croatian army had arrived on the scene. If they had, there was a good chance that the Serbs might reoccupy the airport. Under the General's direction, however, Lieutenant-Colonel Jones, the Van Doos' commander, had prepared for such an eventuality. He had a company dug well in around the runway. Additionally, his TOWs (anti-tank weapons) and mortars were ready for use. According to the UN's directive, peacekeeping troops shouldn't be equipped with missiles or explosives. But, as MacKenzie would later quip in *Peacekeeper,* "Fortunately, of course, we had cheated."

As MacKenzie told a magazine reporter in a telephone interview while watching Hercules transports land at Butmir airport, his current assignment was definitely more challenging than any previous posting he had held. "If you take all of those missions and multiply by a factor of ten, it's still not as difficult as this one," he said. "It's just so unpredictable — so much hatred, so much history involved, such a complex political situation." Certainly, it was difficult, frustrating, and agreements made at the top were often impossible to execute on the street. As MacKenzie concluded: "The [Serbian] leadership and the [Bosnian] presidency can't control everything that's going on: the reality is that there are groups that are pursuing their own agenda."

Another dramatic difference between his mission at Sarajevo and MacKenzie's prior UN service was that this operation was conducted under the glare of the world's media. Hundreds of reporters scuttled around the airstrip in flak jackets, exposing themselves to extraordinary risks to file "the Big Story." MacKenzie even allowed two satellite links to be set up in a protected area near UN Force HQ, on the understanding that everyone would have equal access to them. Additionally, he was always available for briefings. "I never said no comment," he recalled. "I always tried to give them the story, and I never got screwed by anyone." Soon, the General was a familiar sight on screens all over the world: racing his armoured car through the shattered city, dragging a cigarette from his desk, even changing his pants.

Such global exposure made the tough but modest MacKenzie an instantly recognized celebrity. As he later chuckled, "I had no idea the feed was going out to almost everybody." But his overnight television fame was not as ingenuous as it appeared. A modern officer, MacKenzie realized early on that the media were the most effective weapon he possessed. On a number of occasions, in the wake of frustrating negotiations, he'd get to a point where he'd say: "Okay, if that's the way you want it, I'll nail your butt on CNN tonight." This gave him powerful leverage as a moderator. For, as the General put it: "Nobody does their worst in front of the international media."

Because the situation was deteriorating faster than the UN was able to make decisions, the General found himself forced to play a political role no previous UN commander had ever attempted. As he recalled: "Usually there was a co-equal political advisor, who acts as the link back to New York to generate political pressure. I didn't have one." Given the labyrinthine politics of the Bosnian Serb-Croat-Muslim conflict, MacKenzie himself would also become a target. The recipient of many death threats ("death by burning . . . really bothered me"), he was also labelled a "war criminal" by a group of Bosnians for allegedly allowing Serb shells to fall on their residential district during one of the many cease-fires. Deliberately fabricated stories also circulated, including his favourite: that he was soft on Serbs because his wife was a Serb (although she is not). According to the tale, she had been introduced to him by no less a personage than Mila Mulroney herself!

Frequently, MacKenzie's greatest strength, his candour, carried him to the brink of disaster. In New York, the Serbs were viewed as troublemakers. But in a widely televised message from Sarajevo, the General bluntly stated that Bosnians were firing on their own people in the hopes of ratcheting up pressure for further UN intervention. The General later grimaced: "You weren't very popular when you made statements like that, which contradicted New York."

Nor did the General always see eye-to-eye with his own political masters. While Prime Minister Mulroney and External Affairs Minister Barbara McDougall made platitudinous speeches advocating a stronger UN role in Sarajevo, the straight-speaking MacKenzie stated that a beefed-up UN presence would be counterproductive now that the war had started, unless hundreds of thousands of troops were dispatched, as they had been two years earlier during the Gulf War, to pacify the entire country. Anything less would only further inflame the situation; it would probably also make it impossible to get additional humanitarian aid through. Such frank talk, coming from a senior officer, clearly sent a shiver through diplomatically conscious Ottawa.

On his part, MacKenzie was well aware that many Bosnians were disappointed with what the UN had been able to accomplish. Many did not understand that his peacekeeping force possessed only a limited mandate: to secure the airport and ensure the safe delivery of supplies. Certainly, UN troops had little ability to stop the sniping and shelling that claimed lives every day. As MacKenzie's boss, General John de Chastelain, told *Maclean's*, MacKenzie was not equipped to go beyond the constraints of a peacekeeper: "If the aim of the operation was to get both sides to stop fighting, and use force to do it, it would take thousands of troops and large numbers of heavy weapons and aircraft." Tragically, this dilemma dogged the UN effort for over three years.

Such a strictly limited mandate presented a problem for the peacekeepers, too. "Nobody had time to educate the two sides on what peacekeeping means," observed MacKenzie. "There is an anomaly here because there is no peace. Normally, we go in where there is an established peace and a demilitarized zone to park in and observe. Here, there's no cease-fire and no cease-fire line."

By mid-July, the humanitarian assistance program was slowly

beginning to function. Canadian troops positioned their armoured personnel carriers at strategic points along the city's main roads. This made it possible for supplies to travel safely from the airport to the main distribution centre. By week's end, cargo planes carrying 150 tons of food, medicines and other emergency aid had begun arriving from France, Britain, the U.S., Italy, Norway and other countries. Soon, UN officials even began to worry that relief organizations might jam the airport with supplies faster than it would be possible to distribute them.

For the Canadians in Sarajevo, it appeared their mission would shortly be over. The week previous, UN Secretary-General Boutros Boutros-Ghali announced they would be replaced by 1,500 troops supplied by France, Egypt and Ukraine. The Canadians would be returned to their original peacekeeping duties in Croatia. Coming as it did, the announcement struck a particularly poignant note with the normally hard-headed MacKenzie, causing him to tell a magazine reporter: "I've never been prouder of Canadian soldiers." Later, U.S. President George Bush said, "I think the Canadians who stepped forward deserve a great vote of thanks from the entire world for what they're doing."

Shortly afterwards, on July 12, General MacKenzie made what he later described as "the hardest decision of my career": to ask to be replaced as commander of UN forces in Sarajevo. A major factor in the decision was that, while UNPROFOR might be unpopular, it was at least doing some good for the people. But as MacKenzie later stated: "[I had become] an obstacle to the peace process, and the disinformation campaign against me was endangering everyone who worked for me."

Within hours he met with de Chastelain, who was visiting Sarajevo as part of a high-ranking Canadian military mission. The senior commander listened to MacKenzie's logic, which culminated in him telling his superior that he intended to ask General Nambiar to replace him. To his relief, the CDS told MacKenzie that he understood. In fact, he had considered pulling him out earlier. He thought MacKenzie should leave "as soon as possible." But to leave and run was not MacKenzie's style. The two agreed that, if his security could be enhanced, he should stay on until the Van Doos were scheduled to depart.

The outspoken Canadian General reluctantly left Sarajevo on August 1. The UN rumour mill claimed that he had been "pulled" because of his outspoken opinions. MacKenzie dismissed the idea, pointing out that it was only natural that the incoming contingent should serve under commanding officers of their own nationality. Still, when he flew back to New York, MacKenzie could not help noting that his welcome, following his tour of duty, was clearly muted. As he put it: "They were very kind to me. But I had a funny feeling they were a little uncomfortable. They weren't used to [a blue beret] being so high profile."

That evening, MacKenzie set a personal record for media exposure, appearing in the space of four hours on the *MacNeil/ Lehrer News Hour, Larry King Live* and ABC's *Nightline*. In between, the celebrity-status Canadian General gave interviews to *USA Today* and *Time* magazine. Next morning, he was up at 0500 and appeared on both the CBC and NBC morning news programs, followed by interviews with CFRB radio Toronto, *USA Today* and *The Washington Post*.

During the months that followed, MacKenzie travelled extensively, both in North America and abroad, discussing the seemingly insoluble Yugoslavian problem with a number of national leaders such as Queen Elizabeth and various prestigious groups. The question put to MacKenzie was always the same: "We have to do something to help in Bosnia — what can we do?" The quiet Canadian General's answer was always the same: "Stop the war. But you can't do that militarily without killing a lot of people, including your own. If you go in with a big military force . . . the whole thing will flare up again when you leave. You have to force the sides to agree to a constitutional solution that will stand the test of time." During the following years, the General's viewpoint would more than prove its correctness.

After MacKenzie's departure, morale among Sarajevo's peacekeepers plummeted. Different nationalities failed to communicate with one another, and television cameras, starved of a hero who could explain the complicated situation in simple and lucid fashion, disappeared. Meanwhile the butchery raged on. Two months following the Canadian General's departure, the Bosnian government counted more than 11,000 dead, 50,000 missing and believed killed, 128,000 wounded, and more than 1.3 million persons driven from their homes. In the long, bitter months that followed, casualties would continue to mount.

At long last, the Dayton accord, signed in November 1995, ended, if only temporarily it seems, Bosnia's three-and-a-half-year civil war. Today, the country remains a powderkeg, with the clock ticking down to June 1998, when the 31,000-member NATO-led multinational Stabilization Force (SFOR) is due to depart. The major problem also persists of bringing to trial Radovan Karadzic, the Bosnian Serb leader, and other persons responsible for alleged atrocities committed during the civil war. In addition, ethnic groups continue to be bitterly divided. Clearly, difficulties in the region are not over. Still, MacKenzie and the UN force he headed played a crucial role in helping reduce tensions and temporarily stabilizing the conflict, so that peace negotiations could eventually take place.

While the Yugoslavian situation was deteriorating, bureaucrats in the Department of National Defence and Ministry of Finance were deciding that the time was ripe for Canada greatly to reduce its military presence in Europe. Indeed, the changed threat level and the collapse of the Warsaw Pact, the USSR's alliance system, in 1991, were major factors underlying the new reality. Since then, emphasis has been placed on Canada's employing its military in peacekeeping operations in a number of hot spots around the globe, including, in addition to Bosnia and Croatia, countries such as Somalia, Rwanda, Haiti and Cambodia.

With this new focus as background, Canadians should be aware that the many challenges General MacKenzie faced in Sarajevo pale in comparison to problems the UN will face if it gives in to pressures to expand its peacekeeping role. The next time a professional officer such as Lewis MacKenzie puts on a blue beret and goes off to keep the peace between hostile neighbours, he will probably find the task is not as clear-cut as the mandate itself suggests. Probability is high that such a commander will find himself not only hamstrung by the normal day-to-day tasks of peacekeeping, but also frustrated by the undefined nature of his job and ambiguous UN policies.

Although the UN recently celebrated its 50th anniversary, the most pressing problem it currently faces continues to be money. Enthusiasm for the international body's mandate far outpaces its ability to pay for it. Its peacekeeping account is presently a "black hole debt" of approximately a billion dollars. Our country is only one of about 30 member-states that pay their full peacekeeping assessment. In fact, when the Security Council expanded its operations to the former Yugoslavia, it did so without providing financial assistance to participating countries. Should Canada, a nation with less than one percent of the world's population, continue to provide up to ten percent of all UN peacekeeping personnel? And why should hard-pressed Canadian taxpayers get stuck with the globe's peacekeeping tally? Especially, while the U.S. refuses to pay its UN membership dues.

But more than mere money is involved. After returning from Sarajevo, MacKenzie publicly criticized the UN for its inability to command, control and support logistically its burgeoning peacekeeping forces in the field. "Ninety percent of the UN's problems in this area are logistics and communications," the General would claim. "They're only staffed for one or two missions, and they've got ten on the ground right now. In Sarajevo, we crossed our fingers every ten days that our food would arrive — that someone had organized a convoy." Fortunately, the Canadians, as representatives of a rich country, had brought their food with them. On occasion, they even assisted poorer peacekeepers with rations from their own supplies.

And MacKenzie has continued to expand the dialogue concerning the future of peacekeeping. In *Peacekeeper: The Road to Sarajevo,* the memoir he published a year after his tour of duty in the former Yugoslavia, he provides some interesting additional insights. His essential argument is that, when peacekeeping forces were simply keeping the peace, as they were from the first observer missions in 1947 to 1992, communication between the UN and its field commanders functioned well enough. In the 1990s, however, the number of UN peacekeepers deployed around the world has expanded from fewer than 5,000 to more than 60,000. Because of this reality, a full-time UN peacekeeping centre needs to be established as a matter of urgent priority. Also, as MacKenzie notes, it "should be manned by experienced officers with previous UN peacekeeping experience, and it should have a planning capacity."

As already mentioned, the UN also lacks an adequate logistics system or network to support its growing operations. The solution to this problem is not easy, but it has to be addressed. As the General writes: "A chain of logistics bases is required around the world to support UN peacekeeping operations. They must have the necessary equipment on hand, or at least the ability and the budget to purchase it. Such bases exist today; they are American bases."

In "A Soldier's Peace," the award-winning television documentary based on his book, Mackenzie addresses other, more difficult challenges facing the UN: the need to establish a permanent global peacekeeping force; the need to provide peacekeeping missions prior to the outbreak of hostilities (such as the highly successful, but little reported UN mission in Macedonia); also the need for the UN to develop "crystal clear," and easily understood peacekeeping policies or rules.

At present, in the late 1990s, MacKenzie continues to be an outspoken champion of peacekeeping per se. Like most Canadian officers, he and his colleagues worry that our country, generous as it is, will simply not be able to keep up with escalating requests for assistance. Shortly after returning from Sarajevo, the General put the issue into simple perspective when he told an audience that there were more policemen in the Metro Toronto Police Force than there were active infantrymen in the Canadian Armed Forces. Since then, thankfully, the situation has begun to improve.

Commencing with Trudeau's administrations, successive Liberal and Tory budgets have chipped away at defence spending, the federal government's single largest department and expenditure. For awhile, MacKenzie's extraordinary success in Sarajevo and Canada's excellence in peacekeeping, which he personified to the world at large, presented our country's brass hats with a public relations bonanza which helped explain and defend the military budget. As the General declared: "Peacekeeping is a growth industry. It is not going to go away as long as countries, and organizations within countries, pursue their own agendas."

In the early 1990s, as a result of the honeymoon that prevailed between a worshipful public and its military hero of the moment, Lew MacKenzie, his message enjoyed a high priority. Today, however, despite the General's continuing popularity and his own commitment to improving the peace process, his message is often in danger of being forgotten. Although Canadians are proud of their armed forces' record in United Nations missions overseas, they seldom if ever debate their success outside the context of our troops' performance. We owe it to the General, as well as our peacekeepers and ourselves, that the fundamental issues surrounding global peacekeeping and its logistics become a national priority.

SELECTED READINGS

"Interview with Major-General Lewis MacKenzie." *Esprit de Corps: Canadian Military Then and Now* 2:7 (December 1992): 10–15.

MacKenzie, Major-General Lewis. *Peacekeeper: The Road to Sarajevo.* Vancouver: Douglas & McIntyre, 1993.

Rigby, Vincent. *Bosnia-Hercegovina: The International Response.* Ottawa: Research Branch, Library of Parliament, 1994.

"A Soldier's Soldier: Lewis MacKenzie Takes a Familiar Role." *Maclean's* 105:28 (July 13, 1992): 30–31.

Trooper Naomi McFarlane, a Reservist with the Elgin Regiment, applies camouflage during Exercise Trillium Guard, 1995. Courtesy Sergeant Pat McCarthy.

AFTERWORD

Brave Soldiers, Proud Regiments: Canada's Military Heritage appears at a critical juncture in our country's military evolution. During the last decade, the traditional military culture of the Canadian Forces has been under attack, both from increasing "civilianization" and from the public at large who often do not understand military issues. Nor is this a problem for Canada alone. The United States, Germany, the U.K. and France have all become uncertain about the role of their military forces. Certainly many questions are currently being asked concerning the purpose of Canada's soldiers. With the clamour for good policing both at home and abroad at an historic high, should Canada's politicians focus the role of our military far more narrowly on peacekeeping, peacemaking, and peacebuilding? Or, do we need to take a wider perspective? Should territorial defence continue to remain a high priority, even in a post Cold War world? Also, how do we feel about the need for our soldiers to continue to participate in allied operations, both in Europe and elsewhere, in coming decades?

None of these questions is easily answered. One of the major difficulties is that the Canadian public has become largely divorced from the purposes of the military. Nonetheless, as this book has demonstrated, one cannot ignore the fundamental reality that the major role of the Canadian military has been to fight wars and defeat an aggressor (or better still dissuade potential enemies from attacking). While our soldiers were welcomed with open arms during the Oka crisis in 1990 or when helping Manitobans during the recent 1997 flood, or when they add glamour to ceremonial functions, the other side of the coin is harder to accept. When preparing to be deployed in the field under difficult, even extremely dangerous conditions, they do what soldiers must: they train to kill. The same holds true for the military's other branches: the navy and air force. They, too, must hone their skills to protect our way of life and to respond to crises wherever they might occur. It should be remembered that so-called "peacekeepers" cannot suddenly be transformed into soldiers to meet a military crisis; on the other hand, properly trained soldiers can be deployed for peacekeeping.

The various chapters of this volume teach us other lessons as well. Although the Canadian public was much closer to its military in the period prior to 1914 than it is today, and our forces responded to the challenge magnificently, the fact is that we were largely unprepared for the Great War. After the close of hostilities, we virtually disarmed ourselves during the inter-war decades. As a result, we were even more unprepared for battle when World War II broke out. Once again our soldiers contributed to the conflict's outcome in outstanding fashion. But the costs of our military lapses should by now be evident. An even more glaring example of our country's continuing state of military unpreparedness is the minimal role we played in the 1991 Gulf War.

We also require an army strong enough to provide effective *Aid to the Civil Power* — one of the specific roles of the military. As examples, one can cite the role the Canadian Forces assumed during the FLQ crisis of some 30 years ago and in numerous strikes, such as the one in London, Ontario, during the Great Depression.

The basic problem we must address is how to create support for the Land Force and its activities within our Canadian populace. If the public at large is better informed concerning things military, as well as foreign policy and peacekeeping issues, it will be better equipped to tell our politicians exactly what we desire in a future military force.

Despite the public's continuing uneasiness about the Canadian Airborne Regiment, disbanded under a cloud of controversy in 1995, a new airborne unit is being created that can provide a model. The first of four specially trained companies that will soon be deployed across the country, this new unit is infused with a strong sense of purpose and discipline which should ensure our troops' success in almost any undertaking. While the reality is that these new "paras" will probably never go into battle in large numbers, the troops pride themselves on their role as general purpose light infantry, capable of responding quickly to both national and international challenges, and also on their association with famous Canadian parachute units of the past. Additionally, if emergency personnel are required in future — to deal with an air crash or some other emergency in our country's northland — the likelihood is that they will be drawn from the ranks of such specially trained and equipped light infantry.

The elite training such soldiers receive and the unique demands made upon personnel ensure that anyone who survives jump school and earns his paratrooper's badge possesses not only superior physical and psychological attributes, but also has mastered a wide range of challenges, ranging from communications skills and group leadership methods to wilderness movement and survival techniques. Even more importantly, the new airborne units provide an opportunity and test to personnel throughout Canada's infantry and land forces.

Although this book has treated our military heritage rather than directions in which the military is likely to develop in future, some conclusions are possible about the overall training and tasking of our troops, either for peacekeeping or more traditional roles. One is that tougher measures against racism need to be implemented in our military. It is simply not enough to say that the Forces are no more racist than society in general. Given the fact that they are likely to be employed on missions around the globe, Canadian troops have to be able to deal with peoples of all races.

It is evident, too, that our military should be better trained for other aspects of peacekeeping. These include methods of dealing with hostile populations where no clear enemy or situation is evident. The military also has to improve greatly its intelligence function and gathering before it goes on missions. The problems encountered in Somalia and Rwanda are evidence of this. Nor should we ever again send our men and women into a dangerous (even hostile) theatre of operations under rules of engagement that in any way fall short of equipping them for eventualities that may occur.

Overall, as we enter the 21st century, the government needs to assign a clear role to the military. Politicians should address this problem, instead of trying to forget, as they often seem to, the fact that we have a military. They should also resist listening to bureaucrats who want to impose a managerial culture that takes the easy route by focussing on political constraints and budgets. As history teaches us, if we have an unprepared army, or no army at all, we remain at the mercy of any aggressive activity or faction, and completely dependent on the United States. Not least, anthropologists continue to warn us that humanity has not abandoned the aggressive side of its nature. Until it does, odds are high that even a peace-loving country like ours is going to require soldiers who are prepared for any eventuality.

NOTE ON MILITARY
ORGANIZATION

Traditionally, the very essence of the Canadian Army's organization (drawing as it does on the British model) has been the regimental system as it exists in the infantry and cavalry. In the 18th and 19th centuries especially, a regiment had no fixed size. Most infantry regiments consisted of one or two battalions, but they were capable of expanding. The size of a battalion also varied, but an infantry battalion usually consisted of 700 to 1,000 men, divided into eight to twelve companies. A cavalry regiment was generally smaller, with about 300 to 500 all ranks.

A typical regiment, or battalion, of infantry was commanded by a lieutenant-colonel and included three or four majors, nine or ten captains, and some fifteen to eighteen subalterns, or junior officers. A cavalry regiment possessed a similar number of officers.

During the century or more that followed Wolfe's victory, virtually all British regiments were posted to Canada at one time or another. Royal Engineers and units of the Royal Regiment of Artillery also served in its garrisons. Among Guards/Household regiments, however, only the Coldstream Guards were posted to

British North America. Also, few if any cavalry regiments were sent across the Atlantic.

From the American Revolution onwards, British regulars were augmented by regiments of locally raised provincials and militia. The volunteer movement that swept Victorian Britain and Canada (as well as other colonies) would give rise to dozens of militia battalions from coast to coast, destined to form the nucleus of the Dominion's military force by the late 19th century.

Prior to the Anglo-Boer War (1899–1902), the British or Imperial Army, of which our countrymen formed a part, was not systematically divided into field armies, corps, divisions, or even brigades on a regular basis. Instead, the British Army was basically a collection of regiments which were assembled in any order a general saw fit or as need arose.

The sheer scale of the Great War (1914–1918) would change all this. Henceforward, the basic British military formation would consist of the division, a military unit approximately fifteen times the size of a battalion. When the conflict broke out, the Canadian government offered Britain an expeditionary force consisting of a single such division, albeit an over-sized one. The 31,000 men of the Canadian Expeditionary Force (CEF) sailed from Quebec in October 1914. After proceeding to France in 1915, it was shortly joined by a second division. By late 1916, the Canadian Corps, consisting of four divisions at full strength, had come into being.

Technically, a Canadian infantry division, numbering roughly 20,000 men and commanded by a major-general, consisted of three infantry brigades, of four battalions each. A division also included two brigades of field-artillery (each composed of three batteries of field artillery and one of howitzers), three trench-mortar batteries, a machine gun battalion and other requisite arms and services.

Each of the 50 or so battalions making up the Canadian Corps in turn consisted of four companies, and each company consisted of four platoons, each ordinarily made up of four sections. Commanded by a lieutenant-colonel, such a battalion usually numbered 1,000 officers and men. An infantry brigade, led by a brigadier-general, consisted, as already mentioned, of four battalions plus a trench mortar battery. The Canadian Cavalry Brigade had four cavalry regiments, a machine gun squadron and a field ambulance.

Ultimately, the Canadian Army Corps, as it would come to be called in World War I, would number just over 100,000 men, including reserves. Although this was relatively small in terms of overall Allied military organization, the Dominion's force was large enough to exert a significant impact on the Western Front's battles. By the conflict's end, a total of 619,636 personnel had served in the Canadian Expeditionary Force. Although half of the officers, men and nursing sisters who enlisted were British-born, it was in essence a small Canadian army, and reflected a nation in the process of creation.

To meet the demands of armoured warfare during the Second World War (1939–1945) and an army that would eventually see 730,625 men and women serve in its ranks during six years of conflict, the organization of Canada's land forces would continue to evolve and undergo further developments. As in the Great War, the basic military formation consisted of the division, either infantry, armoured, or airborne. An infantry division, led by a major-general, was made up of three infantry brigades of three battalions each. It also contained a reconnaissance regiment, the divisional artillery of three field regiments, an anti-aircraft and anti-tank regiment, engineers, signals, a machine gun battalion and supply, transport, medical, ordnance and workshop units.

A World War II infantry battalion, from which brigades and divisions in turn were constructed, was commanded by a lieutenant-colonel and eventually comprised 38 officers and 812 men. Initially, it consisted of three rifle companies (each usually commanded by a captain or a major), headquarters company (transport platoon, quartermaster and battalion headquarters) and one support company of mortars, Bren-gun carriers, anti-tank guns and pioneers. In August 1943, the number of rifle companies in a battalion was ordered increased to four, each normally commanded by a major with assistance from a captain. A lieutenant commanded each of a company's three infantry platoons, which contained 35 men and was supported by a platoon sergeant. A platoon in turn was further divided into three sections of 11 men each, led by a lance-corporal.

An armoured division consisted of one armoured brigade of three regiments plus an infantry motor battalion, an infantry brigade of three battalions, an armoured reconnaissance regiment and two field artillery regiments. Other arms and services were similar to those for an infantry division.

On the highest level, a Canadian corps, commanded by a lieutenant-general, consisted of two to five divisions (not necessarily all Canadian), an independent armoured brigade and an AGRA (Army Group Royal Artillery) of four or five regiments of medium, field and heavy artillery. Corps troops also comprised an armoured car regiment, anti-tank and anti-aircraft regiments, a survey regiment, and engineer and signals units.

Until the end of the Second World War, Canada's land forces were known by a variety of names. Post-war reorganization, however, gave them the simplest of titles: the Canadian Army. In 1946, the strength of our country's ground force was fixed at 25,000. Although this was a small number, it was by far the largest professional army that our country had supported until this time. Soon, though, the growing Soviet threat, NATO's creation, and the outbreak of fighting in Korea, combined to increase the military's strength. By 1952, the army had 52,000 members, with a brigade group fighting in Korea and another stationed (as it would be for decades to come) in Germany with NATO. Also, during this period, substantial new commitments arose, most notably peacekeeping operations for the UN, which have continued to the present day.

The Canadian Forces Reorganization Act, implemented in early 1968, created a unified armed force, the first time any country in the world had attempted such. The advent of this new entity, known as the Canadian Forces (note: not the Canadian Armed Forces, as it is often erroneously termed), officially ended the separate legal existence of the Royal Canadian Navy, the Royal

Canadian Air Force, and the Canadian Army. Today, in their stead, there is a single unified service. Initially, all personnel were attired in a common uniform of dark green. Since then, however, each of the forces has re-instituted a number of its former traditions; each has also regained the right to wear its own distinct uniform, an important part of its identity.

Today, the Canadian Infantry Corps' cutting edge continues to be provided by its original three "Regular" units: the Royal Canadian Regiment with battalions based in Petawawa, Ontario, and Gagetown, N.B.; the Princess Patricia's Canadian Light Infantry with battalions at Winnipeg and Calgary; and the Royal 22nd Regiment, or "Van Doos," both battalions of which are in Valcartier, Quebec. In addition, four new airborne companies of general purpose light infantry are being trained, soon to be employed at various locations across Canada.

Similar to the Regulars, 49 Militia regiments, some of which date from before Confederation and which also derive their traditions from the British model, are constituted into "named regiments," each with its own lineage and traditions. When "fleshed out" to full battle strength they possess (in theory) the capacity to provide six divisions to supplement the Regulars' single division. During the 1990s, Militia and Reserve personnel have volunteered wherever possible for service with the Regulars; in fact, Canada could not possibly fulfill its UN commitment without such reservists.

Other elements of the Canadian Land Force include the Royal Canadian Armoured Corps, with its three regular regiments, the Royal Canadian Dragoons, Lord Strathcona's Horse (Royal Canadians) and the 8th Canadian Hussars (Princess Louise's), as well as the Royal Regiment of Canadian Artillery, the Corps of Royal Canadian Engineers and other specialized units, including the Royal Canadian Corps of Signallers and the Royal Canadian Army Service Corps.

While present plans call for our military's overall manpower to shrink from 72,000 to 60,000 by the end of the century (including the Militia from 29,000 to 23,000), overall plans for our country's Regular Land Force are more positive: they include expanding our hard-pressed army by 3,500 combat troops, purchasing new armoured personnel carriers, increasing the combat capability of Reserves, and moving to encourage short-term enlistments rather than more (and expensive) career soldiers. Such reforms and others being planned, it is hoped, will ensure that Canada's soldiers are prepared to meet any challenges the 21st century is likely to bring.

INDEX